FROM CHANCE TO CHOICE
Genetics and Justice

A powerful alliance of government, business, and science is propelling society into a new era in which human beings will possess a much greater understanding of the most basic functions of human life. Scientific knowledge of how genes work will empower human beings to cure and prevent diseases. It may also enable us to shape some of the most important biological characteristics of the human beings we choose to bring into existence. No one knows the limits of our future power to shape human lives or when those limits will be reached. One thing, however, is certain: Whatever those limits turn out to be, coping with these new powers will tax our wisdom to the utmost.

This book, written by four internationally renowned bioethicists, is the first systematic treatment of the fundamental ethical issues underlying the application of genetic technologies to human beings. Probing the implications of the remarkable advances in genetics the authors ask how they should affect our understanding of distributive justice, equality in opportunity, the rights and obligations as parents, the meaning of disability, and the role of the concept of human nature in ethical theory and practice.

Unlike any other study of the ethical issues in genetics, the book offers a historical context to contemporary debate over the use of these technologies by providing an ethical autopsy of mankind's first attempts to use the scientific knowledge of heredity to improve human lives: the eugenics movement of the late 19th and early 20th centuries. In addition lucid appendices explain the nature of genetic causation and gene-environment interaction, and expose widespread misconceptions of genetic determinism, as well as outline the nature of the ethical analysis used in the book.

The questions raised in this book will be of interest to any reflective reader concerned about science and society and the rapid development of biotechnology, as well as to professionals in such areas as philosophy, bioethics, medical ethics, health management, law, and political science.

Allen Buchanan is Professor of Philosophy at the University of Arizona.
Dan W. Brock is Professor of Philosophy at Brown University.
Norman Daniels is Goldthwaite Professor of Philosophy at Tufts University, and Professor of Medical Ethics at Tufts Medical School.
Daniel Wikler is Professor in the Program in Medical Ethics and in the Department of Philosophy at the University of Wisconsin, Madison. In 1999 he was appointed Senior Staff Ethicist for the World Health Organization.

FROM CHANCE TO CHOICE

Genetics and Justice

ALLEN BUCHANAN
University of Arizona

DAN W. BROCK
Brown University

NORMAN DANIELS
Tufts University

DANIEL WIKLER
*University of Wisconsin, Madison,
and World Health Organization*

CAMBRIDGE
UNIVERSITY PRESS

PUBLISHED BY THE PRESS SYNDICATE OF
THE UNIVERSITY OF CAMBRIDGE
The Pitt Building, Trumpington Street, Cambridge, United Kingdom

CAMBRIDGE UNIVERSITY PRESS
The Edinburgh Building, Cambridge CB2 2RU, UK
http: //www.cup.cam.ac.uk
40 West 20th Street, New York, NY 10011-4211, USA
http: //www.cup.org
10 Stamford Road, Oakleigh, Melbourne 3166, Australia
Ruiz de Alarcón 13, 28014 Madrid, Spain

First published 2000

Printed in the United States of America

Typeface Sabon 10.25/13 pt   *System* DeskTopPro$_{/UX}$[BV]

A catalog record for this book is available from the British Library.

Library of Congress Cataloging in Publication data
From chance to choice : genetics and justice / Allen Buchanan . . . [et al.].
p.   cm.
Includes bibliographical references.
ISBN 0–521-66001-7 (hardcover)
1. Human genetics – Moral and ethical aspects. 2. Genetic
engineering – Moral and ethical aspects. 3. Eugenics – Moral and
ethical aspects. 4. Medical ethics – Moral and ethical aspects.
5. Human Genome Project – Moral and ethical aspects.   I. Buchanan, Allen
QH431.F8765   2000
174'.25—dc21   99–24025
                                                                    CIP

The views expressed in this book do not represent positions endorsed by the
World Health Organization.

ISBN 0 521 66001 7   hardback

CONTENTS

v

PREFACE

We began thinking about writing this book in the spring of 1991 because we believed that new genetic knowledge and technology posed challenges not only to traditional social practices but also to ethical theory. We believed, as nearly everyone does, that ethics should provide guidance for social practice. We also believed that our ethical understanding – the reasons, principles, and theory we draw on – itself has developed in response to specific challenges of social life. Consequently, we thought, the new human capabilities genetics creates requires an examination of ethical theory, not just an application of it. What distinguishes this book is the conviction that we must look deeply inward to the core of our field as moral and political philosophers as well as outward from it toward the engagement of social practices with new genetic powers.

Because our goal was to produce a sustained and systematic analysis, we have produced a multiauthored book, not an anthology of separate articles. Although all four authors collaborated on each chapter, there was a division of labor. Allen Buchanan is the primary author of the Introduction, Chapters 3 and 7, and the appendix on moral methodology. Dan Brock is chiefly responsible for Chapter 6 and shares primary responsiblity with Norman Daniels for Chapter 5. In addition, Daniels is the primary author of Chapter 4. Daniel Wikler is the primary author of Chapter 2 and of Chapter 8 (with some input from Buchanan). Although Elliot Sober did not work on other parts of the book, he is the sole author of the appendix on genetic causation.

Skillful copyediting by Linda Starke has produced a degree of uniformity in style, but differences among the authors regarding philosophical substance remain, in particular regarding some aspects of the theory of just health care and the place of equality of opportunity in a

comprehensive theory of justice. In a few cases these differences manifest themselves in rather subtle ways in the book. This necessity we
regard as a virtue. The differences among us represent hard philosophical choices at the frontiers of ethical theorizing; we have attempted to
signal their presence clearly to the reader, believing that they add
richness to the discussion and will help dissipate any illusion that there
is one clearly superior ethical framework that best responds to all the
problems.

From the outset of this project the authors were keenly aware of a
fundamental limitation: Although our topic clearly has interdisciplinary dimensions, we are all philosophers, not geneticists, social scientists, or historians. Because of generous funding from the Program on
Ethical, Social, and Legal Implications of the Human Genome Project
(now called the Human Genome Institute), we were able to enlist an
impressive interdisciplinary panel of advisors who provided invaluable
guidance at critical junctures during the course of the project: Mark
Adams, Paul Billings, Robert Cook-Deegan, and Richard Lewontin. In
addition, Robert Cook-Deegan, Thomas Christiano, and Clark Wolf
supplied line-by-line comments on a complete draft of the manuscript.
The authors are also indebted to David Benatar and Jeff McMahon,
who generously commented on several key arguments, and to Diane
Paul, who guided the presentation of the history of eugenics in Chapter
2. We are also grateful for research and logistical contributions by
Sandra Arneson, David Benatar, Ric (Frederick) Bolin, Cindy Holder,
and Dale Murray.

Through the long process of completing this project we were sustained by the generous and enthusiastic support of Elizabeth Thomson,
Eric Juengst, and Eric Meslin, all of the Program on the Ethical, Legal,
and Social Implications of the Human Genome Research Institute
(formerly the Human Genome Project), which supplied funding for
the project as a whole. Special thanks are also due to Terence Moore
of Cambridge University Press for his editorial expertise and his enthusiastic support.

―

ONE

INTRODUCTION

CHALLENGES OF THE GENETIC AGE

A powerful alliance of government, business, and science is propelling society into a new era in which human beings will possess a much greater understanding of the most basic functions of all forms of life. With this understanding will come unprecedented control over living things, including ourselves. Scientific knowledge of how genes work will empower human beings to cure and prevent diseases. It may also let us shape some of the most important biological characteristics of the human beings we choose to bring into existence.

No one knows the limits of our future powers to shape human lives – or when these limits will be reached. Some expect that at most we will be able to reduce the incidence of serious genetic diseases and perhaps ensure that more people are at the higher end of the distribution of normal traits. More people may have long and healthy lives, and perhaps some will have better memory and other intellectual powers. Others foresee not only greater numbers of people functioning at high levels, but the attainment of levels previously unheard of: lives measured in centuries, people of superhuman intelligence, humans endowed with new traits presently undreamt of. One thing, however, is certain: Whatever the limits of our technical abilities turn out to be, coping with these new powers will tax our wisdom to the utmost.

PREVIEWS OF PERPLEXITIES

Consider a few of the perplexities with which the genetic revolution is likely to confront us in the future.

Scenario 1: Genetic Communitarianism

A disaffected member of what the media refer to as a religious cult announces that the group is attempting to implement its vision of the good society by "mass producing" human embryos cloned from the group's leaders. He claims that the group has its own genetics lab and hopes to adapt for use on humans techniques for cloning embryos commonly employed in the commercial production of animals. Several members of Congress express outrage and urge that the government take action against the religious group. A spokesperson for the American Civil Liberties Union says that if we value reproductive freedom and freedom of religion, we must respect the right of religious communities to attempt to transmit their beliefs and way of life to future generations, whether by the traditional methods of teaching and indoctrination or by the application of genetic technology.

Scenario 2: Personal Choice or Public Health Concern?

A single, inexpensive blood test for prospective parents can detect high risk for virtually all serious genetic disorders as well as a broad range of genetic susceptibilities for illnesses. An initiative is afoot to provide mass genetic screening using this test. A government commission examining the feasibility of this proposal notes that the program's cost-effectiveness depends on whether a sufficient number of those tested "act on the knowledge of positive results – that is, whether they choose to avoid conception of affected fetuses." An advocate of the mass screening program says "this is a public health matter; people should not be free to inflict avoidable diseases on their children, especially if we are ever to have an affordable health care system that provides coverage for everyone." An opponent replies that "genetic services of any kind are strictly a matter of personal choice – respect for reproductive freedom requires this. People must be free to act on the test results as they see fit; any program that will result in pressures that limit reproductive freedom would be unacceptable."

Scenario 3: The Quest for the Perfect Baby

Excerpt from the introduction to a dissertation in a history of medicine written in 2040:

In the 1990s, as in the preceding three decades, parents mainly practiced negative eugenics, using tests for major chromosomal defects such as Down syndrome and aborting "defective" fetuses. By 2020 the standards for acceptable babies had been raised: prospective parents routinely aborted fetuses that were otherwise healthy but that had genes that gave them a significantly higher than average risk of breast cancer, colorectal cancer, Alzheimer's dementia, or coronary artery disease. By 2030, the trend was toward even higher standards: Fetuses with any of a range of "undesirable" or "less than optimal" combinations of genes were routinely aborted, including those predicted not to be in the highest quintile with respect to intelligence or even height. Widespread use of these techniques by parents who could afford them began to raise the average level of health, physical strength and stature, and intellectual ability in the population, a trend encouraged by nationalist politicians. But the insistence of many parents that their child be in the upper quintile created a spiral in which no amount of genetic boost ever seemed enough.

Scenario 4: Health Care in the Age of Genetic Intervention

At a congressional hearing, Dr. Philip Jones testifies that the standard benefit package that all insurance companies are federally mandated to offer should be expanded to include what are popularly called "mood enhancer" drugs for all persons who have the "mild depression gene," even though these individuals do not usually meet existing criteria for having bipolar affective disorder. According to Jones, "What is important is whether clinical science can help people live better lives; the fact that a person's mood swings don't qualify as bipolar disorder isn't really important." A spokesperson for the National Association of Health Insurers protests, "Health care coverage stops where treatment for disease ends; there's a right to health care, but there's no right to be happy." Jones, shaking his head with a somewhat patronizing air, replies, "What we now know about the way genes affect the brain and hence the personality renders the distinction between psychiatric disorders and undesirable psychological conditions unimportant."

Scenario 5: The Genetic Enhancement Certificate

Katherine and Bill are applying for the same management position in a large firm. Included in Katherine's dossier is a genetic enhancement certificate from Opti-Gene, Inc. It certifies that the bearer has "bene-fited from cutting-edge genetic enhancement technology" and asserts that those who have had the package of services in question on average have fewer colds and other common respiratory infections, are less likely to suffer depression, and score higher on tests of memory skills. Bill, who cannot afford genetic enhancement, protests that "hiring on the basis of genetic enhancement is just as unfair as hiring on the basis of race or gender – it's a violation of equal opportunity and makes a travesty of the merit system." Katherine replies indignantly, "Merit means the position goes to the best candidate, and I am the best candidate, so what's the problem?"

THE NEED FOR SYSTEMATIC ETHICAL THINKING

Reflection on scenarios such as these prompts two sorts of self-doubt. We worry whether, like the sorcerer's apprentice, we will suffer the consequences of partial knowledge, overestimating our power to pre-dict and control the causal chains we initiate through the application of our newfound knowledge. But we also worry about values. Even if we were more assured than we should be that our technical control will be complete, we would continue to wonder whether we will be able to distinguish between what we can do and what we ought to do. Do we have the ethical resources to use our genetic powers wisely and humanely? Or are we like hapless space-travelers embarking on an interstellar voyage equipped only with a pocket compass? Do existing ethical theories, concepts, and principles provide the materials for constructing more adequate instruments for moral navigation?

In the face of these doubts about whether our values will keep pace with our powers, there is an unfortunate tendency to rest content with inarticulate forebodings about the dangers of "playing God" when confronted with revelations of particular new genetic discoveries or technical breakthroughs. The admonition not to play God is useless, except as a general warning against hubris. It tells us nothing about how we should respond to any particular choice we may confront.

Something more is needed. A systematic vision of the moral char-acter of the world we hope to be moving toward is required. The primary objective of this book, accordingly, is to make a contribution toward answering a single question: *What are the most basic moral principles that would guide public policy and individual choice con-cerning the use of genetic interventions in a just and humane society in which the powers of genetic intervention are much more developed than they are today?*

Accomplishing this will require responding to many other questions, among the most important of which are: What are the most important ethical problems to which greatly increased powers of genetic intervention will give rise? Are these new problems? How adequate are the resources of existing ethical theory to cope with them? And what sorts of ethical principles and distinctions are needed to help a society equipped with formidable powers of genetic intervention avoid the mistakes and evils of the eugenics movements of the late nineteenth and early to mid-twentieth centuries?

GENOMIC RESEARCH AND GENETIC INTERVENTION

The Human Genome Project and Related Genetic Research

Our knowledge of how genes function is growing at an almost imponderable rate. The Human Genome Project is ahead of schedule in achieving its goal of determining the sequence of the three million or so base pairs of nucleotides that make up the complete genetic material of a human being. Presumably the coming years will also bring a great expansion of our knowledge of how particular genes function. Almost daily, newspaper headlines proclaim startling and sometimes disquieting discoveries and feats of technological virtuosity, from the identification of a "fat gene" to the cloning of a sheep from an adult sheep's mammary cell. Eventually these advances will bear practical fruit: the ability to use knowledge of how genes function to intervene in significant ways in human life. The Human Genome Project, in part because of the impetus it has given to the rapid, worldwide sharing of information and technique, does much to guarantee that the stream of genetic knowledge will continue to increase in volume and speed.

Although it is the most highly publicized locus of research, the Human Genome Project does not stand alone. Many other projects for human genetic research are funded by the National Institutes of Health in the United States and by government agencies in other industrial countries. And private, commercial research efforts are increasingly capitalizing on the knowledge base provided by the Human Genome Project and other government-funded research and on the expertise of researchers in academic institutions, many of which are publicly funded. Although the research for this book was funded by

the program for Ethical, Legal, and Social Implications of the Human
Genome Project of the National Institutes of Health, our concern is
broader. We will speak generally of "human genomic research" or
even more broadly of "advances in genetic knowledge," recognizing
that the study of nonhuman organisms has contributed and will continue to contribute to an understanding of how genes function in
human beings.

Modes of Genetic Intervention

As a rough, initial categorization, modes of genetic intervention can
first be divided into direct and indirect interventions. By "direct genetic
interventions" we mean primarily two modes: gene therapy, in which
normal or desirable genes are inserted into either somatic (body tissue)
cells or germline cells (gametes – sperms or eggs – or embryos); and
gene surgery, in which abnormal or undesirable genes are "switched
off" – that is, deactivated so that they no longer produce their distinctive effects.

At present, gene therapy in human beings has been limited to somatic cells. For example, normal genes have been inserted into the
bone marrow of patients who suffer from certain blood disorders due
to the inability of their own genes to produce particular proteins. In
the future, it is expected that gene therapy and gene surgery will be
performed on human germline cells, with genes being inserted into or
deactivated in gametes and embryos (fertilized eggs).

Gene therapy today involves the insertion of cloned normal genes –
genes that occur naturally. Naturally occurring genes may come either
from other human beings or from nonhuman animals. But it may
eventually become possible to create new genes – that is, to synthesize
new sequences of base pairs to produce effects that are not found in
nature. Genes, after all, are just functionally significant sequences of
base pairs.

From a technical standpoint, a fruitful combination of methods – at
least for some conditions – would be to complement gene therapy on
germline cells with gene surgery. The desirable gene would be introduced early enough in the gamete or embryo to replicate and keep
reproducing throughout all the cells of the organism (rather than being
inserted, decaying, and being reinserted into a particular tissue), and
the undesirable gene would be "knocked out." Alternatively, recently
isolated *totipotent* human embryo stem cells may eventually provide

the ideal platform from which to develop a range of gene therapies. (A totipotent cell is one that can develop into any kind of tissue or organ, given the proper biochemical stimulation.)

In contrast to direct intervention, *indirect genetic intervention* means primarily genetic pharmacology and embryo selection. By *genetic pharmacology* we mean the use of knowledge about genes to design drugs that will either substitute for the chemical products that would be produced by a normal gene in an individual who has an abnormal one, augment the chemical products of normal genes or counteract the effects of an undesirable or abnormal gene (e.g., by disrupting the protein it produced; Lewontin 1997). Furthermore, someday novel sequences of base pairs – new genes synthesized in the laboratory – may produce drugs that will either ameliorate or prevent diseases, give individuals new desirable traits, or enhance desirable traits they already have or would have when they become fully developed. Embryo selection involves three main steps: "harvesting" embryos, subjecting them to DNA analysis, and implanting an embryo that possesses the preferred characteristics.

There is a third category of intervention that may be called genetic, though perhaps with some stretching of the term. It involves the application of knowledge about genes but without the use of either modifying genes, genetic pharmacology, or embryo selection. There are two subcategories: when genetic information is used in regard to reproductive decisions and when it is used to prevent or ameliorate genetically based diseases in an already existing individual. For convenience, we call the first group "reproductive genetic testing interventions" and the second "therapeutic genetic testing interventions."

Reproductive genetic testing interventions are done in response to information revealed by genetic testing, where the testing is performed either on persons who intend to have children or, after conception has occurred, on the fetus. In one sense, the difference between these modes of genetic testing and embryo selection is not great: In the latter, testing is done on embryos rather than on prospective parents or fetuses.

If such a test reveals a risk of genetic disease or of some other undesirable condition, any of several steps may be taken to reduce or eliminate the risk. If it is determined that a woman is carrying a fetus with a genetic defect such as the chromosomal anomaly known as Down syndrome, she may elect to abort the fetus. If a couple undergoes carrier testing (by a blood test) and learns that they both carry a gene for cystic fibrosis or Tay-Sachs disease, they may choose not to have children, to have children by sperm or by egg donation, or to adopt. At present we lack the capacity to use gene therapy, gene surgery, or genetic pharmacology in any of these cases. The only way to reduce the risk of having a child with an abnormal or undesired genetic condition is to avoid having that child.

The second subcategory, therapeutic genetic testing intervention, has been widely practiced in the United States in the case of the hereditary metabolic disorder phenylketonuria (PKU) for more than 30 years. A blood test is performed on infants at birth. If it is positive for PKU, a special diet is used to avoid the buildup of an enzyme that causes brain damage.

The gene for another potentially lethal genetic disorder, hereditary hemochromatosis, or inherited excessive iron storage disease, was identified by a private genetic technology company in 1996. A blood test for the two mutations that cause the disease has just become available. The treatment for hemochromatosis, like that for PKU, is remarkably "low-tech," consisting of regular phlebotomies (bloodlettings) to deplete stored iron. Because hereditary hemochromatosis is by far the most common serious genetic disease in the United States (approximately 4 persons per 1,000 of the Caucasian population are homozygous, i.e., have two copies of the mutation, and 1 in 10 is heterozygous, i.e., has one copy), and because treatment is inexpensive and effective, some argue that testing for hemochromatosis should become the next mass genetic screening program in this country.

In addition, knowledge of how genes work will lead to greater knowledge of how genes interact with different environments. Increasingly, we can expect to identify subgroups of the population who have genetic characteristics that may call for special environments if their physical or cognitive development is to be maximized. Here, unlike with PKU and hemochromatosis, tailoring an environment to the special developmental needs of a genotypic subgroup of the population may not be a matter of offering a therapy to treat a disease.

For example, we already know that some children benefit from special environments for learning to read or do mathematics. It may well turn out that there are genetic markers that will help pick out those with special learning needs or special needs for nutrition if their cognitive development is to be maximized. (It is already known that the Tohono O'Odham Indians of southern Arizona and Sonora, Mexico, experience extraordinarily high rates of diabetes on a "normal" white American diet but not when they eat their traditional foods.) Intervening to tailor environments to the needs of genotypic groups may not be genetic intervention as ordinarily understood, yet it is intervention based on knowledge of how genes work in various environments.

Our choice of topics in this book deserves a word of explanation. Only in Chapter 5 are we concerned primarily with the role of genetic testing in reproductive choices. The remainder of the book concentrates mainly on direct genetic interventions and genetic pharmacology, with much of what we say having direct implications for embryo selection as well. The reason for this focus is twofold: First, some of the most fundamental ethical issues arise most clearly in the case of direct genetic interventions and genetic pharmacology. Second, there is already considerable literature on ethical issues in both genetic testing reproductive interventions and genetic testing therapeutic interventions (Cook-Deegan 1994; Andrews et al. 1994; Russo and Cove 1995).

Our reason for giving genetic pharmacology equal billing with direct genetic interventions perhaps warrants explanation. When ethical issues arising from the new genetics are discussed in the popular media – and even in the bioethics literature – the focus is often on "genetic engineering," a phrase that evokes images of scientists splicing genes together to create new kinds of organisms. Nonetheless, genetic pharmacology is likely to be one of the most potent applications of genetic science in the immediate future. (Venture capitalists, including some of the largest pharmaceutical companies, appear to agree with this prediction.) "Engineering" human embryos, if it occurs at all, will probably happen only in the relatively distant future. Dramatic advances in genetic pharmacology are a much nearer and surer prospect. Another alternative to the embryo engineering is embryo selection. Like genetic pharmacology, it seems to be more likely to see extensive use in the nearer future.

THE SHADOW OF EUGENICS

Even the brightest aspirations of the new genetics are from time to time dimmed by the shadow of eugenics. The very term has been in such bad odor since the era of Nazi "racial hygiene" (Proctor 1988) that few people today wish to be associated with eugenics. Indeed, controversies over the new genetics often proceed as if the rival parties assume that if it can be shown that someone's views are "eugenic," they are thereby discredited. Much energy is then spent in trying to attach the label to an opponent or avoid being labeled a eugenicist.

Such exercises tend to be long on rhetoric and short on cognitive content. Attitudes toward eugenics are much like the common view of Marx's *Das Capital* – people know it is wrong though they know little about it – or, more charitably, like the attitude toward Freud's theory of the unconscious: "He was on to something, but he went too far."

At present, neither those who assert that the new genetics is infected by the evils of the old eugenics nor those who indignantly defend the new genetics' moral purity have made a convincing case. Two things are needed for the satisfactory resolution of this controversy: an ethical autopsy on the old eugenics and an examination of the ethical presuppositions and implications of the new genetics. The first task is taken up in Chapter 2; the remainder of the book is devoted to the second.

To evaluate the charge that the new genetics is infected by the evils of eugenics, it is necessary to unearth the ethical assumptions that provide the best justifications currently available for pursuing genetic knowledge and for attempting to use this knowledge to intervene in human lives. As with the attempt to articulate the underlying values of the eugenics movement, our task here requires considerable reconstruction, because those who endorse the expansion of our genetic knowledge and powers of intervention rarely make their ethical assumptions explicit, and they certainly offer nothing like a developed ethical theory.

In part, our attempt to articulate the ethical underpinnings of the new genetics is dialectical. We proceed by stating objections against or worries about the new genetics, and we see how defenders of the new genetics might best reply to them. Chapter 7 contains the most severe criticisms of the new genetics – those voiced by some members of the disabilities rights movement. Answering these criticisms requires making explicit some of the most fundamental moral assumptions that justify the development and use of technologies for genetic intervention to prevent disease and disability. Other chapters provide additional elements of an ethical framework that both justifies the general goal of developing our powers of genetic intervention and provides principles to guide the application of those powers.

TWO MODELS FOR GENETIC INTERVENTION

The Public Health Model

Our "ethical autopsy" on eugenics, in Chapter 2, identifies two quite different perspectives from which genetic intervention may be viewed. The first is what we call the public health model; the second is the personal choice model.

The public health model stresses the production of benefits and the avoidance of harms for groups. It uncritically assumes that the appropriate mode of evaluating options is some form of cost-benefit (or cost-effectiveness) calculation. To the extent that the public health model even recognizes an ethical dimension to decisions about the application of scientific knowledge or technology, it tends to assume that sound ethical reasoning is exclusively consequentialist (or utilitarian) in nature. In other words, it assumes that whether a policy or an action is deemed to be right is thought to depend solely on whether it produces the greatest balance of good over bad outcomes.

More important, consequentialist ethical reasoning – like cost-benefit and cost-effectiveness calculations – assumes that it is not only possible but permissible and even mandatory to aggregate goods and bads (costs and benefits) across individuals. Harms to some can be offset by gains to others; what matters is the sum. Critics of such simple and unqualified consequentialist reasoning, including ourselves, are quick to point out its fundamental flaws: Such reasoning is distributionally insensitive because it fails to take seriously the separateness and inviolability of persons.

In other words, as simple and unqualified consequentialist reasoning looks only to the aggregate balance of good over bad, it does not recognize fairness in the distribution of burdens and benefits to be a fundamental value. As a result, it not only allows but in some circumstances requires that the most fundamental interests of individuals be sacrificed in order to produce the best overall outcome.

Consequentialist ethical theory is not unique in allowing or even requiring that the interests of individuals sometimes yield to the good of all. Any reasonable ethical theory must acknowledge this. But it is unique in maintaining that in principle such sacrifice is justified whenever it would produce any aggregate gain, no matter how small. Because simple and unqualified consequentialism has this implication, some conclude that it fails to appreciate sufficiently that each individual is an irreducibly distinct subject of moral concern.

The public health model, with its affinity for consequentialist ethical reasoning, took a particularly troubling form among some prominent eugenicists. Individuals who were thought to harbor "defective germ plasm" (what would now be called "bad genes") were likened to carriers of infectious disease. While persons infected with cholera were a menace to those with whom they came into contact, individuals with defective germ plasm were an even greater threat to society: They transmitted harm to an unlimited line of persons across many generations.

The only difference between the "horizontally transmitted" infectious diseases and "vertically transmitted" genetic diseases, according to this view, was that the potential harm caused by the latter was even greater. So if measures such as quarantine and restrictions on travel into disease areas that infringed individual freedom were appropriate responses to the former, then they were even more readily justified to avert the greater potential harm of the latter. This variant of the public health model may be called the *vertical epidemic model*. Once this point of view is adopted and combined with a simple and unqualified consequentialism, the risks of infringing liberty and of exclusion and discrimination increase dramatically.

The Personal Service Model

Today eugenics is almost universally condemned. Partly in reaction to the tendency of the most extreme eugenicists to discount individual freedom and welfare for the supposed good of society, medical geneticists and genetic counselors since World War II have adopted an almost absolute commitment to "nondirectiveness" in their relations with those seeking genetic services. Recoiling from the public health model that dominated the eugenics movement, and especially from the vertical disease metaphor, they publicly endorse the view that genetic tests and interventions are simply services offered to individuals – goods for private consumption – to be accepted or refused as individuals see fit.

This way of conceiving of genetic interventions takes them out of the public domain, relegating them to the sphere of private choice. Advocates of the personal service model proclaim that the fundamental value on which it rests is individual autonomy. Whether a couple at risk for conceiving a child with a genetic disease takes a genetic test and how they use the knowledge thus obtained is their business, not society's, even if the decision to vaccinate a child for common childhood infectious diseases is a matter of public health and as such justifies restricting parental choice.

The personal service model serves as a formidable bulwark against the excesses of the crude consequentialist ethical reasoning that tainted the application of the public health model in the era of eugenics. But it does so at a prohibitive price: It ignores the obligation to prevent harm as well as some of the most basic requirements of justice. By elevating autonomy to the exclusion of all other values, the personal service model offers a myopic view of the moral landscape.

In fact, it is misleading to say that the personal service model expresses a commitment to autonomy. Instead, it honors only the autonomy of those who are in a position to exercise choice concerning genetic interventions, not all of those who may be affected by such choices. As we show in Chapter 5, this approach wrongly subordinates the autonomy of children to that of their parents.

In addition, if genetic services are treated as goods for private consumption, the cumulative effects of many individual choices in the "genetic marketplace" may limit the autonomy of many people, and perhaps of all people. Economic pressures, including requirements for insurability and employment, as well as social stigma directed toward those who produce children with "defects" that could have been avoided, may narrow rather than expand meaningful choice. Finally, treating genetic interventions as personal services may exacerbate inequalities in opportunities if the prevention of genetic diseases or genetic enhancements are available only to the rich. It would be more accurate to say, then, that the personal service model gives free reign to some dimensions of the autonomy of some people, often at the expense of others.

A Third Approach

Much current thinking about the ethics of genetic intervention assumes that the personal service model is not an adequate moral guide. However, the common response to its deficiencies is not to resurrect the public health model associated with eugenics. Instead, there is a tendency to assume the appropriateness of the personal service model in general and then to erect ad hoc – and less than convincing – "moral firebreaks" to constrain the free choices of individuals in certain areas. For example, some ethicists have urged that the cloning of human beings be strictly prohibited, that there be a moratorium or permanent ban on human germline interventions, or that genetic enhancements (as opposed to treatments of diseases) be outlawed. In each case the proposed moral firebreak shows a distrust of the unalloyed personal service model but at the same time betrays the lack of a systematic, principled account of why and how the choices of individuals should be limited.

The chapters that follow aim to avoid both the lack of attention to the moral equality, separateness, and inviolability of persons that afflicted the eugenics movement's public health model of genetic intervention and the narrow concern with autonomous individual choice that characterizes the personal service model. We argue that although respect for individual autonomy requires an extensive sphere of protected reproductive freedoms and hence a broad range of personal discretion in decisions to use genetic interventions, both the need to prevent harm to offspring and the demands of justice, especially those regarding equal opportunity, place systematic limits on individuals' freedom to use or not use genetic interventions.

We try to develop a systematic, defensible moral framework for choices about the use of genetic intervention technologies. Our view steers a course between a public health model in which individuals count only so far as what they do or what is done to them affects the genetic health of "society" and a personal service model in which the choice to use genetic interventions is morally equivalent to the decision to buy goods for private consumption in an ordinary market. Because our account locates the ethics of genetic intervention within the larger enterprise of ethical theorizing, it avoids the arbitrariness and lack of system of the moral firebreaks approach.

ETHICAL ANALYSIS AND ETHICAL THEORY

Although we discuss ethical principles for individuals, our focus more often than not is primarily on ethical principles for institutions. In most cases we try to refine, and sometimes reinterpret or modify, institutional ethical principles that are quite familiar. Prominent examples include the principle that the basic institutions in a society should ensure equal opportunity and the principle of individual self-determination (or autonomy). We also evaluate certain distinctions, such as that between positive and negative genetic interventions or between treatments and enhancements, that some have tried to elevate to the status of institutional ethical principles.

Principles for Institutions

One of the main results of our analysis is that a proper respect for individual self-determination in the realm of reproductive choices must recognize an asymmetry between institutional ethical principles and those for private individuals who are prospective parents: In general, parents should have considerably more latitude to use genetic interventions to shape their children than governments should have to shape their citizens. So even though our emphasis is on institutional ethical principles, determining their proper scope and limits requires an exploration of principles for individuals.

A comprehensive ethical theory – which we do not pretend to provide here – would include an account of virtues as well as principles. Our concern is not to attempt to provide a theory of the connection between ethical virtues and choices concerning the uses of genetic interventions. Nevertheless, some of what we say has direct and important implications for the sorts of virtues persons will need to have, both in their capacities as private individuals and as citizens concerned with public policy, in a society of heightened genetic powers. In particular, we have a good deal to say about the attitudes toward genetically based disabilities and the commitments to "the morality of inclusion" that members of such a society must exhibit if our new powers are to be used justly and humanely.

By way of partial preview, this much can be said about the institutional ethical principles we believe are most essential for a just and humane society equipped with robust capabilities for genetic intervention. As a first approximation, we can say that among the most important principles are those of justice and the prevention of harm. This is hardly surprising or controversial. Things become more complex and interesting as we explore different concepts of what justice requires and different understandings of what constitutes harm, and as we attempt to ascertain the scope and limits of the obligation to prevent harm.

Justice

Following Rawls (1971, p. 3), we focus in Chapter 3 on the justice of basic social institutions and only by implication on the justice of particular policies or actions. We identify two main headings under which considerations of justice arise in a society of developed powers of genetic intervention: equal opportunity and the morality of inclusion (the latter concept is introduced at the end of this section).

One important conception of equal opportunity requires protection against limitations on individuals' opportunities imposed by racial, ethnic, religious, or gender discrimination. This principle, we argue, is important but incomplete. We opt for a somewhat more inclusive concept of equal opportunity – a version of what John Roemer has called a level playing field conception, of which Rawls's notion of fair equality of opportunity is the most prominent exemplar. Level playing field conceptions require efforts to eliminate or ameliorate the influence of some or all other social factors that limit opportunity over and above discrimination.

The most direct and compelling implication of this conception of the principle of equal opportunity lies in the domain of just health care. Here we adopt the main lines of Norman Daniels's theory of just health care, as developed in several books and a number of articles over the past 15 years. The core idea is that a just health care system should strive to remove barriers to opportunity that are due to disease. ("Disease" here is understood as any "adverse departures from normal species functioning.")

Regardless of how the term "genetic disease" is defined, the etiologies of many diseases include a genetic component. If just health care puts a premium on eliminating barriers to opportunity posed by disease, the question is not whether or in what sense a disease is genetic, but whether there is an intervention (genetic or otherwise) that can cure or prevent it. Thus the level playing field conception has direct implications for genetic intervention: In general, genetic intervention will be an important means of achieving equal opportunity, at least through its use to cure or prevent disease.

We also argue that equal opportunity, as an important principle of justice, has another bearing on genetic intervention. This principle can impose conditions on access to genetic interventions that go beyond the prevention or cure of disease. If, for example, it should ever become possible to enhance some normal desirable characteristics, a consistent commitment to equal opportunity might rule out an unrestricted market for the dissemination of the relevant technology, for if valuable enhancements were available only to the better-off, existing inequalities in opportunity might be exacerbated. Under such conditions, equal opportunity might require either making the enhancements available to all, even those who cannot pay for them or preventing anyone from having them. How we respond to the fifth scenario sketched earlier – The Genetic Enhancement Certificate – will depend on whether justice requires constraints on unequal access to enhancement technologies.

A deeper and more perplexing question is whether equal opportunity may require or permit genetic interventions for the sake of preventing natural inequalities that do not constitute diseases. On the account we endorse, health care does not include everything of benefit that biomedical science can deliver. Health care, so far as it is a concern of justice, has to do only with the treatment and prevention of disease. However, we argue that some versions of the level playing field conception extend the requirements of equal opportunity, at least in principle, to interventions to counteract natural inequalities that do not constitute diseases.

The rationale for such an extension is straightforward: If one of the key intuitions underpinning a level playing field conception of equal opportunity is the conviction that peoples' opportunities should not be significantly limited due to factors that are wholly beyond their control, then it appears that equal opportunity may require the interventions to counteract the more serious opportunity-limiting effects of bad luck in the "natural lottery," regardless of whether the disadvantage conferred by a person's genes is a disease, strictly speaking, as in our fourth scenario (Health Care in the Age of Genetic Intervention).

Examples such as that of the person with the "mild depression gene" may pull one toward the conclusion that equal opportunity requires genetic interventions in such cases, even if the intervention is not treatment for a disease, for the same reason that equal opportunity requires efforts to counteract the effects of being born into a family of lower educational attainment. In both cases, it seems wrong that a person's opportunities should be limited by wholly undeserved and unchosen factors.

We will also see, however, that there are other interpretations of the level playing field conception that stop short of the conclusion that equal opportunity generally requires interventions to prevent natural disadvantages beyond the realm of disease. One such interpretation, which we believe to be Rawls's, does not hold that all undeserved disadvantages as such, including less desirable genetic endowments, require redress as a matter of justice. Instead, this understanding of equal opportunity only asserts that it is unjust to structure social institutions so as to base persons' entitlements to goods on their possession of natural advantages. According to this view, equal opportunity would not require intervention to prevent any and all instances in which an individual would have less desirable genetic endowments. Natural inequalities as such would not be problematic from the standpoint of justice. These alternative understandings of the level playing field conception of equal opportunity appear to have radically different implications for action: One seems to require what might be called genetic equality, the other does not. Thus, a satisfactory response to cases like our fourth scenario inevitably requires a sortie into the realm of ethical theorizing about the proper understanding and role of equality of opportunity in a theory of justice.

This divergence between different versions of the level playing field conception of equal opportunity provides the first illustration of one of the major aims of this book: to explore how the prospects of genetic interventions with human beings challenge existing ethical theory. The challenge takes two distinct forms. First, the prospect of vastly increased powers of genetic intervention brings with it the inevitability of new choices, the contemplation of which stimulates us to articulate existing ethical theories in greater detail (in this case distinguishing different variants of level playing field theories of equal opportunity, which appear to have different practical implications). Second, by placing within human control features of our condition that we have heretofore regarded as given and unalterable (the fate assigned to us by the natural lottery), the prospect of genetic interventions forces us to rethink the boundary we have traditionally drawn between misfortune and injustice, and indeed between the natural and the social.

Preventing Harm

In Chapter 6, we argue that the most straightforward and compelling case for developing and using genetic interventions is to fulfill one of the most basic moral obligations human beings have: the obligation to prevent harm. People have especially demanding obligations to prevent harm to their offspring, but through the agency of their political institutions, they also have obligations to prevent harm to others.

Taking seriously the potential of genetic interventions to prevent harm pushes the limits of ethical theory in two ways: first, by forcing us to ascertain more precisely the scope and limits of the obligation to prevent harm; and second, by putting pressure on our very under-standing of how harm is to be understood in ethical theory. Meeting the first challenge requires us to determine how the sometimes conflict-ing values of reproductive freedom and the obligation to prevent harm limit each other. Meeting the second requires us to take a stand on a fundamental question of ethical theory: whether behavior is subject to ethical evaluation only if it worsens or betters the condition of partic-ular, individual persons. Some genetic interventions – those that pre-vent a genetic impairment by preventing an individual who would have the impairment from coming into existence – cannot be described as preventing harm, if a harm is a worsening of the condition of a particular individual. If the individual does not exist, then the interven-tion cannot worsen his condition.

In addition, our exploration of the obligation to prevent harm through genetic interventions calls into question common dogmas con-cerning "nondirective" genetic counseling and the right to refuse med-ical treatment in cases of "maternal/fetal" conflict – where a woman who intends to carry a fetus to term refuses treatment that would prevent a disability in the future child. Thus, whether it is morally permissible to require or at least encourage individuals to avoid a high risk of transmitting a genetic disease (Scenario 2: Personal Choice or Public Health Concern?) will depend in part on how the obligation to prevent harm is understood.

Limits on the Pursuit of "Genetic Perfection"

Parents, of course, are typically not just concerned with preventing harm to their children; they want what is best for them. As the capa-bility for genetic intervention increases, however, ethical issues arise concerning the proper expression of this benevolent parental impulse. In Chapter 5, we distinguish between permissible and obligatory ge-netic enhancements, examine the social implications of some of the enhancements that parents might consider undertaking for their chil-dren, and argue that what Joel Feinberg has called the child's right to an open future places significant limitations on what it is permissible for parents to do in this regard.

We also distinguish between the ethical implications of the pursuit of improvements by individual parents and those that might be pur-sued by collectivities in the name of some communitarian vision of human perfection. In that chapter and in our exploration of the morality of inclusion in Chapter 7, we provide some of the distinctions and principles needed for a sound ethical response to the issues raised in the Genetic Communitarianism and The Quest for a Perfect Baby scenarios.

The Morality of Inclusion

The dawning of the age of genetic intervention also pushes the limits of theories of justice in another way – by calling into question the manner in which the fundamental problem of justice is characteristically framed.

Theories of justice generally begin with the assumption that the most fundamental problem is how to distribute fairly the burdens and benefits of a society – understood as a single, cooperative framework in which all members are active and effective participants. This way of formulating the issue of justice overlooks two vital points: first, that increasingly human beings can exert some control over the character of the basic cooperative framework within which the most fundamental questions of fair distribution arise; and second, that the character of the most basic cooperative framework in a society will determine who is and who is not "disabled." In other words, what the most basic institutions for production and exchange are like will determine the capacities an individual must have in order to be an effective participant in social cooperation (Wikler 1983; Buchanan 1993, 1996).

But if the choice of a framework of cooperation has profound implications for whether some people will be able to participate effectively, there is a prior question of justice: What is required for fairness in the choice of a society's most basic and comprehensive cooperative scheme? Attempting to answer this question stimulates us to gain a deeper understanding of the very nature of disability.

In Chapter 7, we distinguish genetic impairments from disabilities that have a genetic component, noting that whether or to what extent a genetic impairment results in disability depends on the character of the dominant cooperative framework and the kinds of abilities required for effective participation in it. We then argue that there is an important but often ignored obligation to choose a dominant cooperative framework that is inclusive – that minimizes exclusion from participation on account of genetic impairments. If obligations of inclusion are to be taken seriously, they too impose significant restrictions on the personal choice model for the ethics of genetic intervention.

Justice in the choice of cooperative schemes turns out to be complex, however. The obligation of inclusion is not the sole morally relevant factor, so it cannot be a moral absolute. There is also the morally legitimate interest that persons have in having access to the most productive, enriching, and challenging cooperative scheme in which they are capable of being effective participants. Where there are significant differences in persons' natural assets, the obligation of inclusion and this legitimate interest can come into conflict.

However this conflict is resolved, we argue, a just society of considerable powers of genetic intervention may require changes in both directions: genetic interventions to enable individuals to be effective participants in social cooperation who would not otherwise be able to, and efforts to design the structure of cooperation in ways that make it possible for more people to be effective participants. Appreciation of the problem of justice in the choice of cooperative schemes leads us to the conclusion that regardless of whether we choose to use genetic interventions to promote inclusiveness or refuse to do so, we are in a very real sense choosing who will and who will not be disabled.

ETHICAL THEORY AND PUBLIC POLICY

Our investigation of ethical principles for a just and humane society capable of powerful genetic interventions is not an attempt to advance concrete policy recommendations for our own society at the present time. We offer no model statutes for regulating genetic interventions. We provide no definitive list of genetic interventions that should be included in the package of benefits required by the right to health care.

Instead, our aim is to explore the resources and limitations of ethical theory for guiding deliberations about public policy. To borrow a metaphor from molecular genetics, we only hope to produce a map featuring the most important moral markers, nothing like a complete sequence of ethical steps into the genetic future. We do this by articulating and refining the basic ethical principles that policymakers ought to take into account in responding to issues on the development and deployment of genetic intervention technologies, and by critically evaluating current attempts in the bioethical literature to narrow the range of permissible policy alternatives by using certain distinctions, such as that between treatment and enhancement or between germline and somatic cell interventions. Our aim is to provide some of the essential materials for constructing a framework for discourse about the ethics of genetic intervention.

The eighth and final chapter draws out the major implications of our analysis for how we ought to think about public policy if we are to avoid the errors and abuses associated with eugenics and to harness our burgeoning genetic powers to help create a more just and humane society. Because our moral map aims to provide guidance for some considerable distance into the future, we have tried to take the longer view. Doing so inevitably means, however, that we do not achieve a fine focus on objects in the foreground. We do not, for example, explore some of the more urgent concrete policy issues our society faces today, such as the problem of genetic privacy or insurance discrimination on genetic grounds. There is already a sophisticated literature on these issues. Our objective is to explore other and in some cases more fundamental issues that are often overlooked or not attacked in a systematic fashion.

SCIENCE FICTION EXAMPLES, REFLECTIVE EQUILIBRIUM, AND THE IDEOLOGICAL USES OF GENETIC DETERMINISM

We began this introduction with several hypothetical scenarios, some more farfetched than others. Is there any reason to include such science fiction cases as the genetic enhancement certificate and genetic communitarianism in serious moral deliberations?

The use of concrete cases – both real and hypothetical, complex and simplified – to stimulate moral reflection is essential to the method we use in this book. Our procedure here is far from novel; we rely on the now-familiar method of reflective equilibrium. (A more detailed explanation of our methodological assumptions is found in Appendix 2.)

The aim of systematic moral reasoning is to develop a coherent set of beliefs that includes moral principles, other elements of moral theory (such as an account of which sorts of beings have rights), and beliefs about what is right and wrong in particular cases – actual and hypothetical – as well as beliefs about how the world is and how people in it behave. Moral arguments appeal to some elements of this system of beliefs in order to bring critical reflection to bear on others. This process aims at what Rawls calls "wide reflective equilibrium"

(Rawls 1971, 1974; Daniels 1996). Our moral beliefs are thus held to be revisable in light of other things we believe or reasonably come to believe (Buchanan 1975).

The Risk of Reinforcing "Gene-mania"

Given the subject matter of this book, there are good reasons to use science fiction examples, and equally good reasons for exercising caution in so doing. Because we are concerned with genetic interventions and because the rate of scientific discoveries about genes is now accelerating enormously, we face a painful dilemma. We can refuse to speculate about how extensive our powers of genetic intervention may become, but at the price of failing to provide guidance for significant choices that our society may well have to make in the future. Or we can speculate about the powers human beings may come to wield, but at the risk of being ridiculed for having been swept away by the religious fervor of what might be called "gene-mania," or delusions of biotech grandeur.

If in an effort to provide ethical guidance for the longer run, we overestimate the developing powers of genetic intervention and the impact of genes on individual and social life, we run the risk of reinforcing genetic determinism. This is more a set of attitudes than a creed. To succumb to genetic determinism is, most simply put, to think of genes as self-sufficient or autonomous causes of traits or behaviors.

Genetic determinism betrays, above all, a failure to understand that genes are always only contributing causes. Whether a given trait will be present depends not just on the gene or genes in question, but also on the environment, including the environment of the organism's body at a particular stage in the organism's development. In the vocabulary of social anthropology, genetic determinism is a variety of fetishism. (A fetish is an object that people endow – in their imaginations – with supernatural powers, or at least with powers that the object does not have.)

The fetishism of genes in our society's popular culture has been eloquently documented by Lindee and Nelkin (1995). A glance at mass media coverage of these issues shows how pervasive gene-mania is. Virtually every week headlines proclaim the discovery of "the gene for X" (obesity, anxiety, homosexuality, etc.). Genetic determinist thinking feeds gene-mania because it goes far beyond the assumption that genes play a significant role in all of the traits or behavior in which we are interested to the patently false claim that genes are autonomous causes.

Genetic Determinist Fallacies

The various confusions and fallacies of genetic determinism are carefully exposed in Appendix 1, written by Elliot Sober, a preeminent philosopher of biology. Sober's analysis of the concept of genetic causation helps clarify an essential point: Genetic determinism is not merely a tendency to make erroneous causal judgments about genes; it is a cognitive error that fosters the abdication of moral and social responsibility.

Genetic determinism promotes a worshipful attitude toward genes and genetic science. Given the assumption that, as James Watson (1989) has said, "our fate is in our genes," our admiration for the achievements of genetic science leads us to look to our genes for the source of all our problems and to molecular biology for their solutions. We thereby conveniently blind ourselves to the uncomfortable possibility that many of our most serious problems result from our social practices and institutions.

Ideological Functions of Genetic Determinism

Genetic determinism thus plays an exculpating role. If academic and economic "underachievement," aggression, depression, "criminal behavior," and sexual infidelity are all caused by genes, then there is indeed a double exculpation. Individuals are not responsible for their behavior (tiny chemical factories embedded within them are), nor are we responsible for critically evaluating and perhaps reforming existing institutions and social practices, since these are largely irrelevant to the problems that most concern us. If there were an all-powerful and all-knowing being who was resolutely committed to shielding the existing social and political order from critical scrutiny, it is unlikely that it could hit upon a better strategy than implanting genetic determinist thinking in peoples' heads.

There is, of course, no such evil demon. There are, however, scientists who sometimes foster gene-mania by a combination of excessive enthusiasm for their own projects and breathless public relations rhetoric aimed at securing social and financial support. And there are biotechnology firms poised to unleash sophisticated marketing techniques that will no doubt encourage unrealistic hopes for genetic so-lutions to all sorts of problems. Finally, there is the interest that ordinary people – especially those who benefit quite nicely from the existing social and political order – have in avoiding anything that might require them to question whether they should continue to sup-port and benefit from the status quo.

As the next chapter shows, the exculpatory functions of genetic determinism attained their most dramatic expression in the eugenic preoccupation with "the problem of degeneration." Despite its heter-ogeneity in other regards, eugenic thought tended to "geneticize" a remarkable number of the most important social problems, and on the basis of remarkably little evidence that genes played any significant role in them.

Those who scoff at the suggestion that our society is in danger of a resurgence of eugenic thinking should ask themselves two questions. Is genetic determinist thinking significantly less prevalent today than it was in the heyday of eugenics? And are the interests in avoiding the conclusion that most of society's problems are to a significant degree rooted in our institutions any less powerful today than they were a hundred years ago? Unfortunately, the answer to both questions seems to be "no" (Hubbard and Wald 1993; Lewontin 1992).

Given the serious risk of encouraging genetic determinist thinking and its exculpatory ideological functions, would it be better to avoid the use of "science fiction" examples of genetic interventions, even if this means that we may fail to consider some ethical issues that our society may in fact have to face? We believe that predictions about which genetic interventions will never become possible are often al-most as unfounded as the extravagant view that virtually everything will eventually become possible. So although we have tried to engage in science fiction, not science fantasy, we have considered some inter-ventions that may become possible while recognizing that they may in fact never actually become so. (For example, in Chapter 3 we consider the possibility that genetic intervention might in the very distant future produce changes that lead us to revise our conception of human nature or even to dispense with it.)

It would be a poor strategy to make our ethical conclusions rest on empirical premises about what will never happen, given the very real possibility that they may prove false. Developing a proactive ethical stance is a better defense against genetic determinism and its politically conservative implications than a policy of failing to engage with the ethical issues by dismissing the possibility that they will arise. More important, our analysis will show that a dramatic expansion of our knowledge of the role of genes as (contributing) causes and a corresponding increase in the capacity for genetic intervention would do nothing to justify a conservative and uncritical attitude toward existing social practices and political institutions.

TWO

EUGENICS AND ITS SHADOW

THE RELEVANCE OF EUGENICS

Optimism and Anxiety

The revolution in genetics, although full of promise for understanding our own constitution and for the power to change human lives for the better, has nevertheless proven profoundly unsettling. Discovery of the genes responsible for certain diseases and traits, and invention of new techniques for manipulating the human genome provoke not only wonder but fear as well. Sensitive to these concerns, James Watson, first director of the Human Genome Project, found it prudent to promise a wary Congress that a significant share of funds allocated to the project would be devoted to studies of the ethical, legal, and social issues it raises. His successor, Francis Collins, has stated that concern over ethical issues, not the remaining scientific and technological hurdles, were the greatest threat to the success of the project, for the project cannot continue without public support.

The source of most of the public's distrust, no doubt, stems from the widespread realization that genetic information may be used to deny insurance and employment. It takes no subtle philosophy to understand that anyone is vulnerable to exclusion from these and other economic and social arrangements should their genes be examined and found wanting. These risks have rightly occupied center stage in bioethical debates over how the new genetics will be used.

Some of this concern, however, may be a faint echo of earlier controversy. The current revolution in molecular biology is not the first but the second large-scale attempt to modify the pattern of human heredity for the better. The eugenics movements of 1870–1950 came

first. These large-scale social movements, originating in England but
ultimately involving public advocates and membership organizations
from Brazil to Russia, located the source of social problems in the
genes of individuals and sought to alter the pattern by which these
genes would be transmitted to future generations. In the United States,
the movement received substantial funding from the great family fortunes, including Carnegie and the Rockefellers, and it was endorsed,
with varying degrees of enthusiasm, by most scientists working in the
field of human genetics. Indeed, eugenics was the motivation for much
of the early scientific research in this field.

Nevertheless, the history of eugenics is not a proud one. It is largely
remembered for its shoddy science, the blatant race and class biases of
many of its leading advocates, and its cruel program of segregation
and, later, sterilization of hundreds of thousands of vulnerable people
who were judged to have substandard genes. Even worse, eugenics, in
the form of "racial hygiene," formed part of the core of Nazi doctrine.
Hitler endorses it in *Mein Kampf*, and once in power expanded both
eugenic research and, borrowing from U.S. models, a program of
sterilization that became the first step toward the murder of handicapped "Aryans" and ultimately millions of victims of the Holocaust.

Eugenics as a Cautionary Tale

Understood as the second of two eras in which the science of heredity
was promised to offer great benefits for mankind, it is inevitable that
today's genetics proceeds in the shadow of eugenics. The current revolution in genetics, in this view, is Round Two. Given this history,
anything reminiscent of eugenics is bound to be suspect. When particular uses of genetic technology and science are branded as "eugenic,"
the label points us to an evil that eugenics represents. It is a powerful
warning.

But what is this evil? If we are to avoid the errors of the past, we
must know what they were. The label "eugenics" denotes the movement of that name, but not a specific tenet or practice against which
we are cautioned. In this chapter, we attempt to specify this evil, giving
content to the comparison between eugenics and current and future
developments in human genetics.

We begin with a short history of the movement, recounting the
growth of mainstream eugenics in the United States and the United
Kingdom but taking note also of the considerable diversity of goals,

beliefs, and proposed policies that could be found in eugenics movements around the globe. We then turn to consideration of eugenics as a doctrine or set of doctrines that represent the kernel of the eugenic ideal in its various manifestations. We provide a moral assessment of these doctrines, an "ethical autopsy," identifying what was indeed evil and what might be considered benign. Finally, we apply our conclusions to the present and future, identifying the questions that must be answered if public policy regarding genetics is to avoid the moral errors of eugenics.

In our own consideration of eugenics, benefiting both from superb reconsiderations of the movement by historians in the last decade and from primary sources, we have been impressed by the complexity of the eugenics movement and by the importance, too often unrecognized by nonhistorians, of informing our moral evaluation of past events and actors with an understanding of how the world seemed through their eyes. Indeed, the historian Leila Zenderland[1] has warned that the history of the eugenics movement exists in two versions, an "official" story of racist, reactionary thinkers and politicians, working with a few marginal scientists, a movement that proceeded directly from Darwin to Hitler; and a "real" story of a bewildering array of thinkers, activists, snobs, socialists, scientific visionaries and crackpots, fascists, and architects of the Scandinavian social welfare states, divided among themselves on nearly every point of doctrine and proposed intervention. The "official story" is what is taught to young geneticists and inhabits the popular imagination; it tells us what we must not do. The "real" story is less tractable, less teachable, and harder to mine for bioethical insights. Attempts to draw lessons from this history require great caution.

Not all would agree, even so, that we can learn very much from the history of eugenics. In this view, the eugenics episode is chiefly a historical curiosity, one that might tell us something about the temptation for political movements to reach for the authority of science, but that sheds no light on contemporary clinical genetics or public policy in the current era.

While respecting the complexity and diversity of the eugenics movement as well as its historical remoteness, we believe that the history of eugenics is instructive for those concerned with the bioethics of the

---

[1] "What was Eugenics?," unpublished paper (the American Philosophical Association, Pacific Division, 1998).

new genetics. It was marked, in its worst moments, by cruel violations of human rights; any steps, whether public or private, that might propel us in this same direction must be identified and countered. While we make a point in the following to correct the common mistake (in the literature of bioethics) of identifying eugenics generally with its Nazi variant, the magnitude of the evil waiting at this extreme terminus of the eugenics movement provides an enduring general caution for genetics in the foreseeable future.

The history of the eugenics movement prior to the Nazi period is instructive as well. While its record of mayhem was overshadowed by that of the Nazis, we can find, even given the most charitable understanding of its leaders' motives, a failure to deal adequately with the tension between social good and individual liberties, rights, and interests, which has long been the moral problem at the heart of the enterprise of public health. We situate the cardinal moral failing of eugenics within this understanding of the ethics of public health, and our book is dedicated in large measure to providing some clarity where in eugenics we find only a blind spot: the relation of genetic intervention to justice.

EUGENICS: A BRIEF HISTORY

Origins and Growth

Although the literature of eugenics extends back to Plato, its modern impetus was the work of one man. Francis Galton, a cousin of Charles Darwin, was impressed by the frequency with which genius seemed to be manifested in some lineages more than others. He sought to investigate the possibility that talents and virtues of character were inherited along with other traits, offering their bearers advantages in natural selection. His research, enhanced by statistical methods developed as he needed them, convinced him that society's stock of talent could be greatly enlarged if members of favored families were to increase their rate of childbearing. The balance should be further improved, he believed, by discouraging from reproducing those who had less to offer. Galton coined the term "eugenics" in 1883 (15 years after publishing his first proposals), defining it as the "science of improving stock – not only by judicious mating, but whatever tends to give the more suitable races or strains of blood a better chance of prevailing over the less suitable than they otherwise would have had."

Galton's influence was nearly immediate. Darwin declared himself persuaded by his cousin's eugenic arguments, and Galton attracted a number of distinguished disciples. In Germany, the Racial Hygiene Society was formed in Berlin by 1905 (Weindling 1989); the English Eugenics Education Society was founded in 1907, with Galton elected honorary president the next year (Kevles 1985, p. 59). In the United Kingdom and the United States, the movement drew on the middle and upper middle classes, including many professionals and academics (Rafter 1988; MacKenzie 1981; Kevles 1985; Searle; Mazumdar 1992). By 1923, when the American Eugenics Society was formed, it boasted 28 state branches (Kevles 1985). During the decades 1890–1920, eugenic ideas were advanced also in numerous non-English-speaking countries as diverse as Norway, Brazil, and the Soviet Union.

Eugenics in the United Kingdom and the United States was both a research program and a popular movement. Galton's work on heredity and statistics was continued by his successor Karl Pearson, and their coworkers in what became the Galton Laboratory, with an endowed Galton Eugenics Professorship. In the United States, the Carnegie-supported Eugenics Record Office, under sociologist Charles Davenport, employed a team of interviewers to collect information for its store of family pedigrees, which it also solicited from the public (Allen 1986, Paul 1996). Eugenics was taught at leading universities and received attention in standard biology textbooks.

The popular eugenics movements, meanwhile, succeeded in rapidly introducing eugenic ideas into public discourse. Accounts of generations of misfits in such "white trash" family lines as the "Jukes" and the "Kallikaks" were widely publicized, warning that an unwise reproductive act could wreak havoc for generations (Rafter 1988). Following British successes at health exhibitions before the turn of the century, American eugenic organizations took a particular interest in maintaining exhibits and events at state fairs and public expositions. The Race Betterment Foundation, under John Kellogg, attracted 10,000 visitors and boasted a million lines of newspaper publicity for its contribution to the Panama-Pacific exposition of 1915 (Rydell 1993).

Eugenicists took over the American Museum of Natural History in New York for a month in 1915, and a similar exhibit there in 1932 drew 15,000 visitors. "Fitter Families" competitions were mounted at state fairs, from Massachusetts to Oklahoma, with governors and senators handing out awards (Rydell 1993, p. 46). By wedding eugenics to the ideal of the "average American" at these fairs and exhibitions, its elite supporters sought out a mass audience – although this populist turn took the movement in a direction quite different from that envisioned by Galton, whose inspiration had been the phenomenon of scientific genius.

Varieties of Eugenics

The content of the eugenic program varied considerably from country to country and within each nation's movement. There were differences, for example, in beliefs about the mechanism of transmission of inherited traits. The French and Brazilian eugenics movements were at least as concerned about neonatal care as with heredity, and their hereditarian thinking was Lamarckian – that is, they believed that parents passed on to their children characteristics acquired during their lives (Schneider 1990; Stepan 1991). If the notion of a Larmackian eugenics seems an oxymoron since eugenics is remembered as a movement that emphasized nature over nurture as both cause and remedy of human failings, a thesis Lamarckians rejected, this is perhaps because our own experience (in English-speaking countries) has defined eugenics narrowly. If we look beyond the Anglo-Saxon experience, William Schneider states, we will understand eugenics as "less a pseudoscientific, failed branch of applied human genetics than a biologically based movement for social reform." Most eugenicists elsewhere accepted Galton's view, buttressed by the "germ plasm" hypothesis of August Weismann, that selection rather than environment determined heredity. Eugenicists tended to draw from this account the implication that medical care frustrated evolution by permitting the unfit to survive and reproduce (although Darwin and a number of others who held this view nonetheless continued to support humanitarian measures).

Eugenicists differed also in their practical proposals and legislative aims. Some favored "positive eugenics" (encouraging the most fit to have larger families), others accented "negative eugenics" (curbing the fertility of those judged least fit), and many wanted both. While action on behalf of positive eugenics was limited to such mild measures as family allowances, some eugenicists (particularly in the United States and, later, Germany) did not hesitate to call for coercive measures, either sexual segregation or, later, involuntary sterilization, to prevent those imagined to have undesirable genes from propagating.

National experiences varied widely. Involuntary sterilization remained rare in England, but was permitted by statutes enacted between 1910 and 1930 in northern Europe, including Denmark and Germany, and in the United States. Involuntary sterilization was practiced on large numbers of people in the United States, where tens of thousands were affected during the Depression, and in Germany, where the greatly stepped-up program following the Nazi rise to power rendered several hundred thousand incapable of bearing children.

In both the United States and Germany, a number of leading figures combined eugenic interests with a focus on race (Roll-Hansen 1988); eugenicists in South America did this less (Stepan 1991; Larson 1995). Eugenicists in the United States supported restrictions on immigration, maintaining that the immigrants arriving after the turn of the century from southern and eastern Europe suffered by comparison with "old American stock" in intelligence and other virtues. They pressed also for laws forbidding interracial marriages.

In Germany, eugenics became an integral element of medical thinking, which envisioned a three-way division of health care involving medical care for the individual, public health for the community, and eugenics for the race (Weiss 1990; Proctor 1988). Eugenics, for some, was an extension of a tradition of a social orientation in German medicine that had produced Rudolf Virchow and other pioneers of public health. In the United States, however, medical schools were slow to include any instruction in eugenics or genetics.

Eugenicists differed among themselves wherever the movement attracted a large following. Historians have generally followed Daniel Kevles's (1986) classification of eugenicists, at least in England and the United States, as either "mainline" or "reform." In the United States and Britain, mainline eugenics was largely (but not exclusively) conservative in political orientation. Galton was but the first of a long line of eugenicists who believed that those who achieved (at least in fields such as science and literature, where social position was insufficient for advancement) were distinguished from others in their possession of great natural, inherited talent. Indeed, the mainline eugenicists tended to believe that a person's station in life reflected his or her capabilities and could thus be used as an indication of the genes likely to be passed down to subsequent generations.

The preoccupation of mainline eugenicists was the social havoc being wrought by the lower classes. Indeed, one historian of the En-

glish movement defined eugenics bluntly as "a middle-class activism
focused upon the pauper class, with a biological view of human failings" (Mazumdar 1992, p. 258). In both the United Kingdom and the
United States, a long list of social ills, including poverty, prostitution,
drunkenness, and crime, were attributed to the "unfit."

In the United States (as in Germany), this class bias was joined by a
virulent racism, which warned of the effects both of miscegenation
and of high birthrates among "inferior" races. These attitudes helped
to win support for the drastic curbs on immigration enacted after the
First World War. Theodore Roosevelt warned that a "war of the
cradle" was being waged between the better and inferior social groups.
To be sure, mainline eugenicists, when speaking with care, took pains
to distinguish the working classes from the degenerate "social residuum," but these fine distinctions were often blurred, and they did not
lessen the offense taken by their socialist opponents.

Nationalism was a third characteristic concern. Mainstream eugenicists were often prone to interpreting the degeneracy thesis in national
terms, identifying nationality with "blood" and fearing that England
(or Germany, or wherever) would lose in competition with nations
that did a better job maintaining the quality of their germ plasm.

The "reform" contingent, often socialists, and including many of
the leading figures in the science of human genetics, accepted eugenic
goals, but were unsparingly critical of the mainline eugenicists' research, biases, and proposals. Hermann Muller, an American geneticist who later won a Nobel prize for demonstrating the effect of
radiation on chromosomes, insisted that natural talent could not be
assessed in a society such as the United States, which did not offer
equal opportunities for advancement to its citizens; only under socialism could the fit be identified as such and then encouraged to multiply.

Eugenics was often found in the political platforms of left-of-center
political parties. A key proponent in Denmark, for example, was Karl
Steincke, a father of the Danish welfare state (Hansen 1996), and
several of the leading Norwegian eugenicists were also Social Demo-
crats (Roll-Hansen 1980). Eugenics was adopted with enthusiasm by
Tommy Douglas, later the pioneer of Canadian social democracy in
Manitoba; by Fabian Socialists in the United Kingdom; and by the
Progressives in the United States, all of whom favored social programs
that, with the help of science, applied resources available to the state
to building a more humane society. Many of these same figures, how-

ever, were indistinguishable from their conservative counterparts in class and racial bias.

Sweden's eugenics programs are an instructive case study, since, as Gunnar Broberg and Mattias Tydén (1996) have shown, they show the compatibility of eugenic thinking to varied political viewpoints. Until the 1930s, the movement was centered in the Institute for Race Biology in Uppsala, under the direction of a traditional eugenicist who would later profess Nazism. The work of the institute focused on physical anthropology and was much concerned with alleged threats to the "Nordic type." After a five-year dispute, a Social Democratic scientist took control, disavowed racism, and emphasized laboratory studies in medical genetics. But the ascendancy of the socialists proved to give eugenics a second wind. The planners of the Swedish welfare state, concerned with the "quality" as well as the quantity of Sweden's then-dwindling population, were eager for the government to use natural and social science for the common good. The modernization and rational ordering of society left little room for the inferior and the deficient, and the government sought to identify and sterilize these citizens. Indeed, Social Democratic intellectuals maintained that these sterilizations were necessary if Sweden were to be able to afford the cradle-to-grave security they championed. Eugenics, in effect, was an instrument for reducing need. Tens of thousands of Swedes, mostly women, fell victim during the next three decades. The contrast between "progressive" and "reactionary" eugenics should not be overemphasized – Swedish eugenics targeted a population of itinerants (*Tattare*, or tinkers), who were imagined to be racially different, and the eugenicists who made a point of disavowing racism and class bias tended to be academics rather than government officials. As in other countries, those who actually bore the brunt of state coercion in the name of the eugenic common good were usually the marginal, the stigmatized, and the vulnerable. But the Swedish eugenicists strenuously denied any commonality with Nazi policies of the same era, and our current tendency to equate eugenics with Nazism distorts this historical record.

While eugenics was supported by most geneticists of the era, a number of the scientists were harshly critical of mainline eugenics. Like his Swedish counterparts, Hermann Muller recognized the movement's racism and class bias, and the worthlessness of the studies of family pedigrees that constituted its source of data. But he, too, was concerned that civilization was interfering with natural selection, and was intrigued by the possibility that humanity might sever the age-old link between biological and social parenthood in favor of "germinal choice" of superior genetic material.

A "Geneticists' Manifesto" signed by Muller and other leading scientists in 1939 insisted that encouragement of eugenic-minded reproduction be part of a wider social program that would provide economic security to parents, equal opportunities to women, public education in biology, and a "socialized organization" that ensures that "social motives predominate in society." The first goal of eugenics, in their view, was health, followed by intelligence and "those temperamental qualities which favor fellow-feeling and social behavior rather than those (today most esteemed by many) which make for personal 'success,' as success is usually understood at present." The goal of eugenics, they held, was "much more than the prevention of genetic deterioration"; they looked to the day, only a few generations distant, when "everyone might look upon 'genius' . . . as his birthright. And . . . this would represent no final stage at all."

The labels "mainline" and "reform" do not do justice to the great variety of viewpoints and goals associated with the eugenics movements. Indeed, as Diane Paul has observed, one sign of the ubiquity of eugenic thinking was the attempt by parties on all sides of particular social disputes to further their cause by demonstrating that their recommendations would have the strongest eugenic effect. Leading figures in the American and British eugenics organizations were political reactionaries. But eugenics, seen as an avenue for the application of science to social problems, was attractive also to some of the architects of the modern welfare state, such as the Progressives in the United States and the Scandinavian Social Democratic parties.

Much of the opposition to eugenics during that era, at least in Europe, came from the right. The eugenicists' legislative successes in Germany and Scandinavia were not matched in such countries as Poland and Czechoslovakia, even though measures had been proposed there, largely because of the conservative influence in these countries of the Catholic Church (Roll-Hansen 1988). The Church opposed eugenics in principle (and it was virtually the only institution to do so), but this was of a piece with its opposition to abortion and contraception: Then, as now, the Church was opposed to limitations on fertility, and its opponents were often on the left.

To be sure, early eugenicists were also opponents of birth control, since they believed that its use by the upper classes exacerbated the degeneration of the gene pool. But not all eugenicists took this position. The eugenic banner was seized also by feminists who argued that control over fertility, along with emancipation generally, permitted women to improve the race through sexual selection.

Today, few people other than historians of science appreciate the range of political viewpoints and causes that were once proudly associated with eugenic doctrine. Historical memory of the movement is colored, perhaps permanently, by the appropriation of eugenics by the Nazi Party.

The Nazi Debacle

Eugenics in Germany, while distinctive in having a medical leadership, had been marked by much the same divergences of opinion as the movements in other countries. Though numerous prominent eugenicists were racist and anti-Semitic, others were avowedly antiracist (and some were Jews), and a number stood on the political left (Weindling 1989). The Nazis imposed a uniformity of viewpoint, securing the allegiance of the many eugenicists who rallied to its cause for a thoroughly racist, nationalist eugenic program that recognized no limits in the pursuit of "racial hygiene."

Eugenics was central to the entire Nazi enterprise, joined with romantic nativist and racist myths of the purebred Nordic. The emphasis on "blood" called for a purifying of the nation's gene pool so that Germans could regain the nobility and greatness of their genetically pure forebears (Burleigh and Wipperman 1991).

As Robert Proctor (1988) and other historians have shown, the subsequent programs of sterilization, euthanasia of the unfit (a program that took the lives of tens of thousands of "Aryans," mostly young children), and eventually the Holocaust itself were part of the unfolding of this central idea. The sterilization and "euthanasia" programs, which did not initially target Jews and other minorities, were an exercise in negative eugenics designed to improve the native German stock from its degenerated condition. Legislation barring sexual relations between Jews and "Aryans," and ultimately the Holocaust were intended to prevent further adulteration of the "pure" German nation with inferior genes. Jews and others who contributed "evil" genes were the disease afflicting the German nation, which Hitler, the physician, would cure.

These measures were complemented by a range of other genetic interventions, ranging from an elaborate system of Genetic Courts passing judgment on the genetic fitness of those thought to harbor defective genes, to marriage advice clinics, to the *Lebensborn* breeding program for SS men and other racially motivated initiatives in positive eugenics (Weindling 1989). The academic fields of anthropology, biology, and medicine were reformulated in racial and eugenic terms, and the profession of medicine in Germany was compromised by its participation in government programs of identification, sterilization, and murder of those deemed unfit (Aly and Prosch 1994; Weindling 1989; Burleigh 1994; Gallagher 1990; Wikler and Barondess 1994).

Nazi eugenics was distinctive in its scale and elaborateness, its ferocity, its racial orientation, and its demands for absolute submission by the individual to the interests of the group. No other eugenic program approached the Nazis' eugenics in any of these dimensions. But the Nazi eugenicists claimed – misleadingly, according to Weindling (1989) – that there were continuities between their eugenics and the programs of the regimes that had preceded theirs.

How should we understand the relation of the Nazi crimes to the doctrine of eugenics? Did the Nazis simply carry out the measures that were inherent in the eugenic program all along, but that others had been unwilling or unable to put to practice? Or was Nazi eugenics a distortion, that is, a perversion, of eugenics, which stemmed not from any barbarism inherent in eugenic doctrine but from its adoption by Nazis, who bloodied and sullied everything they touched? These questions frame much of the debate over the shadow of eugenics.

Decline and Fall

In their first years, Nazi eugenic programs and propaganda won the acclaim of eugenic leaders in the United States. The Nazis flattered their counterparts overseas by pointing to legislation in California and elsewhere not only as precedents but also as models. It is unsettling to compare the notorious Nuremberg laws to the miscegenation and eugenics statutes of California and other states; among other elements, the determination to keep 'races "pure" was carried over intact, although the races were identified differently. The authors of these statutes toured Germany and filed favorable reports upon their return (Kuhl 1994). Harry Laughlin, Director of the Eugenics Record Office and a central figure in American eugenics, was given an honorary degree by a German university, which he accepted with thanks at the German legation in New York.

After the Holocaust and the defeat of the Germans, however, eugenicists in most other countries were quick to distance themselves from German eugenics. Since the Germans had presented themselves as the most consistent and purposeful of eugenicists, the movement itself fell into general disrepute. American eugenic organizations experienced amnesia over their prewar affinity with their German counterparts, spoke out against racism, and urged Americans to consider eugenics as a source of national strength. The *Eugenical News* (23:2–3, 1945) urged its readers to remember that

it can sometimes be as important to live for our ideals and to pass on a goodly heritage, as to die for them when that time comes. The heroes of Valley Forge and Gettysburg . . . will have died in vain if the best of our race also dies. The stork . . . must be kept flying, too, along with the eagle and the bombers. But it must fly to those homes where good environment will bring the best heredity to fruition, socially and biologically.

Despite these efforts, the eugenic societies soon lost their followers. The American society's journal was renamed *Journal of Social Biology*, and what had in prewar years been a virtual consensus in favor of eugenics among genetic scientists disappeared within a decade. The movements' offices were shut down, and the Rockefellers and other funding sources turned their attention to related but more reputable concerns, such as world population control and prevention of birth defects, and to genetics and molecular biology (Kay 1995; Paul 1991).

There is some controversy over the explanation of the sudden disappearance of eugenics from our national consciousness. The account given in the first histories of the eugenics movement was that eugenics was abandoned as the science of genetics progressed, leaving genetic scientists increasingly dubious of the central factual claims of the movement. A revisionist tradition points to the strikingly rapid repudiation of eugenics by reputable geneticists in the mid-1940s, a period marked not by any sudden increase in scientific knowledge but by the scientists' strong interest in distancing themselves from the Nazis. Some would even maintain that the eugenicists did not in fact abandon ship, although they said they did. In this view, the Nazi connection motivated eugenicists to refuse to endorse eugenic ideas under that name, and to support eugenic beliefs and projects in other guises.

These accounts have different implications for the future of genetic policy. If eugenics succumbed to the advancement of science, perhaps the lid on its coffin is nailed as tightly shut as it needs to be. If, however, the retreat from eugenics was simply one of fashion, the movement has not been repudiated on the basis of fact or even principle, and we might unthinkingly (or, worse, consciously) return to eugenics when and if fashion changes again. Finally, if clinical genetics is simply eugenics under a different name, we must achieve a clear understanding of the morality of both.

COMMON THEMES OF EUGENICISTS

Despite the evident variety of eugenic activity, the whole of eugenics can be characterized by a core set of tenets to which the various movements and figures are related, and important currents in the eugenic stream can be identified more precisely. Although there may be few theses to which all eugenicsts subscribed, there are some that nearly all supported. In particular, most eugenicists shared two assumptions about heredity: the degeneration of the gene pool and the heritability of behavioral traits. There was also widespread agreement on the general aims of the eugenic program.

Degeneration

Fears of degeneration haunted European social thought in the late nineteenth century. Before Weismann's theory of the unalterable germ plasm gained wide acceptance, the commonly accepted explanation was environmental, blaming the migration of young men from the healthy countryside to the cities during industrialization, which was claimed to have ill effects on offspring (Soloway 1990). After Weissman's and Galton's views had made an impact, concern shifted to the effects of "unnatural" selection. Darwin's *Origin of Species* seemed to demonstrate that competition, a process with losers as well as winners, is essential if the human race is to improve. Modern society, it was feared, rescues and nurtures the unfit, who, far from falling by the wayside, now flood society with disproportionately large numbers of offspring. The result is that damaging hereditary characters spread through the population, threatening a catastrophic loss of fitness, and hence of all human excellences, with a cumulative effect that increases exponentially by the year.

Others understood degeneration as a result of the loss of racial purity. A German study of interracial offspring among Hottentots in Africa by a scholar who later figured prominently in Nazi eugenics claimed that mixed-race offspring were inferior to the races of both parents. *Parsifal*, Wagner's final, epic opera of degeneration among teutonic Knights of the Holy Grail, has been understood as a warning of the loss of Germanic biological superiority through the mixing of blood; one devotee who may have taken this lesson from Wagner was the young Adolf Hitler. The specter of degeneration, whether understood in racial terms or not, gave urgency to eugenic policies. Without this doomsday scenario, fewer of the movements' followers would have accepted its harsher prescriptions.

Heritability of Behavioral Traits

The belief in the heritability of behavioral traits – talents, proclivities, dispositions, and the like – has earned the eugenicists well-deserved ridicule. Davenport's list of inherited traits, for example, ranged from "pauperism" to such fanciful items as "thallasophillia," or love of the sea, the gene for which he judged to be sex-linked (since sea captains were exclusively male). For many eugenicists, the key to the transmission of character and talent was the single trait of intelligence, and eugenics was intimately associated with the rise of IQ testing and the labeling and grading of degrees of mental incompetence by Henry Goddard and others. At issue was whether the objectionable behavior of the unfit could be traced to lack of intelligence (immorality, in this view, resulting from an inability to understand right and wrong), or to the inheritance of separate incapacities, in particular, lack of self-control and industry.

In view of their belief in genetic transmission of talents and temperament, almost all eugenicists believed that social problems had both a biological basis and, to some degree, a potential biological remedy. The precise relationship between society and biology was understood very differently by, say, "mainline" British conservatives, Nazi racialists, and Marxist radicals. But we can find the same biologizing tendency in proposals as varied as segregation of the "feeble-minded" and the proposal for "eutelegenesis" – the mass insemination of women with the sperm from a small number of remarkable men, which a Soviet eugenicist insisted was necessary for fulfillment of the Five-Year Plan.

Eugenic Ends

Beyond these assumptions, nearly all eugenicists agreed on the overall aim of their movements. The fundamental goal of all eugenics in those countries in which the "hard-hereditarian" genetic theories of Galton and Weismann were accepted was to "improve" the overall quality of the gene pool, whether by positive or negative eugenic means. Because eugenics antedated the current revolution in genetics and molecular biology, its proposals of necessity relied almost exclusively on changing the breeding practices of human beings. Accordingly, reproduction was seen by all eugenicists as an act with social consequences rather than a private matter.

Not all eugenicists concluded that reproduction should be controlled by the state. Galton, for example, wanted to secure voluntary acquiescence with eugenic guidelines by making eugenics a civil religion, and some eugenicists focused entirely on positive eugenics, which could scarcely be compulsory. This social understanding of reproduction was accompanied by a view of the germ plasm as a social resource, its use governed by considerations of the public good – although, once again, eugenicists of different political colorations drew very different implications from this shared premise.

If there was a core belief common to all eugenicists, it would have to be expressed in the most general terms: concern for human betterment through selection – that is, by taking measures to ensure that the humans who do come into existence will be capable of enjoying better lives and of contributing to the betterment of lives of others. This, most would agree, is an unexceptionable aim – and its general appeal helps account for at least some of the wide appeal of the eugenics program. But behind this genial promise lay a multitude of sins.

ETHICAL AUTOPSY

Eugenics is remembered mostly for the outrages committed in its name. Terrible as they were, however, these wrongs do not, in themselves, tell us about the validity of eugenic moral thinking, any more than medical experimentation on human beings can be judged immoral on the basis of experiments at Dachau and Tuskegee. For the history of eugenics to be instructive in ensuring social justice in a society with greater knowledge about genes, and perhaps some ability to alter them, the key question is whether, unlike medical experimentation on humans, eugenics was wrong in its very inception. If so, any eugenics program will be wrong. On the other hand, if the abuses done in the name of eugenics do not necessarily reflect badly on eugenic ideas themselves, then our task will be to ensure that any eugenic interventions of the future avoids these abuses. Our review, which will be simultaneously historical and prescriptive, finds that much of the bad reputation of eugenics is traceable to attributes that, at least in theory, might be avoidable in a future eugenic program. But we believe that problems of social justice and fairness, which reduced the moral stature of eugenics in the past, will prove just as difficult in the decades ahead.

A Creature of Its Time

Eugenics is easy to ridicule. Photographs of "Fitter Family Contests," showing large families at state fairs receiving the same kinds of awards as those handed out for best cows and pigs, need no comment, and the movement's extravagant promises and predictions are ludicrous in retrospect. Indeed, very little of the scientific basis on which the movement was premised – for this was fashioned as an attempt to bring the insights and methods of modern science to bear on social problems – withstands scrutiny.

Though the eugenicists correctly noted the social dislocations of the late nineteenth and early twentieth centuries, their biological explanation – the "degeneracy" thesis – was not correct, either in its Lamarckian or its Darwinian versions. The widespread belief among eugenicists left and right in the heritability of talents, vices, and other traits of character, has not fared much better. Though interest in the genetic basis of behavioral traits and dispositions continues unabated in today's studies of twins (Bouchard et al. 1990) and in sociobiology (Kitcher 1996), which are hardly free from controversy, even those most strongly convinced of a genetic basis for particular behavioral dispositions find little merit in the eugenicists' research methods or specific conclusions.

Nor were the eugenicists' prescriptions for genetic improvement likely to have much effect. They had no way to identify carriers of recessive genes, and so did not know whom to discourage from reproducing; thus their proposed programs could not possibly deliver the benefits they promised. Some eugenicist scientists came to appreciate the relative futility of their proposed measures in bringing about large-scale changes in the distribution of what they imagined were the genes underlying such traits as intelligence and self-control (Paul and Spencer 1995). In their more careful moments, they conceded that the effect of eugenic measures would be very small, although they considered the interventions justified even by these results. Their candor, however, was not matched by the leaders of the movement, who promised rapid, visible social improvement.

The bigotry and racism of mainstream eugenics, like the pseudoscience, is glaring and appalling to the present-day reader. The class prejudices of mainline eugenicists are startling in their ferocity. The feminist eugenicist Marie Stopes spoke of "that intolerable stream of misery which ever overflows its banks" (Stopes 1921); others spoke of "social pests," "sewerage," and "scum" (Searle 1992). The founder of the famous Vineland Training School, E.R. Johnstone, spoke of "waste humanity" (quoted in Popenoe and Johnson 1918). And Sidney Webb, the Fabian socialist, warned of the "breeding of degenerate hordes of a demoralized 'residuum' unfit for social life."

It is chilling, in light of events to come in Germany, to encounter Charles Davenport's social Darwinist perspective on infant mortality:

We hear a great deal about infant mortality and child saving that appeals to the humanity and the child-love in us all. It is, however, always the saving of the lowest social class that is contemplated. I recall the impassioned appeal of a sociologist for assistance in stopping the frightful mortality among the children of prostitutes. But the daughters of prostitutes have hardly one chance in two of being able to react otherwise than their mothers. Why must we start an expensive campaign to keep alive those who, were they intelligent enough, might well curse us for having intervened on their behalf? Is not death nature's great blessing to the race? If we have greater power to prevent it than ever before, so much the greater is our responsibility to use that power *selectively* for the survival of those of best stock; more than those who are feebleminded and without moral control. (Davenport 1914)

These views betray an almost visceral hatred (parading as concern for the victims who would curse us for their rescue). The first step toward atrocity is the objectification, vilification, and ridicule of the victim. The comparison of "feeble-minded" people and others in the underclass to feces, waste, and animals made it thinkable to deprive hundreds of thousands of people of their civil rights, first through institutionalization and segregation, then by involuntary sterilization, and, in the singular instance of Nazi Germany, through murder.

Though the pseudoscience, bias, bigotry, and racism that abounded in eugenics make the movement's bad reputation richly deserved, these features of the historical movement do not in themselves demonstrate that eugenics must be avoided in the future. The eugenics movement was a creature of its time. The science of genetics was in its infancy. Racism, class snobbery, and other forms of bias were openly expressed even by learned scholars; these sentiments, so obviously objectionable today, were invisible then, because, of course, they were so widely shared. There is no shortage of class, race, and national biases today, although they are no longer displayed openly in polite society, and vigilance is needed to ensure that they do not infect social policy involving applications of genetic science (as in every area of social life). Part of the fierce opposition to the theses of Herrnstein and Murray's *The Bell Curve*, which occupied center stage in intellectual debate for a season, can be understood as a response to their disparaging remarks – couched, to be sure, in soothing and reasonable language – about not only the intelligence but even the moral character of both the poor and African-Americans. But, as we note later in this chapter, racism and other biases were not unique to eugenics. A central concern of public health authorities who studied health among blacks was that whites might catch their diseases. For example, Dr. C. E. Terry reported that though the mortality rate was higher for blacks, the white mortality rate was higher than it should be because of "a race infection" occurring as the blacks "mingle with us in a hundred intimate ways" while rendering services (Terry 1913, quoted in Muller 1985). A 1945 report of a tuberculosis control program in Memphis aimed to x-ray "a large proportion of the Negro females in the community" so that housewives could check their health cards before hiring them as domestics (Graves and Cole 1945). This sorry record does not show that we should abandon public health programs, and likewise it does not argue definitively against eugenics.

In short, the central theses of a social movement, including its moral premises, ought not be dismissed because of the intellectual and ethical failings of its adherents. Eugenics is recalled as the Nazis' racial doctrine, which it was, but to be a eugenicist, then or now, is not tantamount to being a Nazi. Reflexive rejection of eugenic ideas because they had unsavory advocates is neither morally nor intellectually serious. What matters is the moral defensibility of the eugenic concepts and values themselves, which must be identified and assessed.

Why Was Eugenics Wrong? Five Theses

We now consider five answers to the question, Why was eugenics wrong? Each goes beyond the movement's poor science and evident prejudice to attempt to locate errors of moral wrongs inherent in any eugenic program. We endorse the fifth, the lack of a concern for the fair distribution of burdens and benefits, but several of the others come close to the mark.

Thesis 1: Replacement, not Therapy Eugenics sought human betterment, but in a distinctive way: by causing better people to be conceived and born, rather than by directly bettering any people. Benefits to people already born would be indirect: freedom from the burdens placed on society by the unfit, sharing in the productivity of the gifted. The distinction has been drawn vividly, albeit in a different context, by Richard Lewontin:

> To conflate . . . the prevention of *disease* with the prevention of *lives* that will involve disease, is to traduce completely the meaning of preventive medicine. It would lead to the grotesque claim that the National Socialists did more to "prevent" future generations of Tay-Sachs [a lethal genetic disease found most commonly among Jews] sufferers than all the efforts of science to date. Genetic counseling and selective abortion are substitutes for disease prevention and cure. (Lewontin 1997; italics in original)

Is eugenics suspect for this reason? We believe not. There are, however, a number of reasonable concerns that might seem to condemn eugenics for this reason. Policies of any sort, eugenic or otherwise, that affect the well-being of future generations by changing the identities of those who will constitute them present a host of apparent philosophical paradoxes and conundrums, as Jan Narveson (1967, 1973) and Derek Parfit (1984) have shown to a generation of moral philosophers. We discuss these "genethical" uncertainties (Heyd 1992) in Chapter 6. For our evaluation of eugenics, we need only note that eugenic policies are by no means unique in having this kind of effect. So do conservation policies, macroeconomic decisions, and commercial advertising, since each affects, in ways large and small, which individuals will be conceived and born. Why, then, single out eugenics? One concern is that those who would better humankind by bring-ing about the conception of "better" humans would make faulty judg-ments on what kinds of people should be conceived and born. The eugenic authorities might favor the wrong traits, and they might not appreciate the value of diversity and differences in points of view over what makes life valuable and worthwhile. A related concern is that any scale of human excellence that eugenicists might use to "improve" the population would automatically stigmatize those people, both liv-ing and those yet to be conceived, whose traits put them at the bottom of the eugenicists' rankings. Both of these concerns are understanda-ble, and we discuss them both in this chapter and in Chapter 7. To be sure, the eugenicists of half a century ago were guilty of intolerance and disdain for those whose like they sought to "prevent" in future generations. This contempt is audible in H.G. Wells's admonition (1905, quoted in Paul 1995) that "the way of Nature has always been to slay the hindmost, and there is still no other way, unless we can prevent those who would become the hindmost being born." Nazi eugenicists took the further step of murdering many of them. Never-theless, this appraisal of eugenics does not point us toward its cardinal sin. In theory, eugenicists could heed concerns over diversity. Objec-tions to the choices eugenicists made, to which we turn shortly, do not necessarily argue against any attempt to choose. And some of the same concerns about stigmatization could be raised in opposition to pro-grams that seek to ameliorate conditions, such as deafness, among existing people: for why try to "cure" a person of deafness unless it is undesirable to be deaf?

This critique also proves too much. As a general argument, it would condemn genetic screening even for very serious conditions, which disabilities rights organizations themselves support. The gene for achondroplasia, for example, a single copy of which produces a (usu-ally) healthy dwarf, is dreadful in combination, and, according to Ruth Ricker (1995), former President of Little People of America, the dwarf community looks forward to the day when dwarf parents can be spared the fear of giving birth to a child with two of these genes. Advocates among the deaf have asked to appreciate the quality of life achievable with hereditary deafness (Wernimont 1997); but the argu-ment we are considering would also condemn any interest in "prevent-ing lives" marked by disabilities that do not permit such a high quality of life. Indeed, we consider in Chapter 6 the case for the moral thesis that this form of "prevention" is not only permissible but morally obligatory for parents given the choice, at least with respect to severe disabilities.

Thesis 2: Value Pluralism   "Who was to set the criteria for ideal man? In a complex modern society no particular human type could be characterized as 'the best' " (attributed to Wilhelm Johannsen 1913, in Roll-Hansen 1989). Is the very idea of a eugenic program self-defeating? If there is no best, how can eugenicists promote it? Eugenicists are rightly blamed for promoting a particular conception of human perfection, failing to appreciate the essential plurality of values and ideals of human excellence. Like others, they assumed that the ideal would be similar to themselves or at least to those they most admired. Mainline eugenicists in the United Kingdom and the United States, largely members of the upper-middle professional classes, hoped for a society in which each person would attain his or her level of virtue, and they despised those who failed to display the proper bourgeois values. Nazi racial hygienists, many of whom considered themselves to be of "the Nordic type," valued the Nordic type. Hermann Muller, the socialist geneticist and eugenicist, extolled a wide range of models, including Lenin, Gandhi, and Sun Yat-Sen – all of whom were, like Muller himself, exceptionally brilliant men.

As the question attributed to Johannsen, a Danish geneticist and reluctant eugenicist, demonstrates, the difficulty of defining human perfection was not entirely lost on the eugenicists, but the strident rhetoric of much of the mainline eugenics literature brooked no opposition and admitted to no doubt over what constituted a "healthy" and virtuous style of life. In a word, the mainstream eugenicists tended to be snobs. Looking down on the manners and values of those they despised was not an incidental feature of their eugenic program; it was one of its driving forces, validating and supporting the self-image and pretensions of the upper-middle classes (Mazumdar 1992). This intolerance and self-glorification was a notable moral failure in mainstream eugenics. A closer examination of the mainstream, pre-Nazi eugenic program, however, complicates the picture considerably. For although mainline eugenicists despised the underclass for not resembling themselves, the traits the eugenicists believed heritable and worthy of cultivation were ones valued by people with widely varying ideals of personal development, plans of life, and family structure. Although some eugenicists did believe there to be particular genes for drunkenness, "shiftlessness," and the like, in the main the eugenicists focused on a very short list of traits about which there is little controversy. Members of the "human residuum" they wished to eliminate would presumably have valued these traits, too. As we have seen, intelligence dominated the list, or was the only item on it; self-control and a few other very general virtues were sometimes added. There is little real dispute over the value of these all-purpose talents, even among those who might disdain the proper airs and manners of the mainline eugenicists; whatever a person's favored pursuit or style of living might be, intelligence and self-control help make the most of it.

It remains true that the mainline eugenicists were anything but tolerant of personal and social ideals that differed from their own. They favored breeding humans with an eye to intelligence and self-control because they thought that these traits were necessary if a person were to lead a proper kind of life. Claims of this kind – for instance, that the poor are too stupid to understand the difference between right and wrong, or to exercise the restraint necessary for the nuclear family – resurface today in such works as *The Bell Curve*. Still, we would not fault the eugenicists (or the authors of the later book) for believing that raising the level of intellectual ability in the population would result in human betterment. What deserve criticism and rejection are a series of beliefs and attitudes that accompanied this element of the eugenic program. These include the assumption that raising intellectual ability would result in more widespread adoption of bourgeois values, and that this would be a good thing; that social problems such as crime and unemployment are the result of low intelligence; and a belief that, on the whole, people of low intellectual ability are of little value to themselves or others.

For the future of genetics, however, pluralism of ideals and values may turn out to be a crucial issue. Parents who choose not to avail themselves of genetic screening or engineering for avoiding short stature in a child might be condemned by neighbors for failing to ensure that their child would be "normal." Less defensibly, deaf parents who wish to abort fetuses that do not test positive for inherited deafness, and dwarf parents who want only a child with the gene for achondroplasia, also hold unconventional values, and their freedom to act on them is likewise at issue in the ethics of clinical genetics. The European Parliamentary panel on genetic engineering, headed by the Green representative to the German Bundestag, R. Härlin, held that genetic screening requires us to decide what is "normal and abnormal, acceptable and unacceptable, viable and non-viable forms of the genetic make-up of individual human beings before and after birth" (quoted in Kevles 1992). And if we ever acquire an ability to influence personality and character through genetic choice or manipulation – to choose, for example, between aggressive and gentle dispositions – this debate will be of crucial importance. In Chapter 6 we discuss the range of choice among alternatives likely to be available in the near and medium term that should be given to prospective parents.

Thesis 3: Violations of Reproductive Freedoms   Apart from the Nazis' crimes, the involuntary sterilization of tens of thousands of Americans and Europeans is the worst stain on the record of the eugenics movements. (Other great wrongs, such as curbs on immigration and the miscegenation laws, stemmed from a variety of causes.) In many instances, those who warn us of a return to eugenics have infringements of reproductive freedoms in mind. Indeed, the eugenic program, once LaMarckian theories of heredity were abandoned, consisted largely in trying to influence (or to dictate) who would breed with whom. This was the sole technique the eugenicists had for influencing the genetic makeup of new generations. It may seem appropriate, then, to identify eugenics with violations of reproductive freedom, and in turn to condemn both on the same grounds. But is this what was wrong with eugenics? Diane Paul (1996) has pointed out that not all eugenicists favored the use of coercion. Galton did not, and surely he counts as a eugenicist. Eugenics was imposed by force, in the form of sexual segregation and sterilization, but in other instances it was entirely voluntary. Today, the eugenics-minded government in Singapore offers singles cruises to educated women in the hope that they will find husbands and reproduce. This is no violation of reproductive freedom, even if is wrong-headed.

Paul has argued that, at least in the United States, reproductive freedoms are sufficiently well-established that we need not entertain serious fears about the return of a coercive eugenics in the wake of the Human Genome Project. Surely she is correct that sterilizations on a mass scale are inconceivable in this country, at least in the near term. The same may not hold in countries with weaker traditions that lack entrenched legal protections for reproductive freedom, however; China, whose recent law on maternal and child health contains eugenic provisions, is a case in point (*Nature* 1995; Qiu 1998). We discuss issues of genetics and reproductive freedom in Chapter 5.

Thesis 4: Statism   In a recent address, James Watson (1997) reviewed the odious history and possible future of eugenics and concluded that the most important safeguard is to eliminate any role for the state. He provided a strong case. The great wrongs visited on vulnerable people in the name of eugenics – institutionalization, sexual segregation, sterilization, and, in Germany, murder on a mass scale – could not have occurred without state involvement. This was as true in Social Democratic regimes, such as Sweden, as under the Nazis. In England, where the state's role was minimal, eugenics may have been offensive, but it did not violate individual rights.

Nevertheless, we take issue with Watson's thesis if understood as implying that the chief ethical problems of eugenics can be addressed by keeping the state out of genetic improvement. Eugenics can be pursued without the state, and arguably even as the unintended result of actions done for other reasons, but the ethical issues can be just as serious. What Troy Duster (1990) has called "backdoor eugenics" threatens to visit harm on the genetically disfavored through the cumulative effect of many private decisions on the part of employers, insurers, and prospective parents. As Robert Wachbroit (1987) has observed, government and society might conceivably switch roles, with the former intervening in private choice in order to preserve the liberties and well-being of those whose genes threaten disease or disability. In such a scenario, denying a role to the state might hasten eugenic evils rather than protect against them. If the backdoor concern is justified, we ought not conclude that the wrongs of eugenics can be avoided as long as the *state* forswears any eugenic intent.

In any case, a strong state role is not essential for a eugenic program. True, it may be difficult to win compliance with eugenic prescriptions without the long arm of the law. That is why Galton, imagining a fully voluntary regime, mused that eugenics might have to be instated as a civil religion in order to induce members of society to make the sacrifices required. Eugenics never attained this status, in the United Kingdom or elsewhere (not even in contemporary Singapore, where the head of state has been an enthusiast). The British eugenics movement was no less "eugenic" for being a citizen's movement relying on voluntary measures, and from this fact it follows that statism is not a source of wrongs inherent in the core of the eugenic program.

Thesis 5: Justice   Daniel Kevles (1985) concludes his magisterial history of the eugenics movement with the observation that eugenics has proved itself historically to have been a cruel and always a problematic faith, not least because it has elevated abstractions – the "race," the "population," and more recently the "gene pool" – above the rights and needs of individuals and their families. (pp. 300–1)

The eugenics movements of 1870–1950 insisted – wrongly, as it turned out – that humankind faced a grave threat (degeneration) and stood to gain a large benefit (more able, fit people) if humans would submit to the kind of breeding programs that had been used to improve plants and livestock. But who would benefit, and at whose expense? The internal logic of eugenics provides the answer. The "underclass" is simultaneously the group of people whose genes were not wanted and the people who, through involuntary sexual segregation, stigmatization and denigration, sterilization, and even murder, paid the price. The injustice of this distribution of burdens and benefits is evident, even when we make the effort to accept, for the sake of argument, the eugenicist's warnings about degeneration and their promise of a better society to come. Thus construed, the central moral problem of eugenics is akin to the perennial ethical quandary of public health, which seeks to benefit the public but in some cases exacts a penalty, such as quarantine or involuntary vaccination, on some individuals. The actual Typhoid Mary, for example, was forced to live out her life on an island in the East River near New York (Leavitt 1996); HIV-positive Cubans today may face restriction to a sanitorium (Bayer and Healton 1989). The search for a balance between public health and personal liberty and other interests will always figure prominently in the ethics of public health. It is notable that eugenicists often portrayed their movement as a campaign for public health. Programs and personnel were often common to both. As Charlotte Muller noted in her insightful review of writing in the *American Journal of Public Health* during this period, the gross differences in health status across racial and income lines tended to be explained in terms of heredity. Martin Pernick (1997) has noted extensive overlap even in the jargon of the two fields, each of which resorted to "isolation" and "sterilization" of the individuals who were thought to pose threats to the well-being of the public. Eugenics was often described in medical terms (Kamrat-Lang 1995), for example, as an effort to prevent the spread of (genetic) disease from generation to generation. Hitler was lauded as the great doctor of the German nation, rescuing the Aryan gene pool from the genetic disease introduced by Jewish infestation (Proctor 1988).

The Public Health and Personal Service Models

It is tempting, in trying to guard against a reversion to bad eugenic policies, to draw a bright line between eugenics as an intervention on behalf of public health and welfare, and clinical genetics, in service to the individual. We called these the Public Health Model and the Personal Service Model, respectively, in Chapter 1. The bright line would distinguish indefensible eugenics from defensible genetics, even if the latter faces moral problems of its own. In our view, the distinction is not as clear as it is alleged to be, nor is the moral difference as sharp. As with other "ethical firebreaks" examined in this book, this alleged distinction is not an appropriate substitute for moral analysis.

According to this proposal, parents do not practice eugenics when they seek "the perfect baby." The reason is that these parents presumably do not employ clinical genetics with the population's welfare in mind. Any testing, or indeed genetic engineering, which they employ will be done because they want their child to have every advantage the new genetics can bestow. The cumulative impact of decisions like theirs may have a substantial impact on the well-being of others, and on society over time, but, in seeking clinical services, this is not their personal concern.

But can these two concerns, one for the prospective child and the other for society, be so neatly distinguished? Consider these statements:

1a. I favor a genetic intervention because I want my child to have the "best" (healthiest, etc.) genes.
1b. We favor genetic interventions (on behalf of each of us) because we want our children to have the "best" (healthiest, etc.) genes.
1c. I favor genetic interventions (for each person in our group) because I want our children to have the "best" (healthiest, etc.) genes.

If 1a is morally acceptable, it doesn't become wrong when voiced by several people (in the form of 1b). And how can one person be faulted for endorsing that group's hope (1c)? 1b and 1c are merely the aggregate of many instances of 1a. One might expect to hear 1c uttered by, say, a health official or a legislator who sponsors a measure that would provide genetic services to large numbers of people. Concern for the welfare of large numbers of people is part of their job descriptions.

Advocates of a bright line between clinical genetics and population eugenics might reply that the health official or legislator who enables parents to make use of genetic services is focusing not on the "quality" of the population but on the desires of the parents. The beneficiaries of these services, in this view, are first of all the parents, and only secondarily the offspring; any effect on the "population" is unintended and incidental. But would funds, either public or private, be allocated if the offspring did not enjoy significant benefits? Again, the difference seems not to be a matter of the principles underlying social policy so much as the vantage point of those in different roles involved in carrying out these policies.

Cost-Benefit Justifications for Genetic Interventions

The difficulty in distinguishing the population perspective of the public health model and the individual concern of the personal service model arises also in consideration of cost-benefit calculations. The *Eugenics Catechism* of the American Eugenics Society (1926) expresses the kinds of sentiments we now seek to avoid:

Q. How much does segregation cost?
A. It has been estimated that to have segregated the original "Jukes" for life would have cost the State of New York about $25,000.
Q. Is that a Real Saving?
A. Yes. It has been estimated that the State of New York, up to 1916, spent over $2,000,000 on the descendants of these people.
Q. How much would it have cost to sterilize the original Jukes pair?
A. Less than $150.

Similar examples abounded in the arithmetic books of German school-children in the 1930s, extending to the cost of keeping institutionalized, handicapped people alive; not long afterward, tens of thousands lost their lives. But cost-benefit arguments in genetics do not necessarily signal a readiness to sacrifice some for the betterment of others. If we offer a cost-benefit analysis in support of a program of genetic screening or other intervention that shows that the sum total of benefits would be greater than the costs, the intended message need not be that the genetic services should be offered to save money. The goal may instead be to ensure that as many children as possible are born with genes that make their lives go well. Given the endless competition that exists for public funds, however laudable their purpose, it always helps if one can argue that the net social cost is zero or better. This

calculation has been a trump card in debates over health care allocation when played by advocates for cost-effective health services such
as perinatal medical care, and it might apply equally well for a program aiming to provide better genes.

A case in point is the current debate over screening for Down
Syndrome and other genetic and chromosomal abnormalities. According to Kevles (1985), a U.S. government analyst estimated in 1974
that $5 billion spent over 20 years to reduce the incidence of Down
Syndrome (by voluntary screening and abortion) would, assuming a
reduction of 50 percent, save the United States more than $18 billion,
and other screening programs had the potential to save another $75
to $100 billion. A more recent proposal to extend a three-level screen-
ing program for Down Syndrome to all pregnant women included an
estimate of cost savings (Elkins and Brown 1993). Is this eugenics?
Carlson (1996) quotes a physician who resolutely avoids the term:
"Sometimes you need to abandon words that have common meanings
that connote the wrong ethics or morals." Carlson adds, "But only the
words have changed."

The line, we believe, is thinner than it is bright. If, as we have
argued, the central ethical problem in eugenics was one of social
justice, the remedy, as we try to ensure that the genetic future is more
just than the eugenic past, is not to disavow any social purpose. The
distinction between social and individual perspectives is not always
clear. Even where this distinction can be drawn, however, must we
disavow any social purpose?

THE SOCIAL DIMENSION OF GENETICS

In our view, the key issue in appraising the shadow cast by the eugenics movement on clinical genetics is not whether those who build
programs of clinical genetics have an individual focus as opposed to a
social one. The social goal is not automatically suspect. What matters
is whether either goal is pursued justly. In particular, the fact that the
prospect of better health – or even enhanced functioning, apart from
health – in the next generation is a worthy goal, other things being
equal, does not in itself show that this goal would justify restrictions
on liberties, social inequalities, or other measures that are suspect from
the perspective of justice. Constrained and guided by concerns of
justice – the chief focus of this volume – the prospect of healthier and
more able generations of human beings in the years to come is an

appropriate and defensible goal of public policy on genetics. Indeed, Rawls, in the brief treatment of eugenics in his *A Theory of Justice* (1971), argues that genetic improvement is a social responsibility: "It is in the interest of each to have greater natural assets. This enables him to pursue a preferred plan of life. . . . [thus] the parties want to insure for their descendants the best genetic endowment (assuming their own to be fixed). The pursuit of reasonable policies in this regard is something that earlier generations owe to later ones, this being a question that arises between generations." The eugenicists were ahead of their time – which was probably a good thing. Since they lacked the means to detect recessive genes in the population, even with full compliance their proposals would hardly make a dent in the distribution of the genes they imagined to be of social importance. More important, their sole instrument of change was the blunderbuss weapon of human breeding (and in extreme cases, sterilization and euthanasia). Humans are notoriously hard to breed; we are animals with hearts and minds of our own. A few scientists, such as Muller and Haldane, permitted themselves the fantasy that people could learn to sever the age-old link between biological and social mating, choosing one person as lover and husband and another (via insemination) as biological father, but this was never to be. There is no reason to think that the eugenicists "improved" the gene pool to any appreciable degree, nor could they have.

Our powers are much more impressive, and humankind's future abilities to rewrite our genetic code are apparently limitless. Davenport would have given anything to have been around in these times. So would Hitler's racial hygienists.

Could eugenicists of the old school make a convincing case for reinstituting their programs, cleansed this time around of bias and pseudoscience and respectful of individual rights? Muller's heirs might insist that now is the time to launch a program to propagate a superior version of ourselves, a Sun Yat-Sen or a Gandhi. Or should we second Elof Axel Carlson's (1981) appraisal of eugenics as "the manure from which the flower of genetics could grow," no more relevant to today's genetics than astrology is to astronomy or alchemy to chemistry?

The core notion of eugenics, that people's lives will probably go better if they have genes conducive to health and other advantageous traits, has lost little of its appeal. Eugenics, in this very limited sense, shines a beacon even as it casts a shadow. Granted, when our society last undertook to improve our genes, the result was mayhem. The task for humanity now is to accomplish what eluded the eugenicists entirely, to square the pursuit of genetic health and enhancement with the requirements of justice. Much of this book is devoted to the pursuit of this end. These considerations of justice can be divided into two categories: constraints on genetic practice and policy, and justice as a goal of those practices and policies. We close by considering these briefly.

Genetics Constrained by Justice

Reproductive Freedoms   Whether the state or any other powerful institution makes a conscious decision to use advances in genetics in the social realm, the widespread use of these increasingly powerful techniques and products will inevitably affect our relationships with each other and with the state. We can look back to the eugenics movement to educate ourselves on how we ought not to proceed, and we can try to anticipate new problems of social justice that will arise as we deploy the developing science of heredity in our very different circumstances.

Since infringements of reproductive freedoms were the most notable wrongs done in the name of eugenics, apart from crimes of Nazi racial hygiene, close attention to the effect of the new genetics on these freedoms is essential. With self-determination supported in the United States both by constitutional law and by geneticists' efforts to ensure nondirective counseling and services, it is tempting to draw another bright line and insist on complete laissez-faire. In Chapter 5, we discuss the tangled moral dilemmas involved in genetic intervention in the conception of a child and find potential harms to these offspring, which may argue against a completely permissive policy.

Natural Inequality and Self-Respect   Eugenics was inspired by the notion that not all people are created equal. Whether the individual eugenicist was inspired by the prospect of social progress brought about by increasing the number of gifted scientists and leaders or consumed with dread over crime, disease, and sin, all eugenicists attached enormous importance to what they viewed as inequalities of endowment. Mainline eugenicists were the most vocal in pointing to and warning about the alleged lack of talent and virtue in the underclass. By the emphasis that they put on measures of IQ and other supposedly unalterable key mental and temperamental attributes, the eugenicists pounded in the message that those least endowed were of least value to their contemporaries, to the future of the race, and even to themselves, in that their lives were impoverished.

Self-respect is, to some extent, a good that can be distributed, both by the functioning of social institutions and by the public rationale for their design and operation, and its value can hardly be underestimated. Rawls observes that self-respect "includes a person's sense of his own value, his secure conviction that his . . . plan of life, is worth carrying out." For "when we feel that our plans are of little value, we cannot pursue them with pleasure or take delight in their execution. Nor plagued by failure and self-doubt can we continue in our endeavors" (Rawls 1971, p. 440). Although we do not yet know how much of the differences in performance and ability exhibited across and between populations will be traceable in any direct way to genetic differences, the prospect points once again to questions of justice that were addressed poorly and injuriously in the eugenics movement and that must be dealt with more adequately in the years ahead. A similar concern has been registered by disability-rights leaders who fear that programs of genetic screening and intervention that target their disabilities will have the effect of stigmatizing people with disabilities. We discuss their concerns in Chapter 7.

Dividing the Risk Pool   Control over genetic data is the single greatest concern among bioethicists and the general public concerning the new genetics. While this is usually conceived in terms familiar from medical ethics – that is, as a right of confidentiality and privacy – its deeper significance is one of distributive justice. As Daniels has remarked, our ignorance of the pattern of distribution of deleterious genes has put us in a single lifeboat, each feeling vulnerable to disease. As the veil of ignorance lifts through genetic testing, those who are free of a given health risk are enabled to draw lines between the vulnerable and the secure (Daniels 1994). And by forming their own risk pools, they can better their lot. Those not identified as having deleterious genes can achieve lower insurance costs; their industries can be made more efficient by avoiding the need to clean up materials toxic only to the few; and they can avoid the prospect of children or grandchildren afflicted by certain genetic diseases. In effect, those who are, relatively speaking, genetically healthier can secede, or can exclude and ghettoize others, and profit from doing so. Where ignorance of genetic differences once provided a sense of a common fate, thus joining a personal motive of self-protection to arrangements that offered mutual support, the fruit of knowledge will require a commitment to principles of justice.

Similarly, only careful attention to the requirements of justice can inform us of the limits, if any, to a social obligation to provide genetic services to those who may want or need them. While we may believe that justice is not compatible with division of the population into different risk pools for health insurance purposes, not all genetic interventions of the future will be addressed to health. If genetic services can be used to enhance as well as to cure, does justice demand that these services be provided upon demand at social expense? Should access to enhancements be left entirely to the market? And what if these enhancements provide "positional goods" – advantages, such as relative height – that are benefits if and only if not everyone has them? We probe these questions in Chapters 3 and 4.

Genetics in Pursuit of Justice

Looking to the more distant future, we may entertain the proposition that genetics be used specifically to bring about a more just society. The mainstream eugenicists pursued this goal, in their own fashion, insofar as they believed that the "unfit" were an unfair burden on the fit. We can reject the eugenicists' notions of what is just without disavowing the possibility of using genetics to achieve greater justice. These prospects are largely speculative today, since there is little that we will be able to do in the near future to rectify social injustices. But what if we could distribute genes as readily as we can (but rarely do) distribute wealth? Would justice require that we create a society of equals? Or, if we discovered that greater efficiency and satisfaction were attainable by creating human beings in five distinct grades of overall ability, as in the society in Huxley's *Brave New World*, would this be the better choice – particularly if the added efficiency added to the well-being of even the lowliest members of society? We have a long time, perhaps measured in centuries, to deliberate about such questions. Still, they are of practical importance if they point toward any near-term policies that might affect such dimensions of social justice as overall equality. In Chapter 3 we ask whether the best theories of justice entail that if we could distribute natural assets equally, we should. The conclusions reached there point toward a moral basis for long-term considerations on the demands of justice on the distribution of genes.

CONCLUSION

Eugenics casts a shadow in large part because of the way in which it was pursued. It is no surprise that Nazis would seize on such ideas as a theme and rationale for a campaign of exclusion, terror, and murder. Although lesser mayhem came from the pursuit of genetic "betterment" by zealous protectors of middle-class mores and interests bent on subduing a troublesome underclass, those unjustly sterilized and segregated in their efforts numbered in the tens of thousands. These abuses, however, do not lend themselves to condemnation of the eugenicists' every thought and goal, any more than Nazi cost-benefit thinking condemns cost-benefit thinking.

Though we agree with the need to be vigilant over any hint of a return of these abuses, our examination of the shadow of eugenics has focused on the less visible issues of morality and justice at its center. These pose questions and challenges as much as warnings and admonitions. Reprehensible as much of the eugenic program was, there is something unobjectionable and perhaps even morally required in the part of its motivation that sought to endow future generations with genes that might enable their lives to go better. We need not abandon this motivation if we can pursue it justly.

THREE

GENES, JUSTICE, AND HUMAN NATURE

DISTRIBUTIVE JUSTICE ISSUES RAISED BY GENETIC INTERVENTION

The genetic revolution in molecular biology will not benefit all equally, and some may in fact be greatly disadvantaged by particular applications of genetic science. The fairness of the distribution of benefits and burdens is a matter of social justice, and has appropriately received considerable attention in bioethical writing on the Human Genome Project. Many of the distributive issues are near-term and quite tangible. They include:

- Whether it is just to exclude individuals from employment or from health, life, or disability insurance if they are known to have genetic diseases or genetic factors that predispose them to diseases
- Whether it is just for only those who can afford genetic services to have access to them, especially since much of the initial research that led to these services was publicly funded
- Whether the right to health care includes entitlements to genetic enhancements as well as treatment and prevention of diseases
- Whether international distributive justice requires that the fruits of genetic science (in medicine and agriculture in particular) be shared with those in poorer countries that cannot afford to develop the technology, as opposed to leaving the distribution of these benefits to the global market
- Whether the direction of genetic research and development should be shaped by expected market demand, as opposed to having ethical principles determine priorities (e.g., channeling funds to cure devastating diseases that afflict large numbers of people

rather than to the enhancement of normal traits for the rich or the discovery of treatments for less serious conditions, such as male baldness) (Murphy and Lappé, 1994).

At a deeper level, some writers have explored a sixth issue: puzzles concerning the use of genetic interventions to prevent serious disabilities, pondering whether the failure to do so can be morally wrong when the only way to avoid the disability is to avoid the birth (or conception) of the individual who would have it.[1]

The first five concerns are all clearly questions of distributive justice. All have already been discussed in the burgeoning literature on the ethics of the genetic revolution. The sixth, which has also been extensively explored, bears on the theory of distributive justice, at least so far as the scope and limits of the rights of future generations are concerned, even though those who consider it have generally spoken only of obligations to prevent harm rather than those of justice. But the broader implications of the possibility of identity-altering interventions for theorizing about justice have not been drawn by those who have explored the sixth concern.

Resolving these issues, with the possible exception of the sixth, does not require a fundamental reorientation in our thinking about distributive justice. They are old questions in new guises.

There is, however, another set of distributive justice issues raised by rapid advances in genetic science that have not yet even been sys-

---

[1] This literature to a large extent takes its departure from Chapter 16, "The Non-Identity Problem," of Derek Parfit's *Reasons and Persons* (Oxford: Oxford University Press, 1984) and from Parfit's earlier paper "Future Generations: Further Problems" (*Philosophy & Public Affairs*, Vol. 11, No. 2, Spring 1982. For discussions that consider genetic interventions, see Matthew Hanser, "Harming Future People," *Philosophy & Public Affairs*, Vol. 19, No. 1, Winter 1990, pp. 47–70; John Harris, *Wonderwoman and Superman: The Ethics of Human Biotechnology* (Oxford: Oxford University Press, 1992); and David Heyd, *Genethics: Moral Issues in the Creation of People* (Berkeley: University of California Press, 1992). Heyd's illuminating work focuses most systematically on identity-altering genetic interventions and is concerned in part with their implications for theories of justice. He does not, however, consider the range of challenges to theorizing about justice discussed in this volume. He concentrates on the question of whether not undertaking identity-altering interventions to prevent serious disabilities violates anyone's rights, rather than on the pressure that the possibility of such interventions puts on our familiar conceptions of equal opportunity, equal resource distribution, and the distinction between the subjects and objects of justice – all of which are discussed in this chapter. Nor does he consider the challenge to our traditional conceptions of the relationship between justice, human nature, and moral progress, which are also explored here.

tematically articulated, much less resolved. As the possibilities for significant and large-scale genetic interventions on human beings come closer to being actualized, we may be forced to expand radically our conception of the domain of justice by including natural as well as social assets among the goods whose distribution just institutions are supposed to regulate, to abandon the simple picture of justice being about distributing goods among individuals whose identities are given independently of the process of distribution, and to revise certain basic assumptions about the relationships between justice, human nature, and moral progress. In this chapter, we are concerned about these more fundamental and less discussed issues of distributive justice.

INCLUDING THE DISTRIBUTION OF NATURAL ASSETS IN THE DOMAIN OF JUSTICE

The Traditional View: Natural Inequalities Are Not a Concern of Justice

At least in the West, systematic thinking about justice begins with Plato's *Republic*. Plato assumed that there are significant natural inequalities – what we would call genetic differences – among human beings. He also believed that differences in the capacity to develop higher forms of intelligence and to cultivate certain virtues are among these natural inequalities. Furthermore, he assumed, without argument, that these natural inequalities (and perhaps all natural inequalities) are not themselves within the domain of justice. For Plato, the (alleged) fact that some are born with a lesser capacity for developing intelligence, or wisdom, or courage, or temperance is not itself something that justice requires efforts to correct. Those who happen to be born with lesser capacities have no claim of justice.

Later theorists have tended to share this assumption about the boundaries of the domain of justice without questioning it – perhaps without even noticing it. Recently, however, some theorists, including Ronald Dworkin and John Roemer, have suggested that justice requires redistributing social goods in order to compensate those with less desirable natural assets. But they have not considered the possibility that justice might sometimes require altering the natural assets themselves, perhaps for the simple reason that until very recently this has been unthinkable.[2]

Challenging the Traditional View

The new molecular genetics challenges the assumption that justice does not require interventions to alter peoples' natural assets because it offers the possibility of selectively, rapidly, and accurately modifying or replacing individuals' genes. Moreover, even if it should never become feasible to achieve large-scale direct genetic intervention to alter or replace genes that significantly influence life prospects, it may well become possible to exert much greater control over a wider range of phenotypic characteristics than ever before through genetic pharmacology.

If precise and safe control over the distribution of natural assets becomes feasible, then those who believe that justice is concerned with the effects of natural assets on individuals' life prospects will no longer be able to assume that justice requires only that we compensate for bad luck in the natural lottery by intervening in the social lottery, rather than by attacking natural inequalities directly. As we shall see, there may be moral reasons for not doing what we would then be able to do, but whether such reasons are available depends on the theory of justice followed.

---

[2] In contrast to what might be called general theorists of justice, including Rawls and Ronald Dworkin, some who write specifically on justice in health care have held that the right to health care includes an entitlement to services or treatments designed to remedy or prevent natural disadvantages so far as these qualify as diseases. The most prominent and systematic representative of this position is Norman Daniels (*Just Health Care.* Cambridge: Cambridge University Press, 1985). However, these writers have concentrated on nongenetic services and treatments, and they have not acknowledged the likelihood that advances in genetic science will greatly expand our ability to respond directly to natural disadvantages. More important, they have not considered the possibility, discussed later in this chapter, that justice (as a matter of equality of opportunity) might require genetic interventions that go beyond the prevention or cure of disease and that, consequently, extend beyond the right to health care, so far as the latter is thought to be a right whose implementation aims at responding to disease and preserving health, understood as the absence of disease. Thus, even theorists of just health care have not taken seriously the broad implications for our conception of the domain of justice of the possibility of intervening directly in the distribution of natural endowments.

Equality of Opportunity

Many contemporary theorists of justice follow Rawls, who holds that the principles of justice include a principle of equal opportunity. There are disagreements, however, about how equal opportunity is to be understood. Three major alternative interpretations of equal opportunity may be distinguished in the historical and contemporary literature (Buchanan 1995):

1. Equal opportunity requires only the elimination of legal barriers to similar prospects for persons of similar talents and abilities (sometimes called "Formal Equality of Opportunity," or "Careers Open to Talents").

2. Equal opportunity requires the elimination of legal and informal barriers of discrimination for persons of similar talents and abilities ("informal barriers" includes extra-legal discrimination based on race, gender, sexual preference, ethnicity, class, religion, etc.).

3. Equal opportunity requires not only the elimination of legal and informal barriers of discrimination, but also efforts to eliminate the effects of bad luck in the social lottery on the opportunities of those with similar talents and abilities. (The "social lottery" here refers to the ways in which one's initial social starting place – family, social class, etc. – affect one's opportunities. Hence, one of the most important measures required by this third conception of equal opportunity is free basic education).

The first and second interpretations are both instances of what John Roemer has called the nondiscrimination conception of equal opportunity (Roemer 1996). According to these interpretations, it is only the limitations on opportunities that result from legal or informal discrimination that are unjust and hence, as a matter of justice, call for elimination. Once the first interpretation is accepted, it is difficult if not impossible, on pain of inconsistency, to refrain from replacing it with the second: Legal discrimination is clearly unjust, but if that is true, then private or informal discrimination appears to be unjust as well. Following John Roemer's terminology, we can call the third interpretation the level playing field concept of equal opportunity.

It is probably fair to say, as a broad generalization, that the dominant view in contemporary liberal political philosophy is that equal opportunity requires at least the elimination of both legal and informal discrimination. Some who would describe themselves as liberals, however, would resist any effort to expand the requirements of equal opportunity further, to encompass the third interpretation. In their view, the fact that some individuals' opportunities are seriously limited by the poverty or lack of education of their families of origin is unfortunate, but calls for no remedy as a matter of justice.

Nevertheless, the third interpretation of equal opportunity has considerable appeal, once the expansion from the first to the second interpretation is granted. Its core idea is that the fact that someone is born into a family with low socioeconomic or educational status should not in itself lead to that person's having lower life prospects than other persons of similar talents and abilities who were born into more fortunate social circumstances.

Two Variants of the Level Playing Field Conception

Two quite different reasons can be invoked to support the idea that the opportunities of people with similar talents and abilities should not be disparate due to the effects of the social lottery. Each gives rise to a different form of the level playing field concept of equal opportunity.

The first is that, at least in societies like the United States, how someone fares in the social lottery is significantly influenced by the ongoing effects of unjust social structures. Perhaps the most obvious example here is the continuing effects that past discrimination has on the opportunities of African-Americans. The distribution of initial social assets would also be influenced, however, by the present effects of unjust inequalities in the distribution of wealth and income that are not due to racial discrimination and that would persist for some time even if appropriate principles of distributive justice were now implemented. Not all past injustices were a matter of racial discrimination; there was also economic exploitation, facilitated by the abuse of governmental power and in some cases lawless coercion.

The first version of the level playing field requires that something be done to counteract the opportunity-limiting effects of bad luck in the social lottery so far as these limitations result from the ongoing effects of unjust social structures. It can be argued that Rawls is endorsing this social structural view when he says that "those who are at the same level of talent and ability, and have the same willingness to use them, should have the same prospects of success regardless of their initial place in the social system" (Rawls 1971). This view does not limit efforts to achieve equality of opportunity to countering the lingering effects of discrimination; it also requires efforts to counter the ongoing effects of other forms of past institutional injustice, including the unjust distribution of wealth. But the emphasis, to repeat, is on limitations on opportunity that originate in unjust institutions, not in natural differences among persons.

The second variant of the level playing field concept is based on a different assumption: the moral intuition or considered judgment that persons should not have lesser opportunities as a result of factors that are beyond their control, in the sense of being unchosen. Thomas Scanlon has labeled this the brute luck view of equal opportunity – the contrast being between matters of brute luck, which are not within one's control at all, and misfortunes that depend on a person's choices (Scanlon 1989). According to this view, persons should not have lesser opportunities due to how they fare in the social lottery – whether born into a poor, uneducated family, and so on, regardless of whether the limitations on their opportunities originate in unjust institutions.

When it comes to the social lottery, the implications of the two variants of the level playing field conception are closely congruent, at least in a society with a history of unjust social institutions. In that case, many of the inequalities in initial social assets (all of which are beyond the control of the individual) will be the result of unjust social structures. But when it comes to the natural lottery, the social structural view and the brute luck view have quite different implications. The former has no direct implications for inequalities in opportunity resulting from the natural lottery – the distribution of natural assets or endowments. The latter does: Equal opportunity, on the brute luck view, requires efforts to counteract the effects of all factors beyond an individual's control. And if anything is beyond a person's control, it is how the individual fares in the natural lottery.

The difference between these two variants can hardly be over-emphasized. The social structural view, like the discrimination conception of equal opportunity, limits the domain of equal opportunity, at least in the first instance, to social inequalities, because it is concerned only with how social structures, and more specifically, unjust social institutions, influence a person's success in competing for desirable offices and positions in society. The brute luck view is much more expansive: It enlarges the domain of equal opportunity to include natural inequalities.

It is worth noting that there are passages in Rawls's much-cited discussion in his book *A Theory of Justice* of how his Principle of Fair Equality of Opportunity and his Difference Principle fit together that might be interpreted as endorsing the brute luck view. For example, in explaining why he rejects the nondiscrimination conception of equal opportunity, Rawls notes that if equal opportunity were construed in this narrow way, this would be inadequate because "the initial distribution of assets for any period of time [would be] . . . strongly influenced by natural and social contingencies." Similarly, he also says that a theory of justice that allows "the distribution of wealth and income to be determined by the natural distribution of abilities and talents" appears to be "defective" (ATOJ, pp. 73–4). Both these passages might at first appear to go beyond the social structural view toward the brute luck view (Rawls 1971).

It is true that the passages do seem to commit Rawls to the view that justice is concerned with both natural and social inequalities. However, a closer reading of the text suggests that Rawls does not seek to address natural inequalities under the heading of equality of opportunity. Instead, he appears to restrict equal opportunity to efforts to counteract the opportunity-limiting effects of unjust social institutions (i.e., the social structural version), while noting that the operation of a distinct principle of justice, the Difference Principle, will do something to mitigate the effects of natural inequalities. (The Difference Principle requires that inequalities in wealth broadly construed work to the greatest advantage of the worst off). In the second passage cited earlier, Rawls may be merely saying that it would be impermissible to base a person's entitlement to a share of social goods on the mere fact that he happens to have been more fortunate in the genetic lottery. That view does not commit him to the brute luck thesis that all natural inequalities require redress or compensation as a matter of justice.

If this interpretation is correct, then Rawls's remarks about the moral arbitrariness of natural inequalities do not signal that he has moved to the more radical brute luck conception. However, they do mean that in some sense he regards natural inequalities as falling within the domain of justice. Other passages in the same discussion lend further support to the hypothesis that Rawls's conception of equal opportunity is the social structural view (e.g., his discussion of how the family influences peoples' opportunities; Rawls 1971).

Our suggestion, then, is that in spite of his recognition that in some sense it is contrary to justice to allow natural inequalities to affect peoples' life prospects by basing their distributive shares on their natural endowments, Rawls opts for a combination of a more restrictive conception of equal opportunity with the Difference Principle, rather than a more radical interpretation of equal opportunity that would require counteracting the effects of natural inequalities or eliminating natural inequalities altogether, if this were possible through genetic intervention.

A proponent of the brute luck view of equal opportunity might at this point say that Rawls's response to natural inequalities is inadequate. If equal opportunity is so important as to enjoy the priority that Rawls accords to it, then the Difference Principle cannot adequately mitigate the opportunity-limiting effects of natural inequalities.

As we discuss in Chapter 4, the matter may not be so simple. Rawls's apparent choice to use the more limited, social structural conception of equal opportunity and to rely on a kind of division of labor between that and the Difference Principle represents a more complex view of how a theory of justice should be structured. One virtue of this approach is that it preserves the historical roots of contemporary notions of equal opportunity in the concept of formal equality or "careers open to talents," which focuses only on limits on opportunity due to the influence of social institutions – more specifically, legal rules that entrench inherited privilege to the detriment of meritocratic competition. However, one can only determine which is the correct choice in constructing a theory of justice – the narrower social structural conception of equal opportunity plus a subordinate principle for the distribution of wealth, or the more radical brute luck view – by evaluating the overall strengths and weaknesses of the rival theories in which these options are situated.

Our purpose here is not to engage in Rawls exegesis. We have suggested that the various passages in A Theory of Justice just cited can be interpreted as an endorsement of the social structural view. We acknowledge, however, that others have interpreted Rawls's concern with natural inequalities as pointing toward the more radical brute luck view. In that sense, Rawls's classic discussion can be viewed as a matrix out of which two dominant strains of contemporary liberal thought on equal opportunity can be generated.

The brute luck view (with various twists) is rather unambiguously embraced by a number of other prominent contemporary philosophers, including John Roemer, Richard Arneson, and G.A. Cohen (Roemer 1996, Arneson 1989, Cohen 1993). Our chief aim is to trace the implications of these two conceptions of equal opportunity for the uses of genetic intervention technology. We shall argue that in spite of the profound difference between these two conceptions as to the domain of equal opportunity, there is a surprising overlap in their implications for how genetic intervention technology ought to be deployed, at least for the foreseeable future.

Each of the two level playing field conceptions has some appeal. The strength of the social structural variant, as noted earlier, is that it preserves a clear connection with the historical roots of the notion of equal opportunity: the idea of careers open to talents, or formal equal opportunity. Like it, the social structural view focuses on the very plausible idea that equal opportunity has to do not with just any inequalities, but with inequalities due to defective social institutions.

Yet the appeal of the brute luck view is simple and straightforward: To many people it seems unfair that some should have fewer opportunities as a result of factors over which they have no control – circumstances that did not result from their choices. Not only are natural deficits as much beyond the individual's control as initial social assets; in some cases they may impose even more severe constraints on opportunities. This is clear enough in the case of a straightforward genetic disorder such as phenylketonuria (PKU), which, if untreated, produces mental retardation, or Tay-Sachs Disease, which causes much suffering and inevitably results in death in early childhood. Whether an individual has certain abilities and talents may depend upon his or her luck in the natural lottery. Restricting our concern about equal opportunity to differences among those with the same talents and abilities seems arbitrary.

Most industrialized societies recognize a societal obligation to use medical interventions to cure seriously disabling congenital disorders, whether their source is genetic or is due to environmental or developmental factors during pregnancy or birth conditions. If a baby is born with a hip deformity, for example, an effort will be made to marshal social resources to pay for surgical repair of this condition if the parents lack health insurance and cannot afford to pay the surgical bill. One obvious and compelling justification for subsidizing this procedure is that it is necessary in order to remove a serious obstacle to opportunity. In this sense, some of our most basic social institutions reflect a commitment to intervening in the natural lottery for the sake of equal opportunity, at least when it is a hereditary or congenital disease that threatens opportunity. And presumably any philosophical account that accords an important place to equal opportunity as a principle of justice must acknowledge the necessity of such interventions.

But an individual's place in the distribution of natural assets can severely limit her opportunities even in cases in which she does not suffer from anything that would uncontroversially count as a genetic disorder or a disease. For instance, suppose that only those whose genetic assets fall within certain parameters tend to develop certain cognitive abilities beyond a certain level. Suppose also that, in general, only those who develop these abilities beyond this level are able to learn the mathematics needed to succeed in all but the very least desirable jobs in a technically advanced society. Under such conditions, those whose genetic constitutions prevent them from reaching the needed threshold of abilities will experience significant limitations on their opportunities unless something is done to overcome this impairment.

Notice that the preceding example of a significant natural inequality that is not a disease is presented as hypothetical. At this point in the infancy of genetic science, no one can say whether there will turn out to be a significant number of genetic conditions that do not qualify as diseases but that seriously limit peoples' opportunities. Notice also that the hypothetical does not buy into anything so gross and problematic as the view that IQ is genetically determined. Instead, it only suggests the possibility that some particular aspect of cognitive functioning might turn out to have two features: First, there are significant inequalities among individuals in its distribution within the range of normal functioning for our species (hence those with lower levels of the skill do not have a disease), and second, because of particular features of the society in question, those with lower levels of the skills experience significant limitations on their opportunities. Our main concern is not whether there are such differences, but rather what the possibility that there are shows us about how we should think about justice.

Roemer provides an example (similar to our Scenario 4 in the Introduction) that is less hypothetical and yet also shows the apparent arbitrariness of restricting equal opportunity concerns to the genetic disadvantages that count as diseases. He considers the case of a child who "is not slow to learn but has an emotional cyclicity, clearly inborn, which makes it harder for him to carry out plans, or succeed in school" (Roemer 1989). His point is that because the child's psychological condition is beyond his control (being inborn) but limits his opportunities, equal opportunity requires that something be done. Notice that Roemer does not say that the psychological condition is a disease, though of course "emotional cyclicity" is broad enough to cover cases of the mental illness known as bipolar disorder.

The point is that there is a continuum of psychological conditions – from mild mood swings to bipolar disorder – and that what really matters is whether a condition limits opportunity and is beyond a person's control (Siever 1996). Whether there are a significant number of cases in which a genetically based condition (whether psychological or physical) that is not a disease substantially limits persons' opportunities is an empirical matter. The facts are in dispute, but genetic research may well document a number of such cases, with the result that we will be less confident about drawing moral lines between opportunity-limiting conditions that are diseases and those that are not.

The message of these examples is not that the concept of disease is so fuzzy as to be unusable. Throughout this book we use a conception of disease proposed by Christopher Boorse and developed and used by Norman Daniels in his work on just health care. Disease, according to this view, consists of conditions that are adverse departures from normal species functioning. So genetic diseases, roughly, would be genetically based conditions that are adverse departures from normal species functioning. What Roemer's example shows is that there can be genetically based conditions that limit people's opportunities, and that what matters, from the standpoint of a general account of equal opportunity, is not whether they are diseases but whether they limit opportunity.

In some cases, of course, a genetically based disadvantage can be remedied by nongenetic means, and the question of genetic intervention will not arise. For example, although PKU is a genetic disease, the mental retardation that it produces can be avoided by administering a special diet to the individual for the first few years of life. Similarly, as noted in Chapter 1, although nonacquired hemochromatosis is caused by a defective gene, it is now successfully treated by nongenetic means (regular phlebotomies, i.e., bloodlettings).

Nevertheless, there are some genetically based conditions for which there is no known environmental treatment or nongenetic remedy, and more are likely to be discovered. The point is that from the standpoint of the brute luck view, the distinction between natural inequalities that are diseases and those that are not is insignificant, at least in principle. The real issue is whether inequalities in natural assets, as one form of brute luck, limit opportunities. If so, then regardless of whether they constitute diseases, they are a concern of justice.

The Social Structural View of Equal Opportunity and the Right to Health Care

As Norman Daniels has argued, the case for a moral right to health care relies, at least in part, on the fact that health care promotes equal opportunity by preventing and curing disease (Daniels 1985).

Daniels has developed a sophisticated theory of just health care based on Rawls's principle of equal opportunity. Rawls himself offers no theory of just health care, though he has endorsed Daniels's project. In *A Theory of Justice*, Rawls notes that he makes a simplifying assumption, which explains why he offers no account of the right to health care: The idealized parties who are to choose principles of justice are to proceed on the assumption that they are normally functioning, full participants in social cooperation. Daniels's Rawlsian theory of just health care relaxes this simplifying assumption, arguing that equal opportunity provides a basis for the right to health care.

Daniels does not endorse the brute luck conception, however, as will become clear in Chapter 4. His view of equal opportunity is closer to what we have called the social structural variant of the level playing field conception. (Moreover, he maintains that it is the latter rather than the former that provides the most consistent interpretation of the totality of Rawls's writings that bear on equal opportunity.)

At first blush, it might seem that it is problematic to take the tack Daniels does, to reject the brute luck view and embrace the claim that equal opportunity requires efforts to cure and prevent disease. At least in some cases, and perhaps many, disease is a result of bad luck in the natural lottery, not the effect of the social structure. So if equal opportunity, as the social structural view holds, is not concerned with natural inequalities as such but only with the opportunity-limiting effects of social structures, how can it serve as the foundation for a right to health care as a response to the natural inequality of disease?

We noted earlier that the social structural view has no *direct* implications for counteracting natural inequalities. This qualification is important. One way of understanding how a Rawlsian theory of equal opportunity can consistently reject the brute luck view and yet base the right to health care on equal opportunity is to focus on an idea we encountered earlier in Rawls's simplifying assumption about heath care needs: the idea of being a normally functioning, full participant in social cooperation.

In the context of concerns about equal opportunity, we can think of being a normally functioning, fully participating member of society as having the characteristics necessary to be a "normal competitor" for desirable social positions. Clearly, diseases – as adverse departures from normal species functioning – can prevent an individual from being a normal competitor. We can think of equal opportunity, then, as being concerned not only to counteract the opportunity-limiting effects of social institutions but also to cure or prevent diseases, insofar as they preclude an individual from being a normal competitor in social cooperation. In other words, equal opportunity has to do with ensuring fair competition for those who are able to compete *and* with preventing or curing disease that hinders people from developing the abilities that would allow them to compete.

In this view, equal opportunity not only requires that competition be fair; it also requires efforts to bring people up to the threshold of normal functioning that enables them to compete under conditions of fairness. This allows a consistent appeal to equal opportunity as a moral foundation for the right to health care without embracing the brute luck view, and with it the thesis that equal opportunity must somehow counteract all natural inequalities, not just those that constitute diseases.

It would be a mistake, however, to conclude that the social structural view as developed by Daniels to include a Rawlsian theory of just health care strictly limits genetic interventions to cure and prevent disease. The significance of disease is that it limits opportunity in the most serious cases, at least, by preventing persons from developing the threshold of abilities necessary for being "normal competitors" in social cooperation. It is possible, however, that some natural inequalities are not adverse departures from normal species functioning but nonetheless so seriously limit an individual's opportunities that he or she is precluded from reaching the threshold of normal competition. In such cases, genetic intervention might be required if it were necessary to remove this barrier to opportunity.

Whether there are such natural inequalities will depend in part upon the nature of the framework for social cooperation. It is not implausible to think that in some cooperative frameworks, persons with certain abilities at the low end of the normal distribution will be prevented from being effective competitors for desirable social positions, and even from participating in the mainstream economic activities of the society. Two possible examples of conditions that fit this description have already been considered: emotional cyclicity that impairs work and personal relationships but is not so severe as to count as the disease of bipolar affective disorder; being deficient in certain genetically based cognitive skills that are required for higher mathematics in a society in which sophisticated quantitative skills are needed for a broad range of jobs.

In Chapter 7, we explore the application of conceptions of justice to the choice of a basic cooperative scheme, insofar as the nature of the cooperative scheme determines who is able to be a full participant or normal competitor in social cooperation. At this point, we only wish to emphasize that while the Rawls-Daniels view avoids the kind of wholesale commitment to genetic intervention – or to "genetic equality" – to which the brute luck view seems wedded, it may require some interventions that go beyond the cure and prevention of disease. Whether it does will depend on what the normal distribution of various characteristics is and how that relates to the most fundamental requirements for successful participation in social cooperation in a given society.

The Brute Luck View and the Scope of Intervention in the Natural Lottery We have argued that the social structural view, at least when developed along the lines of Daniels's Rawlsian account, implies no commitment to regard all natural inequalities as subject to the dictates of equal opportunity. The brute luck view, however, seems to require just such a profound expansion of the domain of equal opportunity. For some, this expansion will seem implausible, if only because it seems to sever the notion of equal opportunity from its historical roots in the idea of "careers open to talents." For, as we have seen, that notion – like the social structural view, but unlike the brute luck view – anchors equality of opportunity to a concern for the opportunity-limiting effects of defective social institutions and is nothing so ambitious as an attempt to free human beings from opportunity-limiting effects of misfortune generally.

It would be a mistake, however, to assess the basic moral intuition underlying the brute luck view solely according to whether it supports an adequate conception of equal opportunity. A number of the most prominent theorists who believe that people's prospects should not be limited by factors beyond their control have attempted to work out the implications of this conviction for a general theory of justice. They would be unimpressed by the criticism that their view does not comfortably fit within the confines of what has traditionally been regarded as equal opportunity.

Resource Egalitarianism and the Domain of Justice

The brute luck view has been advanced in some of the most interesting and rigorous work in the theory of distributive justice in recent years – the so-called "Equality of What?" debate. In initiating this controversy, Amartya Sen asked, Given that a sound theory of distributive justice will include an egalitarian element, what is it that is to be distributed equally? One answer that has been explored in some detail and has attracted the support of several formidable thinkers is resources (Sen in McMurrin 1980; Dworkin 1981a, b; Cohen 1989). Stated as a principle of justice, the resource egalitarian view is simply this: Resources ought to be distributed equally among persons.

According to John Roemer, the chief task for resource egalitarians is to devise a "resource allocation mechanism" to achieve an overall equal distribution of resources among persons by compensating for inequalities in the distribution of natural resources through special redistributions of social resources (Roemer 1985). This requirement, that those with fewer natural resources (genetic endowments) ought to be compensated by redistributing social resources to them, may be called the Resource Compensation Principle.

What is striking is that resource egalitarians have focused exclusively on the Resource Compensation Principle, rather than the Equal Resources Principle itself, to the extent that they have speculated about how institutions should function if they are to achieve justice. They have not explored the possibility of achieving greater equality by intervening directly in the natural lottery by which genetic endowments are currently distributed. Yet from the standpoint of a theory that emphasizes the primacy of resources for distributive justice and that appears to have no room for any fundamental distinction between social and natural resources, there is no obvious reason to restrict the operation of the institutions of justice to the redistribution of social resources. If resources ought to be distributed equally and natural endowments are resources, then we ought to intervene in the natural lottery whenever doing so would be the best way of equalizing resources. In contrast, as we have seen, there is one way of interpreting Rawls's theory – namely, as endorsing the social structural view of equal opportunity rather than the brute luck view – that avoids the implication that justice requires interventions to counteract all natural inequalities.

Individual Liberty and Genetic Intervention

It might be argued that even if resource egalitarians took seriously the feasibility of interventions in the natural lottery, they would have moral reasons for not endorsing them. Most resource egalitarians are liberals; they might argue that respect for basic individual liberties precludes interventions in the natural lottery, requiring instead that social resources be distributed so as to compensate those who fared badly.

This response is unpromising for several reasons. First, resource egalitarians have generally been reluctant to assume that the particular resources Rawls calls the basic liberties are of such extraordinary importance relative to other resources as to enjoy an absolute priority. Consequently, they cannot simply dismiss the possibility of intervening directly in the natural lottery on the grounds that doing so would clearly be incompatible with respecting basic liberties.

More important, if proper regard for individual liberty is to provide a reason for not concluding that resource egalitarianism is committed to a profound expansion of the domain of justice into the natural lottery, it will have to be shown that genetic interventions violate the liberty of either prospective parents or their offspring or both.

Consider the claim that genetic interventions directed toward prospective parents (such as the insertion of genes into embryos or gametes) are precluded by respect for the liberty of the prospective parents. First of all, not all genetic interventions will require treatments to be performed on the parents. Some may be applied directly on the individual who would otherwise have lesser natural assets. In such cases, the priority of the parents' liberty could not be appealed to in order to block the intervention.

Second, even where intervening in the natural lottery requires performing procedures on the prospective parents, these will in many cases be welcomed, since they are for the benefit of their offspring. Thus it is reasonable to assume that in most cases prospective parents would freely consent to genetic interventions to increase their children's opportunities. But if this is so, then it is hard to see how their basic liberties could be an obstacle to extending the operation of equal opportunity to the natural lottery, to the extent that they would willingly cooperate in improving their children's prospects. For if the basic liberties include the right to refuse invasive interventions, they are accompanied by the right to accept them as well (as it is in the case of ordinary medical interventions). Finally, even in cases in which the parents for some reason or other did not consent to interventions on themselves for the sake of their offspring, it cannot be assumed that their interest in avoiding nonconsensual medical treatment always outweighs the fundamental interest that all individuals are supposed to have in equality according to resource egalitarianism.

Consider next the implications for individual liberty of intervening only on the individual for whose sake it is undertaken. If the intervention were early enough in life, it would be implausible to argue that the individual's interest in liberty – in being free from nonconsensual medical treatment – outweighed his or her interest in avoiding significant limitations on opportunity.

This conclusion is buttressed, once we recognize that genetic interventions might in fact be less threatening to individual autonomy and privacy and more likely to succeed at removing barriers to opportunity than the kinds of large-scale changes in family life needed to counteract the opportunity-limiting effects of disadvantages in family culture and early childhood experiences. In some cases, intervening in the genetic lottery might well prove more efficacious and less morally problematic than intervening in the family to correct for disadvantages resulting from the social lottery. A genetic intervention to correct or prevent a disabling metabolic disorder – or perhaps even to improve certain dimensions of memory that would enhance learning – might well be more effective in expanding individuals' opportunities as well as less intrusive than some existing social welfare programs are. It seems, then, that considerations of individual liberty pose no general bar to genetic interventions in the name of resource equality.

To summarize: Neither Rawls nor the resource egalitarians consider the possibility of direct interventions in the natural lottery for the sake of justice. In Rawls's case, there is a plausible interpretation of his theory of equal opportunity, which, when combined with Daniels's theory of just health care, explains why justice requires intervention to prevent or cure disease but does not require any general effort to counteract or eliminate natural inequalities as such. Resource egalitarians, in contrast, appear committed to the thesis that justice requires direct interventions in the natural lottery, and not just to prevent or cure diseases, whenever doing so is the best way to achieve an overall equality of resources. Absent a principled distinction between natural and social resources, it appears that resource egalitarians must either abandon the commitment to equalizing social resources or abandon the view that it is only necessary to compensate for, rather than intervene directly in, the distribution of natural resources.

Genetic Equality?

So far we have argued that, at least from the standpoint of the brute luck view of equal opportunity and resource egalitarianism, the feasibility of genetic intervention requires a profound expansion of the domain of justice. But nothing has been said about which sorts of genetic interventions, under what conditions, are required. In particular, no conclusion has been drawn about the necessity of strictly equalizing the distribution of natural assets.

There are at least two important reasons for avoiding the leap from the thesis that in principle justice requires intervention in the natural lottery to the conclusion that justice requires an equal distribution of natural assets.

First, even if justice ought to be concerned with inequalities in natural assets, what counts as such an asset (or deficit) is at least partly determined by the social structure – and preeminently by which sorts of traits the dominant cooperative framework of a given society favors. (By dominant cooperative framework we mean the set of basic institutions and practices that enable individuals and groups in a given society to engage in ongoing mutually beneficial cooperation.) To take an obvious example, in a pre-literate hunting and gathering society, having a neurological condition that impaired the development of reading skills but that did not interfere with hand-eye coordination, motor skills, and normal oral communication would not be a deficit.

Because the dominant cooperative framework changes over time, the value of various traits also changes. In addition, the value of particular traits may depend not only on their scarcity but on what may be called *complementarity* – that is, the existence, in sufficient numbers, of persons with other traits with which they can be combined in cooperative interaction.

Thus, there is no such thing as a resource per se. Different traits will be resources in different social environments. Recognition of this simple fact imposes a fundamental constraint on any attempt to intervene in the natural lottery in the name of equality of opportunity or of resources.

Nevertheless, there are presumably some very basic characteristics that are what Rawls calls primary goods – maximally flexible assets, characteristics conducive to the successful pursuit of a broad range of human projects in a diversity of social environments. To the extent that the genetic factors that contribute to these can be accurately identified and subjected to safe and effective human control, there is a strong *prima facie* case for undertaking efforts to reduce the impact of inequalities in their distribution. Nevertheless, the fact that what counts as a resource will sometimes vary across social environments makes it misleading to talk glibly about "genetic equality."

The second reason not to leap to the conclusion that justice requires an equal distribution of natural assets is that any thought of literally equalizing such assets would almost certainly betray a failure to appreciate what might be called the fact of value pluralism (or the diversity of the good). What is regarded as a natural asset as opposed to a natural deficit and which natural assets are regarded as most valuable, depend in part on what we assume to be a good human life. And that is typically much more controversial and less capable of being determined by anything like objective, universal criteria than most of us like to admit.

In addition, those who are wary of genetic determinism or reductionism rightly observe that it is extremely unlikely that desirable traits such as "altruism" or "cooperativeness" or "initiative" will be strongly determined by one gene or even by a complex of genes rather than by a complicated interaction of environment and many genes. This important point does not go far enough: It is also a mistake to assume that we all desire the same thing when we say that such traits are desirable.

In some cases, or perhaps many, superficial agreement as to what counts as desirable traits masks deeper disagreement in values. For example, it might be thought that there are some traits, such as "initiative," "altruism," and "cooperativeness," that all or most of us agree are desirable. But serious differences of opinion surface once we begin to think about just what sorts of psychological dispositions we would be seeking to foster. What some consider to be a laudable disposition to take the initiative, others will regard as excessive forwardness or even aggression. What some believe to be the right proportion of altruism in a person's motivational structure, others will condemn as weakness, as a failure to stand up for oneself. And what one person sees as admirable cooperativeness, another may scorn as lack of independence or an excessive willingness to "fit in" at the expense of individual judgment and autonomy.

The point is that the traits we find most desirable are often complex dispositions involving the exercise of evaluative judgments – what Aristotle called virtues. (How cooperative should I be [with these people, under these circumstances]? Should I take the initiative now or wait for a consensus in the group? Should I subordinate my interests to those of my friend in this instance?) Because these traits themselves involve the exercise of complex evaluative judgments, different individuals and communities may have different views about which traits, in which proportions in a person's motivational structure, really are desirable. Thus any sane and responsible attempt to harness the powers of society for large-scale genetic interventions in the name of resource egalitarianism or equal opportunity must recognize the limitations imposed by the fact of value pluralism, which includes disagreements rooted in the complex evaluative nature of some of the traits we find most desirable.

Finally, the proposal to equalize natural assets becomes even less plausible once it is seen that what would have to be equalized, presumably, would be overall packages of natural assets, rather than each natural asset, however the latter are understood. The fact of value pluralism would impose even more serious limits on attempts to compare overall packages of natural assets, making it unclear to what degree there is inequality among packages or even whether they are unequal.

A "Genetic Decent Minimum"?

Taken together, the fact of value pluralism and the fact that the value of traits is relevant to social conditions call for caution about any commitment to genetic equality – and perhaps point toward a more modest goal. At least for the foreseeable future (if not forever), the appropriate objective, from the standpoint of both the brute luck conception of equal opportunity and resource egalitarianism, may be something more like the attainment of a "genetic decent minimum" – to the extent that this can be identified with a reasonable degree of consensus – than the elimination of all inequalities in natural assets.

In practice, this would mean a strong societal commitment to use advances in genetic intervention to prevent or ameliorate the most serious disabilities that limit individuals' opportunities across a wide range of cooperative frameworks. Whether or to what extent such efforts would go beyond attempts to prevent or cure genetically based diseases is largely an unanswerable question at this point. To answer it one would have to know whether there are genetic conditions that significantly limit opportunities but that do not constitute diseases and that we will be able to prevent or ameliorate through the application of genetic science.

Points of Convergence

Thus despite deep theoretical differences, the brute luck conception of equal opportunity and resource egalitarianism, on the one hand, and the social structural view of equal opportunity augmented by Daniels's account of just health care, on the other hand, may have largely similar implications for social policy. Both seem to require that efforts should be directed, for the most part and at least for the foreseeable future, toward the use of genetic interventions to prevent or cure disease. Both views, however, allow for the possibility that justice may require genetic interventions that go beyond that, although the resource egalitarian view allows much greater scope, in principle, for such interventions.

THE COLONIZATION OF THE NATURAL BY THE JUST

We now wish to explore a simple but rather radical way of reinterpreting the distinction that theorists of distributive justice have drawn between natural and social inequalities. We do not offer it as an exegesis of any particular view. Instead, we advance it as a way of avoiding an inconsistency on the part of the resource egalitarians.

The inconsistency, noted earlier, is that those who endorse the thesis that resources are to be equalized seem to be committed to direct and wholesale intervention in the natural lottery, yet opt instead for using social resources to compensate for natural inequalities, rather than attacking them directly. The problem is that the brute luck theorists and resource egalitarians give no good reason to opt for this principle and to eschew direct interventions in the natural lottery (whether for the sake of equal opportunity or for equality of resources, respectively). The apparent inconsistency disappears, however, if we understand the distinction between the social and the natural as that between what is subject to human control and what is not.

Nature, or the natural, is often thought to be not only that which is given but also that which must be accepted as beyond human control. In that sense, to say that something is due to nature is to relegate it to the realm of fortune or misfortune, rather than justice or injustice. (Hence the term "natural lottery," a lottery being a game of chance.) It is not surprising, then, that to a large extent, traditional thinking about justice has associated natural disadvantages with misfortune rather than injustice, since there was little or nothing that could be done to prevent them.

In contrast, nature subdued – nature mastered by human intelligence and directed to human purposes – is no longer the given, no longer that which must be accepted, and hence no longer the domain of fortune and misfortune. Paradoxically, nature brought within human control is no longer nature.

The boundary between the natural and the social, and between the realm of fortune and that of justice, is not static. What we have taken to be moral progress has often consisted in pushing back the frontiers of the natural, in bringing within the sphere of social control, and thereby within the domain of justice, what was previously regarded as the natural, and as merely a matter of good or ill fortune.

Sometimes this is accomplished by simply coming to see that what we took to be natural was all along social, as when the rising bourgeoisie demanded the end of aristocratic privileges that had, for so long, paraded as natural inequalities. In other cases, we actually extend the social by expanding our control (e.g., the annual flooding of a great river is transformed from a fact of nature to an object of administration).

Until now, human beings have achieved this expansion of control mainly through developing technologies for controlling the nonhuman parts of nature. Now we stand on the threshold of a great expansion of the domain of the social. If it becomes within our power to prevent what we now regard as the misfortune of a sickly constitution (a weak immune system) or the catastrophe (the natural disaster) of a degenerative disease such as Alzheimer's dementia, then we may no longer be able to regard it as a misfortune. Instead, we may come to view the person who suffers these disabilities as a victim of injustice. As our powers increase, the territory of the natural is annexed to the social realm, and the new-won territory is colonized by ideas of justice.

Thus we might interpret the resourcists' distinction between social and natural resources as that between resources whose distribution we can control and those we cannot. Then reliance on the Resource Compensation Principle would make perfectly good sense: A commitment to equalizing resources would require that social resources, those resources whose distribution we can control, be distributed so as to achieve an equal distribution of all resources, social and natural, by using social resources themselves to compensate for differences in resources that we cannot control, that is, natural ones.

This reinterpretation would radically transform our understanding of resource egalitarianism. The Resource Compensation Principle would only operate where direct intervention to counteract natural inequalities was either not feasible or for some reason less efficient than compensation. Understood in this way, resource egalitarianism would require that the domain of justice expand as our powers of genetic intervention develop. So even if the practical implications of the Rawls-Daniels social structural view and the resource egalitarian view would tend to converge for a time, they might yield profoundly different implications in the future if mankind's genetic powers continue to develop.

BLURRING THE DISTINCTION BETWEEN THE SUBJECTS AND OBJECTS OF JUSTICE

So far we have seen that both the brute luck conception of equal opportunity and resource egalitarianism appear to yield a profoundly expanded conception of the domain of distributive justice when applied to the possibility of genetic intervention. In both instances, the distribution of what we now call natural assets in principle falls squarely into the domain of justice, at least at the deepest level of theorizing. How much of what we now regard as natural assets actually becomes subject to intervention in the name of justice will depend on the extent to which our powers grow. Now we wish to argue that as the possibilities of what may be called radical genetic intervention come closer to realization, the most fundamental single framing assumption of our ordinary ways of thinking about justice, both in theory and in practice, will be shattered.

The basic problem of distributive justice, as it has hitherto been conceived, is how goods ought to be distributed among persons when their identities, at least for purposes of justice, are given independently of the distribution of goods (Roemer 1985). But if it becomes possible to distribute the genetic bases of all "natural" human characteristics, including those that are partly constitutive of the identity of persons, then this fundamental assumption – this picture of subjects waiting to receive objects through the workings of some distribution mechanism – will no longer be applicable. Yet it is not clear what alternative picture will replace it.

To focus on this problem, we will reserve the phrase *radical genetic intervention* for the use of genetic technology to determine the genetic bases of identity-constituting characteristics in human beings. The basic point is this: If radical genetic intervention becomes feasible, we shall need to reconceive the fundamental problem of distributive justice.

Note that to make this point, a person need not be identified with his or her genes. No variety of genetic reductionism need be assumed. Instead, we can acknowledge that, for fairly obvious reasons, the conception (or conceptions) of personal identity human beings have developed does not focus on genes but rather on phenotypic characteristics, whether psychological or physical or both. But to the extent that these characteristics turn out to be expressions of genes (interacting with environmental factors, of course), the ability to design the genomes of individuals is the ability to design and create individuals with particular identities.

If this is the case, then intervening in the natural lottery by genetic means will not be limited to distributing goods among persons whose identities are fixed prior to the act of distribution. Instead, the distribution of genes itself may in part determine the identities of the persons. (And this is true even if, as some conceptions of identity maintain, a person's identity is also determined in part by factors in the physical or social environment as they shape the individual's development over time.)

To put the same point in a slightly different way, we think of justice as justice to persons. But we may soon have to contemplate the idea of justice in the designed creation of persons. At present we are not well equipped to do this, in part because even the most sophisticated

theories of justice have proceeded on two increasingly obsolete assumptions: that the distribution of the characteristics with which people are born is a given, beyond human control, so that any resulting
inequalities must at best be compensated for rather than attacked
directly; and that the fundamental problem of justice is that of distributing goods among antecedently existing particular persons.

The breakdown of the distinction between the subjects of distribution and the objects of distribution (between persons and goods) seems
inescapable once we are committed either to resource egalitarianism
or to a brute luck conception of equal opportunity (according to which
all unchosen and undeserved significant limitations on persons' opportunities are suspect). However, the breakdown is not inevitable from
the perspective of the narrower, social structural conception of equal
opportunity, according to which the only suspect limitations are those
that are due to unjust social structures or that prevent a person from
reaching the threshold of abilities needed to be a normal competitor in
social cooperation.

No doubt some will take the fact that resource egalitarianism and
the brute luck conception of equal opportunity lead to a blurring of
the distinction between the subjects and objects of justice as a *reductio*
of these theories. Others may bite the bullet and embrace the conclusion that we must learn to think of justice not simply or primarily as
the distribution of goods among persons but as including the distribution of person-constituting characteristics in order to ensure that
whichever persons do exist have equal opportunities (or equal resources). Those who take the latter, bolder path have yet to develop
their own, alternative explanatory metaphors, much less a coherent
theoretical apparatus to replace the traditional ways of framing the
fundamental problem of distributive justice. It would be premature to
conclude that they will not be able to do so but equally unwarranted
to assume that the task will be completed successfully.

JUSTICE, HUMAN NATURE, AND THE NATURAL BASES OF INEQUALITY

Thus far we have discussed bringing the distribution of what have
been regarded as natural assets within the domain of justice and challenging the assumption that the problem of justice is about distributing
goods among persons whose identities are given independently of the

distribution. There is yet another way in which the prospects of genetic intervention require a transformation of how we think about justice. The possibilities of genetic intervention threaten to sever the fundamental connections between justice and human nature that have been assumed in many if not most traditional theories of justice.

It is with some hesitation that we enter this terrain, because the profound sorts of genetic interventions that would call into question traditional assumptions about human nature and its relationship to justice may never become possible. The discussion that follows is therefore even more speculative than most of our explorations in this book, attempting as it does, to peer into an even more distant possible future. We make no assumptions about the degree to which changes in the genetic constitutions of humans will become possible.

In some respects, the most far-reaching insight of the genetic revolution in molecular biology is the realization of the common double-helix structure of all DNA across all species. The basic techniques of manipulating DNA render the so-called barriers between species breachable. More to the point, the very idea of a species becomes less important. Once genetic material from one species can be introduced into individuals in another species, the old definition of species as groups of individuals that can reproduce fertile offspring seems quaint, given the possibilities for creating reproducible, novel kinds of creatures.

Given the common structure of DNA and its ubiquity and fungibility in virtually all living things, we face the prospect of literally changing human nature through the introduction into human beings of genes from other species or even synthesized, novel genes that have never occurred anywhere in nature before. (Once it becomes feasible to construct novel sequences of base pairs of nucleotides, it will be appropriate to speak of creating genes, not just discovering them.)

Human nature has traditionally been regarded not only as that which unites us with one another and distinguishes us from other kinds of beings, but also as unchanging. So the possibility of changing even our "essential" characteristics would seem to render the very concept of human nature obsolete, so far as it includes the idea of an unchanging core of essential characteristics. To the extent that our theorizing about justice has been based on assumptions about human nature, and in particular on the assumption that there is (and will remain) one human nature that provides the basis for the moral equality of persons, the radical malleability of life through the application of genetic science presents yet another basic challenge to our thinking about justice.

Theories of justice (and of morality generally) have been thought of as based on conceptions of human nature. Indeed, advocates of rival theories of justice have typically criticized one another by trying to show that their opponents assumed an inaccurate account of human nature. In some instances, justice has been explicitly identified with acting according to nature or, more specifically, according to our (unchanging) human nature.

According to some theorists, including most famously Aristotle, human nature is simply rationality. According to others, there are other features besides rationality included in human nature. For example, it has been said by Hume among others, that it is human nature to be capable of only limited altruism – that according special priority to our own interests and those of our loved ones and close associates is a characteristic of all human beings, regardless of their culture or location in history. Indeed, proposals for how society ought to be structured are often criticized on the grounds that they fail to take seriously this alleged feature of human nature. Thus a standard criticism of more radical socialist visions of the good society is that they attribute too much altruism to human beings.

The assumption behind all such criticisms is that a conception of justice for human beings must at the very least reflect the motivational and cognitive limitations of human nature. Human nature is thus understood as a constraint on theorizing about justice. But if theorizing about justice begins with a conception of human nature as given, then it is hard to see how it can provide answers to such questions as: Ought we preserve human nature (as we have understood it thus far)? Or, if it is permissible to change "human nature," how should we change it?

Three Conceptions of the Relation of Human Nature to Ethics

The relevance of human nature to theorizing about justice and morality generally is a matter of dispute. There are three quite distinct, major views. Each gives a different sense to the common idea that morality must be based on human nature and that moral theory must somehow reflect this dependence.

First, there is the rather minimal and highly plausible view that human nature has to satisfy certain conditions if morality, and hence theorizing about morality, is to be possible at all. For example, for Aristotle and Kant, human beings must be free and rational if there is to be such a thing as morality (for human beings), and if theorizing about what morality requires is to have any point at all.

Second, there is the view, sketched earlier and attributed to Hume, that even if some features of human nature make morality possible, that nature also constrains the content of morality by limiting the demands it can make on beings like us. (Thus, for example, if we are by nature creatures of only limited altruism, then morality cannot demand that we be wholly self-abnegating.)

A third, much more ambitious – and much less plausible – conception of the relevance of human nature to morality and moral theory is that we can derive the substance or content of morality from a proper understanding of human nature. Some readers of Aristotle have thought that human nature plays this role in his moral theory because they have assumed – probably mistakenly – that his notion of natural function is intended to yield substantive ethical principles. None of the three views takes seriously the possibility that the features of human nature in question might change, much less that human beings might come to have the power to change them.

The appeal of the first view is most evident: Unless human beings are sufficiently rational that they can have a conception of what they ought to do as distinct from what they desire to do and unless they are motivationally capable of acting on this, it is hard to see how they can be thought of as being subject to morality at all. The second and third views, however, are much more difficult to justify, although they have too often been assumed to be correct.

The great difficulty with the second view, of course, is that it runs the risk of mistaking limitations that are due to environmental and social influences for the constraints of our nature. As Marx frequently emphasized, even the most powerful theorists have tended to mistake the distinctive character of human beings in their particular social milieu for human nature (Marx (1844) in McLellan 1984). Indeed, the controversy between those who think that human beings by nature are egoistic and those who attribute more altruism to our species has been simply a matter of assertion and counterassertion, with neither side marshaling adequate empirical evidence to support its case. So even if it is true that human nature constrains morality, the question of what constraints it imposes is no more tractable than other questions concerning the relative contributions of genes and the environment.

The third, most ambitious view of the relevance of human nature to morality and moral theory is even less supported than the second. Although we cannot hope to canvass the objections to the many versions of this view, it is fair to say that the dominant conclusion in ethical theory for at least the past century is that attempts to derive a comprehensive, substantive morality from human nature have failed. Let us then set aside the third, unpromising view of the relationship between human nature and morality, and concentrate on the first and second.

Genetic Causation, Freedom, and the Possibility of Morality

Consider the first view: that morality is only possible for human beings because practical rationality – the capacity to be moved to act by an awareness of good reasons for acting – is part of our nature. There are two ways in which advances in genetic science might be thought to threaten this connection between human nature and the possibility of morality (Brock 1996).

First, there is the possibility that through the misuse of genetic intervention we might destroy those features of our nature that make morality possible for us. French Anderson, a pioneer of gene therapy, suggests a related possibility when he worries that some germline intervention might inadvertently destroy our capacity for the "contemplation of good and evil" (Anderson 1990).

It is perhaps conceivable that a genetic intervention gone awry might result in some particular individual losing or failing to develop the basic rationality required for being a moral agent (just as rationality might be lost through a surgical accident or the administration of a drug that destroyed part of the individual's brain). It is quite another matter, however, to imagine that human beings would deliberately use genetic intervention to destroy their own rationality or that the unintended destruction of human rationality on a large scale through the misapplication of genetic science is a significant possibility. This last, dire possibility is exceedingly remote, if only because it is extremely unlikely that any experiment in human improvement through genetic alteration would include all of humanity rather than some small portion of it.

The second threat from advances in genetic science has to do with knowledge of genetic causation, not with the prospect that intervention might go awry. The fear is that an increasing knowledge of how genes influence human behavior will undermine our conception of ourselves as free.

Consider a widely reported statement by James Watson, co-discoverer of the double-helix structure of DNA and first director of the Human Genome Project: "We used to think that our fate was in our stars. Now we know, in large measure, our fate is in our genes" (Watson in Jaroff 1989). If our destiny is our molecular biology, there seems to be no room for freedom, nor hence for morality so far as it presupposes freedom. Instead of agents choosing the lives we live, what if we are simply the unwitting effects of unseen and unconscious biochemical entities – those tiny protein factories we call genes – whose activities we are only now beginning to understand.

This concern is based on a mistaken assumption, namely, that an increase in knowledge of genetic causation can establish the truth of what philosophers call Incompatibilist Determinism – the thesis that everything that happens has a cause and that universal causation excludes freedom. Incompatibilist Determinism is not subject to empirical confirmation, however. No increase in knowledge of causation can do more than establish the first part of the Incompatibilist Determinist thesis – that everything has a cause. Whether universal causation is compatible with freedom will not be established by any imaginable increase in knowledge of causal interactions; it is a metaphysical or moral-metaphysical thesis.

However, a vast increase in knowledge of genetic causation – or, more precisely, a great expansion of our knowledge of the interaction of genes and environments in the causation of human behavior – might well lead many people to *believe* that human freedom is an illusion. In other words, it may become harder for us to think of ourselves as free. And if this were to occur on a large scale, it might tend to undermine our belief that certain fundamental moral concepts, if not morality itself, apply to us.

An increase in the belief in Determinism, if not accompanied by a clear distinction between Determinism and Incompatibilist Determinism, might undermine the beliefs that support our institutions and practices regarding responsibility.

Some evidence of such a tendency is detectable not only in the history of eugenics but more recently in efforts to exculpate individuals by blaming their criminal behavior on "defective genes." So long as we regard the behavior that is thought to be determined by genes as aberrant and exceptional, there is no threat to our sense of our own freedom. But it might be quite otherwise if there were a great expansion of our knowledge of the interactions of genes and environments covering a broad range of "normal" human behaviors. The point is that even if we learn nothing about genes that shows that human freedom – as a necessary condition for morality – is an illusion, it might still be the case that advances in genetic knowledge might be thought to undermine some of the most basic practices and institutions that give substance to morality.

Consider now the implications of the possibilities of great powers of genetic intervention for the second view about the connection between morality and human nature: The thesis that human nature places substantial constraints on the content of morality (even though, contrary to the third view, it does not fully determine that content). The history of the eugenics movements indicates that it is not so farfetched to think that some human beings might consider it desirable or even obligatory to use a knowledge of how genes work to try to reduce the force of some of the factors they believe constrain the pursuit of moral ideals. Thus, for example, if enough people became convinced that there was a "gene for altruism" and that the moral condition of humanity would be improved if people were engineered or medicated so as to be less egoistic, they might conclude that the time had come to transcend human nature.

We saw earlier in this chapter that the very idea of a gene for altruism, or for any of the desirable human traits that used to be called virtues, betrays a certain naivete. Such traits are exceedingly complex, which masks disagreements about their desirability among different individuals or different value communities. At best, it might turn out that there are some genes or sets of genes that are necessary conditions for altruism. So whether it would ever become feasible to increase our capacity to be motivated by a direct concern for the interest of others is extremely doubtful.

Moreover, we are not now and may never be in a position to determine whether human altruism (or other capacities) does impose constraints on the sorts of visions of the just society that are feasible. Nonetheless, even to consider the possibility of changing whatever constraints our human nature imposes (if any) is to question the traditional view that human nature not only makes morality possible but places constraints on the content of morality.

The results of this section can now be summarized. A theory that purports to base justice or morality generally on a fixed human nature cannot tell us whether justice or morality permits or requires us to alter ourselves in fundamental ways, including ways that change what has been taken to be our nature. Consonance with a fixed human nature cannot be the touchstone for what is just or moral if there is no such thing.

What is less clear is what, if anything, will take the place of appeals to human nature as the touchstone for theories of justice. Perhaps as our powers increase we will come to regard as human nature whatever biological constraints we believe can never be altered. Just as our natural assets will be whatever valuable traits are not within human control, so human nature will be those characteristics that are distinctive of us and that are not subject to our manipulation.

At any given time, we may either underestimate or overestimate our eventual powers to change ourselves. If we underestimate, then once the limitations of our imagination are revealed, we may come to revise our conception of human nature. And this in turn may require revisions in our conception of justice, to the extent that we view human nature as a constraint on the demands of justice. But if we come to regard the constraints of our "nature" as rather negligible, as our ability to change ourselves increases, we may then focus directly on what sorts of characteristics we want our lives and the lives of our offspring to have, whether they are human lives or not.

In some respects, this would be all to the good, since there was never very much to be said for the view that what is important about us, morally speaking, is that we are human beings as opposed, say, to sentient beings or to beings who combine sentience with rationality. Appreciation for the fungibility of DNA, the consequent malleability of life, and the permeability of so-called species barriers thus may add impetus to the efforts of animal rights activists to rid our moral theorizing of parochialism.

The price of this liberation, however, may be high. If we can no longer convince ourselves that human nature provides significant constraints on the pursuit of individual or social good, we may feel cast adrift in a sea of possibilities. In particular, the problem of justice to future generations threatens to become even more mind-numbing than before, since the choices we now make concerning the uses of genetic intervention may determine not just the "nature" of future generations, but also the scope and limits of their ability to change their "nature," and perhaps even their ability to know and evaluate their "nature."

HUMAN NATURE AND THE IDEA OF MORAL PROGRESS

We have seen that the possibility of fundamentally reengineering human beings presents a profound and disturbing challenge to the traditional idea that a theory of justice must be based on a (fixed) conception of human nature. It also calls into question our very notion of moral progress.

At least in the West, we have tended to think of human progress as consisting of a growing awareness of our common humanity, and with it an increasing compliance with universal moral principles based on this common nature. This is especially true so far as moral progress regarding justice is concerned. For example, the struggle to abolish slavery was informed by the recognition that slaves were human beings, too, endowed with the rights of all human beings.

Such a conception of moral progress is broad enough to be accommodated by a broad range of ethical theories. For example, utilitarian views can see the increasing recognition of human rights as progress because, in Rule Utilitarian fashion, a world in which human rights principles are widely respected will be one that maximizes utility. In Kantian or other universalistic so-called rights-based theories, the development of widespread respect for human rights and the recognition of the common moral equality that goes with it is simply what is meant by moral progress.

But if human nature is not fixed, and if we must choose whether and in what way to change ourselves, then this simple idea of moral progress no longer applies. If we seek to justify radical genetic intervention, we cannot do so by viewing it as moral progress in the old and familiar sense – as a step toward a greater congruence between our actions and institutions, on the one hand, and our human nature, on the other. Nor can we view it simply as the fulfillment of our potential as human beings, since the changes we someday produce may provide now unimaginable changes in our potential. Nor can we equate human progress with the growing recognition of and compliance with rights principles that apply to all of us by virtue of our common humanity.

Perhaps more important, we can no longer assume that there will be a single successor to what has been regarded as human nature. We must consider the possibility that at some point in the future, different groups of human beings may follow divergent paths of development through the use of genetic technology. If this occurs, there will be different groups of beings, each with its own "nature," related to one another only through a common ancestor (the human race), just as there are now different species of animals who evolved from common ancestors through random mutation and natural selection. (Perhaps future members of the United Nations will become increasingly uncomfortable with the phrase "Universal Declaration of Human Rights.")

The effectiveness of people's motivation to act consistently on universal moral principles may depend significantly on whether they share a sense of common membership in a single moral community. But whether this sense of moral community could survive such divergence is a momentous question. Even if the correct view of our nature is that we are simply rational beings, and even if (barring some cataclysmic accident) we do not change this, it is quite possible that the sorts of rational beings we happen to be or will become must, as a matter of psychological fact, have more in common with one another than our rationality if we are to be effectively motivated to treat one another as equal citizens in the moral community. For all we know, it might turn out that if differences among groups in characteristics other than a common rationality became pronounced enough, they would not treat each other as moral equals. History is replete with instances in which human beings have failed to empathize with their fellows simply because of quite superficial differences in physical appearance or even in customs and manners.

GENETIC INTERVENTION IN THE NAME OF JUSTICE

Intervening to Prevent Limitations on Opportunity

In contemplating the disturbing challenges that the possibilities of genetic intervention pose for our traditional ways of thinking about justice, it is tempting to conclude that we are ill equipped to make any firm judgments about what justice requires. This temptation, however, ought to be resisted. Some conclusions can indeed be drawn about the requirements of justice in the genetic age.

First, the two most prominent contemporary approaches to liberal theories of equal opportunity – the social structural view and the brute luck view – require genetic interventions for the sake of preventing or curing diseases. Second, both of these approaches, as well as the resource egalitarian theory of justice, allow for the possibility that genetic interventions may be required to counteract the opportunity-limiting effects of natural inequalities that do not constitute diseases.

Regulating Access to Interventions to Prevent a Widening of Existing Inequalities

Much of the current debate over the ethics of genetic interventions centers on the question of whether genetic enhancements of normal traits, as opposed to genetic treatments for disease, are morally permissible. Our analysis of equal opportunity and resource egalitarian theories shows that on some accounts enhancements may be not only permissible but obligatory, as a matter of justice. We have argued that both resource egalitarianism and the brute luck view of equal opportunity appear to be committed to the thesis that justice may require interventions to counteract natural inequalities, whether they constitute diseases or not. So such views are committed to the obligatory nature of enhancements, not just treatments, whenever a natural inequality can best be prevented by enhancement.

In contrast, the social structural view, at least when developed along the lines of Daniels's theory of just health care, supports the position that the distinction between enhancements and treatments is of considerable significance and that, at least generally speaking, treatments are obligatory while enhancements are not. Chapter 4 explores the distinction between genetic enhancements and treatments in detail and assesses its significance for social policy in general and for health care in particular.

It is one thing to say that justice, at least on certain accounts, does not require genetic enhancements or would only rarely do so. It is quite another to say that enhancements are not a concern of justice. There are strong social forces at work that make it extremely unlikely that genetic technology will be limited to preventing or curing diseases. The profit motive – which is both guided by consumer demand and stimulates it through the arts of marketing – may soon extend genetic technology beyond treatments into the realm of enhancements. If this occurs, it may become necessary, in order to prevent existing unjust inequalities from worsening, to regulate access to interventions (Buchanan 1995).

Suppose that it becomes possible to identify, synthesize, and implant in embryos complexes of genes that will greatly increase the probability of an individual possessing certain desirable characteristics to a significantly higher degree than the average person in a given population. Such characteristics might include superior memory, the ability to concentrate for long periods of time, and resistance to common illness (such as colds, common types of cancer, atherosclerosis, and depression). Alternatively, and more likely, suppose that these benefits could be gained by genetic pharmacology. If access to this "enhancement" technology depended solely on ability to pay, then its use would exacerbate and perpetuate disadvantages already suffered by the poor and various minority groups, including disadvantages that are the result of past injustices.

Having a "genetic enhancement certificate" (to refer to Scenario 5 in the Introduction) would be a great advantage, especially in employment. Employers would be more likely to select a person for a desirable career track involving much investment in the individual's training over a long period of time if the individual had a bona fide genetic enhancement certificate. Furthermore, if affordable health insurance continues to be largely employment-based, as it currently is in the United States, and if employers continue to offer health insurance, then they would have an added incentive to hire those who had benefited from genetic enhancement and to shun those who had not.

At present, the number of "sick days" an employee is entitled to without loss of pay presumably reflects the average incidence of sickness. Those whose genetic enhancement conferred a greater resistance to disease would not require as many sick days and would, for that reason, be more attractive to prospective employers. If enough people were able to afford such enhancement, there might even be changes in the way employment contracts were written, with fewer compensated sick days becoming the norm. Those who lacked access to the enhancement would be significantly disadvantaged – indeed, might come to be regarded as disabled – even though they were perfectly normal by our present, pre-enhancement standards.

It is important to see that these effects might occur even if the actual

results of genetic enhancement were somewhat less dramatic than the
purveyors of the intervention portray them. After all, possession of a
college diploma currently serves as a necessary qualification for entering competition for most white-collar jobs, even though in many cases
the educational experience the individual received in college is of dubious relevance to the actual requirements of the job. If access to such
enhancements according to ability to pay exacerbated existing unjust
inequalities, justice might require either that they be made available to
all or that they not be available at all.

The same point can be made by a more familiar example. Originally
the drug Prozac was offered as a treatment for the disease of depression. Now many physicians in the United States prescribe Prozac to
make normal people feel better. This indicates that what people care
about is whether a service is a benefit and whether it is affordable, not
about whether it is a treatment for a disease. In a society in which
market forces increasingly shape the direction of technological development, it would be surprising if the use of genetic interventions
remained restricted to health care properly so-called – that is, to the
treatment and prevention of disease. If genetic interventions emerge
that have a significant impact on equality of opportunity, a sound
ethical response will require that individuals and society attempt to
guide their use according to principles of justice, even if, properly
speaking, they fall outside its primary domain.

Ratcheting Up the Standard for Normal Species Functioning

We have seen that under one conception of equal opportunity and its
implications for the right to health care, the concept of normal species
functioning constrains the range of genetic interventions required by
justice. According to this view, generally speaking it is only those
natural inequalities that cause or constitute adverse departures from
normal species functioning that are a concern of justice. This constraint, though significant, may not be fixed.

It is conceivable that genetic enhancements of normal human functions, if sufficiently valuable and widespread, might lead us to revise
upward our conception of normal species functioning, with the result
that where we draw the line between health and disease, and hence
between enhancement and treatment, would correspondingly change.
If this occurred, we might come to view a certain intervention as being
required by justice even though previously we had regarded it as an

optional enhancement that individuals might be allowed to seek, but to which none was entitled. For example, suppose it were possible to insert into human beings a gene from another species that produced resistance to certain diseases or even perhaps a dimension of visual acuity that had never before been possessed by human beings. If such enhancements became widespread, we might come to regard a person who lacked them as suffering from an adverse departure from normal functioning.

Tailoring Environments to Special Genetic Needs

Finally, there is at least one other area in which equality of opportunity might require constraints on a "free" market in genetic services. As noted earlier, it is reasonable to expect that as knowledge of how genes function progresses, we will identify genotypic subgroups within the general population who would benefit, physically or cognitively, from special environments. Some subgroups might live longer and have more years of high quality of life if they had the benefit of special diets, perhaps supplemented with certain drugs. Others might reach higher levels of cognitive development if they were put in special learning environments, with teaching techniques tailored to their specific capacities.

If access to testing to identify such genotypic subgroups and special environments they need for maximal development were available only to those who could pay for them, then once again we would have a situation in which scientific advances would serve to exacerbate existing inequalities in opportunity. If equality of opportunity matters, then we cannot assume that an unregulated "genetic supermarket" is legitimate.

THE OBLIGATION TO PREVENT HARM

In this chapter we have concentrated on the implications of genetic intervention for how we understand obligations of justice. Justice, however, is not the only source of obligations. In virtually all moral theories, a prominent place is given to the obligation to prevent harm, which in some cases is not assumed to be grounded in justice.

Some genetic defects not only limit opportunities but cause severe suffering. For example, Lesch-Nyhan syndrome, an enzyme deficiency, produces compulsive self-mutilating behavior in addition to severe

mental retardation. Others, including Tay-Sachs disease, lead to years
of suffering, followed by death before the end of childhood. Quite
apart from the obligation to prevent or ameliorate serious limitations
on opportunity, something quite simple – the obligation to prevent
harm – can also provide a moral mandate for intervention.

Some moral theories regard the obligation to prevent harm – at
least where the harm is serious – to be an obligation of justice. In
Chapter 6, we will argue in a more systematic manner that the rights
of prospective parents are significantly circumscribed not only by the
right to equality of opportunity but also by the obligation to prevent
harm, whether it is regarded as an element of justice or not.

CONCLUSIONS

As thoughtful people have pondered the prospects of the genetic revolution, a number of issues of distributive justice have been identified,
from worries about insurance and employment discrimination, to concerns over inequitable access to genetic services, to the fear that the
fruits of genetic research will be shared inequitably between rich and
poor countries. These are all important issues, and our ethical autopsy
on eugenics shows that focusing on them is a step in the right direction, since the greatest single flaw of eugenics was its failure to take
justice seriously. Nevertheless, such concerns fail to penetrate the surface of the implications of genetic intervention for theories of justice.
This chapter has attempted to articulate some of the ways that the
possibility of making hitherto unimaginable changes in human beings
forces us to rethink some of our most fundamental beliefs about justice.

Whether the most dramatic promises of genetic intervention are
realized or not, contemplating them uniquely reveals – and challenges
– the deepest assumptions of theorizing about justice. Among these
assumptions are that justice only requires compensating for natural
inequalities rather than attacking them directly; that the basic problem
of distributive justice is how to distribute goods among persons whose
identities are given independently of the act of distribution; that a
theory of justice must be based on human nature, and that we can
adjudicate among rival theories of distributive justice by seeing which
is most consonant with human nature; and that moral progress consists largely of growing awareness of our common humanity, and with

it an increasing compliance with universal principles of justice rooted in a single, common humanity.

In spite of these perplexing challenges to some of our most fundamental assumptions about justice, we have argued that two major conclusions should guide public policy choices in the age of genetic intervention: There is a principled presumption that genetic intervention to prevent or ameliorate serious limitations on opportunities due to disease is a requirement of justice. And justice may require regulating the conditions of access to genetic enhancements to prevent exacerbations of existing unjust inequalities.

We have argued that the two dominant approaches to equal opportunity, the social structural and brute luck views, have quite distinct implications for the significance of natural inequalities. We have also argued that these two types of theories may well have precisely the same consequences in practice, at least for the foreseeable future: Both will tend to focus primarily, if not exclusively, on the genetic interventions to prevent or cure disease.

There are three reasons why this congruence is to be expected. First, in general the genetic disadvantages that are adverse departures from normal functioning tend to have more serious negative impacts on opportunity. Given that resources are scarce, a reasonable allocation of priority equal opportunity efforts would presumably focus on the prevention and cure of disease first. Second, it is not inconceivable that we would come to reclassify as a disease any correctable genetic condition that has a significant adverse impact on equality, because we would come to regard it as an adverse departure from normal functioning. Third, acknowledging a role for genetic intervention in the pursuit of justice may not require anything so radical as "genetic equality," even according to the more radical (brute luck) theory of equal opportunity or resource egalitarianism.

Properly understood, neither equality of opportunity nor a commitment to attaining a more just distribution of resources requires efforts to eliminate all inequalities in natural assets. Due to value pluralism, in many cases there will be a lack of a rational consensus about what counts as a valuable genetically influenced trait, since in a liberal society there are and will continue to be deep differences among individuals and communities about the character of "the good life." Consequently, a reasonable public policy must proceed in a conservative manner, focusing on efforts to avoid what are clearly deprivations rather than on striving to achieve the greatest equal distribution of natural assets.

This latter conclusion is reinforced by our realization that what counts as a natural asset (as opposed to a deficit) depends on the nature of the cooperative framework within which the individual will operate and on the complementarity of traits. Because cooperative frameworks and the supply of complementary traits change over time (and sometimes rapidly and unpredictably, due to unforeseen technological advances), aiming to equalize natural assets would be a highly fallible and even dangerous enterprise, both for individuals and for society. So long as conscientious efforts are made to prevent or ameliorate genetic conditions that will result in what would uncontroversially count as serious limitations on opportunity in most if not all cooperative frameworks we are likely to develop, it would be imprudent to run the risk of diminished diversity and flexibility for the sake of strict equality. Contrary to what might first appear to be the case, then, acknowledging that the domain of justice extends in principle to natural as well as social assets does not commit us to efforts to achieve "genetic equality" – at least not for the foreseeable future.

There is, of course, another extremely important qualification on our thesis that equality of opportunity will sometimes require genetic interventions and that the required interventions may not always be limited to the cure or prevention of disease. Interventions to remove barriers to an individual's opportunities should not be forced on that individual if he or she is competent and does not consent to the interventions. As with more familiar medical interventions, including nongenetic interventions aimed at removing barriers to opportunity, the requirements of justice are limited by respect for the autonomy of the competent individual.

In this chapter we have argued that certain fundamental elements of justice, in particular equality of opportunity and what we have called the morality of inclusion, speak in favor of genetic interventions in some instances and of regulating access to interventions in others. In Chapter 4 we extend and deepen our exploration of issues of justice by critically examining certain distinctions which some believe would mark important moral boundaries in a just society equipped with formidable genetic powers, including the distinction between positive and negative genetic intervention. In so doing we bring the rather abstract consideration of justice developed above into closer contact with the concrete issues of health care policy, and in particular with the question of how to decide which forms of genetic intervention should be made available to all as a matter of just health care.

FOUR

POSITIVE AND NEGATIVE GENETIC INTERVENTIONS

OLD DISTINCTIONS IN NEW CLOTHES

Positive and Negative Eugenic Goals for Populations

Earlier in this century, the eugenics movement was more concerned with the genetic quality, or "health," of populations than with the health and welfare of individuals. Indeed, as noted in Chapter 2, some in that movement were concerned that keeping "unfit" individuals healthy might have dysgenic effects. This focus on populations rather than individuals is part of what makes the movement and its goals seem so threatening.

We also saw that the eugenics movement had two main goals. Its negative goal was the reduction in dysgenic effects or burdens on the gene pool by eliminating genetic diseases, disorders, disabilities, and other "defects." Negative eugenics aimed to improve the health and performance of the population by preventing reproduction of its least healthy and least capable members. This goal required severe restrictions on reproductive rights, for those with "defects" had to be kept from reproducing, if necessary through the involuntary sterilization of "mental defectives."

The goal of positive eugenics was to improve the health and performance of the population by increasing the rate of reproduction of those harboring its best traits and capabilities. Pursuing this goal also involved modifying traditional reproductive practices, although usually through voluntary measures. For example, as also noted in Chapter 2, to inspire the right marriage choices, there were competitions at county fairs aimed at displaying the best human "breeding stock."

The boundary between positive and negative eugenics did not mark a generally accepted moral boundary for proponents of the eugenics movement, although some attributed moral significance to it. Rather, it reflected two aspects of the same goal of improving a population. The distinction between them rested crucially on drawing a further line between what was considered sub- or abnormal or defective and what was considered normal or even superior. The scope of negative eugenics – that is, what counted as defects to be eliminated – clearly depended on what conception of normal or even superior phenotype and genotype was used. To the extent that "defects" were limited to clear, paradigmatic cases of disease or disability, negative eugenics could be portrayed as a form of disease prevention – although the infringements of reproductive rights committed in its name are disturbing and unacceptable regardless of how benign the categorization of disease happened to be.

A highly idealized or perfectionist view of superior or normal traits would mean that a trait we ordinarily take to be normal would count as "defective." Elimination of these traits would then become the legitimate target of negative eugenics. To the extent that racial stereotypes of "higher" and "lower" races or "socially superior" and "inferior types" were involved in defining normal and defective traits, negative eugenics risked becoming – and in the United States and Germany, dramatically became – racist or even genocidal.

Many of the most serious abuses were actually committed in the name of negative rather than positive eugenics. The seemingly benign goal of disease prevention was transformed into the goal of people prevention (or even elimination), at least for those groups of people harboring "defective" traits. Today, we are at least as horrified at some of the ways the distinction between normal and defective was drawn as we are at the infringements of reproductive rights involved in the pursuit of eugenic goals. We are appalled at the ways in which bad science was harnessed to serve discriminatary attitudes toward race, class, and disability.

Positive and Negative Interventions and the Health and Welfare of Individuals

Today a distinction is commonly drawn between negative and positive "genetic interventions." As noted in Chapter 1, we use the latter term in a very broad sense to include somatic or germline uses of modern genetic technologies and pharmacological applications of those technologies, as well as uses of genetic technology in screening aimed at family planning. As in its earlier use, the negative/positive distinction depends on our being able to distinguish disease, disorder, impairment, or disability from normal traits or capabilities.

In many contemporary discussions, the negative/positive distinction is used to draw a fundamental moral boundary. There is a presumption that negative genetic interventions – ranging from screening and selective abortions to somatic cell and (more problematically) germline replacement therapy – are morally permissible, whereas positive interventions are morally impermissible or at least highly problematic (Anderson 1990, 1980, 1985, 1988; cf. Glover 1988; Kitcher 1995).

The explanation for this presumption, which is surprising in light of the serious abuses committed in the name of negative eugenics, is that negative genetic interventions are in general no different from other medical treatments, whether preventive or curative, of disease or impairment, whereas positive genetic interventions are aimed at the morally problematic enhancement of normal traits and capabilities. The implication is that there is little that is morally problematic about treating disease but there may be much moral controversy about which normal traits, if any, should be enhanced. Obviously, if this negative/positive distinction translates into the distinction between permissible and impermissible uses of genetic interventions, it would be of great importance for public policy, and that explains the interest in this issue and our focus on it in this chapter.

It is important not to confuse the negative/positive distinction with the difference between somatic and germline replacement therapies – that is, between replacing genetic material in the somatic cells of an individual (affecting the expression of some trait solely in that individual) and replacing genetic material in germ cells (affecting the expression of traits for the individual resulting from those germ cells and his or her descendants).

The somatic-germline distinction, so prominent in the literature on genetic technologies, is often used to draw a similar line between morally permissible and morally impermissible or suspect interventions (Council for Responsible Genetics 1993). But it cuts across the distinction between negative and positive genetic intervention. A somatic replacement intervention could be pursued, had we the technology, to correct a defect or to enhance an otherwise normal capability. The same is true for germline replacements. Any systematic differences in risks and uncertainties, in the relation between risks and benefits, or in the prospects for obtaining informed consent of the affected party that support different moral conclusions about the permissibility of somatic and germline interventions will be independent of the distinction between negative and positive interventions (Kitcher 1995), which is our concern here.

Having noted that the shadow of the negative/positive eugenics distinction falls darkly on the negative/positive genetic intervention distinction, it is important to emphasize some decisive differences in the social context (discussed in more detail in Chapter 2). One important difference is that the primary concerns of those interested in either somatic or germline gene replacement today are not the "health" or "capability" of populations or the "quality" of the gene pool, but the health and well-being of individuals and their descendants. In addition, there is a greatly enhanced respect for and legal recognition of individual reproductive freedom, as well as for the requirement that voluntary, informed consent or its legitimate proxy be obtained for all medical (and experimental) interventions.

Contemporary developments in genetics also take place on the heels of the achievements of a highly successful disabilities rights movement. Activists have educated the public about people with disabilities, established strong legal protections for them, and moved the public to broader acceptance of the "diversity" they represent. Finally, the contemporary positive/negative intervention distinction is drawn in a period when we are still highly sensitive to, and frightened by, the historically recent slide from eugenics to genocide.

Together, these differences in the social context do much to dispel the shadow cast by the eugenics movement. Nevertheless, we are still far from a worldwide climate in which racist ideology is no longer a threat. We continue to witness "ethnic cleansing" and genocide in parts of Europe and Africa; even in liberal democracies, we see active racist movements promoting ideology that explicitly invokes Nazi ideas with favor. Echoes of racism underlie the appeal of many of the current "hot" social reform topics in the United States – affirmative action, welfare reform, crime, and gun control. Much but not all has changed. We leave these comments on the social context, however, to concentrate on the moral issues surrounding the positive/negative distinction and its uses.

Moral Boundaries and the Positive/Negative Distinction

The question remains, Can the negative/positive intervention distinction be drawn as cleanly as its proponents imply, and with anything like the moral and public policy implications they suggest? We believe the distinction and the moral implications drawn from it deserve more careful examination for two reasons.

First, the treatment/enhancement distinction on which the contrast between negative and positive intervention rests is used for a very different moral purpose in most medical and medical insurance contexts. Specifically, it is currently used to draw a line between services that it is obligatory to provide to others – for example, in private or public insurance schemes – and those that it is not. But a line between what is obligatory and nonobligatory in insurance schemes is not to be confused with a line between what it is permissible and impermissible for anyone to do with genetic interventions. Obviously, what is obligatory in an insurance scheme is permissible, and what is impermissible for anyone to do cannot be obligatory in insurance schemes. But what is nonobligatory in insurance may be either permissible or impermissible for individuals to do, and what is permissible for individuals to do may be either obligatory or nonobligatory in insurance. So, even given the distinction between treatments and enhancements, we shall have to consider whether this gives us any guidance on the boundary between permissible and impermissible.

Second, the treatment/enhancement distinction itself has been sharply criticized even in its current use for reasons that must be taken seriously. To decide whether the negative/positive genetic intervention distinction has any public policy implications – that is, whether it helps us draw any moral boundaries – we will have to consider more carefully the treatment/enhancement distinction on which it rests. In the remainder of this chapter, we shall consider various objections to the treatment/enhancement distinction: that it is difficult to draw, that it does not give us the boundary between what is obligatory and nonobligatory to provide in medical insurance schemes, and that it leaves us with hard cases that make the distinction seem arbitrary.

To resolve some of these issues, we will have to discuss alternative accounts of our obligations to assist others with medical services, including those based on genetic technologies. Specifically, we shall consider the suggestion discussed in Chapter 3, by one of the more expansive interpretations of the level playing field conception of equal opportunity and by resource egalitarianism, that we drop the distinction between treatments and enhancements altogether in favor of more directly assessing whether an intervention is required because it equalizes opportunities.

On that view, which we dubbed the "brute luck view" (following Scanlon), equality of opportunity requires eliminating all disadvantaging deficits in capabilities for which an individual is not responsible, whether or not they are the result of disease or impairment or merely the result of bad luck in a natural lottery for (otherwise normal) capabilities. A supporting intuition for this expansive account of equal opportunity is the claim that contingencies in the natural lottery are as morally arbitrary as those in the social lottery, so that if equal opportunity is supposed to correct for social contingencies, it also ought to correct for natural ones that produce unchosen disadvantages.

In this chapter, we explore and try to motivate further an alternative, more restrictive approach to the notion of equal opportunity and its implications for our obligations in health care. Described briefly in Chapter 3 as the social structural view, this conception of justice supports a qualified and limited defense of the treatment/enhancement distinction. By drawing out the implications of the social structural view, we will make much more concrete the rather abstract examination of justice in Chapter 3 and bring it into closer contact with basic issues of social policy.

Before trying to defend the distinction between positive and negative intervention or a theoretical perspective that uses it, we first reinforce some of the theoretical doubts about it raised in Chapter 3. We do so by focusing on a range of "hard cases" drawn from actual medical practice, in which use of the distinction sometimes seems especially problematic even though it is part of a widely accepted insurance practice. We then reverse course, defending on both policy and theoretical grounds a more limited goal of maintaining "normal functioning" through health care rather than the more expansive goals that might be supported by the brute luck view. Nevertheless, this approach, though different in its theoretical conception from the more expansive brute luck conception of equal opportunity, comes very close to it in its practical implications. This convergence in practice, which was briefly noted in Chapter 3, is of considerable interest itself.

The limited defense offered here of the treatment/enhancement distinction means it cannot provide a clear or unequivocal guide to the moral boundaries between what it is obligatory and nonobligatory to provide in insurance or between what it is permissible and impermissible for individuals to do. Neverthless, it has a useful, if modest, bearing on each, especially the former. In the remainder of this chapter, we are concerned more with negative genetic interventions and the obligatory/nonobligatory boundary. In Chapter 6, we explore further the general issue of improving our offspring through genetic interventions, both positive and negative.

TREATMENT VERSUS ENHANCEMENT: WIDE USE, HARD CASES, STRONG CRITICISM

Insurance Coverage and "Medical Necessity"

As noted, the treatment/enhancement distinction draws a line between services or interventions meant to prevent or cure (or otherwise ameliorate) conditions viewed as diseases or impairments and the interventions that improve a condition viewed as a normal function or feature of members of our species. Glover (OTA 1988) comments that, like night and day, the distinction may pose boundary problems, but the line it draws is nevertheless useful. We will have to assess whether he is underestimating the challenges to the distinction. Still, the line drawn here is widely appealed to in medical practice and medical insurance contexts, as well as in our everyday thinking about the medical services we do and should assist people in obtaining.

The treatment/enhancement distinction is closely related to the concept of "medical necessity" that appears in legislation regulating public insurance in both the United States and Canada, and in private insurance contracts. Medically necessary services are those that effectively treat physical or mental disease and impairment or ameliorate conditions deriving from them (Daniels and Sabin 1991; Sabin and Daniels 1994). They may effectively produce benefits for other conditions, but those do not count as medically necessary.

For example, insurance coverage is provided by public and private schemes for growth hormone treatment for children projected to be very short, provided that there is an underlying disease condition, such as a diagnosable growth hormone deficiency or Turner's syndrome. If there is no underlying disease condition, insurers do not cover the treatment for children whose parents simply want them to be taller, regardless of how short they will be. Similarly, insurers will generally reimburse – and in some states, like Massachusetts, they are mandated to reimburse – for reconstructive breast surgery following mastectomy or trauma. But they do not reimburse for cosmetic surgery, however strongly a woman may feel that her life will be improved if her breasts are made larger or smaller.

The same distinction plays a role in coverage for mental health therapies. Consider the following cases illustrating coverage policy within the Harvard Community Health Plan (HCHP) prior to 1994, then a staff-model HMO that served more than 550,000 people in New England (the cases are drawn from Sabin and Daniels 1994). An adult patient with a history of bipolar disorder had been stabilized on lithium for some years. He remained shy, however, and was referred to an out-of-plan group therapy situation, from which he clearly benefited over a period of several years. In its original benefit structure, this long-term treatment could not have been covered by HCHP. The plan revised its benefit structure, allowing an "extended benefit" that would cover protracted therapy of this sort without extensive co-pays, provided treatment was for a serious condition. But does treatment of shyness count as treatment of a serious disorder? The psychiatrist managing the Shy Bipolar's case believed that the shyness was the result of the onset of the bipolar disorder; had the disorder not interfered with the adolescent development of this man, who was normally outgoing before its onset, he would probably have been more outgoing. Consequently, the therapist reasoned, the "extended benefit" should be given. Had the shyness not been "diagnosed" as the result of the bipolar disorder, then even if it were comparably serious, there would have been no eligibility for an extended benefit.

The factor underlying this reasoning did not have to do with the degree of suffering involved in being shy; the reasoning depended on the etiology or explanation of the shyness. The point is illustrated by another case in which clinicians distinguished between treatment of illness and enhancement of well-being. An intelligent, professionally successful married father of two children sought treatment because of severe unhappiness associated with marital distress. His wife suffered from a serious mental illness that made her very difficult to live with. The Unhappy Husband was committed to maintaining the marriage. A V code diagnosis ["Conditions not attributable to a mental disorder that are a focus of treatment" (*Diagnostic and Statistical Manual III-R*, p. 359)] (marital problem) was made. In 26 highly productive sessions of psychotherapy, the man was able to clarify some of the pertinent dynamic issues in his marriage and developed a number of adaptive strategies for lessening his distress. The patient wished that his treatment would be covered by insurance, but he agreed that he was not suffering from an illness and that it was fair to expect him to pay.

The Unhappy Husband was probably suffering more than many of the HMO members being treated for illnesses, and psychotherapy definitely enhanced his well-being. What possible rationale could there be for not covering his treatment? The clinician's decision hinged on the question of what the Unhappy Husband is suffering from. By the criteria set forth in DSM-III-R, the man did not have an illness. His suffering arose from the fact that although his wife's unchanging condition caused him great pain, his values precluded divorce. The clinician believed that under the prevailing agreements that govern insurance, individuals like the Unhappy Husband should be responsible for some or all of the cost of ameliorating the unhappiness associated with an unfortunate existential situation. Paradoxically, if the Unhappy Husband expressed his suffering through somatic symptoms and presented to an internist rather than a mental health clinician, insurance would typically cover medical investigation and treatment, which would probably be less effective but costlier than psychotherapy. A 1989 survey of medium and large firms showed that only 2 percent of insured employees have coverage for outpatient mental health services equivalent to other medical services (Scheidemandel 1993, p. 44).

Treatment/Enhancement and Moral Hazard

Some clinicians and some members of the public balk at the line being drawn here. They may be inclined to say that if there is "suffering" involved, as there clearly might be for short children, shy adults, or husbands opposed to divorce from ill wives, then we should relieve the suffering with medical interventions funded through insurance. Nevertheless, there is a very good reason why insurers prefer to insist on a diagnosis of disease or impairment as an eligibility condition for reimbursement for beneficial services, and why they do not simply agree to reimburse for anything that is effective at producing a benefit, at least as perceived by the patient or even the therapist. Without the requirement for a disease diagnosis, insurers would be exposed to what is termed "moral hazard."

Moral hazard refers to the modification of behavior that individuals make in light of the incentives provided by insurance coverage – in particular, behavioral changes that make them eligible for benefits they would not otherwise be entitled to have. For example, someone with extensive fire insurance might seek to make a payoff more likely by setting a fire (here the moral hazard leads to arson and fraud) or by failing to take reasonable precautions against one. Obviously, insurers do not reimburse people for fire damage that is the result of arson the insuree arranges or of gross negligence. Similarly, there is no insurance market for reimbursement for the costs of speeding tickets.

If individuals could define their otherwise normal condition as one that involved "suffering" or one that imposed unacceptable disadvantage, given their expectations, then insurance against such suffering or disadvantage would encourage extensive moral hazard. An insurance market against certain risks can function only if the risks are measurable actuarially and the market does not create conditions (such as moral hazard) that make the risk unmeasurable.

Treatments and the Limits of Obligations

This point about insurance is related to a deeper fact about when we feel obligated to assist others, including when we feel obligated to reduce or mitigate the effects of an inequality that arises among us. Consider the case of the Plain Hero who feels very dissatisfied with his appearance: His face is normal but hardly handsome. He feels he might be more successful in seeking companionship or in "presenting" himself in business relationships if his face or hair better matched some social model of handsomeness. He may have developed elaborate explanations for his failures that excuse himself of any responsibility and place the blame on his appearance and the "superficiality" of others so affected by it. The solution does not lie in changing how he thinks or behaves with prospective social or business partners but in how he appears. Are we obliged to relieve his suffering by providing him with the means to obtain cosmetic surgery?

Some may feel so obliged, but most would not. They would complain that the problem here lies in the beliefs, attitudes, and excuses harbored by our Plain Hero. It is his responsibility to rethink his goals and his means of achieving them. If he is unable to do so, it may indicate some deeper psychological problem, and the treatment he may need is a mental health intervention, not cosmetic surgery. In part, what we resist here is the idea that an individual can develop very expensive tastes or preferences, for example for being one of "the beautiful people," and that others owe him the chance to satisfy those preferences. We resist being held hostage in our obligations to assist others (or to reduce inequality) by expensive tastes. If the Plain Hero wants to invest his own resources in removing what he sees as the obstacle to his success, then let him. We owe him a new face no more than we owe him a Porsche, which he might just as justifiably think would open new doors to him.

The Plain Hero, of course, is to be distinguished from someone who has been disfigured by congenital deformity, disease, or trauma, for whom reconstructive plastic surgery meets a medical need (Daniels 1985, p. 31, note 9; MacGreggor 1979; de Beaufort et al. 1996). Obviously, there will be gray areas in which it is unclear whether plastic surgery meets a medical need or is simply a cosmetic preference.

This concern about social hijacking by extravagant preferences cannot be all there is to the matter. The Unhappy Husband in the example discussed earlier has not adopted extravagant tastes. His aversion to abandoning his ill wife may be the result of some unshakeable moral conviction, perhaps one inculcated in his religious upbringing, or it may be the result of a moral conviction he affirms and takes responsibility for – one that is in fact admirable, as loyalty often is, despite its consequences for him. Still, in general we do not owe it to people to compensate them for all sacrifice and suffering they incur when they live up to what they see as their obligations, although sometimes – for example, with veterans – we may think compensation is appropriate. We are often unhappy in carrying out our moral duties, yet we do not generally think that others owe us something for doing so – that is, other than praise or recognition or moral support. We no doubt owe moral support to the Unhappy Husband in a way we do not owe such support to the Plain Hero.

As a result of this discussion, we might conclude that the treatment/ enhancement distinction derives some support from the general fact that disease and impairment are conditions that we are generally not responsible for (leaving aside the issue of self-induced disease, for the moment).[1] In addition, they are conditions that we can generally agree involve some sort of objectively specifiable burden or harm. For example, the harm might be an impairment of the range of opportunities open to us (see Daniels 1985) because of the reduced functioning or diminished capabilities that result from the disease or impairment. We might also think the "pain and suffering" involved as a result of these conditions can be recognized as typical features of the human condi-

---

[1] Considerable complexity surrounds the notion of "responsibility" for ends and responsibility for a person's own misfortune or suffering. Consequently, clarifying how we draw distinctions between needs and desires ultimately draws us into a tangled web of moral concepts and distinctions that we do not presume to sort out in detail here.

tion. In contrast, we may want to dismiss the pain of the Plain Hero as an "exaggerated" and quite atypical response to the human condition, saying "There need have been no real suffering there, only a change of his attitude."

Hard Cases and the Expansion of Obligations

Unfortunately, if we look more closely at certain difficult cases, we are more hard-pressed to attribute to the treatment/enhancement distinction the weight it is given in medical practice, including insurance schemes. For the sake of vividness, let us put names on the faces of the growth hormone treatment cases.

Johnny is a short 11-year-old boy with documented growth hormone (GH) deficiency resulting from a brain tumor. His parents are of average height. His predicted adult height without GH treatment is approximately 160 cm (5 feet 3 inches).

Billy is a short 11-year-old boy with normal GH secretion according to current testing methods. However, his parents are extremely short, and he has a predicted adult height of 160 cm (5 feet 3 inches). (Allen and Fost 1990, p. 117)

These cases make the distinction seem arbitrary for several reasons. First, Johnny and Billy will suffer disadvantage equally if they are not treated. There is no reason to think the difference in the underlying causes of their shortness will lead people to treat them in ways that make one happier or more advantaged than the other. Second, although Johnny is short because of dysfunction whereas Billy is short because of his (normal) genotype, both are short through no choice or fault of their own. The shortness is in both cases the result of a biological, "natural lottery." Both thus seem to suffer undeserved disadvantages. Third, Billy's preference for greater height, just like Johnny's, is a preference that most people hold; it is not peculiar, idiosyncratic, or extravagant. Indeed, it is a response to a social prejudice, "heightism." The prejudice is what we should condemn, not the fact that they both form an "expensive taste" in reaction to it.

If we return to the case of the Shy Bipolar, we could raise exactly the same points in comparing him to an equally shy but otherwise normal person, the Shy Normal. They will suffer the disadvantages of shyness equally. Both are shy through no fault of their own – assuming normal shyness is a feature that is significantly determined by temperament or by exposure to early learning situations that a person did not choose to be in. And most people would prefer to be more outgoing and to enjoy the relationships we think come with such a posture toward others – the preference to change from being shy is not idiosyncratic or extravagant.

Cases like these raise several questions: Does the concept of disease underlying the treatment/enhancement distinction force us to treat relevantly similar cases in dissimilar ways? Are we violating the old Aristotelian requirement that justice requires treating like cases similarly? Is dissimilar treatment unfair or unjust? Any defense of the moral use to which we put the treatment/enhancement distinction in medical and insurance contexts must respond to this concern. These cases make more concrete the worries raised in Chapter 3 that there is something "morally arbitrary" about addressing the disadvantages produced by disease and impairment and not addressing those imposed by disadvantageous – but normal – allotments of capabilities or talents and skills.

The Microstructure of the Normal and Moral Arbitrariness

Before responding to these questions, we would like to deepen the sense that there may be something morally arbitrary about the use to which the treatment/enhancement distinction is put, and perhaps even about the distinction itself. To do so we appeal, at least hypothetically, to something we may learn from the Human Genome Project and from the greater knowledge we get about how genes regulate growth.

Suppose we learn that some particular pattern of genes explains the extreme shortness of Billy, the child who did not seem to be growth-hormone deficient. Suppose we learn that some particular genes Billy has make some receptors to growth hormones slightly less responsive than the genes that would lead someone to be of average or above-average height; perhaps there are fewer such receptors, perhaps they shut down earlier than in those whose genotypes generally make them taller, or perhaps they slow down production of growth hormones sooner. We learn, that is, just which "losing numbers" in the natural lottery placed Billy in the bottom few percent of the normal distribution for height. Suppose, further, that we also identify a gene that disposes Johnny to develop the brain tumor that caused his growth hormone deficiency. We now have traced both Johnny and Billy's shortness back to specific genes. Billy's genes work directly to make him short; Johnny's work indirectly to do so, by causing a tumor that disrupts hormone production. Why does having one set of genes give Johnny a claim on social resources necessary for growth hormone treatment but Billy no such claim?

Of course, this story really adds nothing new. We already knew that Johnny and Billy's troubles were rooted in their biology. Adding the genetic details only makes things seem more vivid. Still, if we can identify the specific genes that contribute to Billy's shortness, we may be more tempted to think of them as "bad" genes: They lead to Billy's unhappiness or disadvantage in a "heightist" world. We may be more tempted to think of them very much on the model of genetic defects or diseases, especially if they work through mechanisms that have some analogy to pathological defects. We will be tempted, that is, to medicalize what we have hitherto considered normal.

There may be an interesting analogy here to the differentiation into "learning disabilities" of what had earlier been thought of as the "not so bright" end of the school performance trait. In neuropsychology, students whose performances are at variance with their measured intelligence and whose performance discrepancies are not explained by poor teaching are considered likely to have some specific learning disability. The general working hypothesis is that there is a specific information processing problem or deficit – a departure from or impairment of normal information processing – that probably has some neurological basis.[2]

The analogy is to our finding specific growth hormone deficiencies in a person who is otherwise constituted (genotypically) to be taller (in a normal range of environments). In the case of learning disabilities, we disentangle people who were simply grouped as "dull or ineffective students" at the low end of a "normal distribution" of school performance into those with specific disabilities and those who just remain the unanalyzed "dull" students. What happens, however, if we find out that being taller or normally intelligent is nothing more than

---

[2] Throughout this chapter, we equate an adverse departure from normal species functioning (or functional organization) with either disease or impairment. In Chapter 3 we talk about the social construction of disabilities: Some impairments of normal functioning will have an impact on important functions in ways that lead us to view them as disabilities, and others do not. In this chapter, we allow similar room for societally relative "construction" by noting that some impairments do not have enough impact on the individual's share of the normal opportunity range for us to consider them morally important disabilities, just as some diseases may not warrant treatment because they have so little impact on us.

having more of (an appropriate set of) the relevant microstructures or processes? Someone who is very short or dull is then missing more of them. Why is this not seen as just as much a "defect" as having a learning disability or growth hormone deficiency?

The hard cases thus pose this question: What justifies us treating the normal but "bad" or disadvantageous genes differently from genes that lead to growth hormone deficiency or to receptor insensitivity to growth hormone (or to learning disabilities)? If we can remedy the effects of these genes with growth hormone treatment or other treatments, including genetic tampering, we might think it quite arbitrary to maintain the treatment/enhancement distinction.

Two Objections to the Treatment/Enhancement Distinction

The hard cases we have been considering, especially in light of the speculation about what we might learn from the Human Genome Project and related genetic research, really raise two quite distinct kinds of objections to the treatment/enhancement distinction. One is that the distinction, even assuming we can draw a persuasive line between the treatment of disease or impairment and the enhancement of otherwise normal traits, does not have the moral import that is commonly attributed to it – for example, in our insurance practices. Some nondisease conditions seem to oblige us to provide assistance to people for the very kinds of reasons that some diseases or impairments do. If so, the treatment/enhancement distinction does not map onto the boundary between morally obligatory and nonobligatory services, as the defender of our medical insurance practices might have hoped.

The second objection challenges the basis on which the treatment/ enhancement distinction is itself drawn. By implication, this objection then challenges whether we can use the treatment/enhancement distinction to draw further moral distinctions without some kind of circularity. In this view, it is not because there is something biologically distinctive about Johnny's condition as opposed to Billy's that led us to describe Johnny as having a disease and Billy not (although Johnny does have a tumor and Billy does not). Rather, our "social construction" of disease draws on a set of values that happens to have singled out Johnny rather than Billy in this way. But if we come to see that the same value that leads us to consider Johnny's tumor as a disease condition (suppose it is the concern we have to assist people whose conditions put them at a certain kind of disadvantage through no fault of their own) also applies to Billy's condition, then we should reconstruct our view of disease to include Billy's condition.

According to this line of thinking, it is our norms and values that define what counts as disease, not merely biologically based characteristics of persons, and the arbitrariness in these hard cases comes from inconsistently applying our values. Pointing to the line between treatment and enhancement is not, then, pointing to a biologically drawn line; rather, it is an indirect way of referring to valuations we make. We cannot point to such a line as the grounds or basis for drawing moral boundaries since we are only pointing to a value-laden boundary we have constructed.

This objection echoes a worry we expressed in commenting on the positive/negative eugenics distinction: Judgments eugenicists made about "defects" reflected value judgments about what counted as normal or superior traits. Aimed at the treatment/enhancement distinction more generally, the objection is that we are being offered an apparently "natural" baseline between disease (and impairment) and the biologically normal, when there really is none. The effect is that, disingenuously or not, we disguise hidden moral judgments that actually form the basis of the moral boundary we purport to derive.

Are there reasonable replies to this objection? Can the treatment/enhancement distinction justifiably do at least a significant portion of the work we commonly rely on it to do?

A LIMITED DEFENSE OF THE TREATMENT/ENHANCEMENT DISTINCTION AND ITS CIRCUMSCRIBED USE

Treatment/Enhancement and the Obligatory/Nonobligatory Boundary

No reasonable defense of the treatment/enhancement distinction is possible if we expect too much of it. Specifically, we should not expect that distinction to translate without qualifications into the boundary between obligatory and nonobligatory services, even if it justifiably plays an important role in medical insurance coverage decisions. There are good reasons why we are not obliged to provide all and only treatments as opposed to enhancements. For the sake of argument, in much of this section, we shall assume we can draw a plausible line between the treatment of disease or impairment and the enhancement of otherwise normal traits, and we shall revisit the assumption at an appropriate point.

There are two basic reasons why the treatment/enhancement distinction does not coincide with the boundary between obligatory and nonobligatory services. First, resources will be too limited to meet all our needs for the treatment of disease or impairment. Justice then requires that we meet the most important needs first, leaving people to fend for themselves in meeting less important medical needs. In other words, the class of beneficial treatments is broader than the class of services we are obliged to provide, given reasonable resource constraints. Being a treatment is thus not a sufficient condition for our being obliged to provide a service to people. Still, we might believe that being a reasonably effective treatment for a disease or impairment is still a necessary condition, an eligibility condition, for something being included in an insurance package or being thought of as a service we are obliged to provide.

The second reason for limiting the role of appeal to the treatment/enhancement distinction also rules out the unqualified claim that it provides a boundary between the obligatory and the nonobligatory. Society may – indeed does – have certain moral or legal obligations to offer medical services that do not involve the treatment of disease. For example, we would argue (were this the occasion) that society's obligations to respect the equality of women compel it to make abortion a covered service in a national benefit package, just as it is already a covered service in most existing private insurance in the United States. The reason for including it has nothing to do with treating a disease or impairment, since an unwanted pregnancy is neither a disease nor an impairment but rather the result of normal functioning. (President Clinton's proposed Health Security Act [1994] disguised the issue by including nontherapeutic abortions as "pregnancy related services.")

Indeed, the reasons many have for excluding abortion also have nothing to do with the distinction between treatment and enhancement: Some people are opposed to permitting abortions even when continued pregnancy involves a threat to the health or life of the mother and is therefore "therapeutic" or "medically necessary" abortion. If we are right that nontherapeutic abortion services should be included in standard benefit packages because of concerns about the equality of women, then treatment of disease and impairment does not capture the class of services society is obliged to provide once we consider all of our obligations. As we shall see in what follows, sometimes concerns about equal opportunity, whether construed more narrowly, as in this chapter, or more expansively, as in the brute luck view described in Chapter 3, may oblige us to provide some genetic interventions even when they are not treatments of disease.

The Primary Rationale for Medical Obligations

It may still be the case that the primary rationale for claiming that society is obligated to provide people with a medical service is that it meets an important need for the treatment of disease or impairment.[3] This may be the reason people typically agree on and justifiably cite when they think about the moral importance of health care services. If there is a plausible defense of the treatment/enhancement distinction, it will be in the limited role pointed to here: Our *primary* justification for considering a health care service to be something society is obliged to offer people is that it is a reasonably effective treatment for a disease or impairment (and resource constraints permit treating this condition). Other reasons may broaden societal obligations, but the primary justification gives us the core.

This limited use of the treatment/enhancement distinction is elaborated in Daniels's (1985) account of justice and health care, as described in Chapter 3. Disease and impairment, both physical and mental, are construed as adverse departures from or impairments of species-typical normal functional organization or "normal functioning," for short (see Note 2). The biomedical sciences for humans, like the veterinary sciences for animals, study both the variation in the functional organization typical for our species and the departures from normal functioning that we call disease and impairment (Boorse 1975, 1976, 1977; Kitcher 1995).[4] The line between disease and impairment and normal functioning is thus drawn in the relatively objective and nonevaluative context provided by the biomedical sciences, broadly

---

[3] Using Daniels's (1985) account, described in this section, the importance of the need is explained by reference to its impact on an individual's fair share of the normal opportunity range for his or her society. In an abstract way, this characterizes the expectation of disadvantage an individual may have relative to a baseline of talents and skills.

[4] Although we note Boorse's work as one way of characterizing normal functioning, we are aware that it fails to accommodate all cases that a successful account in the philosophy of biology would have to address. We do not believe, however, that we must refrain from using a notion of normal functioning in ethics and political philosophy until a "true" account of functions emerges in the philosophy of biology.

construed. What counts as a disease or impairment from the perspective of these sciences is largely free from controversy in the broad range of cases.

Of course, sometimes value judgments, including prejudices, as well as errors, intrude, and we get examples of conditions or behaviors that are improperly classified as disease or impairment, such as the disease of masturbation (Engelhardt 1974) or homosexuality (Bayer 1981). But just as whales are not fishes, though they were long classified as such, so too these conditions are not diseases,[5] even if complex social conditions and attitudes contributed to their being viewed as such.

We are not, however, interested only in categorizing disease and impairment. Rather, we have an important interest in their effects, since they often cause pain and suffering, shorten life, and quite generally impair to varying degrees the range of opportunities open to us. In Daniels's view, the central moral importance, for purposes of justice, of treating disease and impairment with effective health care services (construed broadly to include public health and environmental measures, as well as personal medical services) derives from the way that protecting normal functioning contributes to protecting opportunity. Specifically, by keeping people close to normal functioning, health care preserves for people the ability to participate in political, social, and economic life. It sustains them as fully participating citizens, as "normal competitors" in all spheres of social life.

By maintaining normal functioning, health care protects an individual's fair share of the normal range of opportunities (or plans of life) reasonable people would choose in a given society. That individual fair share, however, is defined by reference to the individual's talents and skills, suitably protected against mis- or underdevelopment as a result of unfair social practices. Accordingly, a principle assuring fair

---

[5] Our discussion does not depend on a strong claim about the nonnormativeness of judgments about disease of the sort made by Boorse (1976). Such a claim depends on being able to distinguish genetic variation from disease, and, more specifically, on specifying the range of environments taken as "natural" for the purpose of revealing dysfunction. The problem facing this strong claim is that some socially created environments should be counted as "natural" but others not. Our discussion turns on a weaker claim. It is enough for our purposes that the line between disease and its absence is, for the general run of cases, uncontroversial and ascertainable through publicly acceptable methods, such as those of the biomedical sciences. It will not matter if what counts as a disease category is relative to some features of social roles in a given society, and thus to some normative judgments, provided the core of the notion of species-normal functioning is left intact. This qualification is made in Daniels (1985, p. 30).

equality of opportunity should be extended to govern the design of health care systems. (As we saw in Chapter 3, Rawls [1971] simplifies his theory by assuming all are fully functional; Rawls [1993] endorses Daniels's approach.)

By keeping people functioning as close to normally as possible, within resource limits, we discharge our obligations to protect (a suitably extended principle of) fair equality of opportunity. Daniels's extension of "fair" equality of opportunity to health care broadens the level playing field to include socially correctible departures from normal functioning. In doing so, it corrects both for some natural and some socially induced disadvantages.[6] His account, however, stops short of leveling the field further to include the redistribution of otherwise normal but competitively disadvantageous capabilities (as the brute luck view does). We return to consider arguments in favor of this stopping point in the next few sections, after adding an important detail to this account.

The relative moral importance of treating different diseases and impairments can in part be judged by reference to their impact on the range of opportunities open to us. Because this range of opportunities is itself socially relative, being affected by technology, education, wealth, and other cultural factors, judgments about the relative importance of treating different diseases and impairments will have some social variability. (See our discussion in Chapter 7 on the morality of inclusion as it applies to disabilities.) For example, dyslexia is a cognitive impairment in any society, but it is disability and hence important to treat only in literate societies (Daniels 1985). Within a society, relative to its normal range of opportunities, some diseases and impairments are more important to treat than others, and this will affect our decisions about which treatments to offer when we cannot provide all the ones people need.

The appeal to a principle assuring fair equality of opportunity is an attempt to explain why we attribute special moral importance to treat-

---

[6] Rawls (1971, p. 73) defines equal opportunity thus: "those who are at the same level of talent and ability, and have the same willingness to use them, should have the same prospects of success regardless of their initial place in the social system." As Christiano has pointed out to us, this does not rule out using medicine to enhance the prospects of success of an individual by changing natural qualities of persons that are not directly related to the talents they have. The extension of Rawls's account is thus not incompatible with its initial statement and may be less an extension than it appears. In any case, Rawls (1993, p. 184, note 14) seems to endorse the extension that Daniels proposes.

ing disease and disability. If the particular interpretation of equal opportunity is acceptable, it explains the primary rationale for the provision of health care services. Aiming to maintain normal functioning makes a limited, but crucial, contribution to protecting fair equality of opportunity.[7] It leaves considerable room for social relativity about the importance of some treatments compared with others, but much less about what counts as a disease. Still, it is important to keep in mind that the treatment/enhancement distinction does not specify the boundary between obligatory and nonobligatory medical services. Some obligations derive from considerations beyond the primary rationale, and the primary rationale includes a respect for reasonable resource constraints.

Hard Cases and Expansive Views of Medical Obligations

If we return to the hard cases we considered in the last section, we see that we are pulled away from the primary rationale in two directions. In both the growth hormone (Johnny and Billy) and Shy Bipolar cases, we were concerned that people who suffered equal disadvantage from being short or shy were not being treated the same way. If the therapy could be counted as treating a disease (growth hormone deficiency in Johnny's case or the effects of bipolar condition on personality development), then reimbursement for the therapy was assured. But if the therapy counted as enhancement of an otherwise normal condition (shortness for Billy or shyness for an otherwise normal person), then reimbursement was not available.

According to the fair equality of opportunity account of justice and health care (i.e., the "social structural" view), we are concerned about disease and impairment because of their impact on opportunity. But here Billy suffers as much loss of opportunity as Johnny; so too does the Normal Shy person as compared to the Shy Bipolar. We must face this crucial question: Why should we put so much emphasis on the

---

[7] Some might object that the terminology is misleading: The principle actually supported does not really call for equality in opportunity, but only some adequate range of opportunities. Since protecting normal functioning while leaving a "natural" baseline of talents and skills in place leads to individuals having different "fair shares" of the normal opportunity range for their society, equal opportunity does not, after all, assure strict equality of opportunity. The debate about the scope of "equality of opportunity" is pursued in the next main section of this chapter, when we discuss three philosophical models of the principle.

distinction between treatment and enhancement rather than calculate the effect on opportunity directly? The pull here is to equalize capabilities or at least to reduce disadvantages that result from less-than-equal capabilities, regardless of the role of disease or impairment. This pull thus concretely reflects the instability noted in Chapter 3 regarding positions that pursue only partially the level playing field interpretation of equal opportunity. The instability seems to imply that we should either aggressively and completely pursue the level playing field strategy by moving toward a brute luck or equal resources view, abandoning such partial approximations as the treatment/enhancement distinction, or we should abandon the distinction altogether.

The other pull is visible in the case of the Unhappy Husband who is clearly unhappy and finds therapy effective. Moreover, he is not unhappy because he has cultivated exotic tastes – indeed, we think of his compunctions about abandoning his wife as admirable (although we do not ordinarily think we should compensate people for any sacrifices they make in order to meet their moral commitments). He has not in any obvious sense "chosen" to adopt idiosyncratic or selfish or self-serving attitudes or preferences that are the source of his unhappiness. (One qualification is needed here: His religious or moral compunctions about divorce and abandonment of his sick wife may be the result of early childrearing, but we think of these as values that are reaffirmed – and thus "chosen" when we are adults.) Why should such effective therapy not be reimbursable? Some clinicians – call them "expansive" clinicians – think that such a person should be eligible for reimbursed treatment. They think that health care should have the goal of removing sources of unhappiness from which we suffer through no fault or choice of our own. Health care should give people an opportunity to be happy that is just like the opportunity enjoyed by others.

The three positions described here – the primary rationale and the two pulls from other directions – reflect three distinct interpretations of our egalitarian concerns that have been developed in the philosophical literature. More specifically, each can be read as a different gloss on the scope of our concerns about equality of opportunity. If we think that concerns about equal opportunity should guide the design of a health care system, then each leads us to a different view of our obligations to assist others through health care services, including genetic interventions. The primary rationale retains an appeal to the treatment/enhancement distinction, but the other two positions abandon it. Each needs further explanation, and ultimately we shall have to decide whether the alternative positions give us sufficient reason to abandon or modify the primary rationale.

Three Philosophical Models of the Relationship Between Equal Opportunity and the Goals of Health Care

The Normal Function Model   The primary rationale appealed to by Daniels rests on what we shall call a "normal functioning" interpretation of the requirements of what was referred to in Chapter 3 as the social structural view, which Rawls calls fair equality of opportunity (Rawls 1971).

Historically, our understanding of the requirements of equality of opportunity has evolved, as noted in Chapter 3. We have come to oppose allowing certain human traits – originally race, religion, ethnicity, and class origin; later gender, age, disability, and sexual orientation – to serve as the basis for assigning people to jobs or offices. Rather, these traits are seen as "morally irrelevant," and we believe people should be judged by their capabilities to perform in jobs, offices, or educational settings. (This is the "nondiscrimination" conception of equal opportunity described in Chapter 3.)

But we also recognize that past unjust social practices may have distorted the development of peoples' talents and skills, and that we may have to compensate people for the effects of those practices – for example, by special programs aimed at correcting for those distorting effects. Otherwise, expecting people to compete on the basis of the talents and skills they actually have may be expecting them to compete on an unfair basis. This was the idea behind the federal program Operation Head Start, one of the most successful compensatory education programs attempted in the United States, and, more generally, it is the idea behind universal public education.

Whereas the nondiscrimination view of equal opportunity simply requires us to eliminate reference to morally irrelevant traits in determining access to desirable social positions, "fair" equality of opportunity (the "social structural" version of the level playing field view) requires us to correct where we can for the mis- or underdevelopment of talents and skills – that is, for the effects of the social lottery, at least where these are influenced by past injustices.

The normal functioning interpretation of the requirements of equality of opportunity – whether in Rawls's (1971, 1993) general account of distributive justice or in Daniels's (1985) extension of it to health care – assumes that there is a background inequality in the distribution of capabilities, an effect of the natural lottery. Equal opportunity then does not require assuring truly equal chances of success, which could result only if we eliminated this inequality in the distribution of capabilities. The leveling of the playing field goes only so far in the normal functioning view.

Applied to health care and construed as an account of the goals of health care, the normal functioning interpretation of the fair equality of opportunity principle thus ascribes to health care the relatively modest and limited task of keeping people functioning as close to normally as possible. In effect, health care, like compensatory education programs, aims to produce "normal competitors." These are not equal competitors; quite generally, some will suffer the disadvantage that comes from some normal but not optimal or even average capabilities. An unequal distribution of capabilities is left intact, once the distorting effects of past social practices and treatable disease and impairment are addressed.

Why should we take the natural distribution of talents and skills as a baseline, as the normal functioning view does? If we can redistribute or modify some of those disadvantaging talents and skills, why not alter the baseline? This was the key question raised in Chapter 3 and we see it echoed in the pull of the hard cases. If medical technology – whether genetic or not – allows us to redefine the baseline and produce more equal chances of success, are not we committed to doing so wherever we can if we believe in leveling the playing field?

In Chapter 3 we noted some reasons for leveling the field more completely. Here we develop further some reasons for abiding by the normal functioning (or "social structural") view. As noted earlier, these views are further apart in theory than in practice, but for the moment we want to clarify further the theoretical issues.

A fundamental point to note is that our egalitarian concerns in general and our concerns about equal opportunity in particular form only part of our concerns about what justice requires. A theory of justice in general, or of justice for health care, in particular, must combine concerns about equality with those about liberty. And both these must be reconciled with considerations about efficiency and the allocation of resources. Even if the fundamental intuition underlying our concerns about equality of opportunity pushed us toward thinking that we were obliged to take some steps to redistribute capabilities such as talents and skills, rather than treating their "natural" distribution as a baseline, we must reconcile the pull of that concern with conflicting goals regarding liberty and efficiency. The presumption in favor of modifying the baseline, coming from the egalitarian pull of a concern about equality in opportunity, can be defeated by other key components of our concerns about justice. If, for example, we were only concerned about equality of opportunity, we might be indifferent between "leveling down" by reducing the greater capabilities of the better off and "leveling up" by improving the capabilities of the worst off. But considerations of both liberty and efficiency rule out leveling down.

In Rawls's (1971) theory, this reconciliation of equality with liberty and efficiency takes place through the choice of principles that deliberators would make in the Original Position – Rawls's social contract situation. Suppose that contractors knew that it was sometimes possible to alter the natural distribution of talents and skills and that doing so might make it possible to better promote equality of opportunity. They would still have to solve the more general problem of distributive justice posed by the fact that, in general, some unequal distribution of talents and skills can and must be taken as a baseline.

For example, Rawls is quite explicit that environmental factors, including culture, family influence, and individual responsiveness to educational and compensatory educational measures, will unavoidably lead to some ineliminable inequality in the distribution of talents and skills. In the *general* case, it may be better for deliberators, even for those who anticipate they may turn out to be worse off with regard to marketable talents and skills, to *mitigate* the effects of inequalities by redistribution of other important goods than to insist on what may turn out to be a highly inefficient "equalizing" of the distribution of natural talents and skills (or even a more modest elimination of obviously disadvantaging traits). And this general case is what yields Rawls's integration of efficiency and equality concerns through a division of labor between principles. The Difference Principle, which allows inequalities only if they maximally benefit the worst off, provides maximal mitigation of the consequences of the natural lottery, at least in the general case. Insisting quite generally on more direct and radical forms of seeking equality through modifying traits might in fact make those seeking modification worse off than they would otherwise be. Rawls assumes that deliberators in his Original Position would make just such a reconciliation of competing concerns, requiring that the system as a whole can be made to work to the advantage even of those worst off with regard to marketable talents and skills. In specific instances, however, where we can identify a highly efficient intervention to eliminate traits that are obviously disadvantaging, then there is nothing in the the theory to block this course of action, and much to support it, especially since it may be clearly superior in all ways to mere mitigation.[8]

Interpreted in this way, there is no reason to think that Rawls's account or Daniels's extension of it to health care would rule out sometimes being obliged to use genetic technologies to alter the distribution of talents and skills. The Rawlsian reconciliation between equality and efficiency, even if it captures the general case, will not justify treating the natural baseline as if it is an uncrossable boundary. In some special cases, where there might be a particularly good likelihood of inexpensively and safely reducing clear disadvantages, there may well be adequate reason to go beyond our standard notion of equal opportunity to permit some enhancement in the name of eliminating obvious disadvantages.

Even with such case-by-case exceptions, however, the normal functioning conception of equal opportunity retains a central feature of the conception of equal opportunity that is part of our public culture – namely, that not all unchosen competitive disadvantages are unfair and require elimination or compensation. As standardly conceived, we do not think competition is automatically unfair – or that opportunities are automatically unequal – just because some people are naturally endowed with talents or skills that others cannot match. The normal functioning view of equal opportunity, even with the exceptional extensions allowed here, retains the core idea that has long standing in our democratic culture – namely, that a competition for jobs or offices is fair if it tests people for their possession of the relevant capabilities, provided society has not unfairly distorted them. (We return to this point about democratic culture in a later section of this chapter.)

This point about fair competition draws support from other con-

---

[8] In the view described here, what equal opportunity requires is specified only after its integration with other elements of a theory of justice. An alternative view also has some plausibility. In this alternative, when we integrate concerns about efficiency, we simply choose not to realize fully what equal opportunity requires in order to give reasonable weight to other aspects of justice. This view might seem to preserve more of the intuition behind the brute luck interpretation, i.e., that we have a claim on others when we are at a disadvantage through no fault of our own.

texts as well. In athletic competitions, we may sometimes set up categories, such as weight ranges in boxing or wrestling or gender classifications in many sports, to recognize some obvious sources of biological difference that might make competition unfair. We recognize, however, that some people are naturally faster or stronger in ways that no training regimen can correct for, and we do not view such competition as intrinsically unfair. In any case, what is made unlikely by Rawls's account of fair equality of opportunity or by Daniels's normal functioning account is that an individual who finds himself or herself at a competitive disadvantage because of an otherwise normal capability thereby has a *prima facie* claim, based on equality of opportunity, to assistance to rectify that (perceived) deficit.[9] In what follows, we try to clarify this point by examining two alternatives to the normal functioning view. In Chapter 3, we considered a much more demanding and expansive interpretation of the requirement of equality of opportunity – at least in theory – than the normal functioning account. To explore that approach more thoroughly, we examine two variations that appear in the philosophical literature, both of which abandon the treatment/enhancement distinction. The equal opportunity for welfare view explicitly appeals to a principle similar to the brute luck view, calling for compensation whenever a disadvantage or loss of opportunity for happiness comes about through no individual fault. The equal capabilities view actually appeals to a different philosophical idea, the notion of positive freedom – that is, the freedom to do or be whatever we want. We begin with the equal capabilities view.

The Equal Capabilities Model   In a series of articles and books, Sen (1980, 1990, 1992) argues that the object of our egalitarian concerns

---

[9] Should we think of the deficiency in capability as giving rise to a defeasible claim, if not ultimately a defensible claim? On the normal function model, if the deficiency falls within the normal range and is not itself produced by disease, disability, or unfair social practices, then we ultimately recognize no claim here. Is this still a "defeasible" claim, one defeated by these etiological criteria, or should we say that defeasible claims arise only after these criteria are met? For example, reasonable resource limits might still defeat the claim that satisfied these criteria. We are inclined to say that defeasible claims arise only after the criteria that distinguish the theory are met. As we shall see in our discussion of the equal capabilities model, not every disadvantage in capabilities on this model gives rise to a final claim: incommensurable differences do not count. Since the account of commensurability is a distinguishing feature of the theory, however, by parallel reasoning we should not call this a defeasible claim either. Here too, reasonable limits on resources may defeat a defeasible claim that some disadvantage in capabilities is present and gives rise to obligations to compensate.

is equality in what we can do or be.[10] Think of all the things we can do or be as forming a complex set of our actual capabilities. (Sen talks of an "n-tuple of doings and beings" as forming our "capability sets.") To the extent that we are concerned about equality, we should think not simply about the resources we have available to us, but our ability to transform those resources into actual capabilities, since variations in individuals will lead to different capabilities for the same inputs of resources. (In Sen's view, as in Rawls's, we are also not concerned about producing experiential states, like happiness or pleasure.) Sen views this account as an explication of the idea of "positive freedom," but it is not implausible to view it as an account of equality of opportunity. We have equality of opportunity when our capability sets are equal. (If capabilities are not equal because some people have developed certain ones rather than others they could have developed, we may ignore that inequality; we will simply talk about "capabilities" in what follows.[11])

If we could simply translate this claim about equality of opportunity into an account of the goals of health care – which we shall argue we cannot – then those goals would be dramatically expanded from the limits set by the normal functioning rationale discussed earlier. Health care would now have as its task the goal of reconstructing people in ways that make their capabilities more equal. With this expansion, there would simply be no point in drawing a line between treatments and enhancements. Society would be just as obliged to enhance the capabilities of those who function normally but with less-than-equal capabilities as to keep people functioning as close to normally as

---

[10] Others have pursued accounts of capabilities, for example Nussbaum (1998), that may or may not be open to some of the objections raised later in this chapter. We concentrate here on Sen's account because it has stimulated so much discussion and is explicitly raised as a critique of Rawls's account. See Rawls (1993, p. 183–90) for his reply to Sen.

[11] Sen does not want an individual's decision to develop some capabilities at the expense of others to give rise to a further claim on others for resources just because the choice means some capabilities have been sacrificed. A similar point must be accommodated within Daniels's account of the effect of disease on the range of opportunities open to individuals. Daniels distinguishes the normal opportunity range – the array of life plans reasonable people will choose, given their talents and skills, in a given society – from the effective opportunity range that an individual has as a result of choices to develop some talents and skills rather than others. From the perspective of an individual who has a particular plan of life and who has developed certain skills accordingly, the effective opportunity range will only be a part of the fair share of the normal range. For purposes of justice, we ignore the individual assessments of the importance of a given function that derive from particular conceptions of the good. Of course, impact on the effective range may be important in micro-allocation decisions, including those by individuals about whether they want to receive certain services.

possible. (One perhaps disturbing wrinkle in this approach is that we may not be under an obligation to correct for the effects of disease and capability where they work to increase equality in capabilities – for example, by diminishing the capabilities of those endowed with superior capabilities.)

To see why we cannot so directly use the equal capabilities approach to expand the goals of health care, we must examine Sen's account more carefully. A crucial point is one already made: A theory of justice requires integrating concerns for equality with concerns for liberty and efficiency. Sen's claim that our egalitarian concerns really focus on capabilities, not resources or experiential states, or the claim that we explicate the goal of equal opportunity as the goal of achieving equality in capability sets, does not tell us what justice requires us to do. Sen (1992) comments that we must reconcile our concerns about efficiency with our concerns about equality in order to find out what justice requires. In other words, justice might not require us to pursue equality of capabilities so directly after all, if the cost in terms of efficiency were too great. We might instead be required to permit some inequalities and act to mitigate their effects. Sen does not discuss how this reconciliation of justice and efficiency would take place in a theory of justice.

Rawls, as we have argued, does attempt a particular reconciliation: We should take some natural distribution of talents and skills as a baseline (generally, this is the normal distribution). Although those with the least marketable capabilities will have lower prospects in life than those with more marketable capabilities, Rawls mitigates the effects of this basic, residual inequality by requiring that inequalities in primary social goods like wealth and income be constrained so that they work to the advantage of those with the worst prospects in life. In this way, those with more marketable talents and skills must harness their advantages to maximizing the prospects of those who are worst off with regard to talents and skills. In effect, Rawls divides responsibility for meeting our egalitarian concerns between two different principles of justice. The principle governing equality of opportunity leaves the normal distribution of capabilities in place, but the principle governing overall inequality in prospects in life mitigates the effects of doing so.

If health care should be governed by a principle governing fair equality of opportunity, then, for the general case, it too may leave the normal distribution of capabilities in place, concerning itself only with keeping people functioning as close to normally as possible. It would then be necessary to rely on other principles of justice governing inequalities in life prospects to mitigate the effects of this pragmatic decision. The fact that Rawls appeals to the "moral arbitrariness" of the natural lottery for capabilities does not mean that the only reasonable way to address this problem within a comprehensive theory is to devote extensive resources toward equalizing capabilities. It may be that we can do better, even by those worst off with regard to capabilities, by leaving the distribution of capabilities mostly in place and mitigating the effects of doing so in other ways – at least that is his rationale.

This dramatic restriction on the scope of what we can pursue in the name of equal opportunity – as compared to Sen's account – may not be what Sen has in mind, but then we need some clear idea of what restrictions are compatible with the overall demands of justice. (The reader is also reminded that Rawls's rationale for the general case does not preclude a more restrictive, case-by-case assessment of claims that eliminating some obviously disadvantaging [but normal] traits is justifiable on grounds that modestly extend the concept of equal opportunity.)

Even leaving aside the competing claims of liberty, efficiency, and equality, the equal capabilities model does not strictly speaking involve a pursuit of equal capability sets. Sen offers an approach to ranking differences in capabilities. How important a particular capability is will depend on the system of values – the plan of life or conception of the good – adopted by an individual. John may rank capability set A as better than capability set B, but Jane may make the opposite judgment from her conception of the good. We may find some cases in which all can agree that set C is worse than sets A and B, but we may get no rankings for a broad range of capability sets.

In fact, we are most likely to find that the clear-cut cases in which a set (say, C) is ranked lower than others will be cases in which there is a significant departure from normal functioning – a disease or impairment that has a significant impact on capabilities and thus on opportunities. In those cases, Sen's account will tend to agree with the standard model for thinking about our obligations to assist others with medical interventions, including genetic ones. But for a broad range of differences in capability sets, there may be "incommensurability" in the sense that these sets are ranked differently by people with different conceptions of what is good in life. Because of this, our

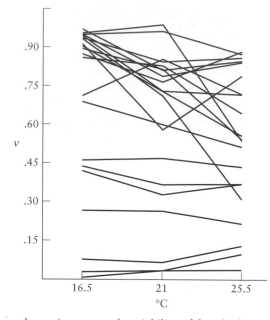

Figure 4.1. Actual reaction norms for viability of fourth chromosome homozygotes of *Drosophilia pseudoobscura*. Figure provided by Richard Lewontin. Data from Dobzhansky, Th., and Spasky, B., *Genetics*, 29 (1944): 270-90.

commitment to pursuing equality of capabilities is seriously limited, since for a substantial range of capabilities, there is no common basis for determining what increases the equality of those sets.

There is a biological point that bears on this incommensurability and on the treatment/enhancement distinction more generally.[12] Consider Figure 4.1 , which reports on the results of an experiment testing how different genotypes from natural populations survive in a variety of environments that vary in temperature.

The same pattern is exhibited for other genotypes in other kinds of environments, since what is portrayed here is a very general fact of nature. In general, genotypes fall into two types: one group is poor at surviving in a broad range of environments, while the other is in the normal range but varies widely in survivorship depending on environments. No genotypes emerge as unconditionally advantageous. Within those whose survivorship puts them in the normal range, however, advantages present in one environment are replaced by disadvantages

---

[12] We are indebted to Richard Lewontin for this point and the citation for the accompanying diagram.

in others. This is the biological analogue of incomensurability when we are considering enhancement of otherwise normal traits. We get convergence on the disadvantages suffered by the group that does badly across environments, which is analogous to the convergence of the equal capabilities and normal function models on those with disease and impairment.

This qualification of the equal capability model has implications for the argument that equality of opportunity pushes us toward a much more expansive model of medical interventions. The equal capability model does commit us to assuring individuals that their capability sets are not clearly worse than those of others, and in this it goes beyond the normal functioning view, at least in its theoretical conception. (In fact, it rather closely resembles what the brute luck view calls for by way of leveling the playing field.) As noted, this suggests that significant diseases and impairments will give rise to medical obligations, as is the normal functioning view.

It may also be the case that when we find clear instances in which even "normal" individuals fall well short of enjoying the capability sets others rank as superior, we may have obligations to enhance their sets. Here, too, the equal capability account does not depart significantly from the normal functioning account, since that model allowed that we might have obligations, deriving from concerns about equality of opportunity, to provide enhancements on a case-by-case basis. (We suggested that nontherapeutic abortions may actually be an example of this.) What the equal capabilities model, properly analyzed, does not seem to imply – although we might have thought it would – is that whenever an individual lacks a capability that others enjoy, he or she has a claim on others for assistance in improving that capability. The shortfall in capabilities, from the individual's perspective, may not be viewed as a significant shortfall from the perspective of others with different plans of life.[13]

We can better see the force of this qualification through an example. Suppose we are parents, and we say to our friends, "Our son has some violin talent, but we cannot afford the best teacher for him. Without the best teacher, he will only be able to play in the Social Center Orchestra later in life, but with the best teacher, he will be able to play

---

[13] Notice how important it is that we have a basis for public agreement on the conditions under which we owe assistance to others – that is, on terms of fair cooperation. Later in this chapter we comment on the importance of the role of publicly acceptable grounds for agreement that abstract from differences in conceptions of the good life.

in the City Orchestra later in life. Other parents are able to secure the services of this teacher for their children, who have comparable potential. We – and our son – are at a disadvantage. Help us pay for the better teacher." If our friends were obliged to help us whenever our capability sets fall short of those enjoyed by others – at least by our own judgments – then they would seem to be hostage to the ways in which we value our capabilities.

Shifting the example to a social context and away from individual friendships does not really alter the point. We do not deny people equality of opportunity if we do not assist them in improving or developing every capability they want that some other people happen to have. If we thought equality of opportunity demanded that we assist people in these ways, we would make the principle hostage to expensive and demanding preferences individuals might have. Just as we do not owe it to our friends or others in general to contribute our resources to making them happy when they are unhappy because they have developed extravagant tastes, we do not owe it to others to improve any and every capability that they judge to be disadvantageous to them, given their plans of life.

This point has specific implications for capabilities that bear on access to jobs and offices, as Cohen (1995) has argued. Suppose Jill succeeds in getting a job as office manager when Jack does not because Jill is better at motivating others to work and at resolving disputes. Does Jack now have a complaint against us: His access to a job he wants is diminished because of a relative lack of the relevant interpersonal skills? Or can we reasonably reply to Jack that he is welcome to practice these skills and improve them – there are courses offered at the local community college – but there are many other jobs he is already well suited to perform, and the social and educational opportunities he has already enjoyed have equipped him to compete fairly for a broad array of jobs. Society owes him nothing further in the name of "equal opportunity," though he is free to invest further in himself.

We turned to the equal capabilities model – whose name is no longer quite accurate (similarly, in Chapter 3, we suggested that the brute luck view requires only a decent minimum of capabilities) – because we thought it supported in a quite natural way a more expansive view of the role of health care (or, alternatively, a recognition that the demands of equal opportunity extend beyond health care). At first sight, it seemed to push us toward any use of biotechnology, whether an enhancement or a treatment, that eliminates disadvantages in opportunity produced by inequalities in our capability sets.

But, appropriately qualified, the model demands much less. In practice – if not in its underlying theoretical motivation – it comes quite close to the actual scope of the normal functioning view. Where there are significant deficits, of the sort induced by serious disease and impairment, we get results similar to those given by the normal functioning view. The normal functioning view allows for special case-by-case leveling up of obviously disadvantaging traits, and the (qualified) equal capabilities view calls for somewhat broader consideration of leveling up. Without clear examples, it is not obvious what the practical difference is. In any event, for a broad range of enhancements of normal capabilities, the equal capability model is actually much less demanding than it might have seemed.

What is particularly striking, however, is that there can be convergence on a practical account of what equal opportunity requires despite some underlying divergence in philosophical rationale. We return to this point later.

The Equal Opportunity for Welfare Model   The other more expansive interpretation of equal opportunity focuses on a central moral intuition – that we have a claim on others for assistance whenever we are worse off than they are through no fault or choice of our own (Cohen 1989 and Arneson 1988;[14] cf. Daniels 1990; and see Chapter 3). This is the single, underlying intuition that we earlier labeled the brute luck view.

If we are miserable because we have chosen to cultivate extravagant tastes or even because we affirm values it is costly to live up to, even if we did not originally choose to have them inculcated in us, or if we have bad "option" luck as a result of choices we make, then we do not have a claim on others. Others do not owe it to us to make up for the bad or costly choices we have made. But if we are miserable because we have had instilled in us – through no choice of our own – certain tastes or values that make it difficult for us to be as happy as others, then our equality of opportunity for welfare has been compro-

---

[14] Cohen (1989) includes welfare, construed as desire satisfaction, within his notion of "advantage," but advantage is broader than mere welfare. Arneson uses a narrower notion of welfare as desire satisfaction. To the extent that advantage includes capabilities, Cohen's account overlaps with Sen's, although Sen, like Rawls, thinks that the target of our egalitarian concerns is not in any way focused on welfare.

mised, in this view. Having had these costly preferences imposed on us is like other forms of bad brute luck, like other bad outcomes we might receive in the natural or social lottery for capabilities that give rise to egalitarian claims on others.

Equal opportunity for welfare obtains when each person faces "an array of options that is equivalent to every other person's in terms of the prospects for preference satisfaction it offers" (Arneson 1988, p. 87). We should picture this in the following way. Imagine that we represent a person's life as a decision tree in which all possible life histories are represented. Equal opportunity for welfare obtains if the best path on each person's life tree *ex ante* (before he actually makes any choices) has the same expected payoff in preference satisfaction. Branches in the tree represent all possible choices, including choices about which preferences to act on or to develop.

We should note, since it is a point relevant to our discussion later, that there is a tremendous "information burden" here. In a given case, how can we really tell whether a preference that makes someone miserable is one that he "chose" to develop at some earlier point in life? (This may point to a deeper incoherence in the account. An unchosen preference may push Cathy, for example, below the happiness she would have had on the "best path" because of some other irrelevant choice about something else she made earlier. Then Cathy is not owed assistance because, say, twenty years earlier, she could have gone left when she went right. Alternatively, it seems possible in almost all cases to construct a counterfactual path where the path chosen would have constituted a "best path" comparable to the best path others enjoy.)

We turned to this equal opportunity for welfare model in order to explain the "pull" toward an expansive view of the role of mental health interventions that we find in a case like that of the Unhappy Husband. But we believe the model does not capture our real concerns about equality or equality of opportunity. We shall argue that unchosen preferences that make us worse off than others do not generally arouse egalitarian concerns unless they can be assimilated to cases of psychological impairment – that is, to cases that would be treated on the standard model because they involve a departure from normal functioning. In that case, they will merit some form of treatment, but not necessarily other forms of compensation. This does not seem to be what is implied by an equal opportunity for welfare account.

The point can be brought out by two hypothetical examples.[15] Suppose John's mother raised him on Mrs. Morgan's Fish Sticks and that as a result he cannot stand the taste of fish (cf. Brandt 1979, p. 120). He becomes interested in the quality of his diet and otherwise quite adventuresome in his eating. Nevertheless, he feels deprived that he is denied access to the broad range of food pleasures that would come from eating and enjoying seafood. He feels ill, however, at the very thought of eating fish. We might even suppose this aversion makes him feel he should not pursue a career as a restaurant critic. If his opportunity for welfare falls below that of others because of this aversion, does he have a legitimate egalitarian claim for compensation?

Suppose Jane's mother raised her to believe that a mother's duty is to stay home with her children and that no woman should pursue a career during her childbearing years. Jane no longer believes that, has had a good career, and now faces the choice about what to do about childrearing. But she feels so guilty at the thought of pursuing her career that she ends up staying home with her children. Not only does this mean she is deeply disappointed about her sacrifice of career, but she resents the burden placed on her by her children and her mother. Should she be compensated because her opportunity for welfare (or advantage) is less than others?

Society is obligated to do something to help John or Jane only if their situations really reflect some underlying departure from normal functioning. Ordinarily, it is expected that someone who does not like fish copes with his unwanted preference by pursuing his other tastes. There's enough else that he likes that we expect him to adapt to his preferences, whatever their etiology. If John was a compulsive or phobic personality, and if the aversion to fish were symptomatic of a more generalized inability to accommodate to his preferences or to reform and revise them over time, then we would be inclined to say that he is entitled to some form of therapy for the underlying disorder. If, however, he then said that he really did not want the therapy, but preferred to "cash it in" for a week snorkeling in Yucatan, then it would be appropriate to refuse him the alternative. What this indicates is that we are not interested in moving John to the point where his opportunity for welfare is equal to others. We are only interested in making

---

[15] The next couple of paragraphs draw on Daniels (1990).

sure that he has the mental capability to form and revise his ends in a normal fashion. Beyond that, we reasonably hold him responsible for his preferences.[16]

Our response to Jane is similar. If she suffers from a more generalized incapacity to form and revise her ends over time, perhaps as the result of some unresolved problems in her relationship with her mother, then we believe she is entitled to access to the appropriate form of therapy or group support. We would not be willing, however, to substitute other forms of compensation aimed at moving her back to equal opportunity for welfare. What does the work here is the belief that there is some underlying handicapping condition.

So it is not explicit choice that matters, but the underlying normal capacity for revising our ends – our goals, values, and preferences – that is at issue. If we have independent reasons to believe that a preference – whether chosen or not, whether identified with or not – cannot be eliminated and is handicapping because of a broader, underlying handicapping condition, then we have reasons to make certain resources available as compensation. It is not the unchosen taste, or the fact that the taste is unchosen, that gives rise to the claim on us. Rather, it is the underlying mental or emotional impairment, and the taste, chosen or not, is but a symptom.

In our hard cases – Billy and Johnny and the Shy Bipolar – we saw that we were pulled in two ways to expand our commitments to assist others beyond simply restoring normal function, which is all that is implied by the normal function model of equal opportunity. These two expansive pulls have their philosophical models in two alternative interpretations of the demands of equal opportunity (or more egalitarian concerns): the "equal" capabilities model and the equal opportunity for welfare model. We looked to these models for support for the view that we "owed" Billy growth hormone treatment no less than Johnny, the Shy Bipolar therapy no more than a normally shy person,

[16] Should we hold people responsible for their ends when they deliberately undertake or court some risks, as in skiing or sky diving? When we want people to internalize the costs of their own choices is a complex question. As Fried (1969) points out in a different context, we all impose risks on others – for example, when we drive to the corner store for a newspaper – for which we do not expect to have to compensate people. There is a reasonable reciprocity in risk imposition here. Perhaps we should accept some further reasonable reciprocity in expecting assistance regarding the risks we take pursuing a reasonable range of human adventures, since all can expect to want to pursue some pleasures (eating, drinking, hiking, running, bicycling, scuba diving) that involve taking risks. (See Wikler 1978.)

or the Unhappy Husband assistance despite his lack of mental disorder.

But our discussion of these two philosophical models suggests they do not support an expanded view of our commitments in health care in any so direct a fashion as they promised. Thus a commitment to the more expansive view that all inequalities in capabilities give rise to a claim on us does not imply the claim is to eliminate the inequality through medical interventions. It may simply force us to mitigate the effects of underserved inequalities through other measures we take in our overall approach to justice. Similarly, there is good reason to resist the suggestion that society owes an individual compensation, and that health care in particular does, whenever she is less happy than others through no fault of her own. If what is making a person unhappy is an underlying psychological impairment, then she may have a legitimate claim for medical assistance (resources permitting). In the absence of an underlying disorder or incapacity in the ability to form and revise our ends or goals, the responsibility for our unhappiness is reasonably placed on our own shoulders.

The Normal Function Model as Better Public Policy

The treatment/enhancement distinction was challenged by our hard cases in two ways, each calling for a more expansive role for medicine, either to eliminate disadvantages in capabilities or to reduce some form of unhappiness. The distinction seemed to provide a reasonable way to delimit the scope of our obligations to use medical services to protect equality of opportunity, at least on the standard interpretation of equal opportunity. But each challenge seemed to draw support from alternative philosophical interpretations of the limits of equal opportunity.

So far we have suggested that neither alternative expansive interpretation of equal opportunity gives strong support to abandoning the treatment/enhancement distinction. This does not constitute a strong, positive argument for the normal functioning interpretation and the way in which it incorporates the treatment/enhancement distinction. It just shows, if we are right, that two challenges to that view are not as powerful as they might have seemed at first, and in any case do not have as significant a practical implication as we might have thought. Still, the hard cases leave a bad taste of arbitrariness, and it is important to see if some other considerations can provide support for the distinction and the normal functioning interpretation it is attached to. Specifically, it may be useful to consider the role played in public policy, in institutions aimed at fair practices that people can agree on, by the treatment/enhancement distinction.

To be useful in a public policy domain, a distinction such as that on treatment and enhancement must pass three tests: Does it make distinctions the public and clinicians regard as fair on reflection? Can it be administered with reasonable effectiveness in the real world? And does it lead to results that society can afford?[17] We believe that the treatment/enhancement distinction and a goal of health care aimed at maintaining normal functioning meets these three criteria better than more expansive views of equal opportunity.

The hard cases we considered brought out points of disagreement among alternative accounts, but we should not let them blind us to the considerable convergence on the importance of treatments for disease and impairment. All developed societies recognize the importance of assisting people in the treatment of disease and impairment; only in a few borderline instances do these societies use their health care resources for cases of enhancement. Where disease and impairment have some significant impact on the opportunities open to us, and where we can effectively respond to them with some form of health care, all three accounts agree on the importance of treatment. Thus where "capability sets" (as in Sen) would be compromised by disease or impairment, so too would there be an impact on individuals' fair shares of the normal opportunity range for their society (Daniels); where there are such effects of disease or impairment, there is likely to be a significant impact on the opportunity for welfare as well. Conversely, where a disease or impairment has little effect on capability sets, it is likely to have an unimportant effect on the range of opportunities open to people, including their opportunities for welfare.

In the case of treatments, medical and psychiatric science gives us elaborate diagnostic categories about which there is considerable agreement: Clinicians can recognize and more or less reliably identify these disorders, and patients can be told about the condition they suffer. For example, although individual cases can pose difficult or insoluble diagnostic dilemmas, psychiatry has developed publicly ac-

---

[17] As Robert Cook-Degan points out (personal communication), a further relevant consideration is whether it leads to stable judgments over time. Advancements in science may make some distinctions less useful, including classifications of disease.

cepted methods – currently embodied in DSM IV – by which agreed upon diagnoses can generally be established.[18] Our very general concern to meet people's health care needs for treatment of disease and impairment can be precisely focused around reliably identifiable instances.

The situation is different for enhancements. We already saw the disagreement that underlies the importance of incommensurability for Sen and the difficulty of unpacking counterfactual claims about choice for the Cohen-Arneson view of equality of welfare. Intuitively, controversy about enhancements is much more widespread. When is being shorter or shyer or less beautiful than we would like a disadvantage that warrants the assistance of others? Whenever we feel it is? When we cannot adapt to our situation through reasonable efforts? When we have set our hearts on particular goals in life?

If we simply take individuals' assessments at face value, then we – as a society or as insurers – again encounter moral hazard, as discussed earlier. If we do not take complainants at face value, how are we to investigate their claims? Have they made reasonable efforts to overcome the condition – participating in social events, asking others for tips on socializing, taking public speaking classes, and so forth? Did they bring it on themselves, as by wishing to consort only with rich, beautiful, and famous people who intimidate them and elicit shyness? We have little idea of how to delve into questions like this. And many of us are very likely to disagree extensively about how to assess these claims.

If the Unhappy Husband invokes the equal opportunity for welfare model and requests treatment on the grounds that he did not choose to be so committed to traditional family values, but was raised to be, similar problems arise. If we do not investigate, we create substantial risk of moral hazard. But if we do investigate, we are faced with a task for which we have few skills – reconstructing the history of his choices and assessing how responsible he is for creating and sustaining the attitudes and behaviors from which he suffers.

Public support for mental health insurance coverage – historically tenuous at best and less secure than coverage for physical health – might be compromised further if the public believed that third-party

---

[18] Of course, as an examination of the successive revisions of the DSM shows, professional agreement at one point in time embodies a host of errors, some of which are recognized in later revisions. Just which agreements have biological validity is something we can only determine in light of the overall state of the biomedical sciences, broadly construed.

resources were subject to even more moral hazard than exists at present. If the public believed that mental health interventions replace reasonable efforts to modify someone's attitudes and behaviors or to extend a person's capacities through learning and practice, support would wane. But this same erosion would occur for physical health care if people saw that scarce medical resources were being diverted into controversial enhancements, perhaps even at the expense of clear cases of untreated disease or impairment. Our willingness to continue to cooperate depends on our assurance that the terms of cooperation remain fair. But opening the door to moral hazard removes that possibility. It might even be more important to us to adhere to a line that seems arbitrary in some occasional hard cases in order to protect the general confidence people place in the fairness of the scheme overall.

Insurance administrators are acutely aware that clinicians can always find ways to circumvent insurance restrictions. No model prevents the possibility of "gaming" (Morreim 1991), and a recent survey of clinicians showed that 68 percent were willing to deceive third-party payers if they believed coverage criteria were unfair (Novack et al. 1989). While clear criteria and monitoring systems make gaming more difficult, the most effective antidote is for clinicians and their patients to understand and endorse the rationale for the model used to determine coverage and to believe in the integrity of the system within which allocative decisions are made (Daniels 1986).

Is the Normal Function Model a Moral "Second-Best"?

Do these policy-based arguments mean that we are really abandoning the clear, clean moral basis underlying our concern for assisting others as an obligation of justice? Are we accepting the treatment/enhancement distinction as a pragmatically forced compromise? Is it not ideal, but only a second-best solution?

Suppose we could agree that there was really one central moral principle or reason (or even intuition) underlying our egalitarian desire to assist others or compensate people who fall short in a relevant way of achieving equality. For the sake of argument, suppose it was the principle appealed to by G.A. Cohen (1989) and Arneson (1988) (referred to in Chapter 3 as the rationale for the brute luck view), namely, that we owe something to people when they fall short of equal opportunity for welfare through no fault or choice of their own. Then an argument that we should nevertheless use the treatment/enhancement distinction because it is more readily administered, or because it more readily provides a focus for public agreement than a criterion that calls for case-by-case evaluation of fault or past choices, might seem like a clear compromise with the ideal rationale. Billy, for example, or even the Unhappy Husband may be denied therapy they may benefit from simply because they do not suffer from a disease or impairment, as recognized by the medical establishment.

The defense of the treatment/enhancement distinction might then look like the kind of defense of a rule that might be offered by a utilitarian: It is simply too costly and inefficient to try to calculate utility directly in each case, but a rule of thumb gives us a practical way to approximate a utilitarian calculation. Just as we remain uncomfortable with this defense of rules when we know that applying them violates the principle of utility in particular cases, we remain uncomfortable with such a defense of the treatment/enhancement rule of thumb when we know we are in a situation that really constitutes a counterexample to it, as our hard cases seem to.

One way to counter this suggestion is to challenge the premise on which it rests – the assumption that we are abandoning a superior moral intuition that should govern this domain of cases. We have already argued that the alternative glosses on equal opportunity do not so readily support expansive alternatives to the standard view of the goals of health care as they might have seemed to. (At the same time, we readily admitted that the normal functioning account does not limit our obligations in health care to the primary rationale.) We here offer a different line of argument: that we should distinguish an area of public concerns about fair distribution of health care (or similar goods) – call it political – from a broader range of contexts in which we (or some of us) may have egalitarian intuitions or beliefs about distribution, and that the normal function account is more appropriate as a political conception than the other glosses on equal opportunity we have considered.

We may begin by asking whether our egalitarian concerns all have one goal or target like the one captured by the claim that we are entitled to concern when we are worse off through no fault of our own. Do all our egalitarian concerns, regardless of context, originate in this one, disarmingly simple intuition? We doubt it; we are skeptical that the egalitarian inclinations we show in diverse moral contexts all have a single explanation. When we are concerned about responding to the needs and preferences of our children, our friends, or our colleagues, or when we chair a department, it is not obvious that our egalitarian concerns are all cut from one uniform moral fabric. The suspicion that they are not grows stronger when we compare our egalitarian concerns in these contexts with our concerns in wider, public arenas. This skepticism about the uniformity of egalitarian concerns across all moral and political domains – a skepticism expressed by Rawls's more complex view of the structure of a theory of justice – stands in contrast with the perspective that underlies the positions taken by Sen, Arneson, and Cohen. They argue as if one target – equal capabilities, or equal opportunity for welfare or advantage – comprehensively captures our egalitarian concerns.

Whether such uniformity exists affects how we should react to the egalitarian concerns is evidenced in certain cases. Suppose that we sometimes do take deficits in opportunity for welfare into account when we think about examples of individuals who suffer from unchosen and unwanted preferences. Perhaps we do this with people we know very well, such as friends or family. Maybe we do this when we understand – or perhaps share – in some detail their conception of the good, and when we have fairly reliable knowledge of what is responsible for their dissatisfaction in life, and perhaps we feel some special responsibility to help them because of our particular relationship to them. Would such responses show that a theory of justice governing basic social institutions must respond to the same egalitarian concerns and have the same target? Is our concern for the relative well-being of others in these instances of a piece with the concerns we might express about how society as a whole should react to inequalities in citizens' relative well-being?

The isolated examples appealed to by theorists like Arneson and Cohen to elicit intuitions about the moral arbitrariness of brute luck do not show that there is a unified target underlying our concerns for the relative well-being of others. Nor do they show that our concerns in the public domain were just "approximations" of what interested us in private settings – for example, that it was "only" for administrative reasons that we "compromised" our concerns in the public domain. What should be of moral relevance in the public domain may not be what is relevant in private domains. What we count as just for basic social institutions may not merely be a necessary departure from what egalitarian concerns "in theory" or "ideally" require. The underlying approach to ethics taken by many philosophers assumes that there will be in all contexts a uniform answer to our concerns about equality. But this is an unargued assumption.

This point has epistemological or justificatory implications: It is not clear what kinds of counterexamples to count as evidence in the debate about the target of equality. Our showing that for purposes of justice we are not and should not be concerned about making choice or its absence as central as Cohen would have it does not show that it is an inappropriate focus for egalitarian concerns in other contexts. By the same token, positive evidence that in some individualized contexts we are concerned with actual choices and their impact on opportunity for welfare would not show that this is the target for theories of justice for basic social institutions. Only if we already believed in the uniformity of our egalitarian concerns would examples in one context count as counterexamples to claims about the target in another kind of context. Without the belief in uniformity, we may only have evidence about how to divide our egalitarian concerns into different domains with different targets.

Rawls's (1971) claim that his principles of justice apply to basic institutions and not to private exchanges opens the door to rejecting the uniformity of egalitarian concerns. Rawls's (1977) replies to Nozick (1974) on this issue elaborate the early form of this argument. Rawls's (1993) more recent elaboration of the claim that his theory is a "political conception" of justice brings a quite different set of arguments to bear on the question of uniformity. It will be helpful to paraphrase this later view, since it is an explicit attempt to argue against the uniformity thesis.

Any political conception of justice must accept certain "general facts" of political sociology. These include the following: There is a diversity of comprehensive religious, philosophical, and moral doctrines (the fact of pluralism); only oppressive use of state power could maintain common affirmation of a comprehensive doctrine; a stable democratic regime requires widespread, free support by a substantial majority; and the political culture of stable democracies normally contains fundamental intuitive ideas that can serve as the basis for a political conception of justice.

A political conception of justice has three main features. First, although it is a moral conception, it is developed and applied only to a specific subject – the basic institutions of a democratic regime. Second, people accept it on the basis of accepting certain fundamental, intuitive ideas present in the political culture. One such fundamental idea is that society is a fair system of social cooperation over time, across generations; another is that citizens are free and equal persons capable of cooperating over a full life. Third, accepting the political conception does not presuppose accepting a comprehensive moral doctrine; nor is the political conception a "compromise" tailored to fit the range of comprehensive doctrines present in the society. Nevertheless, supporters of divergent comprehensive doctrines can achieve an "overlapping consensus" on an appropriate political conception. (We get what might be called "moral epistemology politicized"; cf. Rawls 1993; Daniels 1996, Ch. 8.)

Let us return to the convergence – in practice – on what equal opportunity requires, even given the feasibility of modestly redistributing capabilities. The normal functioning view seems to stay closest to the conception of equal opportunity widely held in our culture since it retains, quite centrally, the idea of competition on the basis of capabilities that might vary naturally. Suppose we take Sen to be articulating a "comprehensive moral view" that gives considerable prominence to the idea of positive freedom. From within that view, the normal functioning view could be justified as an approximation to a slightly more expansive ideal. Similarly, suppose we take Cohen and Arneson to be articulating a principle that involves compensation for unchosen disadvantages – a version of the brute luck view described in Chapter 3.

From the perspective of that comprehensive moral view, the normal functioning account is also justifiable. Both Sen, from one perspective, and Cohen and Arneson, from another, might want to push beyond the normal functioning view, but they can at least support it. If proponents of both other views could come to see that the kinds of reasons needed to pull us beyond the scope of the normal functioning view will derive from "comprehensive" views that not all reasonable people can accept, then they might also accommodate themselves to the political conception that includes only the normal functioning view.

Our intention here is not to defend Rawls's view that we must seek political conceptions of justice. Rather, we have tried to make explicit how such a view bears on the thesis that our egalitarian concerns must all be uniform – that is, subsumable under one central principle or rationale, as they are on Sen's view or the Arneson-Cohen view, regardless of the domain of our concerns in which they arise. Since uniformity is not established, we are unsure how to construe the "evidence" drawn from certain kinds of examples, where we may be tapping into intuitions involving comprehensive views rather than the political conception on which there is overlapping consensus.

The public role that the treatment/enhancement distinction plays is not appropriately tested by matching it to such comprehensive moral views. Instead, the fact that all three models overlap in the importance they attach to treating disease and impairment and that each allows some arguments for enhancement in special cases beyond that suggests this is a politically appropriate core that people who disagree about the demands of equality in other domains might nevertheless agree on.

We conclude this section with a comment that bears on the argument offered here but that has broader implications for this book as a whole. Four philosophers with considerable differences in philosophical beliefs and methods collaborated in writing this book. As noted in the preface, we worked to resolve our disagreements, but we did not fully succeed. One area of lingering tension concerns the usefulness of the treatment/enhancement distinction and the broader issue about the scope of the demands of equal opportunity. Some of us want to push a particular set of intuitions about what equality demands in the redistribution of capabilities; others resist this push, giving more weight to the treatment/enhancement distinction and the related issue of a baseline distribution of capabilities.

This tension has its roots in some broad matters of style: Some of us are more impressed with apparent counterexamples to certain efforts at drawing lines, expecting cleaner principles to underline the distinctions; others find room elsewhere in their own "wide reflective equilibria" to accommodate the examples. The tension may also have its roots in different degrees of acceptance of the idea that justice is "political" and that we may not be able to test the acceptability of principles of justice through appeal to the full range of our considered moral views.

Is the Treatment/Enhancement Distinction a Natural Baseline?

Throughout this section, we have assumed that the treatment/enhancement distinction can be drawn in a reasonably clear fashion, even though there may be some gray areas and hard cases, and we have concentrated on its moral implications. We shall now revisit that assumption, which has been the focus of considerable controversy within the philosophy of medicine, but we shall limit our discussion rather severely. Our concern is primarily with how the central debate affects the ethical implications of the distinction, not the fine details of debates in the philosophy of biology. We believe it is possible to set aside most of the actual controversy, at least for our purposes.

The central conceptual issue, and the focus of considerable controversy, is whether the concept of disease and impairment and the treatment/enhancement distinction can be drawn by reference to a natural baseline, such as departures from species-typical normal functioning, or whether the concept of disease and impairment is fundamentally evaluative. The extreme of the evaluative view is that a disease or impairment is simply an unwanted condition. Earlier, we described the social construction view, which places the evaluation in the hands of some social agency, perhaps the medical profession, or perhaps some broader interaction between the profession, patients, and other cultural and political institutions.

Historically, of course, we can point to many instances in which conditions or behaviors were viewed as examples of disease or impairment – masturbation or homosexuality, or the running-away disease of slaves (Engelhardt 1974) – but these do not show us that diseases and impairments are just what society makes them out to be, given its values. We recognize the error in what was done; it is not simply a matter of social custom, like not shaking hands with the left hand. The real philosophical debate (in the philosophy of biology, not political philosophy) turns on whether we can characterize in the appropriate way, for purposes of theory, certain functions of individuals that are typical for members of that species and distinguish population variation in those functions from cases of disease and impairment. It is this piece of the debate that we cannot enter into here.

Rather, some points we have already made about justice in a pluralist society have a bearing on the part of this debate that is relevant for us. The point behind appealing to a natural baseline that is not itself heavily value-based is that people may agree that it forms a reasonable and relevant basis for public action, despite many other disagreements they may have about other issues of value. Despite numerous other sorts of comprehensive moral views, people may agree that maintaining normal functioning contributes in a reasonable and central way to protecting equality of opportunity. Depending on those other views, they may agree that any inequality in capabilities or capability sets is a source of moral concern. Or they may believe that individuals who are unhappy because of particular attitudes or beliefs they have acquired, through no choice of their own, are owed compensation for their unhappiness. Actually, we may find some disagreement about these matters, with many individuals wanting to hold people more directly responsible for their ends and others taking a more "compassionate" view. But this variation tends to show up outside the core area of agreement about the role of disease and impairment.

The point that emerges here is that the natural baseline has no metaphysical importance: It is not that we must pay some special respect to what is natural, for example, by maintaining or restoring it. Rather, the natural baseline has become a focal point for convergence in our public conception of what we owe each other by way of medical assistance or health care protection. To develop fair terms of cooperation, we should not have to resolve our disputes about these comprehensive moral views, nor should we have to settle an abstract issue in the philosophy of biology.

Suppose that the apparently natural baseline appealed to here does, in various ways, as it has in the past, contain hidden appeals to the values of special groups. Suppose it is a "social construct" after all and draws on some disguised comprehensive moral views. Then our only recourse is to hope that over time there are internal critical pressures within the biomedical sciences that work to expose the special role played by these valuations. Just as we have evidence over time that we have often sneaked valuations into our categorization of diseases, so too we have evidence that we have rooted some of them out. The optimistic view is that there are pressures here that tend to work against any values that are not at least widely shared. This is a partial recognition of the tendency of the sciences to be compatible with pluralism.

The position we are defending, then, does not insist that the natural baseline is completely natural and that no valuations incompatible with pluralism have emerged within it. But we do believe that our best hope of sustaining a point around which we can achieve principled, uncoerced social agreement is one that most assiduously avoids incorporating valuations into its definition of disease and impairment, even if it cannot completely do so. The baseline that emerges over time is most likely one that is compatible with the demands of justice in a pluralist society.

POSITIVE VERSUS NEGATIVE GENETIC INTERVENTIONS
AND THE PERMISSIBLE/IMPERMISSIBLE BOUNDARY

A Reminder about Science Fiction

We have argued that the treatment/enhancement distinction is a useful one provided that we do not expect too much of it. Specifically, we should not expect that it coincides exactly with the boundary between the health care services we are obliged to provide people, given all our obligations, and those that are nonobligatory. Still, it is a reasonable distinction for use within our primary rationale for including services in a health care benefit package. It remains reasonable even in light of expanded ability we may develop to enhance some otherwise normal traits. Dropping it in favor of more expansive views of our medical obligations has distinct disadvantages from a public policy perspective and no compelling arguments for it from a moral perspective.

But as emphasized earlier, we may have other obligations, including those that derive from considerations of justice, such as our concern to promote equality of opportunity, which may compel us to offer some interventions that count as enhancements. Suppose we had a genetic technology that allowed us to enhance immune capabilities beyond those involved in normal functioning (cf. Kitcher 1995). Then, like vaccinations – which have an analogous effect – we might well be obliged to provide this enhancement as part of a medical benefit package (costs and resource constraints permitting). Suppose we had an intervention that allowed us to improve reading or math skills, perhaps through an effect on short-term memory, attention, or some other component of cognitive processing capabilities. Suppose further that its effect is more pronounced for those who perform in the lower half of the normal performance distribution, so that it reduces variance in reading ability by pulling up the bottom. Then, just as we would consider it remiss if educational institutions did not incorporate a pedagogical technique that had the same effects, we might think medical institutions should provide the intervention, costs and resources permitting. Our arguments would turn on the effects on equality of opportunity and on considerations of social productivity. But providing the therapy for some would not be fair without providing it for all (or for all for whom it is reasonably effective). We return to these issues of fairness in enhancements in Chapter 6.

We must now see if the treatment/enhancement distinction has any bearing at all on the moral boundary between permissible and impermissible germline or somatic cell genetic therapies. We shall argue that here, too, the distinction will be of much less use for this purpose, though it may well raise some moral warning flags that require attention.

It is important to emphasize that talk about genetic enhancements is fanciful, given our current knowledge (Kitcher 1995; see also Appendix 1). Our current ability to identify alleles and their effects on a phenotype depends on the mutant form producing large, damaging effects that work for the most part independently of the genome and environment. Because these cases involve a devastating harm, it is more likely that the benefits of intervention outweigh the risks. Our ability to identify genes and to replace them with some precision, as well as the ratio of risks to benefits, all work to make treatments of devastating genetic conditions a more likely scenario than interventions to enhance otherwise normal capabilities. Talking about enhancements, then, presupposes that major gaps in our knowledge and technological capabilities are filled, for otherwise we could never be confident that the direct medical risks of intervention were outweighed by the benefits of enhancement.

The premise behind the rest of this chapter as well as Chapter 6 is that there is some prospect for vastly improving our knowledge and skills. Even so, some scientists are deeply skeptical that for multifactorial traits – like most cognitive functions, strength, height, and immune capabilities – it is anything more than science fiction to talk about their enhancement. On that view, we are engaged in the ethics of science fiction, not applied ethics. Despite this warning, and partly because the issues attract attention in any case, we shall continue our argument.

Negative and Positive and the Permissible/Impermissible Boundary

Just as the treatment/enhancement distinction does not coincide with the obligatory/nonobligatory boundary, it does not coincide with the permissible/impermissible boundary either. Not all treatments will be permissible and not all enhancements will be impermissible. As examples of permissible enhancements, Kitcher (1995) suggests an improvement to the immune system and possibly an intervention to prevent memory loss during aging. These enhancements might be highly beneficial without posing any significant risks. The strength of the immune example comes from its close analogy to vaccinations, which exploit more fully our immune capabilities rather than extending them. The difference seems morally irrelevant. As Kitcher suggests, adapting an old argument from Hume, we are no more playing God by altering people genetically so that they have greater immunity than we are when we give them vaccinations.

Similarly, just because a genetic intervention counts as an effective treatment does not mean we are obliged to include it in our repertoire of permissible medical treatments. Suppose that we could treat a condition through a somatic intervention, with the consent of the patient, or through a germline intervention, for which only consent of the parents were possible. If this were a case where the germline intervention had no additional benefits to the patient (although it might have for offspring), then we might prefer the direct consent of the patient to the proxy consent of the parents. Other moral constraints thus apply, and therefore being an effective treatment is not a sufficient condition for an intervention being permissible.

Treatment/Enhancement and Moral Warning Flags

Even if the treatment/enhancement distinction does not provide us with a simple criterion for deciding what genetic interventions are permissible and impermissible, there is good reason to think that many enhancements will pose serious problems not posed by treatments. For whole classes of cases, certain enhancements may be impermissible for reasons that are unlikely to arise for treatments or for reasons that can be more easily dealt with in the case of treatments. Knowing that something is an enhancement should thus raise a moral warning flag, which is the central implication for public policy.

Three types of warnings about enhancements that we do not encounter with treatments are worth noting here. First, public goods and other coordination problems arise when all parents pursue a course intended to be best for their offspring. For example, gender selection to prevent genetic disease or impairment is pursued only by affected families and has no significant effect on gender ratios in subsequent generations. In contrast, gender selection for economic or religious reasons can modify gender ratios; not only is the gender selection for some of these reasons objectionable for reasons of justice, but the effect may be self-defeating. For example, parents seeking economic advantage for their male offspring may find they contribute to an oversupply of male offspring, making each less valuable.

Second, pursuit of "positional advantage" through enhancement of some traits, such as height, risks being either self-defeating or unfair. If all can do it, it may be self-defeating: no one gains a height advantage if everyone increases in height. If only the wealthiest can pursue enhancement, it seems unfair that advantages so ramify. In contrast, treatment of extreme shortness induced by disease will face neither objection.

Third, we generally agree that eliminating disease and impairment works to the advantage of those who end up functioning normally, but whether some enhancements constitute benefits will depend on the values individuals hold, and parents' values may not always coincide with those of their offspring. So the problems we face determining what counts as a benefit and who should decide that go beyond the problems faced by parents making proxy decisions about treatment of disease and impairment.

This chapter has explored in depth the moral boundary raised by genetic treatments versus enhancements. The next examines more carefully the moral issues raised by parents pursuing "the best" enhancements for their children through genetic intervention.

FIVE

WHY NOT THE BEST?

HAVING THE BEST CHILDREN WE CAN

"Be All You Can Be," the Army recruiting poster urges young men and women. Many parents share the sentiment. They want their children to be the best they can be. For many parents, their most important project in life is to pursue that goal, and they make sacrifices to see it happen. And why shouldn't parents aim to make their offspring the best they can be?

Of course, means matter. That is why we consider in this chapter whether parents should be free to use genetic intervention techniques to produce the best offspring they can. Posed this way, the question immediately raises many antieugenic hackles: Won't screening and selective abortion mean we eliminate many lives that are worth living? And won't it devalue the lives of people with disabilities? Anyway, who is to say what is the "best" (some parents have peculiar ideas)? Won't the economically and socially privileged be those best placed to pursue the "best"? Doesn't "best" for some mean worse for others? Isn't it wrong for parents to think of their children as something they design?

These objections deserve attention, and we will return to them shortly, but it is important to understand the presumption behind the original question. Shouldn't parents seek the best – even through genetics – for their offspring? Don't we expect them to?

What Could Be More Natural Than Parents Seeking the Best?

Parents are generally regarded as having permission, and some would say an obligation, to produce the "best" children they can. They are expected, for example, to keep their children as healthy as possible.

Society expects them to try to keep their children away from drugs, from street crime, from hazardous play. They may be required to put seat belts and bicycle helmets on their children. They are even required to boost their children's resistance to certain diseases, for example, through vaccinations – even if doing so runs counter to their religious beliefs. If genetic techniques gave parents a way to enhance the resistance of their children to certain diseases, and the intervention posed only risks comparable to those posed by vaccination, should parents be free, or even required in some instances, to use them?

Parents are expected to heed nutritional and dietary concerns for their children. We applaud parental efforts to shape their children, even over the children's protests, by moderating their fat intake, increasing fruit and vegetables in their diet, and restricting their access to "junk" foods. Where we have some claims to know scientifically what is "best" for children, we encourage parents to pursue it (although our primarily educational campaigns have their largest effects on the best-educated and best-off sectors of the population). At the same time, parents are allowed considerable leeway to pursue these goals as they see fit – or not at all. For some parents, only a vegetarian diet will do. For others, "good" food is the food they were raised on, whatever their ethnic background. These diets vary in their benefits and risks to children. But parents are allowed to pursue what is nutritionally best for their children as they see it. From a nutritional perspective, this means that parents are allowed to pursue what is not best, as long as it is not so bad that it constitutes neglect or abuse.

Parents also pursue the best for their children – as they see it – through exercise and sports. Some children are enrolled in Little League baseball, soccer, basketball, football, or hockey. They get tennis and swimming lessons or go to running clinics and camps; minimally, they are encouraged to develop their skills at pick-up basketball games or sandlot football. For some parents, the goal is to teach their children a lifelong appreciation of exercise, and they urge them to avoid contact sports that threaten serious injury; for them, athletics is but one dimension of life. For others, contact in sports is ritualized combat, an important preparation for the rigors of competition in life. For still others, the goal is to develop a special athletic excellence that will give their children access to college or even professional sports; for them, athletics is a way up or out. The investment of some parents in tennis or skating or swimming lessons for a child with competitive talent may be enormous.

Of course, parents who have the means often invest in the development of capabilities other than athletic ones: They give their children violin or piano or ballet lessons, enroll them in chess clubs and tournaments, or encourage their computer skills or interest in math teams or science fairs. For some parents, the general strategy is to expose children to many activities, to develop a broad array of capabilities, and to broaden the options open to their children. For others, the key strategy is to spot special skills or talents and to invest heavily in developing these strengths. For some parents from modest backgrounds, the economic sacrifice in developing their children's capabilities is very great; better-off families may quite easily afford whatever investment is necessary. Some scholarship assistance is available for the most talented children from poor backgrounds, at least in some areas of artistic and athletic development, but generally the burden of investment in "human capital" falls on families. For the poorest, both in the United States and elsewhere, seeking the best for their children may mean doing what is possible to assure their survival.

Many parents also aim to make their children the best prudential and moral agents they can be. For them, being the best means having the virtues necessary to planning life and coping and adapting to its vicissitudes. It also means having the virtues necessary to respond well to the needs of others, to stand up for what is right, and to treat others fairly. They place considerable emphasis on teaching children the importance of doing chores and helping others. They insist their children work at jobs to encourage in them an appreciation for the demands of work and the value of money – a work ethic. They compel their children to undergo many hours and years of religious training or participation in community service activities – shaping their sense of belonging to a community, their capacity to respond to others in their group, and their social consciousness and moral conscience.

Here, too, parents are granted extensive leeway to pursue the best as they see it. "Granted leeway" here means only that there is a presumption in favor of not interfering with parents. Raising children to accept the limitations imposed by some religious sects can significantly reduce preparation for other ways of living, but parents may believe this is a way to ensure that their children lead "the good life" as they see it. Our courts have recognized, for example, the rights of Old Order Amish to restrict schooling for their children to age 14 rather than the age of 16 required by state law (*Wisconsin v. Yoder* 1972). Some educational opportunity for these children has been traded for enhanced rights to pursue religious practices and a communal way of life. The "best" as perceived by society at large does not here constrain a religious community's pursuit of its vision of the best for their children.

Some find the court decision in *Wisconsin v. Yoder* problematic (we return to this case later in this chapter): They think educational opportunity should not be restricted in the ways the Yoder decision permits, fearing that children who later want a different way of life will be at a disadvantage in the larger society. But the court argued that the harms imposed on children in this way are speculative and are not of the same quality as the harms that we ordinarily prevent parents from imposing on children. Society prohibits harms that result from malice or neglect, even reserving the right to remove children from parental guardianship if necessary. Despite the leeway granted parents, children are not property to be disposed of as parents wish.

Neglect and abuse aside, however, parents remain free to pursue producing the best offspring they can. Interference with this would be seen by most as interference with the most fundamental elements of the parents' conception of a good life.

Environmental versus Genetic Pursuits

If this liberty of parents to pursue the best for and in their offspring is so fundamental, why not extend it to the use of genetic means? Why are the antieugenic hackles we noted earlier raised so quickly?

The leeway parents are generally allowed to pursue the best for their children may seem unproblematic because there is a tendency to think of their efforts as "environmental" factors that help to develop the capacities or capabilities their children already have or are capable of having. The parents are only "bringing out the best in them," or developing "the potential" that is already there. In contrast, the use of genetic information and intervention (whether somatic or germline) suggests parents are changing their children in some fundamental way, making them different from what they otherwise would have or could have been.

This contrast is problematic. To see why, it is useful to reconsider some of the distinctions noted in our earlier discussion of genetic determinism. When parents use their control over environmental factors to "bring out the best" in their children, much of what they do actually modifies phenotype. Given their children's genotypes, the

range of traits and capabilities – physical and behavioral – that constitute the phenotype, the child we see and interact with is very much a
result of the environments parents and others create. How the child is
fed, for example, will affect height, strength, and resistance to illness.
How the child exercises will affect body shape, muscle development,
strength, and physical capabilities and even neurological development.
How the child is spoken to, read to, and interacted with will affect the
development of cognitive and emotional capabilities. There is no pre-
existing ("essential") "best" in the child that is brought out by parental manipulation of environmental causes; such manipulation has
enormous effects in shaping phenotype.

If parents modify phenotype in pursuit of their goal of producing
the "best" offspring they can, then why not add to their arsenal of
methods whatever genetic interventions may make it easier to accomplish some of those goals? Part of what may disturb us is the (mistaken) belief that genotypic interventions modify the essence or essential features of the individual, whereas environmental interventions
only modify accidental features. The idea seems to be that genetic
interventions result in a different individual, whereas environmental
interventions merely modify the same individual. These metaphysical
metaphors are misleading. The relationship between genotype and
phenotype cannot be reduced to any traditional metaphysical relationship, such as that between matter and form, or substance and attribute, or essence and accident.

The heart of the point can be illustrated by reconsidering some
examples already noted. When an infant is vaccinated, the vaccine
triggers an immune reaction that permanently affects the ability of the
immune system to respond to particular bacteria or viruses. Suppose
the operation of the immune system could be enhanced with similar –
or broader – effect by a genetic intervention. If this were a somatic cell
intervention, we would not think there had been any "essential" modification of the individual, though some cell lines may be permanently
and even essentially modified and immune capabilities will be permanently improved. If this were a germline intervention, we might have
more complicated reactions to the change, but it still seems likely we
would think of this as a change to the same individual or person. If it
were any one of us, we would not be inclined to muse, "I wonder who
I would have been had my parents not altered my immune-system gene
in this way."

We might have similar reactions if we learned our parents had changed our eye or hair color. We might have very different responses if they had altered genes that produced major effects on aspects of the self that are treated as central to our sense of self or personal identity. For each of us, it is particular elements of our phenotype, not every element of our genotype, that we take to be central to our conceptions of self and to our essence as an individual.

There is some irony in the fact that our compunctions about genetic interventions seem to rest on some underlying confusion about genetic determinism ("we are essentially what our genes make us"). The irony is that we allow parents the environmental leeway we do. Understood properly, leaving the extensive room we do for environmental causes should undercut our acceptance of genetic determinism.

WHAT IS THE BEST AND WHO DECIDES?

This section takes up two kinds of worries about using genetic interventions to make the best children possible. The first concerns whether there are adequate or defensible standards for determining what would be the best children possible – that is, what changes would be for the best for our children. The second concerns who – parents or the public – would be making decisions about what kinds of children would be best and then pursuing genetic interventions involving children on the basis of those criteria. The two worries interact, of course.

We postpone until the final section of the chapter constraints on pursuit of the best that might derive from harms to others. Before considering what is best and who decides, it is worth highlighting the specific form of the ethical issue about public policy that underlies the title to this chapter, "Why Not the Best?" The point rests on the familiar distinctions in moral philosophy between actions that are morally required, morally desirable and permissible, bad but nevertheless still morally permissible, and morally impermissible. The permissibility of an action taken by a particular person is a question distinct from the moral permissibility of others interfering with that action.

A Moral Distinction between Actions

The strongest position supporting attempts to perfect children through genetic intervention would be that it is morally required of parents or others to seek to produce the best children possible. This is not a plausible ethical position and not the policy issue which this chapter addresses. It is a general feature of typical attitudes about parental responsibilities in childrearing that parents are not morally required to do everything within their power to produce and raise the best children possible. Parents can legitimately give weight to their own interests and to the interests of others besides themselves and their children in making decisions that involve use of their resources or efforts, and in so doing they do not do all that they might do for their children. This would be an unreasonably high standard.

Moreover, if the standard was to make as perfect children as possible, the standard of what would be the most perfect children possible for particular parents in particular circumstances would be highly morally controversial. It is compatible with rejection of this standard, however, that there might be some specific genetic enhancements that were morally required of specific parents.

A weaker position supportive of genetic enhancements would be that it is morally desirable or morally good for parents to use a variety of means, including genetic interventions, to attempt to produce the best children possible. This is a considerably more plausible position because it allows that there may be other interests that may compete with and override the reasons supporting attempts to produce the best children possible, even if it is always good, other things being equal, to seek to improve our children. The core of the plausibility of this position is that, if we do in fact improve our children by one or another form of genetic intervention, it would seem that we have benefited them, and benefiting them is at least a moral reason for having taken those steps. It is a reason why what we have done is, all other things being equal, morally good or desirable.

A genuinely beneficial enhancement for a child might nevertheless be – all things considered – morally wrong, and so impermissible, if, for example, it prevented the parents from meeting their more important responsibilities to others. But in the absence of any such conflicting moral considerations, genuinely beneficial enhancements, even if not morally required, would be morally permissible.

Of course, in trying to perfect our children by genetic intervention, just as with other means that parents now typically pursue, our efforts might misfire and the attempt to benefit might result in making them worse off. But this is a possibility for any attempt to improve our children, or to prevent harm to them, and does not argue especially against genetic intervention in order to do so.

The weakest position supportive of genetic enhancements, and in that respect the easiest to defend, is that it is within the legitimate authority of parents (or perhaps others) in having and raising their children to use at least some forms of genetic intervention in seeking to improve their children. This position is compatible with having serious moral doubts about whether parents or others should be encouraged to take such steps, doubts that could have a number of different sources, while acknowledging that taking such steps is within the rights or legitimate authority of parents in raising their children. It is also compatible with believing that some genetic enhancements would – all things considered – be bad but still within parents' legitimate authority in raising their children. It is a general feature of both moral and legal rights that they authorize their possessors to take actions that it would be wrong of others to interfere with and that may be unwise or bad, or, on a more extreme position held by some philosophers, may even be morally wrong.

This chapter examines two main questions. First, is the use of genetic interventions to improve children morally good or desirable, other things being equal, in the same way that environmental interventions, such as attempting to give them the best education possible, are often thought to be morally good or desirable? And second, even if some genetic intervention is on balance undesirable, is it nevertheless morally permissible for parents to use it because doing so is within their legitimate authority in producing and raising their children?

Why should anyone think that there is a special problem determining what genetic as opposed to environmental intervention would be best for children? We have already given many examples from nongenetic contexts of parental actions that are uncontroversially good for their children. Some of these are commonly considered to be morally required (such as minimal education), but virtually all are commonly considered morally permissible and desirable. Is there something about genetic enhancements that makes them especially morally controversial?

The history of eugenics movements and the frequency and importance of racist attitudes in them should surely give us pause. Moreover, those movements have often uncritically accepted a variety of other stereotypes and prejudices about what characteristics it would be desirable to produce in children. Individual parents might be just as susceptible to such stereotypes and prejudices as the historical eugenics movements have been. So history alone gives strong grounds for caution about attempts to use genetic interventions to perfect our children.

But this caution should be tempered with recognition of the importance, for both parents and children, of parents having substantial discretion and freedom to decide how to raise their children without interference. Also, it is worth remembering that if stereotypes or prejudices are a problem, they are a problem for environmental interventions as well.

Pursuing the Best for the Child

It is important that the attempts to produce the best children possible be understood as making the life of the child best for the child from the standpoint of that particular child's good, not best from some other standpoint, such as the good of the parents or of society. There are certainly social standpoints from which producing certain kinds of children might be best for the society but would not for the children in question. To take an extreme example, in *Brave New World* Aldous Huxley imagined producing children with significantly limited capacities that would make them well suited for and likely to be satisfied with quite limited and menial roles in the society. If a society has a need to fill such roles, it might be best from its standpoint that sufficient children be produced who will be suited for and content with filling such roles. But that is quite different from claiming that it would be best for the children in question to be created with these limited capacities and expectations.

Our concern is with genetic intervention that purports to be for the good or benefit of the children who are subject to it, not for the good or benefit of others. (We note that this perspective is similar to what is generally thought to be appropriate in providing medical treatments: The focus is on patient welfare and not on the social contribution or value of patients in deciding about appropriate care.)

One way to put the point is to insist that the judgment of parents or others about what would be best for their child as a result of genetic intervention should be made from a standpoint that they can reasonably expect the child to come to share. When, in the course of childrearing, parents impose limits or take other steps concerning their children that the children either oppose or are not yet able to endorse or oppose, a typical justification for doing so is that the child will later come to see and accept that the actions taken were for its own good, and in this sense later come to endorse the earlier action.

In one important respect, this standard is too weak. It is too weak when the actions taken not only change a person's capacities and opportunities in some way, but lead the individual to endorse those changes in ways that he or she might not have done in their absence. The *Brave New World* example took this form: Persons were deliberately created with severely limited capacities but also with expectations that would lead them to be satisfied with those capacities despite the limitations.

There is a more subtle version of this same problem that is more difficult to avoid and that commonly arises in childrearing. Whatever the relative contributions, either in general or in particular cases, of children's genetic endowments and the various environmental factors to which children are exposed, the process of childrearing inevitably shapes in important ways the later standards and values that the child will apply to his or her own life and to other evaluative questions. Thus, for example, when membership in a particular religious group is a deep and pervasive part of the lives of parents and of families, children raised in those families will likely affirm that their membership in the religion in question is an important good in their lives. In this respect, successful religious education leads to the children coming to support the results of that education; they come to endorse their having been subjected to it. The standards the person uses to evaluate what childrearing practices were good for him or her are tainted by the very practices in question.

The case of children who are raised in or have become subject to what are thought of as religious cults shows another version of the *Brave New World* difficulty. Here the very process of initiating children into the group, and inculcating in them the beliefs that the group shares, undermines their capacity to evaluate independently whether having been subjected to this process has been good or a benefit to them. Thus, if the child's later endorsement of the steps that improve or affect him or her is sufficient to justify them, those steps must at least not have destroyed or limited the child's capacity independently to evaluate them.

A further difficulty with this subsequent endorsement standard is that people typically have strong motives to find ways to regard themselves positively. If someone has undergone a procedure that changes in a fundamental way what kind of person he or she is, the desire for positive self-regard provides a motive for endorsing the parents' decision to subject the child to that procedure, even when from other more objective standpoints the choice was not a good one.

The depth of the difficulty can be brought out by considering an example from everyday, noncultist childrearing. Suppose a father, successful in business as a salesman, undertakes to train his somewhat shy and introspective son to be more outgoing and aggressive. As the son matures, having negotiated group therapy sessions, high-school student government elections, and carefully focused parental rewards and punishments, he begins to succeed in his new persona. He acquires his father's values and applauds having been so shaped. Had he not been so cultivated, that shy, contemplative youth might have become a fine writer or scientist, thankful he had dodged forever the "superficial" bustle of his father's world.

There is a similar problem for the notion of individual self-determination if it is understood as individuals choosing their own character uninfluenced by external factors and sources. It is only by a process of interaction with one's environment during child development that a child comes to have values by which to make later evaluations and choices. When those values are endorsed in the right sorts of ways, the later choices using them will be the child's own.

Yet the notion of choosing our own character, where this includes some fundamental values, is incoherent when taken literally. First, one must have a character, in the sense of a set of values, preferences, and behavioral dispositions in order to make any choices, and so there is no way to get behind having those values, preferences, and dispositions in order to choose them. There would be nothing in the person, no character, on the basis of which the choices of character could be made. But if the process of changing and shaping a child leaves the child's critical capacities substantially intact, or better yet helps to develop and improve them, then there is a good deal to be said in support of the criterion that the changes, by genetic means or otherwise, should be ones that the child can be expected later reasonably to affirm as having been for his or her own good or benefit.

Yet the standard of the child's subsequent endorsement is not only insufficient to justify a particular attempt to shape a child's character, it is also not necessary. For example, if a parent recognizes a deep streak of cruelty in a child, the parent might be justified in attempting to reduce or limit it, even if the trait is so deep-seated that the child is not likely later to endorse the efforts. This standard of the subject's later endorsement of the earlier changes cannot put to rest all concerns about what the standard of "best" is for perfecting children.

Harms, Benefits, and General-Purpose Means

In Chapter 6, we discuss many uncontroversial examples of conditions harmful to a child. Why is it that enhancements seem more ethically problematic in their effects on children than treatments, that steps to provide benefits or goods to a child seem more ethically controversial than steps to prevent harms? Why is it that what counts as a benefit to someone seems more controversial than what counts as a harm to that same person? Loss of sight or hearing, or the ability to move a person's limbs, is typically and uncontroversially taken to be a harm, whereas it is more controversial whether gaining the ability to play a musical instrument or to excel in athletics is a benefit. Someone might say, for example, "I couldn't care less about playing the bassoon or competing in the pole vault."

First, we should note that it is not entirely uncontroversial that each of these harmful conditions is indeed a harm. In some views found in disabilities rights movements, the loss of hearing is not uncontroversially a harm and need not create a disability. Some groups stress the deaf culture, the richness of deaf people's alternative sign language, insisting that deaf people should be thought of as "differently abled" but not "disabled." Disabilities rights groups have been important in forcing the broader public to recognize the abilities that disabled persons do possess, despite their disabilities, as well as the ways in which accommodations can be made to disabilities that can remove much or even all the disadvantages they otherwise confer.

To some significant extent, it is because the larger society is structured and ordered for the needs and interests of the "normally abled" that disabilities carry the extent of disadvantage that they often do (see Chapter 7). Despite such cautions, however, it is widely thought that the loss of an ability like sight is uncontroversially a harm in a way that many benefits are not similarly uncontroversial. Why is that?

The typical human's capacity for sight may be thought of as a general-purpose means – useful and valuable in carrying out nearly any plan of life or set of aims that humans typically have. It is a "good" not only from a distinct perspective or plan of life that some may adopt but many others may reject. Instead, there are few perspectives from which the loss of sight is not a harm, and few perspectives from which having sight is not a benefit in carrying out the plan of life a person has adopted. It can be thought of as a "natural primary good," analogous to what John Rawls (1971) has called "social primary goods" – in each case "general purpose" means useful or valuable in carrying out nearly any plan of life.

This is not to deny either that individuals who lose their sight can compensate and adjust their plans so as to still have satisfying and valuable lives, or that loss of sight may make some new goods possible, such as experience of the rich inner life of the blind. But the loss of a general-purpose capacity like sight at the least significantly diminishes the range, and makes more difficult the pursuit, of life plans that humans value and choose.

Not all harms to persons, however, constitute the loss of valuable all-purpose natural capacities. Some are only harms from the standpoint of a particular comprehensive plan of life. And, more important, the relative importance or seriousness of many harms to persons can only be determined from the particular comprehensive perspective or plan of life of the specific individual in question, not from a more general, shared perspective. For example, the loss of fine motor skills in one hand may be devastating to a musician to whom those skills are irreplaceable, whereas it would be a much less serious loss of ability to a person whose work and other activities are largely mental or cognitive and do not make use of those fine motor skills. But this comparison is not between harms and benefits; it is between, on the one hand, general-purpose means whose possession is a good and whose loss is a harm for nearly all plans of life and, on the other hand, specific abilities or capacities whose value and importance depend on the particular plan of life of the person who either has them or loses them.

There are enhancements of capacities and abilities that are as plausibly a benefit from nearly any evaluative perspective as the comparable loss of the capacity or ability would be a harm. For example, a very substantial increase in the capacity for memory of normal humans would also be a general-purpose benefit improving people's capacity to pursue nearly any plan of life. (We assume the enhanced memory is functionally integrated with other cognitive capacities, as is normal memory, and does not, for example, interfere with or intrude on other functions and capacities.) The relative importance of the benefit might significantly differ with different plans of life, but so of course might the relative importance of a harm such as the loss of hearing or sight.

Thus there is no systematic contrast between harms and benefits according to which what constitute harms is uncontroversial and objective from the perspective of any life plan, while what constitute benefits is controversial and subjective, and beneficial only from the perspective of such life plans. Rather, there are both benefits and harms that are uncontroversial because they are general-purpose means or impediments to nearly any plan of life, and there are both benefits and harms whose value or disvalue, and especially whose relative value or disvalue, depends on the particular plan of life of the person in question. So harms and benefits do not systematically differ in a way that would make genetic interventions to improve children ethically problematic or controversial in a way that similar genetic interventions to treat a harmful genetic disease or condition are ethically unproblematic or uncontroversial.

There is a sense in which disease, understood as an adverse deviation from normal species function, is a condition that is at least *prima facie* bad for anyone who has it, although this is compatible with a particular disease not being, all things considered, bad for a particular person in particular circumstances. Genetic intervention to treat disease can consequently be understood as *prima facie* beneficial for any individual who has that disease. A limitation of genetic intervention to treatment or prevention of specific diseases does then provide more objective limits on the use of interventions, although that is in part just because conditions are only judged to be diseases if they are in general harmful.

On the other hand, the use of genetic interventions by parents to make their children "the best that they can be," when no longer limited by the children's given genetic inheritance, are more open-ended and based on various concrete and sometimes idiosyncratic conceptions of parents of what would be best for their children. (Of course, environmental interventions to promote the best may also be based on similarly idiosyncratic or biased conceptions.)

It was noted in Chapter 2 that the old eugenicists have been criticized, with some reason, for failing to take value pluralism seriously. A fundamental feature of liberal political philosophy is that it accepts an irreducible and permanent pluralism among its citizens in regard to concrete, comprehensive values and conceptions of a good life (cf. Rawls 1993). Respecting this irreducible pluralism about the good is one ground of the liberal commitment to state neutrality between different conceptions of a good life.

Many have quite correctly argued that a very strong position of complete neutrality between different conceptions of a good life in all actions and policies of the state is not possible, but there remains an important distinction concerning the degree of neutrality that liberal states, as opposed to nonliberal states, will seek to achieve. This neutrality properly limits enhancements that a liberal state should undertake.

Is there any reason to expect some degree of neutrality between different conceptions of the good as well from parents in shaping and raising their children? That reason would have to be different from reasons grounding the proper neutrality of the liberal state, since the coercive authority claimed by the state over its citizens and its responsibility to promote toleration both distinguish it from the family and parent-child relations. If there is some reason to expect a degree of neutrality from parents toward different conceptions of the good, it could rest in part on a concern about parents using genetic interventions to make their children suitable for only a particular and idiosyncratic conception of a good life that the parents happen to have.

The Right to an Open Future

Although the degree and grounds of neutrality in the kinds of children to be produced properly expected of the state and of parents differ substantially, there is a kind of neutrality that can be expected of parents. Joel Feinberg (1980) has characterized what we have in mind through the concept of a child's "right to an open future." The idea is that parents have a responsibility to help their children during their growth to adulthood to develop capacities for practical judgment and autonomous choice, and to develop as well at least a reasonable range of the skills and capacities necessary to provide them the choice of a reasonable array of different life plans available to members of their society. (We stress the two qualifications of a reasonable range and array, since Feinberg sometimes asserts a stronger right to a maximally open future.)

In this view, it would be wrong for parents substantially to close off most opportunities that would otherwise be available to their children in order to impose their own particular conception of a good life or in order to continue their own community that is committed to that conception of a good life.

Thus, in *Wisconsin v. Yoder*, had the Amish community wanted to withdraw their children from school at the age, for example, of 10 on the grounds that education beyond that age was not necessary for their particular way of life, it would have violated their children's right to an open future to do so. In the actual case of *Wisconsin v. Yoder*, the Amish sought to withdraw their children two years before the age of 16, when any child has the right to withdraw from school on his or her own. Typical state laws that permit children to leave school at age 16 arguably do not violate their right to an open future because children have by then generally received sufficient education to fit them for many jobs and achieved sufficient maturity of judgment to be permitted to decide whether they want to continue their education further. The court in *Yoder* might have argued (indeed, an argument along these lines was made in a minority concurring opinion) that this two-year difference did not make a substantial enough difference in the opportunities available to the Amish children to violate the children's right to an open future.

There is obviously no precise, nonarbitrary point at which genetic intervention, although it makes someone more fit for a specific way of life that parents favor, makes her less fit for a substantial enough range of other ways of life to violate the right to an open future. But any society such as our own, which accepts a very strong commitment to individualism and individual self-determination or autonomy, may reasonably put at least some limits on genetic or other interventions with children in the interest of maintaining reasonable opportunities for those children, even if those interventions might make the child more fit for a specific way of life that its parents favor.

Recognizing the right to an open future is compatible with according substantial discretion to parents to use genetic interventions, just as they would other environmental interventions, to attempt to give their children what they might consider to be the best life possible. What is required is that those interventions do not so narrow children's range of opportunities as to violate their right to an open future.

Whether there is a moral right of children to an open future, much less whether such a right should be enforced and protected by public and legal policy, is of course controversial. Some parents would insist that there are no moral limits on their right to shape their children in the parent's own image, or in any other image they please. But a more plausible reason why the right is controversial is that it comes at a cost in some cases to the child's future welfare.

Some pursuits, such as becoming a professional pianist or tennis player, require early and intense training to make adult success more likely; in other cases, substantial choice leads to anxiety and indecision that firm commitment to a clear path at an early age might have avoided. These considerations must be balanced against the right in interpreting its scope and weight, and what specific interventions, genetic or environmental, would violate it in particular cases. Nevertheless, the limits of such a right on efforts to shape children would not provide any systematic bar to parents using genetic or other kinds of interventions with their children to give them better lives.

The requirement that parents respect their children's right to an open future is important not only because it preserves some prospect of adult autonomy for children, but also because it hedges against various kinds of uncertainty and error. Autonomy aside, the best interests of a child may not coincide with parental judgments about what is best. Parents may erroneously project what is good for themselves onto their children. They may tie their judgments about what is good to what is currently socially valued, not what is of enduring value. Their judgments may be tainted by racism, classism, or sexism. The history of the eugenics movement makes the risks of error all too apparent. A broader array of capacities should usually provide individuals with greater adaptive capacities to correct for the errors and mistakes of their parents.

In current discussions, however, it is not simply error about what is best that is key to reservations about genetic interventions, but the enormous uncertainty about risks that surrounds their use. We revisit the issue of risks at the end of this chapter.

Limits on Pursuit of the Best

Problems in defining and defending a specific account of the best that parents might pursue in genetic interventions for their children, together with children's right to an open future, place some limits on the nature of interventions and the circumstances in which they can be justified. However, besides worries about the nature of the view of the best on which attempts to intervene might be based, there are also concerns about who might be initiating, encouraging, or even enforcing the interventions.

For a variety of complex reasons, social practices and the law accord significant discretion to families in having and raising children. Doing so recognizes deep and important interests of parents concerning their children, the important ways children benefit from membership in at least reasonably well functioning families, and the value of the family in developing capacities for intimacy and in providing privacy, both of which require that the family have significant freedom from external oversight and control. Yet children are not chattels; they are individuals with moral and legal claims in their own right. Nevertheless, considerable but not unlimited discretion in having and raising children is in the interests of children and is a necessary and desirable concomitant of the valuable institution of the family.

However, the family, and specifically an individual child's parents, are not the only persons or institution who might seek to encourage, initiate, or require genetic interventions to give children the best lives possible. Huxley imagined the state taking on some such role in *Brave New World*, and any such prospect raises additional moral worries. We have already noted the ethically problematic nature of any such interventions to produce the best children, when the perspective of the best is society's and not one the children affected could be expected to come to share. And there is reason to worry that interventions undertaken by or at the initiative and urging of the state would be more likely to be motivated by a societal, not an individual, perspective about what kind of children it would be best for the society to have.

An important complexity in the state's proper role in possible genetic enhancements is that it is not plausible to rule out completely enhancements for the benefit of society, as opposed to the subject of the enhancement. For example, there is already some evidence of genes associated with dispositions to violent criminal behavior. Just as the criminal law is a justified coercive social means aimed at preventing or reducing such behavior, society might in the future attempt genetic interventions to do so as well. These interventions would not be made for the benefit of the subject of the genetic intervention (even if that individual also benefited), but for the benefit of the broader society and to protect the rights of its members against violent assault.

While violent behavior is not a disease, these genes would be similar to genes that transmit diseases in that they dispose individuals who have them to deviations from the social norm for violence. But suppose that direct or indirect genetic intervention would reduce the normal human disposition for violence and increase the normal human disposition for cooperative behavior and altruistic concern for others. It is not at all clear why it would be wrong for a society to support or undertake these genetic interventions for the benefit of the society. Genetic enhancements of individuals for the benefit of society cannot be absolutely barred, nor can the need to evaluate the social purpose of the intervention. (A word of caution, however, since we have already seen in Chapter 3 that traits such as altruism – which used to be called virtues – are complex, and that there can be disagreement as to precisely what combination of their constitutive elements, in what proportions, really are desirable. This point receives further attention later in this chapter in the section on "Virtues and the 'Best.' ")

Interventions by the state intended to be for the benefit of children who are subject to the intervention would often raise troubling conflicts with fundamental principles of liberal democracy. The only such interventions that would be compatible with a strong liberal commitment to neutrality between different comprehensive conceptions of the good would be enhancements of capabilities that are what we called natural primary goods – capabilities that are general-purpose means, useful in carrying out virtually any plan of life.

It would be a mistake, of course, to suppose that capabilities are either fully all-purpose means or useful only in some very few specific plans of life. Instead, capabilities fall across a broad spectrum in the breadth of kinds of life plans or conceptions of the good for which they are useful, as well as in the degree to which they are useful. Nevertheless, what we have called general-purpose means are capabilities that are broadly valuable across a wide array of life plans and opportunities typically pursued in a society like our own.

The closer such capabilities are to truly all-purpose means, the less objection there should be to the state encouraging or even requiring genetic enhancements of those capabilities. Most now accept government requirements that parents secure medical care, both acute and preventive, for their children in order to prevent harm to them. Most accept public programs of water fluoridation to enhance normal human capacities to resist tooth decay. Most in our society also accept government requirements that parents ensure that their children receive the benefit of a reasonable minimum level of education. If genetic interventions become possible that would prevent comparable harms, or secure comparable benefits, they could also be justifiably encouraged or required by the state.

The neutrality properly expected of the state in liberal societies, nevertheless, is greater than what is properly expected of individual parents. Indeed, no such neutrality is properly expected of parents in the plan of life or conception of the good that they adopt and pursue for themselves and for their own lives. Strong rights to self-determination or autonomy protect people's right to choose and pursue their own specific plan of life or conception of the good. Nor, of course, would it be desirable or possible for parents to maintain any such complete neutrality about what is a good life in raising their children.

The neutrality that parents must practice toward their children is that required by the child's right to an open future. Parents must foster and leave the child with a range of opportunities for choice of his or her own plan of life, with the abilities and skills necessary to pursue a reasonable range of those opportunities and alternatives, and with the capacities for practical reasoning and judgment that enable the individual to engage in reasoned and critical deliberation about those choices.

Difficult and controversial judgments are involved in distinguishing when parents, in living out their own conception of a good life, also unduly impose that life on their child and excessively close down his or her abilities and opportunities to choose a life. It will often be difficult to know what effects parents are having on their child, and it will be morally controversial how much influence on their child is too much and too constricting. But the general point is that no neutrality is expected in their influence and effects on their children like that expected of the state in a liberal democracy in the genetic or other interventions the state might encourage or require for children.

There is another perspective from which to characterize the limits on parental pursuit of the best for their children. In a recent work, Rawls (1993) describes what he calls "reasonable pluralism." Let us characterize as "reasonable" people who are concerned to live with others on fair terms, assuming the others are so willing. Such people understand that to be fair, the terms of cooperation must be ones that other free and equal persons can accept (Rawls 1993, pp. 48–54; Cohen 1994, p. 1537). Reasonable people, despite their deep commitments to their own comprehensive moral views and conceptions of the good life, must incorporate within their views a view of others who reasonably disagree about such matters (Daniels 1996, Ch. 8).

If reasonable people want their children to be able to live on terms of fair cooperation with others, and we are supposing they do, then they must aim to create in their children the intellectual and emotional capacity to respect as reasonable people those with other reasonable comprehensive views. Inculcating those capacities in their own children, however, requires viewing them as free and equal as well. The suggestion, which we shall not pursue further, is that this view of their own children requires preserving for them much of what the right to an open future requires.

Finally, sometimes it is assumed that decisions about what genetic enhancements would be permitted would be left to scientific experts in basic and applied genetics. Scientific experts certainly have an important role to play in any such decisions – they should be in the best position to inform others of the expected consequences of any genetic interventions under consideration, together with the risks and uncertainty those interventions carry. But their expertise does not extend beyond this to the value judgments necessary to weigh potential benefits against potential risks. Indeed, inevitable professional biases would make them unsuited to be the sole decision makers about these interventions.

Pluralism and Liberalism

So far our discussion has contrasted parental pursuit of "the best" with pursuit of "the best" through the coercive and persuasive powers of the state in the eugenics movement. Our analysis has lent some weight to the view that parents should be free to pursue the best, even through genetic means, by contrasting it with the evil of statist imposition of reproductive goals. However, this picture is too simple.

Individuals do not just contrast themselves with the state and pursue individual goals. They form themselves into associations united by comprehensive moral, political, and religious views about the good life, and these shared views produce communitarian goals. Hence, the standard challenge to liberalism is to respect not just individual autonomy, but the form this autonomy takes when it is expressed through group associations or communities of this sort. The challenge is to articulate a fair basis for social cooperation in the context of an unavoidable pluralism regarding views about the good life.

We currently think of such communities as linked by their shared beliefs and practices. In the presence of a "genetic marketplace," however, communities could try to forge links that rest on more than beliefs or practices. They might try to shape their offspring genetically in ways that facilitate pursuit of their ideals for a good life. (See the Genetic Communitarianism scenario in Chapter 1.) To put this point simply, if fancifully, if their ideals are Spartan, they would pursue particular genetic traits in their offspring that would be of lower priority among Athenians. If they were Christian fundamentalists, they might pursue traits that promote agape or love, but if they were survivalists, they might seek traits that supported fierce independence or even aggression and ruthlessness. The shaping here is not the creation of human nature in their own ideal image but a redistribution of the diverse traits that comprise our varied natures. (We are supposing as well that this fanciful – probably science fiction – scenario could be fleshed out so that it does not involve the erroneous beliefs involved in genetic determinism; see Appendix 1.)

Where we might have thought a genetic marketplace would banish the sorts of concerns about state-based eugenics, we now see a new cause for concern. The effect of old-style eugenic pursuits might be achieved without the coercive role of the state. Indeed, our whole focus in this chapter has been on individual and, now, community efforts to improve offspring, because we wanted to avoid rehearsing the obvious problems of social control involved in national or international eugenic efforts. Defending individual reproductive rights and the autonomy to pursue the best for our children could create the opportunity for some communities, using the strong pressure of group inclusion and exclusion, to shape pursuit of the best, setting the stage for outcomes that are disturbing in many of the ways that state-endorsed eugenics had been.

One troubling outcome of communitarian eugenics, as it might be called, is that it could undermine the possibility of social cooperation among communities within a liberal state in a way that traditional pluralism does not. By altering phenotype through genetic means or through somatic interventions that use genetic knowledge, offspring might be locked into suitability for a particular community in a way that shared beliefs and values do not trap them.

Beliefs and values can be revised. Indeed, one reason members of different communities have for supporting a liberal view of individual liberties is that each can imagine changing those beliefs and values and requiring the liberty to do so, even though each person is as committed as possible to the conception of a good life they have at the moment. If someone has been made more competitive or aggressive "by nature" through parental use of the genetic marketplace, however, it may be more difficult to imagine being in a community bound by love of neighbor and turning the other cheek. Even if an individual is no more locked in by the effects of a parental choice than he or she would have been by unmodified nature, most of us might feel differently about accepting the results of a natural lottery versus the imposed values of our parents. The force of feeling locked in may well be different.

The threat to the political fabric of a liberal society comes from the communities coming to believe that they no longer share a common human nature. Recall that in Chapter 3 we considered the possibility that deliberately produced genetic divergences among groups of humans might undermine the sense of common humanity upon which moral respect is based. Here we consider a related but different possibility: Genetic communitarianism might result in different communities coming to view their differences as no longer the result merely of commitment and persuasion, but of their different "natures," with the result that these differences come to be regarded as irreconcilable. Under these conditions any suggestion of compromise with the values of another community might be regarded as literally a threat to the identity and hence the survival of one's group. Consequently, members of one community might find it harder to see the value of the ways of others, and might reasonably fear that others would find it harder if not impossible to appreciate theirs.

Support for toleration might erode as people no longer believed that we are all "reasonable people" who have come, for complex reasons having to do with the limits of human judgment and facts of history, to believe different things. Even if this perception that a group has come to have a different nature would be no more powerful than many of the cultural factors for group differentiation and identity that now exist, it might still be significant and its results might be quite pernicious.

The threat of locking-in is thus not just a threat to the individual and his or her rights to an open future. It is a threat to the basis for political cooperation in a liberal society that involves a respect for individual liberties and toleration for those who are different. The threat is that people will come to think of themselves as different in ways even more fundamental than they do today.

This threat puts considerable weight – perhaps more than it can bear – on the appeal made earlier to an individual right to an open future. We suggested that right might better be respected if the modifications we seek for our children involve "all-purpose" means – traits that are of value regardless of our conception of a good life. But the boundary between all-purpose means and more specific traits is not always clear or easy to draw. And insisting on it puts us at odds with the autonomy that individuals and communities want to assert. We are left with considerable vagueness in our answer to the question, When can we interfere with presumed parental rights to pursue the best for their children?

Virtues and the "Best"

Some of the ways in which parents want their children to be "the best they can be" involve what are traditionally called virtues. Parents may want their children to possess certain "prudential" virtues: to be temperate or moderate in emotions and appetites, self-controlled, judicious, resourceful, persevering, determined, far-sighted, affable, and reflective. They may want them to possess certain moral virtues as well: to have courage – especially moral courage – and to be fair, benevolent, kind, and forgiving.

Early eugenicists thought that one of their central goals was the production of morally better and socially more efficient societies: They looked to genetics to improve the distribution of virtues in a society. Less desirable traits – like lack of self-control, inability to plan ahead and delay gratification, intemperance, and imprudence – were believed more prevalent among lower classes and nonwhite races. More desirable traits – self-discipline, foresight, creativity, resourcefulness – were thought more prevalent among the ruling classes and races.

The appeal of the Social Darwinists and of the eugenics movement more generally was to the idea of building superior societies – where virtues were more directly selected for. In its current reincarnation, eugenic thinking – bemoaning the low reproduction rates of the upper classes and the high rates of the lower, for example – concentrates on what might appear to be somewhat simpler traits, such as IQ, that are used to explain differential success of different groups. Still, the considerable interest in the sociobiological and ethics literature on the evolution of altruism indicates a continuing belief that moral virtues or character traits have genetic origins.

We limit our discussion here to deepening and drawing the implications of one point advanced in Chapter 3. Most virtues of interest to us because they make people "better," whether prudential or moral virtues, are exceedingly complex traits. They are contextually highly sensitive and specific, they require considerable perception and discrimination for their exercise, and their exercise often requires balancing their appeal with other virtues. Many underlying capabilities or dispositions that might enhance virtues, such as sensitivity to the feel-

ings of others, intelligence, ability to modulate emotional response –
all capabilities that we might think have some significant genetic basis
– can just as easily be put into the service of vice as well as virtue.

Consider Cynthia, for example. Cynthia has great intuition about
the feelings of others. She can read their emotions well, she knows
how to feel their pain and anxiety. Indeed, people find her empathetic:
They see that she resonates with their pain. At the same time, she does
not lapse into pity, and she is not incapacitated by her emotions. She
keeps a level head. She puts people at ease, and is able to say the right
things to them. Without being condescending or pandering, which
would put people off if they too were perceptive, she judiciously exhibits her responsiveness.

Cynthia is blessed in other ways: She is extremely good at planning
a detailed but flexible course of action. She is willing to make sacrifices, even painful ones, in the short term to improve her situation or
that of others she is advising in the long run. She knows how others
will respond to the steps she takes and how to anticipate their reactions. Like a good chess player, she thinks her way through several
courses of action, but she does not seem calculating or cunning to
others so much as careful and thoughtful. She does not seem calculating because she seems responsive to the wishes of others in her planning: She builds on their intentions and encourages their desires to do
well for themselves. She incorporates their desires and goals into her
own planning.

Cynthia exhibits many of the dispositions and traits that would
make her an excellent social worker. She might even win an award for
excellence: Virtuous Social Worker of the Year. Alas, Cynthia is a very
successful con artist, not a social worker: She sells phoney real estate
to unsuspecting retirees. Or at least she was successful until she met
an equally successful former con artist who ran a sting operation for
the FBI. She clearly lacks the direct concern for the well-being of others
that would make her many capabilities serve as components of a moral
virtue.

The moral of Cynthia's story is that we should be leery of any
genetic (or environmental) intervention that enhances a trait or disposition that is merely a necessary condition for having a virtue that
would result in morally better offspring. If we could genetically enhance the various capabilities that contribute to Cynthia's arsenal, it
does not follow that she will be morally virtuous. These are component capabilities, the mechanical underpinnings as it were, not the

virtue itself. Similarly, if her parents had read literature to her in order to make her grasp better the sensitivities of others, the capacity that results may not be moral empathy but the ability to manipulate. We do not intend to make moral virtue mysterious with these remarks, but neither do we want it viewed in a simplistic, reductionist way.

CONSTRAINTS ON PERMISSIONS ALLOWED PARENTS

Thus far in this chapter we have considered the following argument: Parents are given wide leeway to produce the best offspring they can through various environmental interventions. Many of these environmental interventions result in phenotypic changes – for example, in height, strength, resistance to disease, and cognitive and emotional capabilities. Although there may be social agreement on which changes are "best" in some cases (such as improved health), on many others there is no societal consensus, and the "best" is judged from the perspective of different and sometimes incommensurable views of the good life. We respect pluralism and autonomy by allowing parents considerable permission to pursue the "best" as they see it, although a child's right to an open future implies some restrictions on both environmental and genetic pursuits. And last, where genetic interventions facilitate pursuit of these goals without imposing unacceptable harms or risks, and where a child's right to an open future is respected, there should be no objection to parents using genetic interventions to produce the best offspring they can.

This argument leaves open just when parents pursuing the best for their children may involve imposing unacceptable harms or risks on others, and thus when we may have grounds for restricting the liberty allowed them. In this section we address this issue of risk, thus completing the discussion begun in Chapter 4, in our examination of the widely held view that enhancements are somehow more problematic than treatments. We postponed until now a more detailed discussion of when permissions to pursue enhancements might be restricted.

Now we will explore the following claims, each of which, if true, would provide reasons for restricting parents' freedom to pursue genetic enhancement for their children: that seeking competitive advantage through enhancements will, in important cases, be collectively self-defeating and thus harmful or wasteful for everyone; that allowing a market to determine who may pursue competitive advantage will be unfair to those who lack means; and that the pursuit of the best – with the exception of eliminating or preventing disease or disability – will generally involve unfavorable ratios of risks to benefits. We set aside until Chapter 7 a related claim that bears less on enhancements than on the treatment or prevention of disabilities – namely, that restrictions are also in order here because these actions impose harms on people with disabilities.

Enhancements, Coordination Problems, and Harms to Others

In Chapter 4, it was argued that the distinction between treatment and enhancement does not coincide with either of two morally important distinctions. It does not map precisely onto the boundary between interventions we are obliged to help others receive and those for which we have no such obligations, nor does it match the boundary between permissible and impermissible interventions, as some commentators have proposed. At the same time, we suggested that there is good reason to think that many enhancements will pose serious problems not posed by treatments. For whole classes of cases, certain enhancements may be impermissible for reasons that are unlikely to arise for treatments or for reasons that can be more easily dealt with in the case of treatments. Knowing that something is an enhancement thus should raise a moral warning flag. That warning must be examined more carefully now to see what restrictions, if any, it is justifiable to impose on parental pursuit of "the best."

Let us begin with a contrast that is evident in current rather than future practice. To avoid some sex-linked genetic diseases, current genetic counseling practice sometimes calls for screening for the sex of a fetus followed by selective abortion if the fetus is, say, male. This practice raises important moral issues, depending on the severity of the disease and its probability of transmission. Still, it is very unlikely to produce any significant shift in sex ratios, given the frequency of its use. There might be a slightly higher probability that more carriers of the condition will result (females in this case), but that consequence might seem quite predictable and acceptable in light of the alternative, which is more males with a devastating condition. In this example, the selection against males (or against females, in other examples) does not act on or signal acceptance of any general bias or attitude toward one gender or another. It sends no "message" reinforcing such a bias, although it may send a message to those with the disease or disability that is being prevented through these means.

In some parts of the world – India, for example – widespread ultrasound screening is practiced followed by selective abortion of female fetuses. In some cultures, the reason for the preference is that only males may preside at the funeral of a head of household or officiate in other religious rituals. In other cultures, the antifemale selection may be the result of economic considerations favoring male offspring, perhaps in the context of marriage and inheritance customs. In some areas of India and elsewhere, access to ultrasound technology has led to dramatic shifts from the normal 105:100 male to female ratio to ratios approaching 135:75. The problem is so serious that India has imposed legal restrictions on screening for sex selection (as have some other countries).

The reasons for sex selection will affect how people evaluate the consequences of gender imbalance. If the goal is to produce a male offspring to preside at a funeral, a religious (nonconsequentialist) requirement for some Hindus, then it still holds even if the social consequences of the shift impose considerable hardship on the many extra males. The action is thus not self-defeating in light of the reason for performing it. (Even in this case, however, this reason might be outweighed, in the eyes of those making the decision, if the costs to the family of having male offspring who cannot marry and reproduce are seen to outweigh the costs of violating or modifying a funeral custom.)

On the other hand, if the reasons for sex selection are the presumed economic advantages of having more male offspring, then the effect of many people making the same decision will defeat the very reason for the action. In fact, each family that selects for males may be at a disadvantage since it will be even more difficult for those extra males to gain the advantages of maleness that would have existed without sex selection. Whether the reasons are religious or economic, however, the effects are similar: The imbalance in sex ratios makes the situation worse for more families.

Society has good, if not conclusive, reason to restrict the liberties of individuals if the exercise of those liberties undermines a public good. In this case, the public good is the natural balance represented by the biologically determined sex ratio (not equality, but something approximating it). The balance creates a condition that is advantageous to each in the sense that it makes it more likely that each individual can successfully marry and reproduce. It is against the background of a normal sex ratio that the actions of individuals seeking to have more male children makes sense: They "free ride" on the cooperative behavior of others who refrain from disturbing the balance. If too many aim at sex selection, the public good is destroyed and all are worse off. This provides a rationale for limiting the liberty of those who might be inclined to act as free riders.

There are other reasons a society might act to restrict the liberty to select for sex. Where sex selection is achieved by selective abortion, the practice is viewed by some as a form of genocide – specifically, gendercide. But even if the practice did not involve killing female fetuses but only involved avoiding conceiving them, there would be other objections. The practice depends on and reinforces a systematic bias against women. That bias is indefensible on grounds of justice and works in various ways to produce injustice against women. Acting to take advantage of unjust arrangements, or acting in ways that reinforce them, is thus itself objectionable, and permission to pursue "the best" through this means is appropriately restricted. (In Chapter 7, we argue that decisions to avoid disabilities in offspring do not in the same way reinforce discriminatory practices or take advantage of them. Indeed, a policy designed to encourage prospective parents to avoid the birth of persons with serious disabilities might be implemented while still pursuing strong antidiscriminatory policies to support people with disabilities, without any inconsistency. In contrast, seeking more male offspring while at the same time opposing social practices that favor them would be self-defeating.)

One should not assume that all reasons parents have for gender selection can be criticized on these grounds. Some parents might have reasons for wanting a male or female child that do not depend on and reinforce a systematic bias against women. Parents having two or three children of the same sex may just want to have the different experience of raising a child of the opposite sex, for example.

It might be objected that gender selection for nontherapeutic reasons is not really a case of "enhancement." Those who do may see a male offspring as simply "better" than a female one – a better earner, a better ritual-performer – but that judgment does not make this a true case of enhancement since it is not an instance of improving a normal capability, as would be an intervention to improve immune capability or short-term memory. We do not want to argue this issue, for the real point of the example is that nontherapeutic medical interventions, whether they are true enhancements or only resemble enhancements, can have social effects that are very harmful, sometimes unforeseen, and sometimes self-defeating.

Consider how similar points can be made about a true case of enhancement. Suppose it becomes possible to use a germline or somatic intervention to increase the height of offspring by up to six inches, regardless of how tall they would have turned out to be without it. Presumably, parents of children who would have been quite short without it would have a strong reason for approving the intervention. So too would many parents of children who would have been of average height or even fairly tall without it. Some parents would want their children to have the option of playing basketball or of retaining whatever height advantage they might have had prior to widespread use of the new intervention. Let us further suppose that there are no clear medical risks – a supposition that is unlikely to be true. (This supposition is necessary because parents ought not to be allowed to make proxy decisions for children when the risk-benefit ratios are so adverse, a point we return to shortly.)

To the extent that extra height is desirable only because of the competitive advantage it brings with it, widespread use of the intervention is self-defeating. Perhaps some very short people for whom there is true inconvenience living in a world geared to taller people would gain temporary relief, but if the variance in height remains unchanged except that most people are six inches taller, then markets will end up discriminating against the shortest (and tallest) again. Competitive advantage of additional height in (some) sports or in social acceptance would not change from what it was before the intervention. The intervention is thus self-defeating for those whose reasons are strictly competitive.

Actually, the situation is worse than being simply self-defeating, since spread of the technology would create great pressures for people to use the intervention even if they originally saw no benefit of added height. Although they might have been content with their height earlier, they would not be content if they were made shorter than everyone else, or even much shorter (relatively) than they would otherwise have been. If there were slight risks to the intervention, contrary to our original hypothesis, then the pressures to use the intervention become more insidious. People would then feel pressured to take risks, even slight ones, that they would not have had to face before.

There may be a model for this situation in the current hype surrounding mood altering drugs such as Prozac. The (slight) risks – including those of unintended personality transformation – may be worth taking if there is significant depression. But if people in large numbers use such drugs to enhance their personalities, then others may feel pressured to follow suit, fearing that they will be missing out on the advantages that drug users obtain. They will then be pressured to take risks they would not otherwise have considered taking.

Even if there are no risks in height enhancement, however, there are costs. There are the costs of the intervention itself, which might be considerable. There may be other costs as well, such as the expense of redesigning houses, cars, and so on if the population rapidly became much taller. So what seemed advantageous, given the individual cost, on the assumption that few others would do it, becomes collectively self-defeating in several ways. The same point might be made about many other traits that offer "positional advantage." Perhaps "blonds have more fun," but not if everyone is blond; an "exquisite nose" may lose its charm if everyone on the block has one.

Some traits offer an improvement whether or not they provide competitive advantage, and this may mean that coordination problems of the type we have been describing may arise only for some types of enhancements that parents might seek. Someone might prefer a nose to be shaped a certain way whether or not many others are, if that is how the beautiful nose is supposed to appear. Enhanced immune capabilities are beneficial whether or not they offer competitive advantage. Certain cognitive capabilities might contribute to competitive advantage, but provide noncompetitive benefits as well. Slowing memory loss late in life, for example, appears desirable regardless of any competitive advantage it might offer. And increasing memory capabilities or powers of concentration might enable individuals to pursue activities of intrinsic worth to them regardless of whether there are any competitive advantages.

Even our sketchy discussion of this issue shows its complexity. Some "positional" traits that seem desirable largely because they confer competitive advantage will not be desirable for all to pursue. If we could simply demarcate which traits these were, we might argue that no one is worse off if we simply restrict efforts to the "best" in these cases. But many traits that provide competitive advantage also have some instrumental and intrinsic value to people independently of those advantages. For traits valued in these more complex ways, their pursuit by everyone need not produce self-defeating coordination problems. For example, suppose everyone's intellectual performance could be enhanced in certain areas; no competitive advantage would result, but (arguably) society might be better off because of the enhanced abilities of all. Further, other traits may be valued even though they are not positional and confer no competitive advantage: they are just what some individuals view as the best.

These considerations suggest no grounds for blanket prohibitions that cut across all these categories, nor grounds for outright permissions regardless of coordination problems. The policy issue is how to draw reasonable constraints in those cases where the harms or costs are so great that some restrictions seem warranted.

Enhancements and Fairness

The coordination problems described earlier arise if everyone seeks to improve certain traits that confer competitive advantage. But if the technology for pursuing the best is not available to everyone, these coordination problems will not come up. Issues of fairness arise instead, however, especially for positional traits that confer competitive advantage. If only the wealthy could enhance the immune capabilities or the cognitive capabilities of their offspring through genetic interventions, many would consider this unfair. We must consider, then, objections to the pursuit of the best that rest on claims of unfairness.

In Chapter 3 we made the basic case for regulating access to genetic enhancements to prevent inequalities of opportunity. Here we pursue those issues in more detail, in the particular context of parental efforts to improve their children. We may begin by taking some cues from the analogous claims about unfairness that might arise if ability to pay determined access to medical treatments.

First notice an interesting contrast between pursuit of the best through treatments and enhancements. The kinds of self-defeating effects we observed for cases in which everyone pursues a trait that confers competitive advantage are not present for treatments. If everyone pursues elimination of departures from normal functioning, the outcome is not self-defeating. (We ignore the very special case of antibiotics losing effectiveness after widespread use or overuse.) The limited goal of health care, in the view discussed in Chapter 4, is to maintain normal functioning. There is a fairly broad consensus that it is important to restore to the status of "normal competitors" those whose opportunities are diminished by disease and disability. Consequently, the healthy do not – or at least should not – feel a sense of loss when their competitive advantages over the sick or disabled are thereby lost.

Issues of fairness are raised, however, when not everyone can pursue normal functioning. If the poor could not eliminate the competitive disadvantage produced by disease or disability but others could, that would be considered unfair. Similarly, if there is a treatment that only the wealthy can afford and resource limits prevent us from providing it to everyone else, then many feel it is unfair for the wealthy to have the treatment. Some want to prohibit the treatment if not all can get it (Gutmann 1981); others are willing to accept it as regrettable but not something to which we can prohibit access (Daniels 1985, 1993). These issues of fairness arise in similar ways for some enhancements, and not just treatments. Thus, if only the well-off could improve their competitive advantage through genetic enhancements, that too will seem to many unfair (recall the Genetic Enhancement Certificate scenario in Chapter 1).

Three key factors affect these judgments about the unfairness of differential access to either treatments or enhancements. First, if we believe that the socioeconomic inequalities that exist in a social arrangement are themselves unfair and unjust, perhaps the result of classist, racist, and sexist practices, then ramifying or compounding those inequalities with further advantages resulting from treatment or enhancement will seem particularly unfair. Many people think that many of the inequalities we experience in our society are not fair or just. The richest groups enjoy income and wealth many thousand times greater than the poorest groups. With the income and wealth come vast inequalities in political influence and power. The gulf we see is clearly influenced by a history of racist and sexist practices. Over the last two decades in the United States, income and wealth inequalities have been increasing, not decreasing.

Those who object to these inequalities as unjust would have grave objections to the use of genetic techniques that further increase the ability of those who are best off to transmit advantages to their offspring. Of course, others might reply that our society already allows the best off to pursue the best in many other ways: Why single out genetic interventions for special restrictions? Presumably, if it is wrong to ramify one injustice by adding another, genetically produced one on top of it, and the need to avoid this wrong warrants restrictions, then comparable restrictions may be warranted in other, nongenetic cases as well.

If the inequalities in society are just, however, then the additional resources available to the best-off groups are theirs to use as they see appropriate: There are no further claims of others on those resources or the inequalities would not yet be just. So individuals could then use their resources to improve the quality of their lives, to pursue the best as they see it.

The second key factor is the structure of the inequality in access to benefits. A health care system that rations beneficial services to the poorest 25 percent of the population but makes those services available to everyone else seems easier to criticize on grounds of fairness than one whose rationing applies to the bottom 75 or 90 percent of the population and permits extra advantages only to the best-off groups (Daniels 1991). The point is that the poor in the former can reasonably complain that they are being left behind in important ways by most of the rest of society, whereas no minority can feel that way in the latter system. In the latter, but not the former, it is more likely that the worst-off groups are as well off as they can be.[1]

Third, the significance or degree of the benefit or advantage matters crucially. If a treatment has only modest effect on restoring normal functioning, it is less objectionable if it is available to the best-off groups but not to most others than if it has a major effect on health outcomes. If the competitive advantage an enhancement provides is marginal, people will object less to it being available on a market basis only to those who can afford it. If the advantage is decisive or distinctive and highly visible, however, people may object much more strenuously on grounds of fairness.

To see how these factors affect how one should think about fairness, let us explore further the analogy between pursuing the best through genetic interventions and doing so by providing the best education we can afford for our children. In our society, for example, there is a significant private sector for secondary and higher education. Many of the very best high schools and universities are private. It is well known that an education at an elite private high school improves

[1] We are not claiming that the structure of inequality is the sole basis on which to judge the fairness of different cooperative schemes, only that it is a relevant basis. A feudal system that gave special rights, privileges, and wealth to the upper 10 percent of the population but treated all below that level the same way is not, therefore, as fair or just as the British National Health Service, which also has the top 10 percent of the population buying better service, while the remaining 90 percent are treated similarly. The structure of inequality nevertheless is relevant to distinguishing between the British and Oregon systems of rationing health care (for we can then assume rough equality between the populations with regard to the distribution of other important liberties and even with regard to overall wealth of the two systems).

the chances of admission to an elite university. Similarly, admission to an elite university improves the chances for admission to superior professional schools. The "networking" advantages of these superior schools is also a way that initial social, political, and business advantages are maintained.

It is also well understood that alumni and families capable of making substantial charitable contributions to private institutions at all these levels may have some extra leverage in seeking favorable consideration for their offspring: "Legacies" carry weight in admissions offices. Thus inequalities in wealth and income work through an educational market to compound advantages. At the other end of the spectrum, the chances of children from the poorest inner-city ghetto schools finding their way into elite colleges and universities are very small. Inequalities in public school education thus work to compound advantages and disadvantages as well.

Reactions to this situation in the educational system reflect beliefs about all three factors mentioned in connection with differential access to treatments or enhancements. If we are greatly troubled that existing economic inequalities (in the United States) are unjust, we will think the way they work to secure educational advantage is unjust. If we think the public school system is largely adequate, believing that no significant minority is left behind by it and that exceptional educational advantages accrue only to those at the very top, we may find the problem less serious. We might then be satisfied with efforts to add a meritocratic component to private schools through special scholarships for the needy.

If, however, we think the public schools effectively eliminate prospects for higher education for millions of Americans, then we will be much more troubled by the resulting structure of inequality. Finally, if we think that success in life is only marginally advanced by educational advantages, then we might be less concerned by the educational privileges the wealthy maintain for themselves. We might, for example, think that many other factors swamp in importance the advantages gained through an elite secondary school or college. Then we would be less troubled by the workings of the market for educational advantage.

Our reaction to market inequalities in access to genetic interventions that pursue the best will likewise depend on the judgments we are prepared to defend about these same three factors. To the extent that existing inequalities in income and wealth are seriously unjust, this weighs against marketing the means to further advantages. To the extent that access to advantages is denied only to the worst-off groups, rather than available only to the best off, this too weighs against marketing these methods of pursuing the best. And to the extent that the advantages are truly significant, in the sense that they confer increased opportunities on those who already have them and to the extent that most people can agree they are significant, this weighs against a system that makes them available only to those who are best off.

Uncertainty and the Risks of Pursuing the Best

Although we have examined several important reasons for constraints on parental efforts to pursue the best offspring through genetic enhancement, we have set aside until now the main argument in the literature against some forms of genetic intervention. The argument starts, quite reasonably, by pointing out the enormous uncertainties and risks that would face attempts at genetic enhancements, whether somatic or germline, but especially the latter. The claim is then made that there are ethical objections to the types of experiments on humans that might reduce some of this uncertainty.

As we saw in Chapter 4, some infer that it may be acceptable to pursue either somatic or germline efforts to prevent or cure certain diseases, where risk/benefit ratios might prove acceptable, but that genetic enhancements should not be attempted because risk/benefit ratios would always prove unfavorable (Anderson 1990; see also Anderson 1980, 1985, 1989). Others argue that the risk/benefit ratios involved in all germline interventions are too high, and therefore only somatic treatments for genetic disease would be permissible (Council for Responsible Genetics 1993). Both of these arguments attempt to establish a moral boundary between negative and positive uses of genetic engineering, a topic discussed in Chapter 4, to which we return now, this time in the context of parents pursuing the best for their children by genetic means.

Let us consider in more detail the reasons for concerns about the risks of genetic interventions. First, scientists currently lack the ability to deliver a gene to its proper site within a chromosome or to remove a defective gene whose function it is to replace. Instead of precisely repairing the genetic machinery of somatic cells, they simply send the proper gene into the host on a crude vector that deposits it at some location or other, hoping it will function to supply the relevant proteins not produced by the defective gene, which remains where it is.

Without a precise vector or vehicle, however, genetic interventions leave room for many unintended genetic effects with unknown risks (Walters 1991). An analogy might be soldering a circuit board to correct for some defective circuits. If one simply delivered new solder at random, one might make things worse, not better. Such an approach is not only unlikely to produce the desired result, but is likely to produce other problems by destroying even more circuits. Still, germline modification has proved technically easier than might have been predicted, in part because germline cells can take up artificially introduced DNA more readily than more highly differentiated somatic cells (Council 1993, p. 670) can. The modification so far, however, does not solve the problem of the crudeness of vectors.

Second, the crudeness of current technology matters less in somatic interventions than it would in germline interventions. Errors made in somatic interventions do their damage only in the individual being treated. We cut our losses with the affected individual. It would be unconscionable, however, to use such crude vectors in germline interventions, where misplacement of genes can do serious damage that could be disseminated more widely to further generations. For example, as the Council for Responsible Genetics notes, "Introduction of a foreign gene (even if there is a copy of one already present) into an inappropriate location in any embryo's chromosomes can have unexpected consequences . . . the offspring of a mouse that received an extra copy of the normally present *myc* gene developed cancer at 40 times the rate of the unmodified strain of mice" (Council 1993, p. 670 citing Leder et al. 1986).

Third, current capabilities focus on corrections of catastrophic defects caused by malfunctions in single genes. In such cases, the risks of nonintervention are enormous and certain: the disease is manifest and often life-threatening or severely debilitating. Accordingly, the risks of intervention, however large and uncertain, may seem worth taking after a careful risk/benefit assessment. Enhancements, however, are an attempt to improve on what is already functioning normally, if suboptimally. The worst-case scenario for nonintervention is no improvement on the suboptimal but normal functioning. In contrast, the uncertainties and risks of intervention may be very great. That is why Anderson and others have concluded that sound risk/benefit assessment would lead us to avoid all enhancements.

Fourth, interventions to correct for defects in single genes, however complicated and uncertain, are far simpler than what would be involved in multigene or multifactorial cases. Yet most diseases that are influenced by genetic factors are likely to involve the functioning of many genes. Similarly, most functions one might want to enhance will also be causally influenced by many genes. The uncertainties thus grow geometrically for these cases.

The problem does not derive simply from the likelihood of technical error, but also from the inability of biologists "to predict how genes or their products interact with one another and with the organism's environment to give rise to biological traits. It would have been impossible to predict, *a priori*, for example, that someone who has even *one* copy of the gene for a blood protein known as hemoglobin-S would be protected against malaria, whereas a person who has *two* copies of this gene would have sickle cell disease" (Council 1993, p. 670). This source of uncertainty must be added to the reasons already given for thinking germline interventions are riskier than somatic interventions and for thinking that enhancements generally will have worse risk/benefit ratios than treatments of disease.

Fifth, special uncertainties surround the ability to integrate improvements in a component function so that overall functioning actually improves as well, rather than being harmed. For example, suppose it becomes possible to boost a particular component of memory, say short term memory, and the goal is to improve some more comprehensive level of functioning, such as language learning or mathematical abilities. It would be necessary to know that improvement in this particular component of memory will actually be integrated properly into overall functioning by higher-level or coordinating functions. Otherwise, we might simply create interference with the overall function – the distraction of inescapably intrusive memory, for example, perhaps modeling the capabilities of some "idiot savants" suffering from autism. The analogy here is to upgrading memory on a computer: One cannot simply add more memory chips unless there is appropriate hardware and software to integrate the additional capacity. This sort of uncertainty arises even where we have good information about the kinds of interactions genes and gene products have with environment, and even where, using that information, we have evidence we can improve some particular function.

Sixth, the only way to eliminate some of the sources of uncertainty about risks would be through human experimentation, but some of the kinds of experiments we would need to perform may not be performed for ethical reasons. Even if, for example, some seriously ill adults were allowed to consent to risky experimentation on somatic interventions, there would be special problems with germline interventions, since consent cannot be obtained from future offspring who might be affected, nor from the embryos upon whom the intervention would be performed.

Many of these concerns about risks are serious and have important policy implications. It does not follow, however, that there should be permanent prohibitions on germline interventions or enhancements. Let us consider more carefully what conclusions should be drawn from the six concerns about risks.

It is certainly true that a proper vehicle for precise genetic repair is currently lacking, and it is also true that this problem poses greater risks for germline therapies. What follows from this current limit on our capabilities is the need for very careful scrutiny of any protocols for experiments involving these interventions, which in fact is current practice. Is this a short- or long-term problem? At present, no one can make well-grounded predictions about how long this technical problem will persist.

If one went back a century and surveyed predictions made by scientists in different fields about technological changes that have actually occurred in our time, one would place little confidence in the ability of contemporary geneticists and microbiologists to predict where their fields will be a century from now. Some are true believers and the source of great hype about astonishing progress. Others, concerned to remain staid and cautious scientists, want to discuss only what seems to be a very modest extension of current technology. But we cannot place much weight on predictions that particular technical problems will be intractable, and so taking a long-term view of the prospects of genetic intervention seems a reasonable flirtation with the future, provided it does not undermine the extreme caution that should be exercised in the short run.

Even with significant breakthroughs in the ability to make precise substitutions in DNA, it will still be true that germline interventions pose important risks that somatic interventions do not. But that implies only that we should proceed very cautiously with these interventions, scrutinizing carefully each protocol. It does not mean that the possible transmission of harm to future offspring through germline interventions makes such interventions never worthwhile.

The argument that risk/benefit ratios are generally more problematic for enhancements than for treatments of disease has some plausibility. Still, the strong conclusion drawn by some that no enhancements would be justifiable does not follow. There is likely to be considerable agreement among persons about the seriousness of certain diseases and the value of avoiding their effects. To the extent that disease impairs opportunities for individuals, there may even be a clear basis for thinking that we are obliged to assist in restoring functioning where we can. There is likely to be more disagreement about the value of many enhancements, for reasons already indicated. Different individuals, judging from the perspective of different conceptions of a good life, may value enhancements quite differently. (The same can be said for the effects of some diseases or disabilities.) But if individuals – or groups of individuals – value some enhancement very highly, they may well be willing to take significant risks to produce it in themselves and even in their children.

A parent who detects musical or athletic potential in a child may begin to push that child into a rigorous course of training that dramatically shapes a child's life all the way through adolescence and beyond. This is a serious gamble: Will the talent be there and will it be developed adequately to pay off the sacrifices made? If not, there may be great frustration and a sense of great loss at the forgone opportunities and the narrowed prospects for success. Being free to take such gambles, however, is a highly valued liberty, and a society restricts it only at great cost and with great reason. A medical perspective on the risk/benefit assessment of a potential enhancement may vary widely from a parental assessment, even assuming full knowledge of risks and uncertainty.

The difference between treatment and enhancement does warrant very careful examination of any experimental protocols for enhancements, and greater caution may be merited here than in the case of potential treatments. It might also be wise to insist on a research priority – and funding priority – for treatment of disease. But we do not think what follows is a long-term prohibition on enhancements or research leading up to them. It may be possible to produce great benefit for individuals and even for society as a whole through some kinds of enhancement, as our earlier discussion suggests.

Some enhancements may come to be regarded as things society is obliged to make available to everyone, just as some treatments are. To assimilate the value of all enhancements to the level of the value of purely cosmetic surgery is unfair to the potential of enhancements. And our society does permit people to take the risks of cosmetic surgery, albeit at their own expense.

The fifth concern, that enhancements are likely to be multifactorial and quite complex, is no doubt true. But this is also true for many treatments. As we acquire knowledge appropriate to intervening in the case of diseases that are multifactorial, then we will be in a better position to consider some enhancing interventions as well. Again, extreme caution in experimentation is the only plausible policy recommendation. This caution should make us more skeptical of enhancment protocols than of treatment protocols, and of multifactorial interventions as opposed to single-gene interventions, but what counts as appropriate caution is a function of knowledge at the time of the decision, not knowledge we now have.

Finally, what about the serious worries about consent to experimentation when the risks will fall on those not making the decisions? In the case of treating diseases through genetic interventions, it might be preferable to get consent from the affected person where possible by waiting to attempt a somatic intervention rather than attempting a germline intervention. However, this strategy cannot cover an important range of cases. Many somatic interventions would be too late to prevent some manifestation of the effects of the condition, and in general it would be better to prevent the problem than to treat it. So it will often be necessary to weigh the greater benefits of a germline intervention against the possibly greater harms, including those in later generations. Without examining particular cases and protocols, it would be unwise to make a blanket prohibition against germline interventions because of uncertainties in subsequent generations (cf. Kitcher 1995 for a similar conclusion).

Cloning

A particular technique of genetic manipulation that has received a great deal of recent attention is cloning. Following Ian Wilmut's announcement of the cloning of an adult sheep in early 1997, the possibility of human cloning no longer seems merely science fiction. In the process of cloning by nuclear transfer, the nucleus from the cell of an adult mammal is inserted into an ennucleated ovum (an egg from which the nucleus has been removed) and the resulting embryo develops following the complete genetic code of the mammal from which the inserted nucleus was obtained. Public and professional responses to the prospect of human cloning were often highly emotional and did not await a careful assessment of the reasons for and against the practice. We cannot undertake that full assessment here but will touch on a few issues that are related to our earlier discussion in this and the preceding chapter.

Some critics of cloning have argued that it would rob an individual of a sense of freedom or spontaneity in creating a unique life for him or herself and thereby violate what we earlier called, following Feinberg, a right to an open future (Jonas 1974; Feinberg 1980). Jonas argued that human cloning in which there is a substantial time gap between the beginning of the lives of the earlier and later twin is fundamentally different from the simultaneous beginning of homozygous twins that occur in nature. Although contemporaneous twins begin their lives with the same genetic inheritance, they also begin their lives or biographies at the same time, and so in ignorance of what the other who shares the same genome will by his or her choices make of his or her life. To whatever extent one's genome determines one's future, each begins ignorant of what that determination will be and so remains as free to construct a particular future from among open alternatives, as are individuals who do not have a twin.

A later twin created by human cloning, Jonas argues, knows, or at least believes he or she knows, too much about him or herself. For there is already in the world another person, one's earlier twin, who from the same genetic starting point has made the life choices that are still in the later twin's future. It will seem that one's life has already been lived and played out by another, that one's fate is already determined, and so the later twin will lose the spontaneity of authentically creating and becoming his or her own self, of freely creating one's own future. It is tyrannical, Jonas claims, for the earlier twin to try to determine another's fate in this way.

One difficulty with this argument is its apparent assumption of an indefensible genetic determinism according to which one's entire life course is fully determined by one's genetic inheritance. But that assumption is plainly false as we have frequently emphasized because it neglects not only the range of phenotypic expression of specific genes, but also the importance of environment and an individual's choice in constructing a unique life.

One might try to interpret Jonas's objection so as not to assume either genetic determinism or a belief in it. A later twin might grant that he is not determined to follow in his earlier twin's footsteps but that nevertheless the earlier twin's life would always haunt him, standing as an undue influence on his life and shaping it in ways to which others' lives are not vulnerable. But the force of the objection still seems to rest on a false assumption that having the same genome as his earlier twin unduly restricts his freedom to choose a different life from the one the earlier twin chose. A central difficulty in evaluating the implications for human cloning of a right either to ignorance or to an open future, is whether the right is violated merely because the later twin may be likely to *believe* that his or her future is already determined, even if that belief is clearly false and supported only by the crudest genetic determinism. It seems more plausible to say that if the twin's future in reality remains open and his to freely choose, that someone's acting in a way that unintentionally leads him to believe that his future is closed and determined has not violated his right to ignorance or to an open future. Likewise, suppose you drive down the twin's street in your new car that is just like his, knowing that when he sees you he is likely to believe that you have stolen his car and, therefore, to abandon his driving plans for the day. You have not violated his property right to his car even though he may feel the same loss of opportunity to drive that day as if you had in fact stolen his car. In each case he is mistaken that his open future or car has been taken from him, and so no right of his to them has been violated.

So, our argument in this chapter that genetic enhancements or interventions must respect the right to an open future does not provide a reason to oppose human cloning. This is not to say that there are not strong, even decisive, reasons to oppose attempts at the present time to clone humans based on the risks of the procedure. One version of this objection to human cloning concerns the research necessary to perfect the procedure, the other version concerns the later risks from its use. Wilmut's group had 276 failures before their success with Dolly, indicating that the procedure is far from perfected even with sheep. Further research on the procedure with animals is clearly necessary before it would be ethical to attempt to use the procedure on humans. But even assuming that cloning's safety and effectiveness are established with animals, research would need to be done to establish its safety and effectiveness for humans. Could this research be ethically done? There would be little or no risk to the donor of the cell nucleus to be transferred, and his or her informed consent could and must always be obtained. There might be greater risks for the woman to whom a cloned embryo is transferred, but these should be comparable to those associated with IVF (*in vitro* fertilization) procedures, and the woman's informed consent could and must be obtained.

What of the risks to the cloned embryo itself? Judging by the experience of Wilmut's group in their work on cloning a sheep, the principal risk to the embryos cloned was their failure successfully to implant, grow, and develop. Comparable risks to cloned human embryos would apparently be their death or destruction long before most people or the law consider them to be persons with moral or legal protections of their lives. Moreover, artificial reproductive technologies now in use, such as IVF, have a known risk that some embryos will be destroyed or will not successfully implant and will die. It is premature to make confident assessment of what the risks to human subjects would be of establishing the safety and effectiveness of human cloning procedures, but there are no unavoidable risks apparent at this time that would make the necessary research clearly ethically impermissible.

Could human cloning procedures meet ethical standards of safety and efficacy? Risks to an ovum donor (if any), a nucleus donor, and a woman who receives the embryo for implantation would likely be ethically acceptable with the informed consent of the involved parties. But what of the risks to the human clone if the procedure in some way goes wrong or unanticipated harms come to the clone? For example, Harold Varmus, director of the National Institutes of Health, has raised the concern that a cell many years old from which a person is cloned could have accumulated genetic mutations during its years in another adult that could give the resulting clone a predisposition to cancer or other diseases of aging. Moreover, it is impossible to obtain the informed consent of the clone to his or her own creation, but of course no one else is able to give informed consent for his or her creation either.

We believe it is too soon to say whether unavoidable risks to the clone would make human cloning unethical. At a minimum, further research on cloning animals, as well as research to better define the potential risks to humans, is needed. But we should not insist on a standard that requires risks to be lower than those we accept in sexual reproduction, or in other forms of assisted reproduction. It is not possible now to know when, if ever, human cloning will satisfy an appropriate standard limiting risks to the clone.

If and when safety concerns are satisfied for human cloning, we will have to assess what benefits and harms might come from letting it take place. As best we can tell at this time, human cloning is not the unique answer to any great or pressing human need and its benefits would be at most limited. Nevertheless, there are a few circumstances in which individuals might have good reasons to want to use human cloning. First, it would allow women who have no ova or men who have no sperm to produce an offspring that is biologically related to them (Eisenberg 1976; Robertson 1994b and 1997). Second, it would enable couples in which one party risks transmitting a serious hereditary disease, a serious risk of disease, or an otherwise harmful condition to an offspring to reproduce without doing so (Robertson 1994b). Of course, by using donor sperm or egg donation, such hereditary risks can generally be avoided now without the use of human cloning. But those procedures may be unacceptable to some couples, or at least considered less desirable than human cloning because they introduce a third party's genes into their reproduction, instead of giving their offspring only the genes of one of them. Third, cloning a later twin would enable a person to obtain needed organs or tissues for trans-plantation (Robertson 1994b; Harris 1992), so long as it is done in a way compatible with respecting the rights of the donor clone.

Fourth, human cloning would enable individuals to clone someone who had a special meaning to them, such as a child who had died (Robertson 1994b). There is no denying that if human cloning were available, some individuals would want to use it for this specific pur-pose. However, that desire usually would be based on a deep confu-sion. Cloning such a child would not replace the child the parents had loved and lost, but rather would create a new different child with the same genes. The child they loved and lost was a unique individual who had been shaped by his or her environment and choices, not just his or her genes, and more importantly, who had experienced a partic-ular relationship with them. Nevertheless, if human cloning enabled some individuals to clone a person who had special meaning to them and doing so gave them deep satisfaction, that would be a benefit to them even if their reasons for wanting to do so and the satisfaction they in turn received were based on confusion.

In addition, human cloning and research on human cloning might make possible important advances in scientific knowledge, for exam-ple about human development (Walters 1982; Smith 1993). Each of these possible benefits needs much more careful assessment for its extent and probability, but at this time we believe human cloning does not seem to promise great benefits or uniquely to meet great human needs.

Typical feared harms from human cloning are even more speculative than its possible benefits. They include various possible psychological harms to a later twin, for example a diminished sense of one's own uniqueness and individuality (McCormick 1993; Verhey 1994). Even if such an effect, like the possible feeling of a loss of freedom and an open future discussed earlier, is grounded in a confused and false belief in genetic determinism, the psychological distress could nonetheless be real. Opponents of human cloning also fear social harms, such as lessening the worth of individuals or diminishing respect for human life. For example, human cloning might result in persons' worth or value seeming diminished because we would now see humans as able to be manufactured or "hand-made" and replaceable. This demystification of the creation of human life would reduce our appreciation and awe of it and of its natural creation. It would be a mistake, however, to conclude that a human being created by human cloning is of less value and less worthy of respect. Others fear that individuals using cloning to create children genetically identical to themselves represents a narcissistic attitude to parenting that could be harmful to the family.

Human cloning is a means of reproduction. Consequently, individuals' important interests in reproductive freedom, discussed in Chapter 6, do establish a moral presumption for permitting its use in some circumstances. In a few circumstances, human cloning could be the only or best means for individuals to pursue successfully their reproductive interests. It could be argued, however, that use of human cloning is not properly part of reproductive freedom because whereas current assisted reproductive technologies and practices are remedies for inabilities to reproduce sexually, human cloning is an entirely new means of reproduction; indeed, its critics see it as more a means of manufacturing humans than of reproduction. Human cloning is a means of reproduction different from sexual reproduction, but it is a means that can serve individuals' interest in reproducing. If its use is not properly part of reproductive freedom, that must be not because it is a new means of reproducing but because it has other objectionable moral features or harms.

Fortunately, concerns about safety are sufficient that human cloning should not go forward at this time, and so society has time for continued public and professional debate to clarify and evaluate people's concerns and objections to cloning, together with the reasons to permit it. Such a continuing debate will be especially important in arriving at informed and reasoned public policy on such a new and complex issue which generates in many people strong but often not well-articulated reactions.

CONCLUSION

In Chapter 4, we began to examine whether firm moral boundaries could be drawn among different categories of genetic interventions (including interventions using genetic knowledge). We argued that the distinction between treatment or prevention of disease and disability and enhancement of otherwise normal traits does not provide us with a clear moral boundary between what we are obliged to do for people and what may be merely morally permissible. There may be no obligation to provide such treatments, and some enhancements may be obligatory. We also argued, however, that the boundary between treatment and enhancement offers a plausible, publicly usable boundary for saying what society's primary obligations are in the delivery of health care. We also argued that certain moral warning flags should be heeded when we consider using genetic (or other medical) technologies to pursue the enhancement of otherwise normal traits.

In this chapter we have pursued the issue of enhancements in more detail, focusing on the scope and limits of parents' moral authority to pursue the best for their children. Our main goal was to show that a different moral boundary, between the permissible and impermissible, does not coincide with the boundary between treatments and enhancements, contrary to arguments some have made. To motivate our skepticism about calling genetically based or influenced enhancements impermissible, we examined the considerable liberty parents have to pursue the best for their children. Their pursuit seeks to influence phenotype in ways that confer competitive or other advantages on children. We found no reason to object in general to using genetic influences any more than environmental ones in the pursuit of such advantages. We did, however, find that some efforts to pursue advantage (whether genetic or environmentally influenced) may reasonably be restricted. In some cases, these are self-defeating and pose threats to public goods. In others, they raise objections of fairness. In still others, the risks involved in the pursuit may make them unacceptable.

Our discussion has "complexified" rather than simplified. Rather than finding the clear moral boundaries that some claim, we find quite blurred ones. Even where we raise objections to some efforts of parents to seek the best for children as they see it, the guidance we can give to limits on these efforts is limited to offering principles that are themselves plagued by unavoidable vagueness. Just what, for example, is meant by preserving an open future for children? Just which differences in benefits create unacceptable problems of fairness? Our defense for muddying the waters is that the moral world is often complex and defies simplified heuristics for drawing moral lines in the sand.

In Chapter 6 we consider in detail a quite different reason for constraining the use of genetic interventions, whether undertaken willingly by parents or required by social policies designed to prevent harm: the claim that the attempt to prevent genetic impairments devalues persons with disabilities.

SIX

———

REPRODUCTIVE FREEDOM AND THE
PREVENTION OF HARM

THE WIDER CONTEXT: CONFLICTS BETWEEN LIBERTY AND HARM PREVENTION

A common diagnosis of one of the major moral wrongs done by the old eugenics was its infringement of many individuals' reproductive freedom, most blatantly in widespread sterilization programs, more subtly in discouraging those thought to have "bad genes" from reproducing. Our ethical autopsy of the old eugenics in Chapter 2 confirmed this assessment. In our own era, reproductive freedom is again being challenged by new genetic knowledge and technologies. But if we are to respond properly to the challenges to reproductive freedom posed by the new genetics, we need a systematic analysis of the scope, limits, and content of reproductive freedom, as well as a clear view of the moral values that ground its importance. To provide this is one aim of this chapter.

New knowledge about the risk of genetic transmission of diseases and other harmful conditions will give individuals both the opportunity and the responsibility to choose whether to transmit such harms to their offspring or to risk doing so. The information of genetic risk could be used by individuals prior to conception to decide whether to conceive when risk is present, or after conception but before birth to decide whether to abort an affected fetus. New genetic knowledge may also allow genetic or other interventions *in vitro* or *in utero* to prevent the development of the harmful condition. As these new options become possible, individuals must decide whether to seek to prevent these harms to their offspring.

The choices they face will include what actions and interventions would be morally permissible to prevent the harms – for example, some individuals will decide abortion is not a morally permissible intervention – and what actions and interventions would be morally required to prevent harm. Some genetic interventions will be added to other behaviors, such as abstaining from excessive alcohol use or substance abuse during pregnancy, which many people now consider morally required in order to prevent harms to the fetus and the child it will become.

This new genetic knowledge will also create new societal choices about public policy on the use of this knowledge and the interventions it makes possible to prevent harm. Some people will conclude that society should observe a strict neutrality regarding use of this information – that is, that public policy should not require or encourage individuals to use genetic information in particular ways in their reproductive choices. This position extends to genetic interventions the current conventional view supporting value-neutral, nondirective genetic counseling.

Others, however, will conclude that public policy should abandon strict neutrality. There is a large range of possible social influences on the use of genetic information in reproduction that vary in the degree of pressure exerted on individuals' choices and in other morally significant respects. For example, public policy might be restricted to education and other means of encouraging individuals to take some actions to prevent genetically transmissible harms. Or it might intrude further into individuals' choices by using legal measures designed co ercively to require individuals to take some actions to prevent genetically transmissible harms.

In support of this last position, it could be emphasized that the fundamental aim of the coercive force of the criminal law is to prevent individuals from causing a variety of harms to other persons. The prevention of harms to others – as opposed to other uses of the law, such as to prevent offense, to prevent harms to oneself, or to enforce morality – is the least ethically controversial ground for the criminal law's coercive interference with individual liberty. In nongenetic contexts, coercive prenatal interventions to protect a fetus, such as forced cesarean sections, forced drug rehabilitation for pregnant women, and forced *in utero* surgery, as well as even involuntary sterilization of mentally retarded individuals to prevent them from conceiving, have received some public and professional attention and support, although all remain highly controversial. Each of these issues forces society to clarify the proper scope and limits of reproductive freedom.

In this chapter we focus on another challenge to the extent of reproductive freedom: the prevention of genetically transmitted harms. In some cases this will involve applying relatively familiar ethical principles and arguments to the genetic context; in others, it will lead us to less familiar and more philosophically perplexing problems that cannot be adequately addressed within the limits of standard moral principles and theories. Of course, at this time we can only speculate about the precise nature of the interventions to prevent genetically transmitted harms that will become possible in the future; a more complete analysis of concrete cases must await the details of those situations. In broad terms, we have characterized the concern of this chapter as the conflict between reproductive freedom and the prevention of harm, and so we begin by exploring the nature or scope of reproductive freedom and the ethical interests or values that ground its importance and support its protection.

WHAT IS REPRODUCTIVE FREEDOM?

Rights and Freedoms

We shall not attempt a full analysis of reproductive freedom, but shall concentrate on the aspects of it most relevant to the issues raised by interventions to prevent genetically transmitted harms that are possible now or may become possible in the future. John Robertson characterizes "procreative liberty," which we take here to be effectively equivalent to reproductive freedom, as "freedom in activities and choices related to procreation," but notes that "the term does not tell us what activities fall within its scope" (Robertson 1986). In order both to understand when reproductive freedom comes into conflict with other values such as the prevention of harm to others and to address which values or interests should prevail in those conflicts, we need a relatively full characterization of reproductive freedom.

It is common in discussions of these issues to speak from the outset of a right to reproductive freedom – a moral, not just legal, right. For the most part, we will not use the language of a moral right to reproductive freedom. Instead, we will speak of the scope of actions and practices that are properly understood to be a part of reproductive freedom. We will first describe the various components of reproductive freedom, leaving open both the moral value of these various components and when they may justifiably be limited or infringed. We shall then turn to the main reasons or grounds for the moral value or importance of reproductive freedom.

Some or all of our reasons or grounds for the moral importance of reproductive freedom have been used by others to support a moral right to reproductive freedom. We shall not pursue this moral right both in order to avoid the diversion of having to develop and defend a theory of moral rights, and because doing so is unnecessary. Having described the scope of reproductive freedom and defended the main moral grounds of its value or importance, we will be in a position to directly address when it can justifiably be limited or infringed in order to prevent genetically transmitted harms and hence what the broad contours of a legal right to reproductive freedom ought to look like. That is the central moral issue of concern in this chapter, and no side excursion into a theory of moral rights is needed to address it.

This is not to say, however, that we reject moral rights to reproductive freedom. Readers who prefer an approach to these issues in terms of a moral right to reproductive freedom can use our analysis of the scope and grounds of reproductive freedom as a basis for asserting that there is such a right and for understanding its nature. Here it is important to emphasize that assertions about moral rights are not beginning points in ethical analysis. Assertions about rights require support, and the only effective support, in our view, is to show how giving certain important interests and choices the special priority and protection that the concept of a right conveys serves those interests and choices. In the case at hand, it is the interests in reproductive freedom that are the key to making a case for a moral right to reproductive freedom and to articulating the content, scope, and limits of that right. Moreover, our analysis, like an alternative analysis in terms of a moral right to reproductive freedom, supports a legal right to reproductive freedom, but with greater clarity about the proper scope and moral grounds of that legal right than simple appeal to a moral right to reproductive freedom provides.

Positive and Negative Freedom

A common distinction in moral and political philosophy is between negative and positive freedom or liberty, although different theorists draw the distinction in different ways. As we shall understand it here, negative freedom exists when others do not act in particular ways that would restrict a person's freedom – for example, your freedom of speech requires that others not prevent your speaking on a particular occasion. Positive freedom or liberty can require others to act in ways necessary to enable a person to exercise the freedom or liberty – for example, a person's freedom of speech might require others to secure access to the media for the individual to exercise that freedom. Important freedoms referred to in moral and political discourse are typically complex combinations of both negative and positive components. Freedom of the person, for example, is typically understood to require both that others not assault the individual and that society use its police power to protect a person from assault.

Reproductive freedom also contains both negative and positive components – for instance, requiring that others, such as the state, not interfere with individuals' use of genetic information in reproductive decisions and requiring that important genetic information be made available to women who would otherwise not have access to it. Some theorists would not consider the failure to enable individuals to obtain relevant genetic information a limitation on reproductive freedom, but we so characterize it because of its effect in limiting individuals' pursuit of their important reproductive interests. Although negative components of reproductive freedom typically have a positive correlate, it does not always follow that if interfering with a negative component of reproductive freedom would be wrong, failure to do what is required by its positive correlate must be wrong as well. For instance, it may be morally wrong to interfere with a woman's use of some very expensive genetic intervention that she has secured with her own funds, but it would not be morally required, because of the great cost and limited benefit, to make that same genetic intervention available at public expense to anyone who wants it.

A particularly controversial moral issue about reproductive freedom is the scope and extent of the positive components that must be secured for persons – what actions, services, positive aid, and circumstances must others secure for individuals as part of their reproductive freedom, and who is required to do so. But it is the negative component – limiting the interference of others with reproductive choices – that is most important to our concerns in this chapter.

The remainder of this section contains, in brief summary form, the main components of reproductive freedom relevant to the issue of genetic interventions for the prevention of harm. We underline that what follows is a descriptive account of the scope of reproductive freedom – that is, what it consists of. We do not claim that it is never morally justified to interfere with or limit any of these aspects of reproductive freedom. Indeed, the central issue of this chapter is when the prevention of genetically transmitted harm morally justifies some limitation on or interference with reproductive freedom.

The Choice of Whether to Procreate, with Whom, and by What Means Reproductive freedom involves, first, uncoerced choice about whether to procreate at all, or, more precisely, whether to participate in procreative activity with a willing partner. There are activities and choices intended to lead to reproduction, and other activities and choices designed to prevent reproduction. Both are part of reproductive freedom. Reproductive freedom thus can include access to new reproductive techniques and to genetic information important to a choice about whether to reproduce, although that access might justifiably be limited because of the costs of some reproductive services or information.

The Choice of When to Procreate The advent of modern methods of contraception and procreation make the choice of when to reproduce an increasingly important component of reproductive freedom. Contraception provides control over when a person will not reproduce, while new reproductive techniques make it possible for women to reproduce at ages when it would have been either unlikely or impossible for them to do so in the past.

Control over the timing of reproduction is important – on the one hand, for example, to enable women to avoid pregnancy when they are too young to be able to or to want to assume the usual responsibilities of parenthood, and on the other hand, to enable women, and sometimes men as well, to work or pursue careers before they begin families. The age at which women reproduce also affects the degree of risk of passing on some genetically transmitted disabilities to their prospective children.

The general point is that the timing of reproduction within a person's life can have myriad, complex, and important impacts on that life, over which reproductive freedom can provide some control.

The Choice of How Many Children to Have Reproductive freedom includes control over the decision about how many children to have. This aspect of reproductive freedom has been an important feature of recent debates about human cloning, which would make it possible to produce many genetically identical individuals from the genetic material of one individual. Full reproductive freedom would include the freedom to have whatever number of children a person wishes, as opposed to the freedom to have only some limited number of children, but this freedom might be justifiably limited in certain social conditions by such considerations as the need to control population growth.

Different components of reproductive freedom can have different importance, both in general and in particular cases, and this is illustrated by the different importance of the freedom to reproduce and to be a parent at all, and the freedom to have whatever number of children a person wishes. There are at least two reasons for the greater importance of reproducing and parenting at all. First, some of the interests that support these activities – for example, the desire to have the psychologically and emotionally deep experience of parenthood – do not support, or only more weakly support, having a large number of children. Second, significant portions of the costs of having children are externalized in virtually all societies – that is, borne by others besides the parents (or children). The more this happens, the greater a claim these others might make to have some say in, or control of, the costs imposed on them.

One implication of the distinction between the interest in becoming a parent and the interest in having additional children is that the prevention of genetically transmitted harm to others may more easily justify limiting the number of children than reproducing and parenting at all.

The Choice of What Kind of Children to Have   One of the most controversial components of reproductive freedom is the freedom to choose what kind of children to have. It is also one of the aspects of reproductive freedom that can most directly conflict with genetic interventions to prevent harm to offspring.

The enormous increase in knowledge of human genetics that has taken place in recent years, together with techniques of prenatal genetic screening of potential offspring, has already produced substantial abilities to control the nature of our children. This control now takes the largely negative forms of genetic testing of parents to determine whether they have a risk of transmitting a particular genetic disease or condition to their children, or genetic testing of a fetus to determine whether it has or has an increased risk of having a genetically based disease or disability. Parents can then use this information in choosing whether to seek to conceive, whether to conceive without the risks by use of sperm donation, oocyte (egg) donation, or use of another woman's embryo, whether to abort an affected fetus, or whether to use treatment *in utero* when that is possible (Faden and Beauchamp 1986).

The Human Genome Project in combination with other genetic research will vastly increase individuals' ability to detect the risks or presence of harmful genetic conditions and to prevent them by forgoing conception, conceiving without the risk to the fetus, treating the fetus *in utero*, or aborting it. When genetic diseases or disabilities can be treated during pregnancy, a woman's right to one or any of these choices will typically be based on more than her reproductive freedom. A pregnant woman's right to decide about such treatment for her fetus will often be based as well on her own right either to bodily integrity, on her right to decide about her own health care (e.g., if the treatment involves surgical invasion of her own body), or on her right as the potential infant's mother to make medical treatment decisions for it. When her decision is to treat such a disease, it will usually be in the interests of her future child and so supported both by any right she has to decide, based in either her own reproductive freedom or her right to give informed consent to medically invasive treatment, and by her future child's interests.

It is cases of failure to use available genetic testing and counseling to detect genetic risks and/or to take the steps necessary to prevent serious harm to a fetus and the child it will become that are the central concern of this chapter. (The use of genetic engineering to affect positively or enhance the genetic traits of offspring, as opposed to eliminating genetically based diseases and disabilities, is discussed in Chapters 4 and 5; see also Glover (1984).)

The Choice of Whether to Have Biologically Related Children One aspect of the choice of what kind of children to have – biologically related or not – deserves separate attention. When reproductive partners are able to reproduce and have no reason to believe that doing so would result in their children having any genetically transmitted disease or harmful condition, the issue of whether to have biological children typically does not arise. But when one or both partners are unable to reproduce by "natural" means, then even if adoption is an available alternative, they may choose to use a variety of means of artificial assistance in reproduction, even including human cloning if it becomes possible in the future, in order to achieve and experience pregnancy and/or to have a biologically related child. For many people, the desire to have a biologically related child as opposed to becoming a parent through adoption is powerful, although we do not know how much this desire is socially and culturally determined.

When one or both reproductive partners risk transmitting a harmful genetic condition to their offspring, then adoption or the use of some means of artificially assisted reproduction that eliminates one or both parents' biological tie to the offspring may be necessary to reduce or remove that risk. An ethical evaluation of the parties' choice in this situation depends in significant part on the importance of the interest in having biologically related children. This interest is properly considered a part of reproductive freedom, but how much weight it should be given is problematic.

Social circumstances, such as important religious or cultural norms and practices, can make it reasonable for one or both prospective parents to give substantial weight to this interest. This interest might also have substantial weight if having children who are not biologically related, either by adoption or other means, would substantially undermine the experience of parenting. But we know from experience with adoption that many people fully or substantially satisfy their interest in parenting without having biologically related children. Absent some special impact of having children who are not biologically related, this aspect of reproductive freedom – like the aspect of having as many or as few children as a person wishes – is usually of substantially less importance than the interest in becoming a parent at all.

The Social Conditions That Support Reproductive Choices   It is our view that reproductive freedom is properly understood to include the social conditions necessary to ensure persons a reasonable range of reproductive choices without undue burdens or unjust impacts from those choices. We characterize these social conditions as part of reproductive freedom, while recognizing that others will want to insist they are social conditions that make possible and facilitate reproduction and childrearing, and not part of reproductive freedom itself. The important point, however, is that individuals' interest in reproduction includes an interest in the background social conditions necessary for them to have a reasonable and effective array of reproductive alternatives.

Sometimes these background conditions amount to the absence of restrictions on the setting for reproductive choices. For example, reproductive freedom includes some control over and choices about whether reproduction will take place inside or out of marriage, or in a heterosexual or homosexual relationship. In other cases, the background conditions necessary for a reasonable range of reproductive choices without unjust burdens involve a wide range of background social and legal practices that affect and facilitate the practices of having and raising children, such as maternal and paternal leave in the workplace and legal policies that forbid various forms of discrimination related to childbearing and parenting. In the specific genetic context, these supporting conditions include at least some access to genetic screening and counseling services.

Even if it is agreed that reproductive freedom should be understood to include the conditions necessary to permit reproductive choices in circumstances that do not result in unjust deprivations or other unjust impacts on those who choose to reproduce, or who choose not to, there will often be ethical disagreement as to whether a particular impact of a choice is unjust and if so what services must be provided to prevent such impacts.

Summary of the Scope of Concern

We now have a brief sketch of the main relevant components of reproductive freedom. This sketch shows that the common understanding of reproductive freedom as essentially concerned with preventing pregnancy by contraception or procreation by abortion is far too narrow. Even a broader understanding that includes access to the means of enhancing or creating fertility by new reproductive techniques is too narrow, because it too ignores many important effects of reproductive choices on women's, and to a lesser extent men's, lives that properly fall within a concern for reproductive freedom.

Our principal concern so far has been to describe the scope of concern of individuals' interest in reproductive freedom, not to argue for its moral importance. We turn now to a brief consideration of the chief moral values that together determine the moral importance of reproductive freedom. A clearer understanding of these values will allow us to consider when the obligation to prevent genetically transmitted harms is strong enough to justify limiting or interfering with reproductive freedom.

THE INTERESTS AND VALUES THAT DETERMINE THE
MORAL IMPORTANCE OF REPRODUCTIVE FREEDOM

The proper moral protection that reproductive freedom should have, and how it should be balanced against the prevention of genetically transmitted harms when the two are in conflict, depend on what moral interests or values support preserving and protecting reproductive freedom. We will sketch three different accounts of reproductive freedom's moral importance – they will be discussed only briefly because a fuller development would take us too far into issues of moral and political philosophy that cannot be pursued further here.

The first moral basis for the importance of reproductive freedom, and perhaps the most common argument in support of it, is individual self-determination or autonomy. The second moral basis – most natural within, though not exclusive to, utilitarian or general consequentialist moral views – is the important contribution that reproductive freedom typically makes to individuals' good or well-being. The third moral basis appeals to a principle of equality – in the specific version we sketch here, equality of expectations and opportunity between men and women.

It should be emphasized that these three different bases are not mutually exclusive, forcing us to choose among them. Each captures something morally important about reproductive freedom, so that a full account of the moral values of reproductive freedom must incorporate all three. Moreover, they suggest the way in which quite different general moral theories converge in assigning substantial moral importance to reproductive freedom, even though those theories explain and defend that importance in different ways. This convergence is desirable in a pluralistic society, since it makes consensus possible about the moral importance of reproductive freedom among people holding otherwise different moral views.

Self-Determination

In a sentence, people's interest in self-determination is their interest in making significant decisions about their own lives for themselves, according to their own values or conception of a good life, and having those decisions respected by others. John Rawls has characterized this interest as based in people's capacity to form, revise over time, and pursue a plan of life or conception of the good (Rawls 1971). Of course, reference to a plan of life should not be taken too literally, as implying that people sit down at any point in time and lay out a fully detailed plan for the rest of their lives. Instead, the idea is that because individuals have conceptions of themselves as beings who persist over time, with both a past and a future as well as a present, they have the capacity to form more or less long-term plans, projects, and intentions for their lives. Other things being equal, the further into the future they look, the less detailed and fixed these plans will typically be.

In addition to desires to pursue various activities and experiences, human beings have the capacity to value having particular desires or motivations. Other animals share with us a capacity for goal-directed behavior, and so perhaps a capacity in some sense for intentional behavior. Unlike other animals, however, people have the capacity to engage in reflection about their aims, ends, and motivations, and to affirm or deny them as their own and as defining not just who they happen to be, but also what kind of persons they want to be or value being.

It is this capacity that makes it sensible to say that, unlike other animals, human beings have a conception of the good, which is more than simply having desires and motivations, the feature they share with other animals. When, as happens to everyone to a greater or lesser extent, people's desires are not as they want them to be, they can, within limits, take steps to change them to bring their actual motivational structure into closer conformity with the character that they value or want for themselves.

It is through this capacity for critical reflection about what they value having, doing, and becoming that people are able to form and then act on a conception of their good, rather than simply being guided by instinct and environmental stimulus. Of course, none of this is to deny that people's social and natural environment deeply affects their values and conception of the good. By having their choices about the life they want for themselves respected by others, in the sense at least of not being interfered with even if others disagree with the choices they make, people are able to take some control and responsibility for their lives and the kinds of persons they become.

Self-determination so understood includes both the reflective, critical process of forming a personal conception of the good and the capacity to identify or decide upon the particular aims and ends that give that conception concrete specification on particular occasions, as well as liberty of action in not being interfered with by others in the pursuit of personal aims and ends. The exercise of self-determination in these respects might be summarized as the process by which individuals help shape their own unique identity.

Rawls has characterized people's interest in self-determination as a "highest-order interest," meaning, at least in part, that it is of a higher order of importance than the particular aims and values that give content to their conception of the good or plan of life at any point in time (Rawls 1980). These aims and values, we know from our own and others' experience, can and will change over time in both predictable and unpredictable ways. People's interest in self-determination, however, is their interest in being valuing agents, able to guide their own lives in this way. The capacity to be or become self-determining is a central condition of personhood.

We initially characterized self-determination as people making significant decisions about their own lives for themselves and according to their own aims and values, but these two components are distinct. Most people value making important decisions about their lives for themselves, rather than having the decisions made for them by others, even if others might make better decisions even as evaluated from the perspective of those individuals' own values. In this respect, self-determination is part of a moral ideal of the person, not simply valuable in maximizing the satisfaction of people's other desires and interests. More specifically, the value of individuals making decisions concerning their own reproduction does not lie solely in their being able to make the best or wisest decisions, but also in this exercise of self-determination being part of an attractive moral ideal of the person, and one important aspect of individuals helping to define their own identity.

A second necessary point about the value of self-determination is that its exercise can be more or less important or valuable on different occasions and in different decisions. One of the most important determinants of this differential importance or value is the nature of the decision and subsequent action in question. Deciding what to have for breakfast tomorrow is vastly less significant than deciding what career to pursue, whom to marry, or whether and under what conditions to have children. Other things being equal, the more central and far-reaching the impact of a particular decision on an individual's life, the more substantial a person's self-determination interest in making it. This is why self-determination is so important in many of the decisions or choices that we have suggested comprise reproductive freedom. Few decisions that people make are more personal than these (in the sense that the best choice depends on personal aims and values) or more far-reaching in their impact on people's lives.

Another dimension of self-determination commonly accorded great respect and deference is the exercise of religious liberty. Religious liberty is important for reproductive freedom because many reproductive choices implicate and are guided by people's religious beliefs.

While these aspects of reproductive freedom do centrally affect women and, to a lesser extent, their male reproductive partners, they also affect others – most important, the person created by their reproductive activity, but other persons as well. Virtually nothing that people do has no effects on anyone, no matter how insignificant, and self-determination would be empty of moral importance if it were limited to such cases. Instead, the impact of people's actions on others is properly understood as a competing moral consideration that sometimes places limits on the exercise of self-determination. The appeal to self-determination will provide the strongest protections against interference by others, other things being equal, when the actions in question also have only minimal impacts on others.

This point is important for all aspects of reproductive freedom that involve creating and thereby affecting another being. It is especially important for a particular aspect of reproductive freedom – the choice of what kind of children to have. Shaping the nature of children greatly affects a person's own life and so is properly encompassed by self-determination. However, it is not primarily a matter of individual self-determination but as well and, more important, the determination of another. This is so both for choices about genetically-based conditions or traits viewed to be undesirable or harmful and for genetic screening or engineering designed to enhance an individual's genetic inheritance – whether it be sex selection or the much broader powers that may be available in the future.

Having and raising children is a central part of many people's lives, and self-determination lends significant support to parents shaping their children's genetic inheritance, just as it supports their shaping their children's character and lives in other ways during childrearing. The overall moral case for determining what another is like, however, even in the context of parent and child, is substantially weaker than the moral case based in self-determination for individuals shaping their own lives.

In most societies, parents are accorded significant discretion and control in the raising of their children, including decisions about education, religious exposure and training, and more generally the values passed on to children. Some significant discretion of this sort is necessary for whoever is assigned primary responsibility for the rearing of children. This parental self-determination is not unlimited, however, either in morality or the law. The fundamental interests of the child place moral limits on this parental self-determination, as is reflected in typical child abuse and neglect laws. Thus the interests of the child and of the person the child will become are one source of moral limits on this parental self-determination (United Nations 1959).

The more difficult issue is whether, and if so to what extent, society can legitimately claim a role in such decisions. The collective effect of individual decisions by parents to prevent undesired traits or to enhance desired traits may have a substantial impact on the nature of the overall society of which they are members. Moreover, the decisions do not solely, or even principally, affect the parents – their primary impact is on the nature of the persons created through this prevention or selection of genetically transmitted traits or conditions – that is, on those who will be the future members of the society.

In a broad sense, parents help shape, although it is unclear and controversial to what extent, the nature of society in the future. Thus a pregnant woman's or parent's interest in self-determination, understood as in part the making of significant decisions about his or her own life, cannot establish an absolute right to decide whether to prevent or enhance genetically transmitted conditions. Because those decisions help shape the nature of the society in which others will live, there is some case for collective societal decision making. For instance, democratic decision procedures and public policy might define at least the broad parameters or limits within which choices to prevent or enhance particular genetically transmitted traits might be made as a part of the exercise of reproductive freedom.

The moral importance of reproductive freedom over a wide array of choices can thus be based in part on the moral importance of individuals' general interest in self-determination. But the greater the harm would be to another as a result of respecting a particular reproductive choice, the weaker is the overall moral case provided by self-determination for respecting that choice. (What we have called here self-determination is often in the law called either "privacy," as the courts in the United States have constructed the right of privacy, or a "constitutionally protected liberty interest.")

Individual Good or Well-Being

A second line of moral argument in defense of reproductive freedom appeals to the contribution it makes to the welfare, well-being, or good of individuals (we shall usually use here only the notion of individual "good," though these concepts are not interchangeable in all contexts) whose reproductive freedom is respected. The precise form this argument takes will depend in part on the account of individual good used. It is common in the philosophical literature to distinguish three main types of theories of the good for persons. Each looks at what is intrinsically good or valuable in a life – that is, roughly, good independent of its consequences and relations to other things; many other things are instrumentally good because they lead to what is intrinsically good in a life.

Conscious experience theories hold that people's good consists of certain kinds of positive psychological states, often characterized as pleasure or happiness and the absence of pain or unhappiness. Preference or desire satisfaction theories of the good for persons hold that what is good is the satisfaction of people's desires or preferences. Finally, what can be called objective good theories deny that a person's good consists only of positive conscious experiences or desire satisfaction; they hold that some things are good for people even if they do not want them and will not obtain pleasure or happiness from them (Brock 1992; Griffin 1986). Although various objective good theories differ as to what is objectively good for persons, typical accounts appeal to the achievement of certain virtues or ideals of the person and having specific kinds of valuable experiences.

Many difficult and complex issues are involved in attempting to give a full and precise account of any of these alternative kinds of theories of the good for persons, and some of those issues have substantive implications for a defense of the moral value of reproductive freedom. Nevertheless, it is clear that there is at least a broad connection between people's good and securing their reproductive freedom on each of the main accounts of that good. Securing and respecting the various components of individuals' reproductive freedom that we just distinguished usually makes a positive overall contribution to their happiness, since competent individuals typically are the best judges of what reproductive choices will best promote their happiness. Moreover, when people's reproductive choices are blocked they usually experience displeasure and frustration. Likewise, respecting individuals' reproductive freedom usually permits them to best satisfy their desires concerning reproduction. And finally, respecting individuals' reproductive freedom usually will promote some typical objective components of their good (e.g., taking responsibility for important parts of life, and having deep personal relations, such as that between parent and child). Nevertheless, it is important to emphasize that each of the foregoing claims about the tendency of reproductive freedom to promote the good of persons (variously understood) is only plausible if accompanied by the qualification "usually" that we have given it.

This qualification implies that the contribution of the various components of reproductive freedom to persons' good cannot support an absolute or unlimited protection of or right to reproductive freedom. That is as it should be, because this ground of reproductive freedom – the appeal to a person's own good – can sometimes support paternalistic limitation of reproductive freedom. It is necessary to assess the contribution of a particular aspect of reproductive freedom to a particular individual's good in particular circumstances in order to determine what weight this moral defense of reproductive freedom should be given on a particular occasion. With that said, however, respecting most of the components of individuals' reproductive freedom distinguished earlier does usually promote their good, and in those cases this is one significant part of the overall moral case for respecting their reproductive freedom.

Equality of Expectations and Opportunity

The third moral argument in support of respecting reproductive freedom is based on a moral principle of equality. On the one hand, the equality defense best illuminates why some specific components of reproductive freedom just discussed but often not included within reproductive freedom are morally important components of it. On the other hand, some other components that we discussed seem not to be supported by the equality defense, and so their support must originate elsewhere.

The first step of the equality defense is the premise that whether someone is male or female is a morally irrelevant property of persons in the sense that it morally ought not affect people's fundamental social and economic expectations in life and their opportunity to attain desired positions and benefits.[1] In this respect gender is like race, and the premise about its moral irrelevance should be as morally uncontroversial as the analogous claim regarding race.

This premise is not a denial of natural differences between men and women, since it is a banal truism that only women get pregnant. This is a natural fact of biology that it is not now possible to change and by itself represents no unjust inequality. The unjust inequalities that women suffer are either forms of straightforward gender discrimination that disadvantage women or situations in which natural sexual differences, such as the fact that only women get pregnant, are related in ways subject to social change and control to other systematic social and economic disadvantages to women. And, of course, in most of the world today both these kinds of gender discrimination are common.

Reproductive freedom then serves equality in two important ways: first, it can help mitigate those unjust gender disadvantages that women suffer that are specifically tied to reproduction; second, it can help mitigate the effects of other forms of gender discrimination against women that are not tied specifically to reproduction.

To illustrate this relation between reproductive freedom and equality, consider the components of the reproductive freedom of women that involve, first, access to genetic testing to determine whether a fetus has a serious genetically transmitted disease that will prevent it from ever developing an independent life or having meaningful social relations with others, and, second, the choice of whether to abort a fetus found to have such a disease. Even with the best social, economic, and psychological supports, having and raising such a child typically has deep and far-reaching effects on its parents' lives, but especially on its mother's life, since women typically bear a disproportionate share of the burdens of childrearing.

The effective choice and control over whether to continue or terminate such a pregnancy gives women the opportunity to decide whether to undertake a disproportionate share of the burdens of having such a child. Other aspects of reproductive freedom also help women mitigate

---

[1] There is a substantial debate about what the object of egalitarians' concern should be. The principal alternative positions include equality of welfare, of resources, of opportunities, and of capabilities and functionings. Our appeal here to "expectations" in the equality defense of reproductive freedom aims to be neutral between these different positions, although, of course, a full equality defense of reproductive freedom would have to spell out the specific conception of equality used.

the effects of a variety of unjust gender-based inequalities on their lives. But reproductive freedom does not support gender equality only because it mitigates the effects of other injustices. There may be some ineliminable gender inequalities associated with reproduction that are not the consequence of any unjust social arrangements. Reproductive freedom gives women the choice of whether to accept those inequalities in their own lives.

The equality defense of reproductive freedom, like the self-determination defense, supports some aspects of reproductive freedom more clearly and persuasively than others. We have already mentioned how the choice about what kind of children to have can have substantial implications for the gender-based inequalities that will attend childbearing and childrearing. The connection between reproductive freedom and equality is most essential, however, in making clear why a variety of social and legal conditions and practices that form the social and legal context of reproduction and childrearing are properly considered an important part of reproductive freedom. A central purpose of these conditions and practices is either to prevent or to compensate for gender-based inequalities in expectations and opportunities that would otherwise attend reproduction. In weighing what should predominate in conflicts between reproductive freedom and the prevention of genetically transmitted harm, it is necessary to evaluate the extent to which the particular aspect of reproductive freedom in question is supported by considerations of equality between men and women.

USE OF GENETIC INFORMATION TO PREVENT HARM

In summary, our argument thus far in the chapter is that there are distinct components of reproductive freedom that have differential moral importance both generally and on specific occasions. There are also at least three distinct lines of moral support that apply in complex ways to these different components of reproductive freedom, grounded in self-determination, the promotion of a person's good, and equality, respectively. Our discussion of reproductive freedom thus far is not intended to support any simple, general conclusion about its nature and moral importance, but instead to unpack some of the complexities that must be attended to when weighing specific conflicts between reproductive freedom and prevention of genetically transmitted harms.

The remainder of the chapter addresses moral issues in the use of genetic information to prevent harm. More specifically, the focus will be on when individuals are morally required to acquire and/or use genetic information to prevent genetically transmitted harm to offspring, and on some of the moral problems raised by public policies to enforce those requirements.

In the foreseeable future, choices about prevention of genetic harms will usually be made by individuals, and so we consider them here in that context. Further into the future, larger-scale social programs of genetic engineering might become possible. Such programs might leave certain choices less in the hands of individuals or even deprive them of some choices altogether.

It should be emphasized that societal efforts to prevent genetically transmissible harms and the reproductive freedom of individuals are not necessarily or even usually in conflict. The vast majority of prospective parents have a direct and deep concern for the well-being of their prospective children and will voluntarily or even eagerly make use of available genetic information or interventions to prevent harms to or remove harms from them. Most will do this out of simple concern for the well-being of their prospective children and not because they have decided that doing so is morally required or because public policy and the law encourage or require it.

In a variety of cases that now arise, however, and in more cases that will arise in the future, prospective parents will have one or another reason not to make use of genetic information or interventions to prevent harm to their prospective children, and so both they and public policy will need to decide when they are morally required to do so. This question will often arise in the context of genetic counseling, in which prospective parents request advice and guidance about these issues – requests that will make the traditional counseling norm of value-neutrality difficult to justify or maintain. Moreover, as a society we must address when, if ever, we should adopt policies that encourage in a variety of ways, or require by law, that individuals obtain and make use of genetic information and interventions to prevent harm to their prospective children and other related individuals.

Distinguishing Cases

In order to clarify the moral issues in the conflicts and trade-offs between reproductive freedom and the use of genetic information to prevent harm, several distinctions between different kinds of cases are important. Because these distinctions will require us to address a number of different, complex issues, it is useful at the outset to sketch them in broad outlines.

First, we need to distinguish cases in which the genetically transmitted disease or condition is so severe as to make the individual's life from that individual's perspective not worth living from those cases in which the harm is significant but still leaves the individual with a worthwhile life. (Cases in which the genetic intervention does not prevent a harm but is an enhancement that confers a benefit on the individual are discussed in Chapters 4 and 5.) A life not worth living is not just worse than most peoples' lives or a life with substantial burdens; it is a life that, from the perspective of the person whose life it is, is so burdensome and/or without compensating benefits as to make death preferable.

Second, we need to distinguish cases in which the genetic information is obtained or intervention is pursued before conception from cases in which it is obtained or pursued after conception of an affected fetus, but prenatally. And both of these need to be distinguished from cases in which information is obtained or intervention pursued postnatally.

Third, we need to distinguish cases in terms of the relative burdensomeness of the interventions to prevent the harm, as well as the relative seriousness of the harms to be prevented when the child will be left with a worthwhile life whether or not the intervention occurs; in both types of cases burdens and harms occur along broad spectrums in terms of their relative seriousness.

Last, we need to distinguish cases in which the genetically transmitted disease or condition can be corrected or prevented by some intervention either pre- or post-conception from cases in which the prospective parents can only conceive with a risk or certainty of genetically transmitting a harmful disease or condition. We will use these four distinctions and others to develop an ethical framework for addressing the ethical issues that arise in the use of genetic interventions to prevent harm.

For the many kinds of cases of genetically transmitted harms that can arise, two philosophical problems will be of special concern here. Both problems stem from apparent difficulties in applying conventional, commonsense, and philosophical accounts of harm and harm prevention to cases in which the only way the harmful condition can be avoided is for the affected individual never to exist at all – that is, never to be brought into existence. In these cases, the creation of an individual inextricably creates the harmful condition as well. Standard accounts of harm compare the condition of an individual before a putative harm has occurred with the condition of that same individual after the putative harm has occurred; the individual has been harmed only if he or she is worse off in the latter condition as a result of the adverse effect of an action or event on his or her interests. But when the only alternative to the putatively harmful condition is not to exist, or not to have ever existed at all, there is no unharmed condition, because there is no unharmed individual with whom to make the comparison.

The first instance of this problem – cases of so-called wrongful life – has received special attention and engendered considerable perplexity in the law. Courts have worried whether it is even sensible to claim that an infant's or child's quality of life is so bad that he or she would have been better off never having been born at all.

The second instance of the problem, and the philosophically more difficult one, concerns cases that we shall call wrongful disabilities, in which an individual has a significant genetically transmitted disability, but one that is not so serious as to make life not worthwhile. The disability could have been prevented by the child's mother, but only by conceiving at a different time and/or under different conditions, in which case she would have had a different child without the disability. (The claim that this would have been a different child does not commit us to personal identity being determined by genes, since the other child would have a different history in the world and other different properties as well as different genes.) But if the disabled child she did have has a worthwhile life from the child's own perspective, and the disability could only have been prevented by the child never having existed at all, then the child appears not to have been made worse off, and so not to have been harmed, by the disability. And if this is so, then it seems that if the mother does nothing to prevent transmission of the adverse genetic condition, she cannot have violated an obligation to prevent harm.

An adequate moral account of these two kinds of cases appears to require resources beyond those found either in commonsense moral thinking or conventional ethical theories. In wrongful life cases, we shall argue that courts that have held that the necessary moral judgments supporting wrongful life claims are not coherent or sound have been mistaken; conventional moral theories and accounts of harm do have the resources to warrant morally sound wrongful life judgments.

In wrongful disability cases, we shall argue that while standard accounts of harm cannot be applied, those accounts can be revised or extended to fit the circumstances of wrongful disabilities; wrongful disability cases do in fact constitute serious moral wrongs. In each case, we can coherently weigh the harmful condition that would come to the conceived child against the reproductive freedom of the child's mother.

Post-Conception Interventions to Prevent Harms Compatible with a Worthwhile Life

We begin with a class of cases in which standard analyses of harm are essentially adequate. Here, the information about the genetic transmission of the harmful condition is acquired after conception, the intervention to prevent harm to the child will be done during pregnancy, and the harm to the child if not prevented would not be serious enough to make its life not worth living. Since these are cases of interventions affecting a fetus, it might be thought that they raise the very morally, politically, and legally contentious issue of the moral status of the fetus, which has so polarized the abortion controversy. But that would be a mistake. Whatever the moral status of the fetus at different points in its development, so long as the pregnant woman intends to carry it to term, it can be expected in time to become a full moral person with all the moral protections that includes. Therefore, concern for that person, not only for the fetus, provides the stimulus for post-conception harm prevention (Feinberg 1986). Let us spell out and defend this claim.

We assume that the moral status of the child the fetus will become includes a moral claim (hereafter, we shall say a "moral right," although we put the claim in terms of a moral right only for ease of exposition) expressed by the following principle:

M: Those individuals responsible for a child's, or other dependent person's, welfare are morally required not to let it suffer a serious harm or disability or a serious loss of happiness or good, that they could have prevented without imposing substantial burdens or costs or loss of benefits, on themselves or others.

Some principle like M underlies common moral views, as well as legal requirements, concerning parents' responsibilities to care for their children, including their responsibility to secure necessary medical care for them. Child abuse and neglect statutes that exist in all states make this a legal responsibility of parents and authorize state intervention to remove the child from the family if necessary in order to secure such care.

The requirement not to let one for whom one is responsible suffer "a serious loss of happiness or good" is less clearly a part of either common moral views or legal practice than the requirement to prevent serious harm or disability. Much ordinary moral thinking contains lesser (or even no) requirements to secure benefits than to prevent harms to others. But whatever the relative stringency of preventing harms versus securing benefits, M must be formulated to allow some weighing of harms prevented against benefits secured. In people's own lives they often cause or do not prevent a harm in order to secure a greater benefit. Likewise, in acting for others for whom one is responsible it is also often justified to cause or not to prevent a harm to them in order to secure a greater benefit for them (e.g., a parent may have to submit her child to the pain of a tooth extraction to prevent greater dental damage). M should be understood as requiring this weighing of harms prevented against benefits secured when both are in question.

There is an important feature of cases of prenatal interventions that may appear to make them significantly different morally speaking from typical cases of child abuse or neglect, and thus to make M's application to them problematic. This is that they can arise before the point at which many believe the fetus has become a moral person, and so a moral principle like M may be thought not to apply to the fetus. If the fetus is not yet a moral person, and so killing it is morally permissible, how can failure to prevent a much less serious harm be impermissible or wrong? Must we settle the extraordinarily contentious question of when the fetus becomes a person before we know when M begins to apply to it?

If we must, then there are also implications for another class of cases – actions that take place before the fetus is even conceived, but that result in predictable harms to it when or after it is conceived. If a fetus, which is often thought of as a potential person, is not morally protected by principles like M before it becomes a person, then surely before conception has taken place merely possible persons are likewise not morally protected. If the point is put in terms of rights, neither possible persons (before conception) nor potential persons (after conception) are commonly understood to be the kind of beings that can have moral rights.

The flaw in this reasoning is thinking that the harm to be prevented is a harm only to the fetus or, even more implausibly, only to a possible person before conception. In each case, the harm to be prevented is a harm that will come to the child that the fetus will later become, a child who will uncontroversially be a full moral person. The important difference in this harm is that it can only be prevented by actions that must be taken before the individual becomes a full person.

Put in terms of rights, failure to act earlier, when the child was a fetus, will violate the moral right that the child now has to have had the harm prevented when it was possible, earlier, to do so. The moral wrongness of actions that result in harms to distinct individuals in the future, over temporal distances, should not be any more problematic than the more familiar cases of wrongful actions that result in harm across spatial distances. Understood in this way, prenatal but post-conception genetic interventions are no different from interventions with born children intended to prevent harm to them. Principle M applies straightforwardly to both of them.

Just as with moral and legal issues about child abuse and neglect, applying principle M in concrete cases often will require difficult and controversial judgments about when the harms to be prevented are of sufficient seriousness that they are not outweighed by the burdens or costs imposed on the mother (and/or others) by the interventions necessary to prevent the harm, together with any other moral considerations counting against the interventions. Obviously, no one possesses, nor will possess in the future, any precise metric on which the harms prevented, the burdens imposed by the intervention, and other morally relevant considerations can all be measured and balanced. Two examples, however, will help make the issues more concrete.

When the prenatal interventions to prevent harm to the fetus and the child it will become involve invasive surgery on the mother with significant risks, her reproductive freedom and her right to make decisions about her own health care will outweigh most harms that can now be prevented in this way to the fetus and child. So she should be left free to decide.

Her responsibility to undergo surgery to prevent harm to the child would be weightier if she were responsible for the child needing intervention – for example, if its condition resulted from her recklessly exposing herself to toxic substances during pregnancy. But even in an instance in which a woman would be morally required to accept an invasive intervention, it might be problematic for others to coerce her to do so.

In contrast, the burdens of the screening and special diet necessary for women to prevent the severe harms of mental retardation and other disabilities that would be caused by PKU disease in their children are sufficiently limited in comparison with the severity of the harms to the child to make the screening and diet morally required. Even confinement during part of a pregnancy might sometimes be morally justified if necessary in order to prevent this very serious harm to her child.

As new cases multiply in the future, there often will be factual disagreement about the consequences of intervening or failing to intervene for the fetus and child who would be affected by the intervention. For example, the degree of risk of passing on the disease or condition, as well as its likely severity, will often be uncertain and/or disputed. Similar disagreement will often also arise concerning how those who suffer the burdens of the intervention will be affected, most especially the pregnant woman. What medical risks to her does prenatal intervention pose, for example, and what would the short- and long-term emotional and psychological consequences be of public policy imposing such interventions against her wishes, and so forth?

Even when there is agreement about the likely consequences of possible alternative actions or policies, there will often be disagreement about the relative moral weight to be given the different consequences. What moral weight or importance does the particular aspect of her reproductive freedom at stake have, for example, and what moral weight or importance does her responsibility under a principle like M have?

Our earlier discussion of the different aspects of reproductive freedom together with their different moral bases was designed to provide a framework for addressing these questions in concrete cases. Different genetically transmitted diseases or conditions that might be prevented in a particular case must also be assessed for the relative importance of their effects on the child's well-being and opportunities over the course of its life.

Other things being equal, the more serious and probable the harm that might be prevented, the less serious and probable the risks or harmful effects on the fetus and/or others of doing so, and the less weighty the aspect of the mother's reproductive freedom that is at stake, the stronger the moral case for intervening to prevent the harm.

At some point, preventing the harm will be morally required, although whether that point has been reached in a particular case sometimes will be morally controversial. There is no way to remove either the need for sensitive and careful judgment in particular cases or the ethically controversial nature of that judgment in balancing the genetically transmitted harms that might be prevented against the mother's claim to reproductive freedom.

Prevention of Harms across Many Generations

The argument in the last section may seem to omit a crucial consideration special to the moral assessment of the prevention of genetically transmitted harms – their repeated transmission over successive generations. Broadening our perspective from the harm to the immediate individual fetus and the person it will become suggests vastly larger cumulative harms that might be prevented by any steps, such as nonconception, germline therapy, or abortion, that would block the transmission of harm to successive generations when they reproduce.

Viewing the genetically transmitted harm to be prevented from this longer-term perspective shifts our standpoint from that of the genetic counselor advising a woman regarding the harm to her fetus to concern with the vastly magnified harms to be prevented to successive individuals as genetically transmitted diseases or conditions are passed down across successive generations. Imagine, this argument asks, the enormous harms that would have been prevented if we could have stopped a disease like Huntington's chorea after the first genetic mutations that led to its appearance. This kind of concern was central to much eugenic rhetoric earlier in this century, as we saw in Chapter 2.

Even if we can rarely or never intervene at the outset of a genetic disease's appearance, intervening in any single case to prevent its transmission can prevent harms of great magnitude when viewed over long periods of generational transmission. If the concern is also with harms to society caused by the spread of the harmful condition over time, and not just with harms to a larger number of individuals, the concern is properly considered eugenicist. This broader and longer-term perspective suggests that intervening to prevent genetically transmitted diseases or conditions causing only quite minor harms to any one individual suffering them would be clearly morally required in order to prevent the vastly larger cumulative harms to individuals or society from their transmission across generations. Even aspects of reproductive freedom of fundamental moral importance might be outweighed by the great cumulative harms that could be prevented over time. This longer-term perspective might seem to warrant mandatory abortion or sterilization to stop the transmission of even minor harms. As we saw in Chapter 2, it was characteristic of eugenic thinking to take very seriously the cumulative effects of particular dysgenic reproductive acts.

There are at least three considerations that largely undermine the force of this argument. The first is uncertainty about whether the individual who will have the genetic disease or condition if it is not prevented would pass it on to future generations. (The condition could be prevented by the individual not being conceived, being aborted once conceived, being sterilized, or receiving germline therapy; we will stop spelling out these various means of preventing transmission, but shall simply speak of preventing it, although there are, of course, important moral differences in these different means of harm prevention.) Even if this individual has the harmful genetically transmitted disease or condition, it will still not be passed on to future generations if the person does not have children.

Moreover, typically only a risk, not a certainty, will exist of passing on the harmful gene(s) to any children the individual has. And these uncertainties about whether this individual will pass on the harmful genetically transmitted disease or condition to the next generation will exist again for each successive generation. Viewed from this longer generational perspective, it is also increasingly likely that treatments, cures, or other means of prevention will be developed for the disease or condition. Thus there are a variety of uncertainties about whether the harm will in fact be passed on across many generations.

The second factor undermining the argument that it is ethically required to prevent even minimally harmful genetic diseases or conditions is the problematic assignment of moral responsibility to the present generation for the potential harms caused to all future generations. Each successive generation of individuals with the harmful gene will have the choice of whether to pass on, or to risk passing on, the disease or condition to their children. If they choose to do so, the moral responsibility for that will rest with them, not the previous generation that passed on the disease or condition to them. It is therefore problematic to assign moral responsibility to individuals in any one generation for harms that are passed on to all successive generations.

There is a third reason why the great cumulative harm from passing on indefinitely even minor genetically transmitted harmful diseases or conditions does not justify overriding fundamental aspects of the reproductive freedom of individuals who now have the harmful genes. The point concerns justice between generations and limits on the sacrifices that present generations should reasonably be expected to make in order to produce indefinitely large future benefits over an indefinitely long future, even though the benefit to any single future individual is very small.

In assessing what would be reasonable sacrifices or limitations of the reproductive freedom of individuals with harmful genes today for the benefit of future individuals, at least one important perspective is the comparison of the moral importance of the sacrifice of reproductive freedom that would be made by an individual today with the moral importance of the benefit that would be obtained by any future individual, not just with the cumulative future benefits. Only this one-by-one comparison of the sacrifices and benefits of individuals will tell us whether the distribution is fair to the individuals affected over time. It would be unfair to impose a very great sacrifice or limitation of reproductive freedom on the present generation in order to produce aggregate future benefits that are greater only because very small benefits to any one individual reach a great many individuals over an indefinite future. This has been called the "aggregation problem" in the literature on rationing between contemporaries, and it has an analogue in the economic literature on just savings rates across generations (Daniels 1993).

Pre- and Post-Conception Interventions to Prevent Harms Incompatible with a Worthwhile Life

In what have come to be known as "wrongful life suits," parents have brought legal actions on behalf of their child against physicians or other health care professionals or institutions, charging that their child has been harmed by having been brought into existence and that it would not have existed except for the negligent conduct of those against whom the suit is brought. The cases typically involve either a failure to diagnose and inform the parents before conception about a risk that their child will have a devastating genetically transmitted condition or a failure to determine and inform the parents after conception that the child has such a disease or condition. The defendant's action is not the cause of the child's harmful disease or condition, which is genetically caused, but it is the cause of the parents' either conceiving the child or failing to abort it, as a result of the defendant's negligence.

The special feature of these cases that distinguishes them from other negligence cases and that has vexed many of the courts confronting them is that the disease or condition is claimed to be so harmful and irremediable that it makes the child's life not worth living. Thus the wrong done to the child is having been brought into existence or given life in this condition. Moreover, the genetically inherited conditions and diseases that typically have been the subject of wrongful life suits are incurable, irremediable, and cannot be prevented except by preventing the conception or birth of the individual with the condition or disease. So the wrong to the child is its very existence with the harmful condition, and the legal actions in wrongful life cases have maintained that except for the negligent actions of the defendants, the child would never have been conceived, or would have been aborted before birth.

The issue that has concerned the courts has principally been how existence itself could be a harm and so a wrong to an infant or child and, if it is, how to assess damages for it. As noted earlier, our principal concern is with the philosophical and moral claim that life with conditions like Lesch-Nyhan disease or Tay-Sachs disease is so burdensome and without compensating benefits to the individual with the disease that it is worse than never having existed at all. Life itself is a harm, and in turn a wrong, to an individual in that condition.

Some persons might challenge wrongful life claims along vitalist lines, on the grounds that life itself is always a great good, no matter what the quality of that life, and so can never be bad for or a harm, and in turn a wrong, to a person. But for a small group of diseases or conditions like Lesch-Nyhan and Tay-Sachs, the existence of the person with the disease is so unremittingly awful that this vitalist position is difficult for most people to accept.

While data, to our knowledge, do not exist regarding people's attitudes about life under such conditions, surely most people would choose not to conceive if told that their child would have such a devastating disease. And if they did not believe abortion was wrong even in cases like this, surely most people would abort a fetus that they learned had such a disease. Although their motivations would no doubt in part be self-regarding – their concern for the terrible burdens such a child would impose on them – they would almost certainly include concern for the child, for not imposing such an awful existence on it. Since existence without the disease is not possible for such a child, the only alternative to the awful existence with the disease is never to bring the child into existence at all.

The Subject of Harm   There is a different and deeper source of the concern that wrongful life claims are incoherent. The conventional understanding of a harmful action is an action that makes an individual worse off than he or she was before. That is, to say that an individual has been harmed, it must be possible to compare the different conditions of the individual before and after the putatively harmful act is done. But as noted earlier, the pre-harmed condition in wrongful life, the condition that is claimed to be better for the infant than its burdensome life, is the condition of not ever having existed at all. Yet nonexistence is not any kind of condition, so it is clearly not a condition that could be better for the infant than the existence it has. When the alternative is nonexistence, there is no individual who is made worse off by being conceived and born. Nonexistence is not a condition that is better for an individual than actual existence only in rare cases like having Lesch-Nyhan or Tay Sachs disease; it is no condition at all, and so it is not better or worse than any other condition. So it seems that an individual cannot be harmed by receiving life itself, no matter how awful that life. If the wrong in wrongful life is the harm done, as it is generally assumed to be, there can be no wrong of wrongful life in being given life.

We shall examine later the assumption that being wronged requires being harmed, since it is central to what we have called wrongful disability cases, but for now we want to concentrate on the objection to wrongful life cases that there is no coherent sense to the claim of harm in them, since being harmed requires being made worse off than one otherwise would have been. We begin by noting that in deciding whether to use or forgo life-sustaining medical treatment, patients typically make a comparison, which they take to be meaningful, of life in particular conditions with nonexistence. They ask themselves whether the best quality of life that they can expect in the future with life-sustaining treatment would be sufficiently poor that that life would be worse than no further life at all. Typically, when patients do decide to forgo life-sustaining treatment, it is because they judge further life in their condition to be unwanted and not a benefit or a good.

It also appears to be sensible to compare two overall lives such as the following. One life ends at the age of 80 after a full and independent life; the second life is identical with the first except that it extends beyond age 80 for three years, during which the person suffers both extreme cognitive disability with no possibility for any meaningful social interaction with others, and a painful, physically debilitating disease. The only difference between these two lives is that one extends for a period of three years with an awful quality of life, while the other ends before this period. In other words, the only difference is a comparison of three years of suffering versus nonexistence.

Most people would almost certainly judge the first life the better life, a judgment reflected in the common belief that individuals who die "in their sleep" after a full life are lucky in comparison with others who die after a long, painful, debilitating illness. Now this is still comparing two lives, one shorter and one longer, which may seem different from comparing total nonexistence with a short life. It might be that adding three years of extreme cognitive disability and unremitting suffering to an otherwise satisfying and already complete life only makes that life worse because the new longer whole life is not better than the shorter whole life. We need not compare a short, awful life with complete nonexistence in this case. But setting aside effects on others, a short life with terrible burdens and no compensating benefits for the person whose life it is does seem an evil for that individual and not preferable to the alternative of nonexistence, even if the alternative of nonexistence makes the comparatives "better" or "worse" problematic. Looking only at that life, and without comparing it to nonexistence, there is nothing in it to make it a good for the person whose life it is; instead, its nature makes it only a burden and torment.

Joel Feinberg has made essentially the same point with the fanciful scenario of a person dying and facing God, who makes him choose between being reincarnated with Tay-Sachs disease and immediate and permanent extinction; Feinberg quite plausibly claims that most people would choose immediate extinction (Feinberg 1986). So although nonexistence is not a condition with any quality of life – good, bad, or indifferent – that could be better or worse than the quality of life of the child who is the subject of a wrongful life claim, that is not necessary to make sense of the judgment that such a child's quality of life could be so poor as to make it only a burden or evil for him or her. The child in wrongful life cases has been given something – life – that because of its awful quality he or she should not have been given and has thereby been wronged.

Rights and Existence   Wrongful life claims have also been challenged on the ground that they imply both that someone had a duty to an as-yet-nonexistent person and that the nonexistent person had a right not to be born in such a condition, which was violated by its being wrongfully brought into existence. But, the objection goes, we cannot have duties to nonexistent beings, merely possible persons; nor can nonexistent persons have rights.

We have already shown the mistake in this line of reasoning. The right in question is the right of the child who does exist with a life not worth living not to have been brought into existence with such a life. There is no right that a mere possible – that is, an as-yet-nonexistent – child has; nonexistent beings cannot have rights. But any existing child can and does have a right not to have been brought into existence with a life not worth living. The act of creating the person also creates the right that it violates – the person and his or her rights come into existence together. That is why the act of creating the person is wrong.

This right might seem problematic because in wrongful life cases it seems that the right is simultaneously violated when the child and it are brought into existence, but if such a child is not brought into existence, then the right does not exist and so also cannot be respected. How can there be a right that it is not possible to respect, this objection asks? The mistake here is thinking that only individuals who are conceived with lives not worth living have a right not to be born with such a life. Instead, all individuals have such a right, and for the vast majority of individuals who are conceived with a life worth living, their right not to be born with a life not worth living is respected. It is only for the very few individuals with a life not worth living that this right everyone has not to be born in such a condition is violated.

It is not necessary to attribute to beings that do not yet exist rights not to be brought into existence at some future time with a life not worth living. If the child never is brought into existence, there never is a being with the right that would have been violated had it been brought into existence with a life not worth living. This is no different from other harms caused to a child by actions done before its conception.

For example, if waste known to be hazardous to a developing fetus is negligently left in an area and causes a child born several years later to have serious birth defects, the child has been wronged and his or her right not to be negligently harmed has been violated. The child, and so the child's right, did not exist when the negligent act took place, and had the child never been conceived its right – which was later violated – never would have existed either. The child's right not to be negligently harmed comes into existence with the child, and so can only exist and be violated if the child does come into existence. That there will be no right, and so no rights violation, unless the child comes into existence need be no barrier to there being a right and a rights violation if and when the child does come into existence.

Essentially the same point holds with regard to duties – wrongful life cases do not imply that there must be duties to nonexistent beings, only that there are duties to any existing child who has been wrongfully brought into existence in such conditions. A person's action or inaction at one time violates a duty to, and the rights of, a child who exists at a later time only if that child comes into existence, thereby creating the harmful effect of the earlier action. The unusual feature in a wrongful life case is that the action or inaction in question is bringing the child into existence.

Wrongful life legal cases have typically been brought against physicians or laboratories that failed to diagnose either the risk of the child having a devastating disease or the fetus actually having that disease, in either case preventing the parents from making an informed choice not to conceive or to abort the affected child. Our analysis makes clear that in principle the moral claim of wrongful life could as well be made against the parents if they knew before conception that their child would have such a disease, or knew after conception of the risk or certainty that their fetus did have such a disease, and yet allowed it to come into existence in that condition. Suppose that their reason for failing to act in the post-conception case, however, was a moral belief that abortion is seriously wrong even when the fetus will have a life not worth living. There is no inconsistency in believing that someone does not have a life worth living, but also believing that it would nevertheless be wrong to kill him or her. Such views are common in other contexts, such as when people believe that a very seriously disabled or dying patient does not have a life worth living, but that it would still be wrong to kill her without her consent.

Others who do not believe abortion is wrong may still view the parents' choice not to abort as morally wrong, and a wrong to their child. Should public policy and the law require so deeply intrusive an action as an abortion against the parents' own deeply held moral views, and allow civil or criminal charges against them for failure to do so? These "pro-life" parents would deny that there are any post-conception wrongful life cases because the only way after conception to prevent a child from being born, even knowing it will have a life not worth living, is by aborting it, and they believe doing that is not morally permissible. Its life may not be worth living, but it is not in this view a wrongful life.

It is crucial for understanding the deep difficulty of this case for public policy to recognize that the conflict between a "pro-choice" and "pro-life" position is in an important respect even deeper than the disagreement about abortion generally. Abortion is an issue about which some people acknowledge that the positions of others with whom they disagree nevertheless are not unreasonable, irrational, or simply mistaken. They acknowledge that abortion is a moral issue about which reasonable people can and do disagree. On many such issues there is good reason for public policy and the law to leave individuals free to act on their own convictions. In matters of largely self-regarding personal preference, such as how to decorate one's house, this policy has much to recommend it.

The controversy about abortion, of course, is so intractable and heated because it is different in several respects. First, many people consider others with whom they disagree about abortion to be simply and seriously mistaken and wrong; it is not just a matter about which they believe reasonable people disagree. Second, it is not a disagreement about a largely self-regarding action, but about an action viewed by one party as the murder of an innocent and defenseless person. Pro-choice individuals may accept a public policy that lets persons have or not have abortions according to their own moral convictions about it, since this ensures that abortion is legally available to any woman who wants it. But pro-life individuals who believe abortion is simply murder will not – nor should they, given these beliefs – accept that others should be legally permitted to choose it; doing so is not a neutral middle ground between pro-life and pro-choice positions.

A public policy that permitted prosecution of a post-conception wrongful life case against a woman who allowed her child to be born with a life not worth living because she believed the only way to prevent that happening – an abortion – would have been deeply and seriously immoral would take the abortion dispute to an even more profound level. Although public policy now permits women to obtain abortions that pro-life individuals consider clearly wrong, it at least does not require that pro-life individuals themselves have abortions. Requiring a pregnant pro-life woman in a post-conception wrongful life case to have an abortion to avoid a charge of wrongful life would do exactly that. On the other hand, in the pro-choice perspective, according to which abortion is not seriously wrong, preventing wrongful life by abortion is also a matter of protecting an innocent, defenseless third party from the great wrong of being born with a life so dominated by suffering and without compensating goods that it is a life not worth living.

It has long been clear that a public policy on abortion neutral between and acceptable to both pro-choice and pro-life positions is elusive. There is even less reason to expect that such a policy is possible about post-conception cases of wrongful life – moral conflict about abortion drives an even deeper wedge, blocking a mutual compromise over wrongful life. However, this is a book about some moral and philosophical problems raised by advances in genetics, not about abortion, and so we limit ourselves to showing the connections between the issues of the prevention of genetic disease, wrongful life and abortion, but cannot pursue the moral and policy complexities of abortion itself.

Public Policy and Wrongful Life Issues It is perhaps fortunate that, despite the great expansion of genetic information that will be available in the future both from pre-conception testing for genetic risks to potential offspring and from prenatal diagnosis of the genetic condition of a fetus, public policy may be able largely to avoid the most contentious and intractable wrongful life issues for at least two reasons. First, only a very small proportion of genetic abnormalities and diseases are both compatible with life and also so severe as to result in the affected child having a life not worth living. Second, courts and legislatures are likely to continue to be reluctant to permit wrongful life legal suits, both because damages covering the child's medical and extra care expenses can usually be obtained by a suit brought in the name of the parents instead of a wrongful life suit in the name of the child, and because uncertainty exists about how to assess damages for wrongful life. But regardless of what occurs in the courts, moral choices about whether conceiving a child or carrying a pregnancy to term would constitute an action of wrongful life will be increasingly faced in the future by parents or would-be parents.

A complicating factor is that the woman or couple making the choice will often face only a risk, not a certainty, that the child will not have a life worth living and that risk can vary from very low to approaching certainty. Whether it is morally wrong to conceive in the face of such risks will depend in part on the woman's willingness and intention to do appropriate prenatal genetic testing and to abort her fetus if it is found to have a disease or condition incompatible with a worthwhile life.

As noted before, pursuing the moral complexities of abortion would take us too far afield here. Nevertheless, suppose, as the authors of this book believe, that the fetus at least through the first two trimesters is not a person and so aborting it then is morally permissible. Aborting a fetus found during the first two trimesters to have a disease that would make life a burden to the child prevents the creation of a person with a life not worth living; no wrongful life then occurs, so there is no question of moral wrong-doing. Even conceiving when there is a relatively high risk of genetic transmission of a disease incompatible with a life worth living could be morally acceptable so long as the woman firmly intends to test the fetus for the disease and to abort it if the disease is present.

On the other hand, a woman may intend not to test her fetus and abort it if such a disease is present, either because she considers abortion morally wrong or for other reasons. In that case, the higher the risk that her child will have a genetic disease or condition incompatible with a life worth living, the stronger the moral case that she does a serious moral wrong to that child in conceiving it and carrying it to term.

If a mother or anyone else knowingly and responsibly caused harm to an already born child so serious as to make its life no longer worth living, that would constitute extremely serious child abuse and be an extremely serious moral and legal wrong. In that case, however, the child would have had a worthwhile life that was taken away by whomever was guilty of the child abuse; the wrong to the child then is depriving it of a worthwhile life that it otherwise would have had. That is a different and arguably more serious wrong than wrongful life, where the alternative to the life not worth living is never having a life at all, and so not having a worthwhile life taken away. The wrong in nearly all cases of wrongful life is bringing into existence a child who will have a short life dominated by severe and unremitting suffering – that is, being caused to undergo that suffering without compensating benefits.

How high must the risk be of a child having a genetic disease incompatible with a worthwhile life be for it to be morally wrong for the parents to conceive it and allow it to be born? There is, of course, no precise probability at which the risk of the harm makes it morally wrong to conceive or not to abort; different cases fall along a spectrum in the degree to which undertaking the risk is morally justified. How seriously wrong, if a wrong at all, it is to risk the conception and birth of a child with such a life will depend on several factors. How bad is the child's life, and in particular how severe and unremitting is its suffering? How high is the probability of the child having a genetic disease incompatible with a worthwhile life? How weighty are its parents' interests in having the child? For example, is this likely its parents' only opportunity to become parents, or are they already parents seeking to have additional children? How significant is the possibility of the parents having an unaffected child if this pregnancy is terminated and another conception pursued? How willing and able are the parents to support and care for the child while it lives?

These factors, and no doubt others unique to specific cases, will determine how strong the moral case is against individuals risking having a child who will not have a life worth living. It is worth underlining that any case for the wrongness of parents conceiving and bringing to term such a child depends on their having reasonable access to genetic testing, contraception, and abortion services, and this can require public provision and funding of these services for those who otherwise cannot afford them.

We hope that our analysis so far makes it clear why we believe that there are some cases, albeit very few, in which it would be clearly and seriously morally wrong for individuals to risk conceiving and having such a child. However, use of government power to force an abortion on an unwilling woman would be so deeply invasive of her reproductive freedom, bodily integrity, and right to decide about her own health care as to be virtually never morally justified. Allowing the child to be born and then withholding life support even over its parents' objections would probably be morally preferable. The government's doing this forcibly and over the parents' objections would be extraordinarily controversial, both morally and legally, but in true cases of wrongful life, the wrong done is sufficiently serious as to possibly justify doing so in an individual case. However, at the present time and as a practical matter, the common and strong bias in favor of life, even in the face of serious suffering, makes it nearly inconceivable that public policy might authorize the government forcibly to take an infant from its parents, not for the purpose of securing beneficial treatment for it, but instead to allow it to die because it could not have a worthwhile life. Moreover, the risk of abuse of such a governmental power to intervene forcibly in reproductive choices to prevent a wrongful life is too great to warrant granting that power.

There is a stronger moral case for the use of government coercive power to prevent conception in some wrongful life cases. Similar power is now exercised by government over severely mentally disabled people who are sterilized to prevent them from conceiving. In such cases, the individual sterilized is typically deemed incompetent to make a responsible decision about conception, as well as unable to raise a child. Forced sterilization of a competent individual is more serious morally, but the harm to be prevented of wrongful life is more serious than the harm prevented in typical involuntary sterilization cases where the child would have a worthwhile life if raised by others. Nevertheless, the historical abuses of "eugenic sterilizations" discussed in Chapter 2 are enough to warrant not giving government the coercive power to prevent wrongful life conceptions unless their occurrence was very common and widespread. Wrongful life conceptions are sufficiently uncommon, and practical and moral difficulties in using the coercive power of government to prevent them sufficiently great, to rule out policies that prevent people from conceiving wrongful lives. Coercive government intrusion into reproductive freedom to prevent wrongful life would be wrong.

Pre-Conception Interventions to Prevent Conditions Compatible with a Worthwhile Life

The Human Genome Project and related research will produce information permitting genetic screening for an increasing number of genetically transmitted diseases, or susceptibilities to diseases and other harmful conditions. In the foreseeable future, our capacities for pre-conception and prenatal screening for these diseases and conditions will almost certainly far outstrip our capacities for genetic or other therapy to correct for the harmful genes and their effects. The vast majority of decisions faced by prospective parents, consequently, will not be whether to pursue genetic or other therapy for their fetus or child, but instead whether to test for particular genetic risks and/or conditions and, when they are found to be present, whether to avoid conception or to terminate a pregnancy. Moreover, the vast majority of genetic risks that will be subject to testing will not be for conditions incompatible with a life worth living – the wrongful life cases – but rather for less severe conditions compatible with having a life well worth living.

These genetically transmitted conditions and diseases will take different forms. Sometimes their disabling features will be manifest during much of the individual's life, but still will permit a worthwhile life, as with most cases of Down syndrome, which is caused by a chromosomal abnormality. Sometimes the disease or condition will result in significant disability and a significantly shorter than normal life span, but not so disabling or short as to make the life not worth living, as with cystic fibrosis. Sometimes the disease or condition, although devastating in its effects on the afflicted individual's quality of life, will only manifest symptoms after a substantial period of normal life and function, as with Huntington's chorea and Alzheimer's dementia.

When the genetically transmitted conditions could and should have been prevented, they will constitute what we have called cases of wrongful disability. But in which cases will the failure to prevent a genetically transmitted disability be morally wrong? Again, different cases fall along a spectrum in the degree of moral justification for undertaking or not undertaking to prevent the disability.

Whether failure to prevent a disability is wrong in specific cases will typically depend on many features of that case. For example, what is the relative seriousness of the disability for the child's well-being and opportunities? What measures are available to the child's parents to prevent the condition – such as abortion, artificial insemination by donor, or oocyte donation – and how acceptable are these means to the prospective parents? Is it possible, and if so how likely, that they can conceive another child without the disabling condition, or will any child they conceive have or be highly likely to have the condition? If the disability can only be prevented by not conceiving at all, do the couple have alternative means, such as adoption, of becoming parents? When the condition can be prevented or its adverse impact compensated for, what means are necessary to do so?

These and other considerations can all bear on the threshold question: Is the severity of a genetically transmitted disability great enough that particular parents are morally obligated to prevent it, given the specific means necessary for them to do so; or is it sufficiently limited and minor that it need not be prevented, but is instead a condition that the child can reasonably be expected to live with?

Different prospective parents will answer this threshold question

differently because they differ about such matters as the burdensomeness and undesirability of particular alternative methods of reproduction that may be necessary to prevent the disability, the seriousness of
the impact of the particular disability on a person's well-being and
opportunity, aspects of reproductive freedom such as the importance
of having children and of having biologically related as opposed to
adopted or only partially biologically related children, the extent of
society's obligation and efforts to make special accommodations to
eliminate or ameliorate the disability, and their willingness to assume
the burdens of raising a child with the disability in question.

Because there are these multiple sources of reasonable disagreement
bearing on the threshold question, and because the aspects of reproductive freedom at stake will usually be of substantial importance,
public policy should usually permit prospective parents to make and
act on their own judgments about whether they morally ought to
prevent particular genetically transmitted disabilities for the sake of
their child. But there is a systematic objection to all preconception
wrongful disability cases that must be met in order to clear the way
for individual judgments about specific cases.

To fix attention on the general problem in question, which is not
restricted to cases of genetically transmitted disease, let us imagine a
case, call it P1, in which a woman is told by her physician that she
should not attempt to become pregnant now because she has a condition that is highly likely to result in moderate mental retardation in
her child. Her condition is easily and fully treatable by taking a quite
safe medication for one month. If she takes the medication and delays
becoming pregnant for a month, the risk to her child will be eliminated
and there is every reason to expect that she will have a normal child.
Because the delay would interfere with her vacation travel plans, however, she does not take the medication, gets pregnant now, and gives
birth to a child who is moderately retarded.

According to commonsense moral views, this woman acts wrongly,
and in particular, wrongs her child by not preventing its disability for
such a morally trivial reason, even if for pragmatic reasons many
people would oppose government intrusion into her decision. According to commonsense morality, her action is no different morally than
if she failed to take the medicine in a case, P2, in which the condition
is discovered, and so the medicine must be taken, after conception and
when she is already pregnant. Nor is it different morally than if she
failed to provide a similar medication to her born child, in a case, P3,

if doing so is again necessary to prevent moderate mental retardation in her child. It is worth noting that in most states in this country, her action in P3 would probably constitute medical neglect, and governmental child protection agencies could use coercive measures, if necessary, to ensure the child's treatment.

This suggests that it might only be because her reproductive freedom and her right to decide about her own health care are also involved in P1 that we are reluctant to coerce her decision, if necessary, there as well. On what Derek Parfit has called the "no difference" view, the view of commonsense morality, her failure to use the medication to prevent her child's mental retardation would be equally seriously wrong, and for the same reason, in each of the three cases (Parfit 1984). But her action in P1, which is analogous in relevant respects to preconception genetic screening to prevent disabilities, has a special feature that makes it not so easily shown to be wrong as commonsense morality might suppose.

What is the philosophical problem at the heart of wrongful disability cases like P1? As with wrongful life cases, in which the necessary comparison of life with nonexistence is thought to create both philosophical and policy problems, so also in wrongful disability cases do the philosophical and policy problems arise from having to compare a disabled existence with not having existed at all. But the nature of the philosophical problems in wrongful life and wrongful disability cases are in fact quite different. The philosophical objections we considered to wrongful life cases centered on whether it is coherent to compare an individual's quality of life with never having existed at all – that is, with nonexistence – and whether merely possible persons can have moral rights or be owed moral obligations. In wrongful disability cases, a person's disability uncontroversially leaves him or her with a worthwhile life. The philosophical problem, as noted earlier, is how this is compatible with the commonsense view that it would be wrong not to prevent the disability.

The special difficulty in wrongful disability cases, which Derek Parfit has called the "nonidentity problem," is that it would not be better for the person with the disability to have had it prevented, since that could only be done by preventing him or her from ever having existed at all. Preventing the disability would deny the disabled individual a worthwhile, although disabled, life. That is because the disability could only have been prevented either by conceiving at a different time and/or under different circumstances (in which case a different child would have been conceived) or by terminating the pregnancy (in which case this child also never would have been born, although a different child may or may not have been conceived instead). None of these possible means of preventing the disability would be better for the child with the disability – all would deny him or her a worthwhile life.

But if the mother's failure to prevent the disability did not make her child worse off than he or she would have been without the intervention, then her failure to prevent it seems not to harm her child. And if she did not harm her child by not preventing its disability, then why does she wrong her child morally by failing to do so? How could making her child better off, or at least not worse off, by giving it a life worth living, albeit a life with a significant disability, wrong it? A wrong action must be bad for someone, but her choice to create her child with its disability is bad for no one, so she does no wrong. Of course, there is a sense in which it is bad for her child to have the disability, in comparison with being without it, but there is nothing the mother could have done to enable that child to be born without the disability, and so nothing she does or omits doing is bad for her child.

So actions whose harmful effects would constitute seriously wrongful child abuse if done to an existing child are no harm, and so not wrong, if their harmful effects on a child are inextricable from the act of bringing that child into existence with a worthwhile life! This argument threatens to undermine common and firmly held moral judgments, as well as public policy measures, concerning prevention of such disabilities for children.

Actual versus Possible Persons   David Heyd has accepted the implications of this argument and concludes that in all of what he calls "genesis" choices – that is, choices that inextricably involve whether a particular individual will be brought into existence – only the interests of actual persons, not those of possible persons such as the disabled child in case P1, are relevant to the choice (Heyd 1992). So in case P1, the effects on the parents and the broader society, such as the greater childrearing costs and burdens of having the moderately retarded child instead of taking the medication and having a normal child a month later are relevant to the decision. But the effects on and interests of the child who would be moderately retarded are not relevant. In cases P2 and P3, on the other hand, Heyd presumably would share the commonsense moral view that the fundamental reason the woman's action would be wrong is the easily preventable harm that she allows her child to suffer. In these situations, the preventable harm to her child is the basis of the moral wrong she does her child.

In Parfit's "no difference" view, the woman's action in P1 is equally wrong, and for the same reason, as her action in P2 and P3. We share with Parfit, in opposition to Heyd, the position that the woman's action in P1 is wrong because of the easily preventable effect on her child. But we do not accept the "no difference" thesis. We will suggest a reason why her action in P1 may not be as seriously wrong as in P2 or P3, and also suggest that the reason her action is wrong in P1 is similar to but nevertheless importantly different from the reason it is wrong in P2 and P3.

As Parfit notes, the difficulty is identifying and formulating a moral principle that implies that the woman's action in P1 is seriously wrong, but does not have unacceptable implications for other cases. Before proceeding further, we must emphasize that we cannot explore this difficulty fully here. The issues are extraordinarily complex and involve testing the implications of such a principle in a wide variety of cases outside of the genetic context that is our concern here (e.g., in population policy contexts and, in particular, avoiding what Parfit calls the "Repugnant Conclusion" and explaining what he calls the "Asymmetry"). Its relationship to other principles and features of a moral theory must also be explained, including that to the principle applicable to P2 and P3 (Parfit 1984).

The apparent failure to account for common and firmly held moral views in the genetics cases of wrongful disabilities like P1 constitutes one of the most important practical limitations (problems of population policy are another) of traditional ethical theories and of their principles of beneficence – doing good – and nonmaleficence – not causing or preventing harm. Where the commonsense moral judgment about cases like P1 is that the woman is morally wrong to go ahead and have the disabled child instead of waiting and having a normal child, the principles of traditional ethical theories apparently fail to support that judgment. New or revised moral principles appear to be needed. What alternatives and resources, either within or beyond traditional moral principles or theories, could account for and explain the wrong done in wrongful disability cases?

Person-Affecting Moral Principles   Perhaps the most natural way to account for the moral wrong in wrongful disability cases like P1 is to

abandon the specific feature of typical moral principles about obligations to prevent or not cause harm which generates difficulty when we
move from standard cases of prevention of harm to existing persons,
as in P3, to harm prevention in genesis cases like P1. That feature is
what philosophers have called the "person-affecting" property of principles of beneficence and nonmaleficence. Recall that earlier we appealed to principle M: Those individuals responsible for a child's, or
other dependent person's, welfare are morally required not to let her
suffer a serious harm or disability or a serious loss of happiness or
good that they could have prevented without imposing substantial
burdens or costs or loss of benefits on themselves or others.

The person-affecting feature of M is that the persons who will suffer
the harm if it is not prevented and not suffer it if it is prevented must
be one and the same distinct individual. If M is violated, a distinct
child or dependent person is harmed without good reason, and so the
moral wrong is done to that person. Since harms to persons must
always be harms to some person, it may seem that there is no alternative to principles that are person-affecting, but that is not so. The
alternative is clearest if we follow Derek Parfit by distinguishing "same
person" from "same number" choices.

In same person choices, the same persons exist in each of the different alternative courses of action from which an agent chooses. Cases
P2 and P3 above were same person choices (assuming in P2 that the
fetus is or will become a person, though that is not essential to the
point) – the harm of moderate retardation prevented is to the woman's
fetus or born child. In same number choices, the same number of
persons exist in each of the alternative courses of action from which
an agent chooses, but the identities of some of the persons – that is,
who exists in those alternatives – is affected by the choice. P1 is a
same number but not a same person choice – the woman's choice
affects which child will exist. If the woman does not take the medication and wait to conceive, she gives birth to a moderately retarded
child, whereas if she takes the medication and waits to conceive, she
gives birth to a different child who is not moderately retarded.

The concept of "harm," arguably, is necessarily comparative, and
so the concept of "harm prevention" may seem necessarily person-
affecting; this is why harm prevention principles seem not to apply to
same number, different person choices like P1. But it would be a
mistake to think that non–person-affecting principles, even harm prevention principles, are not coherent. Suppose for simplicity that the

harm in question in P1 from the moderate retardation is suffering and limited opportunity. Then in P1, if the woman chooses to have the moderately retarded child, she causes suffering and limited opportunity to exist that would be prevented and not exist if she chooses to take the medication and wait to conceive a different normal child. An example of a non-person-affecting principle that applies to P1 is:

N: Individuals are morally required not to let any child or other dependent person for whose welfare they are responsible experience serious suffering or limited opportunity or serious loss of happiness or good, if they can act so that, without affecting the number of persons who will exist and without imposing substantial burdens or costs or loss of benefits on themselves or others, no child or other dependent person for whose welfare they are responsible will experience serious suffering or limited opportunity or serious loss of happiness or good.

Any suffering and limited opportunity must, of course, be experienced by some person – they cannot exist in disembodied form – and so in that sense N remains person-affecting. But N does not require that the same individuals who experience suffering and limited opportunity in one alternative exist without the suffering and limited opportunity in the other alternative; it is a same number, not a same person, principle. N allows the child who does not experience the suffering and limited opportunity to be a different person from the child who does; that is why the woman's action in P1 is morally wrong according to N, but not according to M. If the woman in P1 does take the medication and wait to conceive a normal child, she acts so as to make the suffering and limited opportunity "avoidable by substitution," as Philip G. Peters, Jr. has put it (Peters 1989).

A different way of making the same point is to say that this principle for the prevention of suffering applies not to distinct individuals, so that the prevention of suffering must make a distinct individual better off than he or she would have been, as M requires, but to the classes of individuals who will exist if the suffering is or is not prevented, as N does (Peters 1989; Bayles 1976). Assessing the prevention of suffering by the effect on classes of persons, as opposed to distinct individuals, also allows for avoidability by substitution – an individual who does not suffer if one choice is made is substituted for a different person who does suffer if the other choice is made. A principle applied to the classes of all persons who will exist in each of two or more alternative courses of action will be a non–person-affecting principle.

The preceding discussion referred only to the prevention of harm or loss of opportunity because that is the focus of this chapter. However, it should be noted that N allows, for the same reasons as does M, the weighing of securing happiness or good against preventing suffering and loss of opportunity. If it did not, but required only preventing serious suffering, then N would require not creating a child who would experience serious suffering, but also great happiness and good, in favor of creating a child who would suffer less, but experience no compensating happiness or good, even though the latter child on balance would have a substantially worse life. We note as well that we have not defined "serious" as it functions in either M or N; it is difficult to do so in a sufficiently general yet precise way to make the application of the principle simple and straightforward for a wide range of cases. Judgment must be used in applying N. The seriousness of suffering and loss of opportunity, or loss of happiness and good, that could be prevented must be assessed principally in light of their potential impact on the child's life, the probability of that impact, and the possibility and probability of compensatory measures to mitigate that impact. Applying N requires judgment as well regarding what are "substantial burdens or costs, or loss of benefits, on themselves or others." For example, how serious are possible moral objections by the parents to the use of abortion, and how great are the financial costs or medical risks of having an alternative child using assisted reproduction technologies, and so forth?

We do not claim that all moral principles concerning obligations to prevent harm, or of beneficence and nonmaleficence more generally, are non–person-affecting, and so we do not reject principle M. In typical cases of harm where a distinct individual is made worse off, the moral principles most straightforwardly applicable to them are person-affecting. Our claim is only that an adequate moral theory should include as well non–person-affecting principles like N. How these principles are related, as well as what principles apply to different number cases in a comprehensive moral theory, involves deep difficulties in moral theory that we cannot pursue here. In this respect, we do not propose a full solution to the nonidentity problem.

Doing Wrong versus Wronging a Person   Even acknowledging these limitations in our proposal for avoiding the nonidentity problem, there are at least two apparent difficulties with it that need to be explored further. The first is that it does not account for the important aspect of the commonsense moral judgment about P1 that the woman specifically wrongs her child by not preventing its disability; her child is the victim of her wrong, and so has a moral grievance against her. But according to N, the disability should not have been prevented for the sake of that child, since doing so would have made that child worse off, or at least no better off (it would never have had its worthwhile life). Rather, according to N, the disability should have been prevented for the sake of less overall suffering and limited opportunity, or for the sake of the class of persons who would have existed if the suffering and limited opportunity had been prevented.

Joel Feinberg has argued that moral rights provide individuals with moral standing as a source of special moral claims against others that they respect those rights and as a source of special moral complaints against others who violate those rights (Feinberg 1970). In typical cases of causing or failing to prevent harm, like P3, person-affecting principles like M also correctly direct us to the victim who has suffered the harm, and who has a special moral complaint against the individual who violated M by causing or not preventing the harm. That is why standard accounts of harm as well as standard moral principles concerning our obligations to prevent or not to cause it take a person-affecting form. Does this imply that non–person-affecting principles like N are inadequate in cases like P1?

We believe it does not because we believe the common intuition that in a case like P1 the woman wrongs her child should, on reflection, be abandoned. In P1, the child who suffers the moderate retardation is not a victim she has made worse off than he or she would have been. So her child does not have a special moral complaint against her for her failure to prevent harm to him that our moral principles must account for. Her child cannot claim to have a special complaint against the mother, because the child is better off, or at least not worse off, as a result of her not meeting her obligation under N. In P1, and in wrongful disability cases more generally, there is no victim with a special moral complaint from having been made worse off as a result of the woman's action, and so no need for a person-affecting harm prevention principle, such as a moral right not to be harmed, to direct us to the standpoint of a victim of the harm.

This suggests that non–person-affecting principles like N may not only be adequate for cases like P1, but that they are indeed preferable there to person-affecting principles like M precisely because they do not direct us to the special standpoint and complaint of a victim who has been made worse off. Moral principles applicable to P1 and other wrongful disability cases should not direct us to a victim in that way because there is no victim who has been made worse off and who therefore has a special complaint. Abandoning person-affecting principles of beneficence and nonmaleficence to account for wrongful disabilities may thus be a promising approach to them, especially if reflection on such cases leaves us confident that the woman in P1 acts wrongly, but weakens our initial confidence that she also wrongs her child in letting it be born disabled.

The belief that she wrongs her child may be further weakened by reflection back on wrongful life cases. We argued that wrongful life occurs only when the child has a life that is so bad overall as to not be worth living, a life that is worse than no life at all. That is the correct threshold for the mother having wronged her child in conceiving and/ or carrying it to term while knowing how bad its quality of life would be. But since in P1 her child's quality of life does not fall below that threshold and could also be prevented only by not conceiving it, or by terminating her pregnancy after it had been conceived, she does not wrong it by allowing it to be born. She does act wrongly, but nevertheless wrongs no one, as N correctly implies; there is no wrong to her disabled child nor any violation of its rights that our moral principles must account for.

Resistance to this view, we believe, probably comes principally from the persistent presence of the disability that the child in P1 has. But if a child suffered a similar disability from natural causes and the disability could only have been prevented at the cost of the child's life, no one would insist that the existence of the disability implied that someone who could have prevented it had wronged the child by not doing so. When the disability arises from natural causes, no one need have acted wrongly, whereas in P1 the woman does act wrongly. But in neither case is the child wronged by the fact that its disability was not prevented at the cost of its life. We conclude that the first apparent difficulty with abandoning standard person-affecting moral principles of nonmaleficence in wrongful disability cases – the fact that they fail to identify a victim who has been wronged – in favor of impersonal principles like N is no difficulty after all.

It is worth pointing out one implication of our argument that moral principles that best fit the features of wrongful disability cases will be non–person-affecting. Others have attempted to solve Parfit's non-identity problem by seeking to show that standard person-affecting principles can be successfully applied to it, and so, by implication, to wrongful disability cases like P1. For example, James Woodward has argued that the general principle implicit in the formulation of the nonidentity problem and in our statement of the problem posed by case P1 – that one individual's action cannot wrong another person unless that other person is overall worse off as a result of the action – is false. To take Woodward's example, an African American refused an airline ticket by a racist clerk has suffered an injustice and been wronged even if the plane the person was barred from crashes, killing all the passengers (Woodward 1986; Parfit 1986).

Woodward's argument suggests that an appeal to moral rights may be possible in cases of wrongful disability like P1 because moral rights protect specific interests, and so a person's moral right can be wrongly violated even if the violation does not harm the person by making him or her overall worse off. What moral right of the child would be violated in P1 is not clear, but Woodward's argument shows that an appeal to a moral right of the child in case P1 might explain and characterize the wrong its mother does the child. Woodward takes it to be an advantage of his account that it both shows how the woman wrongs her child and how her child suffers a loss by her action.

Moral rights principles are person-affecting moral principles, and so no appeal to non–person-affecting principles like N would be necessary if Woodward's account is correct. We shall not pursue the details of Woodward's argument here, but even if he is correct that standard accounts of moral rights can be applied to cases of wrongful disability like P1, our argument has been that person-affecting moral principles will mischaracterize the wrong done in such cases. The very features of person-affecting principles that Woodward takes to be their advantage – that they make the wrong a wrong done to the child and the loss from the wrong a loss suffered by the child – we have argued mischaracterize wrongful disability cases. Non–person-affecting principles correctly fit wrongful disability cases because the nonidentity problem at the heart of those cases makes the wrong that is done not done to the child and the disability not a loss suffered by anyone. No person-affecting moral principles will correctly fit wrongful disability cases.

The Place of Non–Person-Affecting Principles in an Overall Moral Theory The second apparent difficulty with our appeal to a non–person-affecting principle like N for wrongful disabilities concerns its place in an overall moral theory. Our point is not that standard person-affecting principles of beneficence and nonmaleficence should be rejected in favor of non–person-affecting principles like N. Typical cases of harm prevention and rights violations are properly assessed with standard person-affecting principles like M. Moreover, not preventing the same disability to a born child, as in case P3, may be more seriously wrong than not preventing it in a genesis case such as P1. This is because in P3 there is a victim who has been wronged and who can correctly think that his or her life could have been better if the mother had prevented the disability. This grievance present in P3, but not in P1, is a reason for rejecting the "no difference" thesis regarding P1 and P3; not only do different principles apply to them, but P3 is more seriously wrong.

Our argument for the non–person-affecting principle N is only that it is needed, in addition to the person-affecting principle M, for cases like P1. How person-affecting and non–person-affecting principles are coherently and consistently combined in a comprehensive moral theory is an important unsolved problem (McMahon 1996).

A further problem concerns whether, and if so how, non–person-affecting principles like N can be extended from same number cases, in which they give us the desired result, to different number cases, where they have ethically problematic implications. Some of these implications can be indicated, but not explored here. The intuitive point underlying principle N is that it is good to prevent suffering and promote happiness even if doing so reduces no person's suffering and increases no person's happiness. But in different-number cases, that implies Parfit's Repugnant Conclusion:

For any possible population of at least 10 billion people, all with a very high quality of life, there must be some much larger imaginable population whose existence, if other things are equal, would be better, even though its members have lives that are barely worth living.

Extending a principle like N to cases with different numbers of persons would imply that we should increase total happiness slightly by vastly increasing the population, even though we thereby make every existing person much worse off. Only person-affecting principles seem likely to avoid unacceptable implications like the Repugnant Conclusion, since only they require that a reduction in suffering or an increase in happiness be to a distinct individual. No comprehensive theory – Parfit calls it theory X to signify an as-yet-unidentified theory

– has been identified that adequately accounts for both same number and different number cases.

Wrongful Disability, Different-Number Cases   But are all wrongful disability cases same-number cases, so that principle N can be applied to them? A possible different number wrongful disability case occurs if the parents would be unable to have a nondisabled child instead. For example, the parents are virtually certain to genetically transmit the disability to any child they conceive. If they choose not to have a child with a disability and can have no other child instead, the result is one fewer children – a different-number case. But if having the disabled child is the only way the parents can satisfy their important reproductive interest in having children, and if that child will have a worthwhile, though disabled, life, they do no wrong in having the child; it is not a case of wrongful disability.

Different-number cases of wrongful disability might also arise where the parents could only have substituted two or more normal children for the disabled child. It is difficult to imagine how such cases would arise; perhaps if the only way to substitute for the disabled child was to use a form of artificial reproductive technology that typically results in multiple births by parents deeply opposed to abortion. We believe that if it is only possible to substitute more than one nondisabled child for the disabled child, then all other things being equal that would not make it any less wrong to fail to do so. But we acknowledge having no comprehensive solution to the application of principles of beneficence and nonmaleficence to different number cases.

The Nondirectiveness Norm in Genetic Counseling   The practice of genetic counseling is typically guided by a strong norm of nondirectiveness. The counselor's role is only to provide the counselee with information about the harmful genetic condition the counselee's child may or will have. The counselor enables the counselee to make an informed reproductive choice but should not, according to this norm, seek to influence that choice. The counselee's values, not the counselor's, should guide the choice. One important rationale for this norm has been to keep genetic counselors out of the morally and politically contentious issue of abortion. (The norm of nondirectiveness may also be a protective strategy to disassociate genetic counseling from the taint of eugenics.)

Our analysis shows that in cases of both wrongful life and wrongful disability the nondirectiveness norm is morally problematic. Although reasonable disagreement exists about whether some failures to prevent harmful genetically transmitted conditions would be morally wrong, in other cases, such failures would be as clearly and uncontroversially wrong as cases of child abuse and neglect whose wrongness is not seriously questioned. Just as nondirectiveness about those cases of child abuse and neglect would be indefensible, so too is nondirectiveness about genetic transmission of comparable harmful conditions. The norm of nondirectiveness in genetic counseling may function as a useful reminder of reasonable disagreement about whether prevention of a particular harmful condition is morally required, but it is indefensible as an inflexible and systematic norm to guide all genetic counseling.

CONCLUSION

The issues of reproductive freedom and the obligation to prevent genetically transmitted harmful conditions explored in this chapter are in some respects familiar because they are similar to issues that arise outside the genetic context. The account we developed of the different content or components of reproductive freedom, together with the distinct moral grounds of reproductive freedom, obviously applies outside the context of the prevention of genetically transmitted harmful conditions. We developed our account of reproductive freedom in some detail for two reasons. First, one of the worst wrongs of the old eugenics was its disregard for reproductive freedom; to avoid making the same mistake, it is necessary to have a clear understanding of and appreciation for reproductive freedom. Second, when there is moral conflict about the prevention of genetically transmitted harmful conditions, it is reproductive freedom that typically must be put in the balance in order to determine whether preventing those harmful conditions is morally required.

Of course, as we noted much earlier, in the great majority of cases there will be no conflict between reproductive freedom and the prevention of genetically transmitted harmful conditions because most prospective parents will voluntarily, even eagerly, avail themselves of genetic information and interventions that will prevent harmful conditions for their children. The presumption that prospective parents will act in the best interests of their children is well founded, but it does not hold true in every case, either because some prospective parents evidence little concern for their children's well-being or because there are genuine and unavoidable conflicts of interest between parents and their children.

We distinguished several different kinds of cases in which moral issues about the prevention of genetically transmitted harmful conditions can arise, and focused our closest attention on the philosophical and moral complexities at the heart of the failures to prevent harmful conditions that we called wrongful life and wrongful disability. Neither wrongful life nor wrongful disability are unique to the genetic context, but the genetic context will soon contain, if it does not already, their most common and important instances.

We have tried to show how relatively familiar principles of harm prevention can be interpreted and extended so as to apply in these new and often perplexing cases. But it has not always been possible simply to apply familiar ethical principles to these new problems and contexts. We have found here, as elsewhere in this volume, that ethical problems raised by the new genetic knowledge, together with the new interventions that knowledge will likely make possible, uncover and illuminate some important limits of contemporary ethical theories and help point the way toward extending and enriching them.

This chapter has focused on the circumstances in which parents are morally required to undertake genetic interventions to prevent harmful conditions in their offspring. But the moral principles we have appealed to also assert a responsibility to secure benefits for offspring. Chapter 7 explores the limits of what it is permissible for them to do in order to improve their children's lives through genetic interventions.

SEVEN

GENETIC INTERVENTION AND THE MORALITY OF INCLUSION

OBJECTIVES

The Morality of Inclusion

So far this volume has examined ethical issues concerning how, when, and by whom genetic intervention technologies should be employed. Until now, the tacit assumption has been that the project of using genetic science to improve human lives is not only ethically permissible but laudable. The present chapter articulates, analyzes, and evaluates an arresting critique of this basic assumption that has been advanced by some members of the disabilities rights movement. Addressing the radical disabilities rights challenge will reveal how the prospect of advances in genetic knowledge and genetic intervention pushes the limits of ethical theory by raising profound issues about what we referred to in Chapter 3 as the morality of inclusion.

These two objectives are intimately related. The critique by disabilities rights advocates is a profound challenge to the reassuring assumption that the new genetics avoids the exclusionary features of the eugenics movements that were noted in Chapter 1. The concept of the morality of inclusion provides the key to articulating the various dimensions of exclusion and understanding their moral significance.

At the deepest level, a theory of the morality of inclusion would articulate criteria for membership in what might be called the primary moral community, specifying the characteristics that individuals must have in order to qualify as worthy of equal consideration and respect. Such a theory would also delineate the scope and limits of our obligations to include other individuals or groups in various mutually beneficial cooperative arrangements and hence make them eligible not only for the concrete benefits of participation in those arrangements but for the status of equality that is accorded to those who stand in relations of reciprocity with one another.

Here the concept of a cooperative framework, which we introduced and expanded upon in Chapter 3, is of critical importance. The term covers a wide range of structures within which cooperation can occur, from the internal organization of business firms to the most basic institutions of a society. In the United States and other "developed" societies, the most basic cooperative framework consists, to a large extent, of the competitive market system. The more fundamental and pervasive a cooperative framework is in a society, the more debilitating it is for an individual if he or she cannot participate effectively in it. In some cases, the gap between the capacities an individual possesses and the requirements for participation in the cooperative framework is so wide that it can be said, without much exaggeration, that the individual is excluded from participating. In most cases, however, exclusion is not total; instead, there are limitations of varying degrees of severity upon the effectiveness with which an individual can participate.

Individuals may be unable to participate effectively in a framework for cooperation in several different ways. Hence different strategies will be required for overcoming exclusion. If existing law excludes certain people, we can fulfill our obligations of inclusion by changing the law, allowing those who have the requisite capacities to participate in our cooperative endeavors to do so. But in other cases there is a mismatch between what the cooperative framework demands of participants and the capacities of some individuals. Even if they are not legally prohibited or otherwise actively barred, they cannot participate effectively. Some cooperative frameworks are more vital for a person's prospects, interpersonal relationships, and self-esteem than others. When a mismatch between a person's abilities and what may be called the dominant cooperative framework of society occurs, the results may be devastating.

When this happens, a theory of the morality of inclusion should be able to tell us whether and to what extent we are obligated to undertake efforts to enable those individuals to participate. This could occur either through changing the cooperative framework so that its demands do not exceed their capacities or through enhancing their capacities so that they can meet the demands of the cooperative framework.

An adequate theory of the morality of inclusion would answer at

least three questions: Which beings qualify as members of the primary
moral community? Under what conditions are participants in a cooperative framework obligated to include individuals who can participate
effectively? And to what extent is there an obligation to ensure that
the nature of society's most fundamental framework for cooperation
renders it more rather than less inclusive? (More generally, to what
extent should our choice of frameworks for cooperation be guided by
a commitment to making more individuals able to participate effectively in them?)

This question is of crucial significance not only because whether an
individual can participate effectively in the dominant cooperative
framework will have dramatic effects on his or her life prospects for
tangible social goods such as income and access to rewarding occupa-
tions. In addition, and in some ways more important, those who are
excluded from participation in the dominant cooperative framework
are relegated to the inferior status of dependency. They are not regarded, and tend not to regard themselves, as fully equal to those
whose relationships with one another are characterized by the reciprocity that binds together active participants in the dominant cooperative scheme. Instead of being regarded as fundamentally equal subjects of relations of justice, they may be regarded as objects of charity.

Neglect of the Morality of Inclusion in Ethical Theory

Traditional and contemporary ethical theories have frequently grap-
pled with the question of who qualifies as members of the primary
moral community, with different theories offering different criteria.
(Kantian theories focus on the capacities required for rational agency;
utilitarian theories require only sentience – the capacity for pain and
pleasure.) The other two questions about the morality of inclusion
have rarely been addressed, however, in a systematic manner, and in
many theories are never explicitly raised at all.[1]

Whether an individual is able to participate in the most basic coop-

---

[1] For an articulation of some of the issues that a theory of the morality of inclusion would
address and a selective historical survey of the failure of mainstream ethical and political
theories to do so, see Buchanan (1993). As an example of a contemporary theorist who
discusses some issues of membership but does not consider whether there are obligations
to modify cooperative arrangements to include those now unable to participate effectively
in them, see Walzer (1983), especially Chapter 2, pp. 31–62. To that extent, the morality
of inclusion is a neglected but important part of ethical theory.

erative framework of society usually determines the share of social wealth to which the person has access. Hence it would be assumed that theories of distributive justice would address issues of inclusion. But theorizing about distributive justice often proceeds on a simplifying assumption that obscures the third question: namely, that the basic framework of social cooperation is one in which all or most individuals who are members of the primary moral community are able to participate effectively (Rawls in Sen and Williams 1982; Rawls 1993). Given this assumption, the fundamental problem of justice is taken to be: How are the burdens and benefits of social cooperation to be distributed among the members of a society considered as participants in one basic cooperative framework?

Unfortunately, what most theorists of justice overlook is that proceeding in this familiar way slides over a prior question of great significance: How does the choice of a cooperative framework influence who will be able to participate effectively in that effort? Given their capacities, some individuals will be able to participate effectively in some frameworks but not in others. Choosing a framework for cooperation will amount to choosing who will be disabled – unless special efforts are made through genetic intervention or otherwise to achieve a match between the demands of a cooperative framework and the abilities of all individuals. As the new genetics increases our control over which abilities individuals will have, this third question of the morality of inclusion becomes more pressing.

The Allegation That the New Genetics Is Exclusionary

Some of the most passionate criticisms of the new genetics come from those who claim that efforts to use a knowledge of how genes work to cure or prevent disease and disability is exclusionary. For these critics, efforts to draw a clear line between the old eugenics and the new genetics obscure a sinister shared characteristic: Both promote exclusion rather than inclusion.

The old eugenics excluded "defective" individuals from the primary moral community, branding them as dangerous carriers of inferior germ plasm who threatened humanity with moral and physical ruin. The new genetics is seen by some members of the disabilities rights community as a tool for excluding individuals with "bad genes" not only from particular tangible benefits such as insurance and employment, from the most basic good of all – the equal respect and consid-

eration that are owed all members of the primary moral community –
and even from life itself through selective abortion. In addition, some
advocates for the rights of persons with disabilities charge that the
effort to develop more sophisticated capacities for preventing genetically based disabilities is fundamentally misguided: Instead of changing individuals to fit society, we ought to change society to accommodate individuals.

All these complaints about the allegedly exclusionary character of
the new genetics can be subsumed under the three questions that a
theory of the morality of inclusion ought to address. The remainder of
this chapter concentrates on the second and third concerns about
exclusion: the complaint that the effort to use genetic science to eradi-
cate diseases and disabilities denies those with "defective" genes their
status as persons entitled to equal moral worth, and the charge that
instead of attempting to eliminate disabilities by changing individuals,
the goal should be to change society so that the genetic conditions
some individuals have are not disabling.

The more obvious and tangible issue of exclusion – the risk of
genetic discrimination in insurance and employment – will not be the
focus of our inquiry. This topic has been exhaustively examined elsewhere (Capron 1997; Rothenberg 1997). Our emphasis will be on
what we take to be more subtle yet more basic issues of exclusion that
the new genetics raises and with its tendency to push the limits of
ethical theory.

Before proceeding to what we take to be less obvious dangers of
exclusion, however, it may be useful to emphasize one point that has
not received sufficient attention in the public discussion of employment
and insurance discrimination on genetic grounds.

That point is quite simple, but important: Unless something is done
to eliminate the threat of widespread genetic discrimination in employment and insurance, the chief public justification for using tax monies
to finance the Human Genome Project and related genetic research
will be discredited. That justification was that public monies were to
be used to benefit the public. If the knowledge that this infusion of
public funds produces is systematically used to the disadvantage of
citizens at higher genetic risk for certain diseases, then it cannot be
said, without serious qualification, that these public funds are being
used to benefit the public. Instead, at most we can say that they are
being used to benefit some members of the public and to harm others.

Furthermore, if individuals are able to avoid insurance or employment discrimination only by not being tested for genetic conditions (which is now often the case), then they will not benefit from the knowledge that the public's support helped to create (even if they are not harmed, as they would be if they were tested and then suffered discrimination as a result). For those who might benefit from genetic testing but are afraid to avail themselves of it lest they suffer discrimination, all the fine rhetoric about the need to support genetic research so that "we" can gain knowledge to better "our" lives will ring hollow.

THE PUBLIC PROMISE OF THE NEW GENETICS: BETTER LIVES FOR ALL THROUGH MEDICAL GENETICS

Nobel Prize–winning molecular biologist Walter Gilbert described the mapping and sequencing of the human genome as "the grail of molecular biology." Those who know Gilbert and respect his sophistication would no doubt hasten to point out that he does not in fact attribute supernatural powers to mastery of the sequence of base pairs that make up the total human genetic complement. They would plead that he ought to be forgiven for indulging in public relations rhetoric to garner support for the Human Genome Project.

Nevertheless, his choice of metaphors is revealing: The implication is that possessing a comprehensive knowledge of human genetics, like possessing the Holy Grail of legend, will give us miraculous powers. Hyperbole aside, such rhetoric seems to appeal to the best of the Western tradition's zeal for progress – the idea of improving human lives through the practical application of scientific knowledge. The search for the grail is a noble quest – the pursuit for the greater good of humanity as a whole, not a self-interested endeavor or an effort to achieve a benefit merely for some.

In other words, the rhetoric of the supporters of the Human Genome Project and of genetic research generally is explicitly inclusive, in part no doubt to distinguish the new genetics from the exclusionary old eugenics. Genetic science is now to serve human beings generally, rather than any particular people or nationality or "race." Indeed, the very idea of the Human Genome Project appears to highlight what all human beings have in common rather than what differentiates them one from another: The human genome that is the object of an international network of mapping and sequencing projects is a composite, not the genome of any particular person or even a composite representing any one subgroup of humans.

Moreover, the official rhetoric has tended to equate the new genetics with medical genetics – the emphasis has been on the prevention and cure of diseases, rather than on the other uses to which genetic knowledge and technology might be put, including the enhancement of normal characteristics or the production of novel traits. One consequence of this emphasis on disease is to minimize the danger that the new genetics will be hijacked for the pursuit of those dubious ideals that were prominent in the racist eugenics of the past. In this sense, the official rhetoric of the new genetics is that of an inclusive, medical genetics.

Enthusiasts for the new genetics react defensively to any suggestion that current scientific endeavors harbor the taint of eugenics. After all, what could be controversial about the goal of improving human life through the application of a scientific knowledge of genes? Surely the difference between the old eugenics and the new genetics is unmistakable: The former was particularistic and exclusionary, condemning as defective all those who failed to meet supposed criteria of racial purity or human perfection; the latter is universalistic and inclusive, seeking to prevent suffering for all of humanity through the eradication of genetic disease. In addition, the exclusionary vision of the old eugenics was aided and abetted by faulty science, whereas the new genetics is truly scientific.

CHALLENGING THE RHETORIC: THE RADICAL DISABILITIES RIGHTS ADVOCATES' COMPLAINTS

Where enthusiasts for the new genetics see inclusion and progress, some in the disabilities rights movement see exclusion and moral retrogression. The charge is that the very conception of progress that lies at the core of the ideology of the new genetics radically devalues individuals with disabilities, inflicting on them what may be the gravest injury of all – a denial of their equal moral worth and even their very right to exist.

The source of injury is said to be a fundamentally flawed conception of the value of human lives (International Association of Societies for Mental Disabilities 1995). Lives that include impairments are assumed to be without value if not a positive evil to be eradicated. Thus the disabilities rights advocates' view stands the new geneticists' claim to universalistic progress on its head. Not only is the alleged universalism indicted as exclusion, but also the very notion of progress is said to rest on a distorted view of the basic value that is supposed to guide the quests for progress. Scientific control over natural endowments will not mean improvements for all of humanity. Instead, it will result in harm to the fundamental interest of some human beings – those with disabilities.

The disabilities rights advocates' critique of the new genetics appears to be nothing short of a rejection of the basic idea of striving "to make human lives better by selection based on genetic knowledge" (International 1995). "Selection" here includes not only choosing who will be born and who will not (through genetic testing and abortion to avoid the birth of individuals with certain conditions) but also choosing the characteristics of those who will be born by genetic interventions on gametes (sperm and egg cells) or embryos (fertilized eggs) to eliminate or counteract genetic influences that would cause disease.

Furthermore, the charge is not simply that the effort at improvement through selection in either of these ways is unwise or in some way morally questionable. The claim is that it is unjust – that it violates the most fundamental rights of people with disabilities and is nothing less than a degradation of the core of morality, the proper appreciation of the value of human lives. What is striking about the radical disabilities advocates' critique, then, is that it is directed squarely against medical genetics – which proponents of the new genetics have taken to be the most laudable and uncontroversial application of genetic knowledge. Taken at face value, this critique condemns any effort to eliminate disabilities through medical interventions, genetic or otherwise (although it is true that the radical disabilities rights critique has focused primarily on genetic intervention). For if taken literally the slogan "change society, not individuals" does not merely insist that we try to make the social world more accessible to those whose impairments cannot be corrected; it would require accommodating those with impairments *rather than* using medical science to prevent or correct impairments.

Given the universalistic and progressive self-image of those who engage in or support the new genetics, this critique evokes incredulity and indignation. Indeed, it is tempting to dismiss the radical disabilities advocates' objections as hysterical, paranoid, or extremist. This, however, would be a mistake, as we shall see. For there is some truth in this critique. Humanity's emerging powers of genetic intervention do raise important and in some ways novel issues of justice and exclusion – issues the rhetoric of universal progress obscures. On closer examination, however, it will turn out that neither the disabilities rights advocates nor the enthusiasts for the new genetics have grasped the fundamental implications of genetic intervention for our understanding of justice, of the moral significance of disabilities, or of the morality of inclusion.

SORTING OUT THE CONCERNS OF DISABILITIES RIGHTS ADVOCATES

Several distinct objections can be discerned in the disabilities rights advocates' critique. Here we will concentrate on what we take to be the objections that strike at the heart of the legitimating rhetoric of the new genetics, those that challenge the claim that, at least so far as the application of genetic science is restricted to the prevention of disease, the new genetics is nonexclusionary and benign.

The Loss of Support Argument

Before proceeding to the most fundamental objections to the new genetics, however, we should note a different criticism of "improvement through selection" that is often voiced by those from the disabilities rights movement. This is the charge that as the application of genetic science reduces the number of persons suffering from disabilities, public support for those who have disabilities will dwindle. Although we discuss this "loss of support argument" mainly to distinguish it from what we take to be more fundamental objections, three points merit consideration.

First, the objection rests on a sweeping empirical generalization: that as the number of persons with a certain disability decreases, support for those who have that disability will decrease, and that this is true for disabilities generally. Without attempting to settle the empirical issue, we would only point out that it is not enough to state the generalization. Data to support it must be marshaled. To our knowledge, those who advance the "loss of support argument" have not borne this burden of evidence. Moreover, we do know of at least one instance in which a reduction in the incidence of a genetic disease (achieved through voluntary carrier testing) resulted in more resources being used to support the decreasing number of those who had the disease. This was the case of the Thalassemia testing program in Greece (Kitcher 1995).

Second, whether or not support will diminish in a particular case will depend on a number of factors, not the least significant of which is whether the public is alerted in advance to the danger of reduced support. In fact, the prediction that support will decrease as science reduces the incidence of genetic diseases is much less plausible today than it would have been twenty years ago, precisely because the disabilities rights movement has succeeded in awakening the public and policy makers to the need for support.

Third, even if there should turn out to be some loss of support for certain genetically based diseases as their incidence declines, it would not follow that seeking to reduce their incidence is wrong, all things considered. The most fundamental problem with the loss of support argument is that it only considers the interests of those who will have disabilities in a world in which disabilities are less common. It entirely neglects the legitimate interests that people have in not having disabilities. (In addition, as we argue later, this argument also fails to recognize that those who are not disabled and who are not at significant risk of being disabled can have legitimate interests in reducing the incidence of disabilities.)

Consider first the interest a person has in not having disabilities. Surely this is a morally legitimate interest. It is true that in some cases this interest is not relevant, because the disability is avoided only by preventing the existence of the person who would have been born with it. Obviously, in this case, one cannot justify the intervention by citing the interest some person has in not having the disability.

But there are other interventions that do serve the interest that individuals have in not having disabilities. For example, it will very likely become possible to correct some genetic anomalies by intervening on the embryo. In this case, it will be correct to speak of preventing an identified individual from having a disability and to justify the intervention by appealing to that individual's interest in not having a disability. Similarly, genetic science will be able to prevent disabling genetic conditions in other, perhaps less dramatic, ways, not by manipulating the genes of embryos but by administering drugs that mimic the products of normal genes or that counteract the deleterious effects of abnormal genes. In these cases, too, we may correctly say that the application of genetic science makes identifiable individuals' lives better by preventing genetically based diseases, and that such individuals have a legitimate interest in avoiding the damage to them that would occur without the intervention.

Once it is recognized that the incidence of genetically based diseases may be reduced without preventing the birth of individuals who would have disabilities, it should be evident that the loss of support argument must be rejected. It fails to give any weight to the legitimate interests that individuals have in avoiding disabilities. This can be seen more clearly once we recognize that the general form of this argument has nothing peculiarly to do with genetic interventions. If the risk of loss of support is a reason for not undertaking genetic interventions, then it is also a reason for not undertaking conventional medical interventions as well. By this logic, it would be wrong to treat babies' eyes at birth to prevent blindness due to contact with gonococcus bacteria during vaginal delivery. But surely it is not only permissible but morally obligatory to prevent babies from being blinded, if this can be done safely and effectively, even if it could be shown that there is some significant risk of loss of support for the blind.

The risk of loss of support is familiar in the case of so-called orphan drugs. When the number of individuals suffering from a particular malady is small enough, it may not be profitable for pharmaceutical companies to produce drugs valuable to these individuals. In the United States, special legislation provides financial incentives for companies to produce such drugs by increasing the length of patents so that companies have more time to cover their costs.

The situation of orphan drugs illustrates an important point: There is a societal obligation to maintain support for those who are ill or disabled, but it does not follow that this generates a valid claim on the part of those individuals that society must ensure that their numbers do not diminish. So even if proponents of the loss of support argument could do what they have not done – supply strong empirical evidence for the generalization that loss of support would result – this would not suffice to show that any limitations on efforts to prevent disabilities are called for.

One last example will reinforce this point. Suppose that Jill is a young adult who faces life with paraplegia unless she undergoes a surgical procedure. If she has the surgery, she can look forward to a life with all the opportunities that go with normal mobility.

She chooses to have the surgery. As a result of her choice, the ranks of the disabled will diminish by one. Does her action harm people with disabilities? Presumably not – her cure is very unlikely to make much of a difference. Suppose that many people in her situation make the same choice, with the result that there is a significant reduction in the number of people with paraplegia. Have those who had the surgery harmed the people with paraplegia who cannot be cured or who for some reason chose not to be cured? If by harming someone is meant worsening their condition, then it may well be true that large numbers of surgical cures for paraplegia might harm those who remain paraplegic. It does not follow, however, that widespread use of the curative surgical intervention should be prohibited or that it would be morally wrong.

It is necessary here to distinguish between being harmed and being wrongly harmed. Even if the minority who remain uncured are harmed by widespread use of the surgical intervention it would not follow that they have been *wrongly* harmed, unless one is willing to make the implausible claim that those who elected to be cured had no right to make this choice. But whether they have a right to make such a choice will depend primarily upon whether they have a legitimate interest in avoiding being disabled and whether that legitimate interest is of such moral weight that it warrants the special protection implied in the notion of a right. Having a right to do something means having a sphere of discretion to do what might otherwise be wrong, including what may contribute to a worsening of the condition of others. For example, if you have a right to compete with me for a certain prize, then the fact that your entering the competition worsens my condition does not show that you wrong me by competing.

As will become more evident later in this chapter, our critique of the loss of support argument reveals quite general features of other arguments advanced on behalf of persons with disabilities. First, whether their proponents recognize it or not, these arguments are not limited to interventions to prevent genetic diseases. They apply to all disabilities regardless of their etiology, and their general implications are highly implausible. Second, like the loss of support argument, the other arguments considered here are flawed because they consider only some of the legitimate interests at stake. They give no weight to the legitimate interests that persons have in not having disabilities. Thus, ironically, their arguments are exclusionary.

The Justice Trumps Beneficence Argument

We have just seen that the "loss of support argument" overlooks the legitimate interests that people have in avoiding disabilities. This interest is not merely legitimate – that is, not subject to any moral criticism as such. As we saw in Chapter 3, it is the basis of a claim of justice. There we argued that there are cases in which justice requires interventions to correct or prevent genetic defects. The chief basis for this conclusion is that an adequate account of justice includes a commitment to equal opportunity, and that genetically based disabilities, like other disabilities, impair opportunity.

The conclusion that genetic interventions can be required by justice has a direct and devastating implication for another argument advanced on behalf of persons with disabilities and against genetic intervention. This is the "justice trumps beneficence" argument. This argument asserts that while only beneficence, not justice, speaks in favor of genetic intervention to prevent disabilities, the widespread use of genetic interventions to prevent disabilities puts disabled persons at risk of suffering grave injustices (International Association of Societies for Mental Disabilities 1995). More explicitly, the argument is:

1. Genetic intervention to prevent disabilities is not required by justice but only by the value or principle of beneficence.
2. The widespread use of genetic intervention to prevent disabilities would create a serious risk of injustices to disabled people.
3. Justice trumps beneficence (when the pursuit of beneficence creates a risk of serious injustice, the avoidance of injustice should take precedence).
4. Therefore, widespread genetic intervention to prevent disabilities ought not to be undertaken.

In a nutshell, the "justice trumps beneficence" argument contends that it is wrong to act on the principle of beneficence to the detriment of the principle of justice.

Consider premise 2. Our critique of the loss of support argument has already shown that even if a reduction in the incidence of disabilities does put disabled persons at risk for loss of support, it does not follow that we should forgo the effort to prevent disabilities by genetic or other means. In the next section of this chapter we examine another interpretation of premise 2 of the "justice trumps beneficence" argument, one that focuses on a different risk to those with disabilities.

There we evaluate the allegation that genetic intervention to prevent disabilities expresses a radical devaluation of persons with disabilities, which violates their right to be recognized as persons of equal moral worth. But here we wish to attack the third premise, which is false for two reasons.

First, some benefits are not "mere benefits." Achieving a great good or avoiding a great harm can in some cases be obligatory, not merely commendable or desirable. Indeed, there can be instances in which the obligation to achieve a great good or to prevent a great harm trumps obligations of justice, because those particular obligations of justice are less weighty.

To fail to consider this possibility is to make the mistake of assuming that obligations of justice are the weightiest obligations in all circumstances. What distinguishes these obligations from others, including obligations to provide benefits and to avoid harms, is not their relative strength, but their grounds – the kinds of considerations that are appealed to in justifying the assertion that there is an obligation (Buchanan 1987). So even if it were true that beneficence but not justice speaks in favor of genetic intervention to prevent disabilities, it would not follow that we ought never to intervene when intervention creates a risk of injustice.

Second, we have shown in detail in Chapter 3 that justice – and more specifically, equal opportunity as one component of justice – sometimes requires genetic intervention to prevent disabilities. And in Chapter 6 we saw that our obligations to prevent harm can also require genetic interventions, whether these obligations are understood to be obligations of justice or not. So it is a mistake to say that the prospect of genetic intervention to prevent disabilities pits mere beneficence against justice, even if it can be shown that such intervention would put people with disabilities at risk of being treated unjustly.

The justice trumps beneficence argument portrays an unequal contest between the need to protect people with disabilities against the most fundamental injustice, on the one hand, and the merely desirable goal of conferring benefits, on the other. But this is inaccurate. Instead, we have either a conflict between obligations of justice (or to prevent serious harms) and obligations to minimize the risk of injustice. Whether we should underake genetic interventions to protect equal opportunity (or for the sake of preventing serious harm) or refrain from intervening in order to avoid the risk of injustice to people with disabilities will depend on the nature of the injustice for which people with disabilities are put at risk and the likelihood that this injustice will occur.

But if this is so, then we can proceed to examine the claim that the widespread use of genetic intervention to prevent disabilities puts people with disabilities at risk for being treated unjustly and we can dispense with the justice trumps beneficence argument, which we have seen is unsound anyway because of its oversimplified conception of strength of obligations of justice relative to those of beneficence.

The Expressivist Objection

This objection, or rather this family of objections, focuses on what may be called the expressive character of decisions to use genetic interventions to prevent disabilities. The claim is that decisions to intervene – and indeed the whole enterprise of developing the knowledge and technology to make such interventions possible – express negative judgments about people with disabilities, and that these judgments themselves constitute a profound injustice to those people.

The negative judgments allegedly expressed in the enterprise of genetic intervention are said to betray a profound miscomprehension of the core concept of morality: the value of human life. The mistake is to assume that only "perfect" human lives are of sufficient value to be allowed to exist or to come into existence.

According to the expressivist objection, this error is not merely a mistake in ethical theory. To express these negative judgments about people with disabilities is itself an injury to them, a violation of their most fundamental right – the right to be regarded as persons of equal worth.

In addition, the social acceptance of the enterprise that expresses these negative judgments, the project of using genetic knowledge for improvement through selection, puts persons with disabilities at risk in more concrete ways. Those who are not regarded as members of the community of persons with equal worth, those whose fundamental value is denied, are likely to be neglected and abused, if not exterminated. The negative judgments allegedly expressed in the new genetics, then, are these:

1. The lives of individuals with disabilities are not worth living.
2. Only perfect individuals should be brought into the world. (Imperfect individuals have no right to exist.)

Disabilities rights advocates rightly reject both judgments. Those who advance the expressivist argument are quick to emphasize that the first judgment reveals an ignorance of the joys and fulfillments that even severely disabled individuals can experience. The second judgment is rejected on the grounds that it rests on a false assumption about what makes individuals worthy of equal respect and concern, and hence of life. It is not whether or not someone measures up to some supposed standard of perfection that matters so far as equal worth is concerned, but rather an individual's humanity (or, on some accounts, person-hood).[2]

It is no doubt true that people who have not experienced serious disabilities themselves, or been close to people who are seriously disabled, sometimes – perhaps often – fail to appreciate the quality of life of people with disabilities. They may focus only on the suffering and limitations the disability entails, underestimating both the positive experiences people with disabilities can have and the remarkable capacity that human beings have to adapt their expectations and goals to changes in their abilities (Buchanan and Brock 1989).

Even if this is true, however, it does not follow that all or even most of those who are not disabled believe that disabilities as such, or even serious disabilities, make life not worth living. It may well be true that many people believe that there are some disabilities so severe that they make life not worth living. And it may be that some interventions to prevent disabilities are undertaken out of this belief. But from this it does not follow that whenever we intervene to prevent a disability our action betrays a belief that the lives of disabled persons are not worth living.

What, then, would lead some disabilities rights advocates to conclude that the enthusiasm for using genetic science to reduce the incidence of disabilities expresses the judgment that the lives of disabled people are not worth living or that such people ought not to exist? The answer, apparently, is that they believe that central to the new genetics is the decision to prevent disabilities by avoiding the birth of individuals with disabilities – and that this decision must rest on the

---

[2] A human being (in the biological sense) is simply a member of the species *homo sapiens*. To be a person in what might be called the moral sense is to be an individual who has the capacity for acting on reasons, and, according to some accounts, a sense of himself or herself as a being who persists over time. Given these definitions, not all human beings are persons (e.g., those who are permanently unconscious), and there may be some persons who are not human beings (extraterrestrial individuals).

judgment that life with disabilities is not worth living or that less-than-perfect individuals ought not to exist or have no right to exist (Asch 1995).

As a general form of argument, the expressivist objection is invalid. An example that has nothing to do with genetic intervention will show why this is so. Suppose that a woman can either conceive a child when she has German measles (rubella), knowing that if she does there is a significant risk that the child she bears will suffer a serious impairment, or she can delay conception until her illness passes. Surely the woman's decision to postpone conceiving a child need not be an expression of the belief either that if the child were born with an impairment its life would not be worth living or that were it born with an impairment it would have no right to live or be unworthy of equal respect and concern.

To reveal more conclusively the weakness of the expressivist argument, we must clarify what it means to say that a decision expresses (or presupposes) a particular judgment. This happens if and only if either, as a matter of psychological fact, one could only be motivated to make this judgment if the person ascribed to the judgment (i.e., that one could not psychologically make the decision if he or she did not believe to be true what the judgment affirms), or one cannot rationally make the decision without believing what the judgment affirms. So the expressivist objection is that decisions to use genetic intervention to prevent disabilities rationally or motivationally presuppose either the judgment that the lives of disabled individuals are not worth living, or the judgment that less-than-perfect individuals ought not to exist, or both.

Preventing Disabilities without Terminating the Lives of Individuals with Disabilities It should be clear that the expressivist objection only applies to those genetic interventions that prevent disabilities by preventing the existence of individuals who would have the disabilities in question. If the disability is prevented in other ways, there is no reason whatsoever to believe that the decision expresses a judgment that life with those disabilities would not be worth living or that the individual who had those disabilities ought not to exist.

This is a significant point because some modes of genetic intervention do not prevent disability by preventing the existence of individuals who would have the disability. To see that this is so, it is useful to distinguish the following four types of intervention:

- Preventing a genetic condition that would be disabling by "switching off" the gene that produces the disabling condition or by inserting normal genes either into embryos or gametes or into individuals after they are born.
- Avoiding conceiving a fetus with a genetic condition that would produce a disability by using contraceptives when genetic testing reveals a significant risk of the condition.
- Avoiding conceiving a fetus with a genetic condition that would produce a disability by using artificial insemination or embryo transplant.
- Preventing the birth of an individual determined to have a genetic condition that would produce a disability or to be at high risk of having that condition by aborting the fetus.

Opting for the first form of intervention in no way presupposes – either motivationally or rationally – a judgment that only perfect individuals should exist or that people with disabilities ought not to exist, any more than performing conventional surgery to restore a blind person's sight does. In either case the motive may be, and often is, simply the desire to remove serious limitations on the individual's opportunities and to avoid needless suffering. One can be motivated by this desire and can rationally decide to act on it without believing either that the individual's life with the limitation is not worth living or that only perfect individuals should exist. If Jill decides to undergo the surgical procedure to cure her paraplegia, she need not believe that her life or anyone else's life as a paraplegic is not worth living, nor need she consciously or unconsciously believe that only perfect individuals should exist.

Similarly, the second and third modes of intervening to prevent disabilities need not express either of the negative judgments the expressivist argument attributes to those who advocate genetic interventions. To be willing to undertake either of these options, all that is necessary is the desire not to bring into the world an individual whose opportunities will be severely limited and who may also experience considerable suffering.

A number of beliefs may account for this desire, any of which would make the decision fully rational. First, someone may simply wish to be spared avoidable and serious strains on his or her marriage or family. Or he or she may wish to avoid putting additional pressure on limited social resources needed for the achievement of distributive justice in health care and in other areas, including the support of existing individuals who have disabilities.

In the second and third interventions, using contraception, artificial insemination, or embryo transplant, acting on these desires does not violate anyone's rights because there is no existing individual who has rights that might be violated. It is the coming to be of an individual that is avoided. No existing individual's life is terminated. So even if one believes that fetuses are persons with all the rights that persons have, including the right not to be killed, avoiding disabilities by avoiding conception of individuals who would be disabled neither violates anyone's rights nor necessarily expresses any negative judgments about the lives of people with disabilities. Furthermore, to judge that it is morally permissible to avoid bringing a disabled person into the world, a person need not judge that disabled persons ought not to be born any more than judging that it is not wrong to refrain from getting a Ph.D. commits someone to the judgment that no one ought to get a Ph.D.

Only the fourth mode of intervention has any prospect of being vulnerable to the expressivist objection, because it is only in that case that there is a decision to terminate a life that will involve a disability. This point is extremely important because it shows that even in principle the expressivist objection cannot provide a reason for abandoning or restricting genetic interventions per se, but at most only one mode of intervention.

Genetic Intervention and the Status of Fetuses   Notice, however, that even in the fourth type of intervention the decision to intervene – to abort a fetus with a disabling genetic condition – need not express either of the two negative judgments about people with disabilities. Someone who decides to terminate a pregnancy after learning that the fetus she is carrying has Down syndrome may simply be motivated by the very same desire that motivates the decision to undertake any of the other three modes of intervention: the desire not to bring into the world an individual with seriously limited opportunities. Nor is there anything illogical or irrational about acting on this desire while firmly rejecting the judgment that the lives of disabled people are not worth living or that people with disabilities have no right to exist.

In the case of the fourth mode of intervention, as with the other three modes, the desire to avoid the birth of an individual with disabilities may be based on any of several quite morally unexceptionable considerations. A person may wish to avoid serious strains on a marriage or the ability to fulfill responsibilities to existing children, or to avoid diverting scarce resources needed for the achievement of distributive justice – and yet the individual may consistently believe that the lives of many or even of all individuals with Down syndrome are worth living and that every child and adult with this genetic condition has the same right to life and to recognition of equal worth as any other person. Nor need the person believe that only perfect individuals ought to exist. An individual can rationally decide to abort a fetus with a genetic defect while nevertheless believing that persons with disabilities are of equal worth if he believes that fetuses (or at least fetuses up to and including the stage at which the abortion is performed) are not persons and hence do not have the rights and equal moral status of persons.

To believe that it is permissible to avoid a serious disability by selective abortion one need not believe that individuals with that disability ought not to be born. All that is necessary is the belief that the fetus has no right to be born. Furthermore, one can – and many people apparently do – consistently believe both that fetuses, whether they will have disabilities or not, have no right to be born (because they are not persons) while believing that all persons, including those with disabilities, have a right to exist, and hence a right not to be killed, because they are persons.

Similarly, there is nothing inconsistent or motivationally incoherent about believing that one ought not bring a disabled child into the world and believing that it is not the case that individuals with disabilities ought not to be born. (Someone can believe that she ought not to marry without believing that marriages ought not to occur.)

Perhaps those who advance the expressivist argument will still not be convinced of our rebuttal. The appeal of the argument is its simplicity. Thus a person who herself has a disability, impatient with the subtleties and hair-splitting of the preceding arguments, might reply:

No analysis of the possible motives or of the coherence of the possible reasons for preventing disabilities can erase one simple fact: When you endorse the use of genetic science to prevent disabilities, you are saying that people like me ought not to exist. And when you say that people like me ought not to exist, you devalue me in the most fundamental and threatening way imaginable. Your conception of the value of human life denies that my life, imperfect as it is in your eyes, has value.

Recall, however, that to say that it is permissible to avoid disabilities by genetic interventions is not to say that we ought to reduce the incidence of disabilities, much less that disabled persons ought not to exist. In Chapters 3 and 6 we argued that there can be obligations of justice, as well as obligations to prevent harm, that require genetic interventions. From this perspective, we are committed to the judgment that in the future the world should not include so many disabilities and hence so many individuals with disabilities. But it is not the people with the disabilities that we devalue; it is the disabilities themselves. We do not wish to reduce the number of people with disabilities by taking the life of any individual who has a disability.

Devaluing Disabilities, Not People with Disabilities   We devalue disabilities because we value the opportunities and welfare of the people who have them. And it is because we value people, all people, that we care about limitations on their welfare and opportunities. We also know that disabilities as such diminish opportunities and welfare, even when they are not so severe that the lives of those who have them are not worth living, and even if those individuals do not literally suffer as a result of their disabilities. Thus there is nothing irrational, motivationally incoherent, or disingenuous in saying that we devalue the disabilities and wish to reduce their incidence while valuing existing persons with disabilities, and that we value them the same as those who do not have disabilities.

Another example may help to dispel the charge that when we seek to reduce the frequency of disabilities we thereby devalue people who have them. Suppose that a parent encourages her child to work hard in school by pointing out that if he does not, his career options will be limited to "menial" jobs in which there is little potential for development of new skills and little prospect of advancement. Must we say that such a parent devalues persons who do "menial" jobs? No such attitude is implied in the reasons the parent gives to the child for working hard in school or in her motives for doing so.

Of course, it may be true that some parents who have always engaged in "white-collar" work tend to underestimate the opportunities for development of skills and for satisfactions that some of the less skilled "blue-collar" jobs sometimes offer. Nevertheless, the advice the parent gives may be sound. She may be correct both in her judgment that this individual would be happier and more fulfilled with a different kind of job and in her prediction that doing well in school is a prerequisite for getting such a job. She may only be expressing concern for the well-being of her child in the light of a realistic estimate of the educational and economic facts of life, without in any way denigrating persons who perform menial labor.

None of this is to deny that some white-collar workers look down on blue-collar workers, nor that some "abled" persons devalue the "disabled." Nor is it to deny that some blue-collar workers have more job satisfaction than some white-collar workers or that some people with disabilities have more fulfilling lives than some people who do not have disabilities.

One last hypothetical will clarify our observation that devaluing disabilities need not imply devaluing individuals with disabilities. Suppose God tells a couple: "I'll make you a child. You can have a child that has limited opportunities due to a physical or cognitive defect or one who does not. Which do you choose?" Suppose that the couple answers as follows: "Lord, we choose the child without the defect; but if you should decide to give us the child who has disabilities we will love it as much as we would the other." There is surely nothing illogical or motivationally incoherent in this admirable response.

The proponent of the expressivist objection might concede this point but offer one additional argument:

Even if the decision to use genetic interventions to prevent disabilities does not necessarily express negative attitudes, such attitudes are all too common in our society. In fact, negative attitudes are so widespread and pronounced that many individuals with disabilities experience greater limitations on their opportunities as a result of stigma than from their physical or cognitive impairments. Undoubtedly, these negative attitudes are part of the motivation for the willingness to develop and use genetic interventions. We should not encourage these attitudes by using social resources to create vehicles for their expression and perpetuation.

This argument might be telling if there were nothing of moral significance to be lost by following its advice. There is something to be lost, however: the chance to avoid or correct serious limitations on individuals' opportunities and to reduce human suffering. Accordingly, the wiser course of action is to continue the laudable fight to change negative attitudes toward people with disabilities while developing genetic intervention technologies to accomplish the same goal that has inspired the greatest triumphs of the disabilities rights movements in overcoming physical barriers in the social environment. For it is crucial to remember that the strongest argument in favor of removing physical barriers is that this is necessary to achieve equal opportunity, and that all individuals have a right to equal opportunity.

Summary of Response to Expressivist Objection   It may be useful at this point to summarize the main points of our complex discussion of the expressivist argument against genetic intervention. To be sound, the argument either must show that it is motivationally impossible or irrational both to devalue and seek to avoid disabilities while at the same time valuing equally individuals who have disabilities or it must defend the view that fetuses are persons, with all the rights that persons have, and that avoiding disabilities by aborting fetuses with disabilities is the moral equivalent of reducing the incidence of disabilities by exterminating disabled children and adults.

The first alternative is unconvincing. There are many instances in which we devalue (and seek to avoid) certain characteristics that some individuals have without devaluing individuals who have them. The second alternative comes at a steep price: Not only must the disabilities rights advocate articulate and defend an account of personhood that shows that fetuses are persons, he must also acknowledge that the fundamental error of those who advocate selective abortion to avoid disabilities is not that they devalue individuals with disabilities but that they fail to recognize that fetuses, whether disabled or not, are persons. The argument, then, would have nothing to do with disabilities as such.

Moreover, even if it were assumed that fetuses are persons and that hence killing them to reduce the incidence of disabilities is morally indistinguishable from exterminating disabled children and adults, this would have no negative implications for the other three modes of genetic intervention to avoid disabilities. None of these involves killing a fetus, so none can be described as killing a person, even if we assume that fetuses are persons. Therefore endorsing these modes of reducing disabilities need not express and does not presuppose the judgment that existing individuals with disabilities have no right to live.

To repeat: Advocating the fourth mode of intervention (selective abortion) is tantamount to saying that people like you (who have disabilities) have no right to exist only on the highly controversial assumption that fetuses are persons. Opting for the first, second, and third modes of intervention has no implications at all for the worthiness or unworthiness of "disabled lives," regardless of which view of the moral status of fetuses is correct. What appeared to be a distinctive objection to a new technology turns out to be a familiar objection to the age-old practice of abortion.

None of this is to deny that some members of the disabilities community are genuinely offended by what they take to be the misplaced zeal to harness the powers of science to prevent disabilities. Granted the shameful history of discrimination against and insensitivity toward persons with disabilities, their taking offense is perfectly understandable. However, it is one thing to say that certain behavior is offensive to a particular group, and quite another to say that the fact that the group is offended constitutes a violation of anyone's rights.

In general, a liberal society cannot count the occurrence of offense, as distinct from rights violations, as a sufficient ground for curtailing liberty, whether it is the liberty of a person to choose a surgical procedure that will cure her own paraplegia or that of her child, or the liberty of a researcher to try to develop a technique for preventing a genetically based impairment (Feinberg 1984).

The Deaf Culture Argument

As a supplement to our critique of the expressivist argument, we must consider one final, striking argument that has recently been advanced by some members the deaf community. This argument has been advanced in response to a surgical intervention to alleviate deafness, but it is of broader interest, encompassing genetic interventions as well. What is fascinating about this anti-interventionist argument is that it directly challenges a basic assumption of our rebuttal of the expressivist argument – namely, that because disabilities limit opportunity, they ought to be prevented.

Some individuals who are deaf have argued that even though being deaf limits some opportunities, the deaf community has developed a rich culture that provides unique and valuable opportunities and benefits to its members. In particular, it is said that the "deaf culture" provides exceptional solidarity as well as a sign language that is uniquely expressive. The claim is that the goods conferred by membership in the community of persons who are deaf outweighs or at least counterbalances the limitations on opportunity that deafness entails.

The first thing to notice about this argument is that it is not easily generalizable as an argument against interventions to prevent disabling impairments generally. It is not so plausible to argue that there is a paraplegic culture or a Down syndrome culture, much less a Lesch-Nyhan or Tay-Sachs culture. Nevertheless, proponents of this argument have done an inestimable service by calling to our attention the fact that there is such a thing as the deaf community, that it possesses at least some of the important features of a culture, and that belonging to this community brings important benefits.

What the argument overlooks, however, is that there is an asymmetry between the limitations on opportunity that deafness brings and the goods of membership in the deaf community. Without an enormous expenditure of social resources, the limitations imposed by being without hearing in a world in which most people hear are quite severe. Not being able to hear excludes a person from effectively pursuing many options, some of which are generally very important for most people.

But the benefits provided by membership in the "deaf community," while important and impressive, may not in fact be available only to those who are deaf. Solidarity is certainly available to members in other communities – religious groups, political groups, and any number of other forms of community can and do provide solidarity for many people. Nor is it at all obvious that an appreciation of the uniquely expressive character of sign language is unavailable to those who are not deaf. (It is no doubt true, of course, that a person who is not deaf will have less incentive to learn sign language and hence will be less likely to reap its unique benefits.)

But even if it could be shown that the distinctive benefits of sign language are only available to the deaf, it is one thing to say that those who are deaf gain a great good from this mode of communication. It is much less plausible to say that a reasonable person confronted with a choice between suffering the limitations of deafness while gaining the benefit of this mode of expression and avoiding the limitations of deafness but not being able fully to appreciate the unique expressive power of sign language would choose the latter. Yet it seems that the appropriate standpoint from which to decide whether to intervene to prevent children from being born deaf or continuing to be deaf is that of a reasonable person confronted with a choice *ex ante*.

Notice that this response to the deaf culture argument does not commit us to the view that a competent deaf individual ought to be subjected to hearing-restoring surgical intervention against his or her will. Our claim is only that the appropriate perspective for estimating whether to prevent or restore loss of hearing in an individual who is not competent to decide for himself or herself (a fetus or a child) is that of a reasonable person confronted with the choice of whether to be deaf or not. Nothing we have said about the commitment to removing barriers to opportunity warrants overriding the purely self-regarding choices of competent individuals. The point, rather, is that the fact that being deaf can bring special benefits is not a sufficient reason for one person (a parent) to choose that another, nonconsenting person (a child) should suffer this impairment.

It may be possible to imagine a world in which a reasonable person, confronted with such a choice, would choose deafness, but this is not our world. To make such a choice reasonable for most people would require an enormous reallocation of social resources, indeed a radical restructuring of our modes of production and social institutions, in order to make it true that for most people who are deaf, the benefits of membership in the deaf community outweigh the limitations on opportunity that deafness brings.

The next sections of this chapter take up the issue of the scope and limits of the obligation to change society in order to reduce the opportunity-limiting effects of disabilities. There we argue that although such an obligation exists, it is a limited obligation. It is limited by the legitimate interest that persons without disabilities have in being able to participate in cooperative schemes that are suitable to their own capacities.

A proponent of the deaf culture argument might not be convinced, however. He might respond as follows:

Everything you say about being deaf is equally true of being black or being gay. In our society, being black or gay imposes significant, often severe, limitations on a person's opportunities. But surely this is no reason to prevent the birth of blacks or gays. Indeed, there is something grossly immoral about the very idea of striving to have a world in which there are no gays or blacks on the grounds that we ought to avoid bringing people into the world who suffer the limits on opportunity that people from these two groups often suffer. (Suppose there turned out to be a "gay gene" or complex of genes that significantly increased the probability, across a wide range of prevalent social environments, that an individual would be gay. Suppose also that the presence of this gene or complex of genes could be accurately detected in fetuses.)

There is, however, a fundamental difference between the limitations on opportunity that result from being deaf and those that result from being gay or African-American. The limitations a gay or black person suffers are injustices in a quite uncontroversial sense: They are forms of discrimination. While deaf people and others with disabilities certainly do continue to experience discrimination, they would continue to suffer limited opportunities even if there were no discrimination against them. This difference is significant, because it has an important implication for how we ought to regard the costs of eliminating limitations on opportunity that result from being deaf as opposed to those that result from being gay or black.

The fact that it is costly to remove barriers of discrimination against blacks or gays has no moral weight because no one can have a morally legitimate interest in preserving unjust arrangements. (Achieving a fair distribution of the costs of reform is another matter, of course.) However, as we will argue in detail in the next section, the costs of changing society so that having a major impairment such as deafness imposes no limitations on individuals' opportunities are not so easily dismissed. Those costs count from a moral point of view, because there is a morally legitimate interest in avoiding them. Understanding what this interest is and how it can conflict with the interest that persons with disabilities have in being able to interact socially without limitations on their opportunities takes us to the heart of the theory of the morality of inclusion.

THE SOCIAL CONSTRUCTION OF DISABILITY AND THE MORALITY OF INCLUSION

Thus far we have examined and evaluated the allegation that the new genetics, even when restricted to the apparently benign enterprise of preventing or curing genetically based diseases, is nonetheless exclusionary, like the old eugenics. One complaint frequently raised by some members of the disabilities rights movement remains to be considered. As we noted earlier, it takes the form of an arresting slogan: We should direct our energies to "changing society, not people." Addressing the view behind the slogan forces us to face squarely the last of the three questions that a theory of the morality of inclusion should answer: To what extent is there an obligation to ensure that the nature of society's most fundamental framework for cooperation renders it more rather than less inclusive?

The slogan that we ought to "change society, not people" is an exhortation to modify our cooperative schemes to enable those who are now disabled to function effectively in them, rather than using genetic or other medical interventions to prevent or remove the characteristics of persons that make them unable to function effectively in cooperative schemes as they are now structured. Initially, at least, proponents of this slogan have focused on modifications of the physical features of the social world – installing curb breaks to make streets navigable for those in wheelchairs, ramps so that these individuals can enter public buildings, braille signs in elevators, and so forth.

But in principle the slogan has much more radical implications. Some people we now regard as disabled are barred from effective participation in various activities not because they lack physical access to them, but because a mastery of the complex rules, procedures, and symbolic manipulations required for these activities is beyond their cognitive or perceptual capacities.

Taken literally, then, the disabilities rights slogan urges us to simplify our cooperative schemes, if necessary, to make them more inclusive. Furthermore, the implication is that modifying our cooperative schemes is always or at least generally morally preferable to modifying people so that their capacities better match the demands of our cooperative schemes.

Distinguishing Disabilities from Impairments

The force of the disabilities rights slogan stems from a recognition of the fact that disabilities are at least in part socially constructed. To clarify what this means and why it is relevant to the morality of genetic interventions to prevent disabilities, it is first necessary to distinguish a disability from a physical or mental impairment.[3] Building on this analysis, we will argue that in some cases it is not only permissible but morally preferable to modify individuals rather than the social environment.

By a physical or mental impairment we mean an impairment of some aspect of normal functioning for our species. For example, a lesion on the optic nerve that results in abnormally poor vision, whether caused by a gene, an infection, or trauma, is an impairment of (visual) functioning. Although we will sometimes simply speak of an impairment, an impairment of normal species functioning is what we will mean.

Impairments often result in disabilities, but they need not. A disability is inherently relational: Being disabled is being unable to do

---

[3] What we refer to here as an impairment may also be called a defect; however, some find the term offensive, given the unfortunate tendency of some to slide from talking about "a person who has a defective gene" to "a defective person."

something. More specifically, to have a disability is to be unable to perform some significant range of tasks or functions that individuals in someone's reference group (e.g., adults) are ordinarily able to do, at least under favorable conditions, where the inability is not due to simple and easily corrigible ignorance or to a lack of the tools or means ordinarily available for performing such tasks or functions. Each of these elements of the analysis of a disability warrants further explication.

First, someone may be unable to perform a certain range of tasks or functions but able to perform many others. Accordingly, in ordinary parlance we distinguish, somewhat misleadingly, being partially and totally disabled – even though many if not most of those who are labeled totally disabled are in fact able to perform a wide range of tasks and functions.

Second, disabilities are relative to a reference group. Where no members of a certain group are able to perform certain tasks and where the group is identified by reference to features other than this inability, we usually do not speak of any one of them being disabled. For example, because no infants are able to drive cars, we do not say that any infant is disabled in this regard.

Third, disabilities are inabilities that cannot be fixed by simply providing information or by supplying tools or means ordinarily available. If someone is unable to perform some task only because he or she has not been given the instructions for doing so (and most people, or most people who, like this individual, are competent adults, would not be able to perform that task without being supplied instructions), the person is not disabled relative to that task (e.g., a man who is unable to tie special knots but could readily tie them if told how to do so does not have a knot-tying disability). If someone is unable to do something only because he or she lacks the tools ordinarily required for doing it, the person is not disabled (e.g., a woman who is unable to hammer a nail only because she lacks a hammer is not disabled in this regard). On the other hand, if someone is blind and as a consequence of that blindness is unable to perform some tasks that others who are otherwise like the individual can perform and that the person could perform but for the blindness, then that individual has a (visual) disability.

Disabilities thus understood are not the same as physical or mental impairments, although impairments, if not compensated for, corrected, or prevented, can result in disabilities. Whether an impairment of the functioning that is normal for our species results in a disability depends on the social environment of the the individual.

A simple illustration will bring home the significance of this crucial point. Suppose that someone has a hearing impairment due to sustained exposure to very loud noises. Damage to the auditory nerve makes the person unable to hear sounds in a certain range of frequencies, sounds that members of the human species with normal hearing can detect. However, the range of frequencies the individual cannot hear results in no disability because, given that person's social environment, nothing he or she is likely to be required to do or would benefit from doing requires the ability to distinguish sounds in that range.

To summarize: Although every impairment of normal functioning constitutes an inability (to perform a normal function), not all impairments result in disabilities. Impairments become disabilities in one sort of social environment but not others.

Once the social nature of disabilities (as distinct from impairments) is understood, we can fully appreciate the force of the slogan that we should change the social environment, not people. The point is that if we are willing and able to change the social environment in appropriate ways, we can prevent an impairment from being a disability. If the social environment does not demand that individuals have a particular ability, then their lack of that ability due to an impairment of normal species functioning is not a disability.

Earlier we argued that justice may require genetic interventions to prevent disabilities because equality of opportunity is a component of justice and disabilities limit peoples' opportunities. The point of the disabilities rights movement slogan is that it is a mistake to assume that the only way or the preferable way to prevent disabilities – and hence to achieve equal opportunity – is by preventing the physical or mental impairments that result in disabilities. Instead, we can break the connection between having an impairment and being disabled – if we are willing to make sufficient changes in our social environment.

It is quite correct to emphasize that there are two ways, not one, to prevent disabilities. One is by preventing impairments; the other is by modifying social arrangements so that impairments do not result in disabilities. But we still need an account of why we should, as the slogan says, prevent disabilities by modifying social arrangements rather than by modifying people.

Options for Eliminating Disabilities

According to the foregoing analysis, a disability is a mismatch between an individual's abilities and the demands of a range of tasks. Given that this is so, there are four basic ways in which a better match could be achieved.

- Changing the individual through education, training, or some other nonmedical means.
- Changing the individual by medical means, including interventions to change her genome or to modify or counteract the effects of genes through genetic pharmacology.
- Changing relevant features of the physical infrastructure of social interaction.
- Changing the nonphysical – that is, the institutional – infrastructure of social interaction.

This last option is less familiar than others, but is in principle far-reaching in its implications. A small-scale, greatly simplified example will illustrate. Suppose that we wish to play a card game in which everyone in a mixed group of individuals ranging in age from 5 to 50 years can successfully participate. The "institutional infrastructure of social interaction" here is (mainly) the rules of the game. Choosing an institutional infrastructure means choosing which game, defined by which set of rules, will be played. If the game chosen is contract bridge, then some individuals in the group – namely, the 5 year olds – will not be able to participate effectively. There is another option, however: A simpler game (a less demanding infrastructure for social interaction) can be chosen so that everyone will be able to participate successfully. We can play "go fish."

The question before us then is this: Why should we systematically favor modes of preventing disabilities that involve changing the physical or institutional infrastructure for interaction rather than changing the individual?

CHOOSING A DOMINANT COOPERATIVE FRAMEWORK

The Concept of a Dominant Cooperative Framework

Suppose that instead of looking for a card game to occupy us for a few hours, we are choosing what might be called the dominant cooperative scheme for our entire society for the indefinite future. Doing this means we are choosing who will be disabled and who will not. The same individual may be disabled relative to one cooperative scheme, but "abled" relative to another (Wikler 1983; Buchanan 1993, 1995, 1996).

The dominant cooperative scheme in the United States and other industrial economies is highly complex. Among its more important elements are these: an institutional structure that includes a private and a public sector, each with its own distinctive norms of conduct; the dominance of competitive markets in the private sector; a complex division of labor; a legal system that defines "competent" individuals and confers on them an extensive range of civil and political rights, including the right to engage in exchange relationships under the law of property and contracts; and a thoroughgoing reliance on written language and symbols. This sort of cooperative scheme, which for convenience we can call "the industrial-symbolic economy," requires individuals to have a complex array of literacy and numeracy skills if they are to participate effectively in it. These skills may not be needed to thrive in other, "developing" societies, where the division of labor is not so elaborate, where contractual relations and interactions over large distances and across long stretches of time are not so common, and where communication is exclusively oral. Accordingly, some individuals may be disabled in our sort of society, but not in others.

There are other prerequisites of successful participation in the industrial economy that may be less obvious. This sort of cooperative framework operates on the assumption that, for the most part, individuals (as opposed to families or clans) are to gain the materials of life through their own labor, which is to be sold in the market. The paid labor activities that are available to individuals in this economy in turn require certain minimal levels of physical strength, mental alertness, and stamina, and these in turn cannot be sustained without a certain minimum caloric intake, as well as rudimentary shelter and clothing.

Economists who specialize in economic development have begun to emphasize that in many parts of the world there are thousands of individuals who lack the basic resources for participation in the industrial-symbolic economy. They are unable to sell their labor or at least are unable to work long enough hours at a high enough wage to be able to purchase the food and shelter needed to live reasonably long lives, much less to thrive in the new cooperative framework that is rapidly replacing traditional modes of production. In the most extreme

cases, malnutrition during childhood and the enervating effects of lifelong parasites produce generations of individuals who are cognitively
impaired and so physically weak that they are unemployable, except
perhaps at very low rates for brief periods during childhood. Developmental economics, then, gives concrete examples of what it means
to be excluded from effective participation in a dominant cooperative
framework – and of how devastating the consequences of exclusion
can be.

There are other, more subtle ways in which individuals can be
excluded from effective participation in the dominant cooperative
framework than by lacking sufficient material resources to be mentally
or physically capable of meeting its demands. In our society, many
individuals are excluded because they are deemed to be "incompetent." Typically, rough and ready classifications of abilities along with
equally crude legal conceptions of the level of these abilities an individual must possess to qualify as "competent" serve to qualify some and
disqualify others from entering into contracts, marrying, disposing of
property, and so forth. It is tempting to assume that these "gate-
keeping" standards are, at least in principle, grounded on purely paternalistic considerations – that is, that minors or the seriously retarded are to be excluded from entering into contracts, for example,
solely in order to protect them.

On reflection it becomes apparent, however, that those who are
able to participate effectively in such complex interactions have an
interest in excluding from participation those who are not. As the
example of the very young children attempting to play contract bridge
shows, participation by "disabled" individuals can cause "discoordi-
nation" and reduce the benefits that the "abled" might otherwise reap
from complex forms of cooperation. The abled – those whose capacities can meet the demands of the more complex scheme of cooperation
– have an interest in having that scheme chosen. Let us call this interest
the "maximizing interest," to distinguish it from the "interest in inclusion," the interest that individuals have in being included in the dominant cooperative framework of their society.

It is important to note that dominant cooperative frameworks for
entire societies have never been chosen, strictly speaking. Instead, they
have emerged not according to any overall conception or plan or as
the result of collective deliberation concerning alternatives, but rather
from the cumulative and largely unanticipated effects of many individuals' actions over many generations.

At certain critical junctures in a society's history, however, it may be possible to exercise some degree of control over some important elements of the dominant cooperative scheme, including those that will have a significant impact on who will be disabled. On the threshold of the genetic revolution, we find ourselves at such a juncture.

The opportunity to choose key elements of a dominant cooperative framework arises if three conditions are satisfied. First, it is recognized that new technologies are emerging that will have a significant impact on the dominant cooperative framework. Second, there are political institutions that enable some or all citizens to have an effective voice in consciously determining whether or how the emerging technology will be deployed. And third, a sufficient number of politically influential citizens or government officials are motivated to try to exert some control over the character of the framework. If these conditions are satisfied, important features of the dominant cooperative scheme may become objects of social choice, just as certain features of the physical infrastructure for interaction already have become, as the result of the campaign for physical access to public spaces for the disabled. Whether the third condition is satisfied may depend in part on whether there is an awareness that society has obligations of inclusion. For this reason, getting clearer about the morality of inclusion may be of some practical importance.

Why the Choice Is a Matter of Justice

The choice of a dominant cooperative scheme is a matter of justice because it determines who is disabled and who is not and because whether a person is disabled has profound consequences for his or her status in society, opportunities, and overall life prospects. Because of the economic and social advantages of being able to participate effectively in the dominant cooperative scheme, individuals have a fundamental interest in not being disabled, that is, in the dominant cooperative scheme being one whose demands are matched by their abilities. This is the interest in inclusion. That this is a morally legitimate interest seems clear enough, because inclusion is in general a necessary condition for protecting a person's most basic interests – in well-being, in having a wide range of opportunities, and in self-esteem.

There is another reason, however, why the choice of a dominant cooperative scheme is a matter of justice. There is an opposing interest that a just social order will accord some weight: the maximizing interest. Each individual has an important and morally legitimate interest in having access to a cooperative scheme that is the most productive and rewarding form of interaction in which he or she can participate effectively. Just as those whose abilities do not satisfy the demands of the dominant cooperative scheme are at a disadvantage, so do those who could participate in a more productive and rewarding scheme but are barred from doing so by restrictions designed to make the scheme more inclusive lose something of value. The problem with the slogan that we should "change society, not people" is that if taken literally, it ignores the legitimacy of this second interest.

The fact that there are two legitimate interests, not one, at stake in the choice of cooperative schemes is tacitly recognized in the most significant legislation addressing the needs of people with disabilities to date, the Americans with Disabilities Act (ADA). This federal legislation recognizes as legitimate the interest in inclusion by requiring private and public employers to undertake accommodations to the special needs of those with disabilities.

We have argued that a commitment to equality of opportunity requires efforts to prevent disabling impairments. At present, however, biomedicine's powers of prevention are very limited. The requirement that workplaces be modified to accommodate persons with disabilities is a reasonable response to the inadequacy of the preventive strategy. In that sense, the same moral considerations that lead us to try to prevent disabling impairments also support the requirement of accommodation (Daniels 1997).

It is important to emphasize that the ADA adds the qualifier that all that is required in the name of equal opportunity is "reasonable" accommodations. The addition of this qualifier signals a recognition that the interests of employers, of workers who do not have disabilities, and of consumers of the goods and services that public and private organizations produce are also legitimate and should be accorded some weight.

The choice of a dominant cooperative scheme is a matter of justice because justice is concerned, among other things, with achieving a proper balance of conflicting legitimate interests. A closer look at our earlier example of a card game will make it clearer that the two interests in question are really in opposition, and that they are both legitimate.

The youngest persons in our imagined example have an interest in the chosen game being one in which they can participate effectively, and this means a simpler game. The older persons have an interest in the chosen game being one that is more challenging and complex, since this will be more enjoyable for them. This is not to say that the opposition of interests between the two groups need be total. It may be that some of the older people have an interest in being in a game that includes everyone (perhaps they are the grandparents of the youngest children). However, when the choice of a dominant cooperative framework is at stake, and extremely large numbers of unrelated people are involved, we cannot count on such an interest in inclusion being universal or dispositive.

There is another feature of the choice of a card game that is absent in the choice of a dominant cooperative framework for society that makes it more plausible to say that the latter choice is a matter of justice. In the card game, it may be feasible to resolve the conflict of interests simply by forming two different games, suited to the respective capacities of the two groups. Generally speaking, this is not an option in the case of the choice of dominant cooperative frameworks under modern conditions. The global economy is increasingly homogenizing the dominant cooperative schemes of all societies, forging a single world society defined by a single dominant cooperative scheme – that of the industrial-symbolic economy. Most people will have no choice but to try to participate in this emerging globally dominant cooperative framework. The conflict between the interest in inclusion and the maximizing interest cannot be avoided by sorting the parties out into different, noncompeting cooperative frameworks.

Overlooking a Basic Problem of Justice It is not simply the advocates of the slogan that we should "change society, not people" who have failed to see that the choice of cooperative framework is a problem of justice. Theorists of justice have not only failed to supply a principled account of how these conflicting interests ought to be balanced; they have almost without exception failed to identify the problem as one of justice. Instead, they have framed the first problem of justice as that of how to determine the fair distribution of the burdens and benefits of social cooperation, proceeding on the assumption that the basic character of the cooperative scheme is given, and that most or all individuals to whom distributive justice is owed are participants in that cooperative scheme. There is a prior problem of justice, however, as we have just seen: that of choosing the cooperative framework itself.

We have emphasized that because both of the opposing interests are morally legitimate, the prior problem of justice cannot be resolved by ignoring one of the interests. Instead, there must be a balancing of interests. Presumably a proper balancing will give greater weight to the interest in inclusion, at least where the pursuit of greater inclusiveness does not result in a cooperative framework that is unable to deliver a reasonable degree of prosperity and a reasonable range of challenges and fulfillments for those who could have effectively participated in a more complex and demanding framework. Under these conditions, it is plausible to conclude that being excluded from effective participation is worse than simply not being able to participate in the most rewarding and fulfilling cooperative framework among those that a person can participate effectively in.

However, to say that the interest in inclusion is generally speaking weightier than the maximizing interest is not to say that the latter interest should be given no weight at all in the choice of cooperative framework. In some instances, a proper balancing of the interest in inclusion and the maximizing interest – or, more positively, an effort to achieve a better fit between individuals' abilities and the demands of the dominant cooperative framework – may require changing individuals. Moreover, as we have already argued, this way of achieving a better fit cannot be ruled out on the grounds that it necessarily expresses negative judgments about the worth of disabled individuals or denies their right to exist. In a just society in which the powers of genetic intervention are highly developed, both society and individuals will be changed in order to reduce the incidence of disabilities, both for the sake of those who would have been disabled and for the sake of others.

Justice as Self-Interested Reciprocity versus Subject-Centered Justice

We have just seen that the debate over the use of genetic interventions to prevent disabilities raises a fundamental issue for the morality of inclusion: to what extent, if any, does justice require that social resources be used to help achieve a better fit between persons and the dominant cooperative framework, so that more persons can be full participants or normal competitors? Here it is important to point out that how this question is answered depends on a root choice among types of theories of justice (and of ethical theories generally).

Two basic types, justice as self-interested reciprocity theories and subject-centered theories, yield radically different answers about obligations of inclusion generally, and hence about the scope of societal obligations to use genetic interventions to promote inclusion. While the prospect of increased powers of genetic intervention does not uniquely raise this watershed issue in ethical theory, the debate between the proponents of genetic intervention and those who regard it as inherently exclusionary makes the theoretical choice more vivid and pressing.

Theories of justice as self-interested reciprocity hold that whether an individual is a member of the community of subjects of justice – individuals who have rights – depends on whether that individual can make a net contribution to social cooperation. Examples of this type of theory are woven through the history of philosophy in the West; variants are found in Epicurus, Hobbes, Hume, and, with the greatest sophistication, in the work of David Gauthier (Buchanan 1990). The core idea is that obligations of justice are based ultimately on rational self-interest and that consequently we have no obligations to those who have nothing to contribute to our well-being. Chapter 2 noted that the tacit acceptance of some version of justice as reciprocity may explain the strident tone of moral indignation that some eugenicists leveled at those "inferior types" whom they regarded as "useless eaters," nothing but a drain on social resources.

In contrast, theories of subject-centered justice do not make an individual's membership in the community of beings with rights depend on the ability to make a net contribution to social cooperation. Different variants of subject-centered theories pick out different characteristics that confer membership in the community of subjects of justice: Kantian theories emphasize the capacity for practical rationality (the ability to be motivated by the thought of what one ought to do); utilitarian theories emphasize sentience (the capacity for pain and pleasure, or more broadly, for happiness and unhappiness).

Subject-centered theories, unlike justice as self-interested reciprocity theories, provide the basis for taking the morality of inclusion seriously. According to these, persons are entitled to basic moral respect regardless of whether they have the capacity to make a net contribution to social cooperation. Since exclusion from the dominant cooperative framework is damaging in many ways, such theories require that we manifest our equal respect for all by undertaking efforts to enable individuals to be full participants in the dominant cooperative scheme. Justice as self-interested reciprocity theories, in contrast, recognizes no such obligations of inclusion; efforts to include individuals in a cooperative scheme are only required (as a matter of prudence) if the contribution they will be enabled to make exceeds the costs of including them.

It is not within the scope of this volume to mount a systematic argument to show why we believe subject-centered theories to be superior. Here we will indicate only how radical justice as self-interested reciprocity is and how discordant it is with the general framework of moral assumptions within which our inquiry has proceeded. Put most simply, subject-centered theories are consonant with some of our most confidently held general considered moral judgments, including the conviction that there are human rights and that the most severely disabled people are entitled to equal moral respect. Human rights, by definition, are those that individuals have simply by virtue of their humanity, and being a net contributor to social cooperation is not a necessary condition for being human. (For a systematic criticism of justice as self-interested reciprocity, see Buchanan 1990.)

For our present purposes, the key point is that if an endorsement of the use of genetic intervention to prevent disabilities is to avoid the charge of being exclusionary, it must be unambiguously grounded in a rejection of justice as self-interested reciprocity. The first step toward developing a theory of the morality of inclusion to guide personal choice and social policy in a society of greatly enhanced genetic powers, then, is a resolute commitment to subject-centered justice.

How Genetic Interventions Might Affect the Character of the Dominant Cooperative Scheme

To revert to one of the scenarios sketched in the Introduction, suppose that advances in immunology based on increased knowledge of genes make it possible to enhance resistance to common illnesses, including the common cold, flu, depression, and cardiovascular diseases. The mode of intervention might be gene therapy or, more likely, genetic pharmacology. Those who can afford health insurance that covers these interventions will be sick less often and their illnesses will be less severe.

Suppose also, as is now the case, that most people in this country have access to health insurance and hence to these beneficial interventions but, as is also the case, that a significant segment of the population – say 15 percent – lack insurance and cannot afford the interventions. Under these conditions, which are far from fanciful, standard employment contracts, as we saw in Chapter 3, might come to be geared to the health needs of those who have benefited from these enhancements. The number of sick days allowed to employees without loss of wages might decrease significantly, reflecting the lower risk of illness that now characterizes the "enhanced" majority.

In these circumstances, those who lack access to the interventions in question would face severe limitations on employability because they would be unable to meet prevalent expectations for work performance. They would be disabled relative to their social environment in the way that people with chronic illnesses are in our present social environment. Unequal access to enhancement technology would function to exclude them from the dominant cooperative scheme. Their position would be analogous to that of individuals in developing countries who are unable to compete in the labor market because they lack the minimal caloric intake or are severely weakened due to malaria or other parasites.

A somewhat more speculative example is based on the fact that the dominant cooperative framework in developed countries is increasingly shaped by sophisticated information processing technology. Suppose that advances in our knowledge of how genes code for proteins that affect brain functions eventually make it possible to enhance certain significant aspects of cognitive and perceptual performance that are relevant to the ability to use information processing technologies, including ever more sophisticated computers.

Those who are fortunate enough to be able to afford access to these interventions have faster rates of neural processing, can recognize and recall more accurately longer sequences of complex strings of symbols, and can perform more quickly the complex operations required for the optimal use of sophisticated information processing equipment. If a majority or a substantial portion of the population enjoyed such enhancements, their greater capacities might influence the direction of technological development – just as the increase in average height of recent generations has influenced architectural specifications, the length of beds, and the distance between the driver's seat and the brake pedal in automobiles. Computer hardware and software might exploit these enhanced capacities, with the result that those who lacked them could not operate the new systems optimally or even with acceptable proficiency. In this case, genetic intervention that provided enhancements for some would result in exclusion for others.

This is not entirely a science fiction example. Persons with visual disabilities and deficits in motor skills involving the use of their hands are already barred from access to most computing technologies simply because the operating mechanisms (keyboards, screens, the mouse, and so on) are designed for those who do not have these disabilities. If new information technology continues to evolve without any attempt to widen access to it, then the limits on opportunity that people with disabilities already face may be greatly exacerbated, as employability and educational advancement come to depend more and more on the ability to use this technology effectively.

There is at the time of this writing at least one large-scale grant project that addresses an important aspect of the general problem: access to the "information superhighway" and related computer technologies (Perry 1996). The aim of this project is to help ensure that equipment will be designed to minimize barriers to access to the Internet and its successor technologies. The rationale for the project rests on the same insight that our hypothetical example is meant to convey: If technology is designed with reference to "normal" abilities, then it may restrict rather than widen opportunities for some, and this is true regardless of whether those who do not have "normal" abilities suffer from genetic or other impairments or are simply too poor to afford the interventions that set a new level of "normality" with reference to which new technologies are designed.

The preceding examples reveal how the availability of genetic interventions according to ability to pay might result in some people being excluded from the dominant cooperative framework or at least from certain important parts of it. But it must be emphasized that genetic interventions can prevent disabilities as well, by preventing the impairments that, given the features of the existing cooperative scheme, result in disabilities that seriously limit peoples' opportunities.

KNOWLEDGE OF GENETIC DIFFERENCES AND THE MORALITY OF INCLUSION

Advances in genetic knowledge will force us to confront the basic issues of the morality of inclusion even when there is no possibility of genetic intervention to create a better fit between the abilities of individuals and the demands of the dominant cooperative framework.

In many cases, the most valuable knowledge concerning genes will be information about the interactions of specific genes with specific environments. In particular, it is very likely that we will learn that individuals with particular genotypes require particular environments, both physical and social, if they are to flourish. And in some cases, the needed environment will not be the one that now exists.

In this sense, the great expansion of knowledge that is made possible by the Human Genome Project and related genetic research may make the nature/nurture debate moot rather than resolve it. Instead of asking Which is more important (for this problem, this characteristic), genes or environment? the question will increasingly be Which combinations of genes and environments will produce the desired outcome? Better knowledge of how genes function will be knowledge of how they function in various environments, and this will enable us to identify and to select or construct the most beneficial environments for achieving desired results, including the goal of having more individuals as effective participants in the dominant cooperative framework.

Again, examples will clarify. Greater knowledge of the functioning of genes that influence sensory and neural processes involved in learning to read may lead us to the conclusion that there is no one optimal environment for learning to read for all people. Instead, we may learn to group individuals by genotypes and then develop different environments that are tailored to the needs of different groups. Increased genetic knowledge may lead to more effective environmental intervention, rather than to genetic intervention.

Knowledge of how different genotypes react differently in different environments may therefore open up new options for eliminating barriers to equal opportunity. However, the existence of these options raises new and perplexing problems of justice. The environment that is beneficial for one genotypic subgroup may be suboptimal or even dangerous for others. But tailoring an optimal environment for each genotypic group will, in some cases, be either impossible or extremely costly. If the majority learns to read or learns mathematics quite readily in one type of environment, but we discover that there is a minority of individuals who will do poorly unless provided with a special and rather expensive environment, what cost is society obligated to bear to provide it?

This question is already being debated in discussions of educational policy for persons with learning disabilities. It has become evident that tailoring learning environments to the special needs of students can produce significant benefits but that doing so is costly, partly because of the loss of economies of scale and the need for special training for teachers. Not surprisingly, parents of children who do not need these special environments are sometimes concerned that the resources allocated to construct them represent an unacceptable subtraction from what is available to their children. As increased genetic knowledge enables us to sort people into groups having conflicting interests in how public funds are to be allocated and how public institutions are to be designed, problems of justice of this sort will arise with increasing frequency and urgency.

Knowledge of how different genotypic groups can be benefited or harmed by the same environment may also enormously complicate the task of designing just and effective public health policies. We have tended to think of public health measures as universalistic – as quite general interventions that are in the interests of all members of society, and hence as a form of social action that reinforces solidarity rather than creates divisions of interest. Everyone benefits from cleaner water and purer food, the elimination of the major infectious diseases of childhood through mass immunizations, and so on.

New genetic knowledge, however, may in fact serve to divide us one from another. For example, advances in genetic knowledge might lead to the conclusion that the majority of the population could benefit by introducing a particular chemical into water supplies, but at the risk of increasing the incidence of cancer for a minority. Similarly, devising effective public education programs to encourage healthy lifestyles will be much more difficult if we learn that what is good for some is bad for others. It might turn out, for instance, that ingesting at least 60 grams of protein daily (which some nutritional experts now recommend) has beneficial results for many people but heightens the risk of colon cancer for others, or that vitamin C supplements reduce the risk of cancer for the majority but cause liver damage for a minority.

It has often been remarked that new knowledge of genotypic differences may result in stigmatization and perhaps reinforce racism and similar exclusionary and discriminatory attitudes. What has not been sufficiently appreciated is that increased knowledge of genetic differences will force us to confront the most basic issues of the morality of inclusion. Among the most important of these is the extent of the obligation to commit social resources to ensuring that genotypic minorities – whether they be people with what we now recognize as disabilities such as blindness, or individuals who simply need a different environment in which to learn to read – do not experience limitations on their opportunities because the social world they inhabit has been designed by others, for others.

The possibility that new knowledge of genetic differentiation will create or exacerbate problems of just allocation of resources illustrates the general structure of the problems that a developed theory of the morality of inclusion must address. On the one hand, there is the morally legitimate interest in inclusion, on the other, what we have called the "maximizing interest." What a theory of the morality of inclusion ought to supply is a principled, defensible way of balancing these interests. No such theory is offered here. Something can be said, however, to indicate the kinds of choices that would have to be made in constructing such a theory.

How much weight the interest in inclusion should be given vis-à-vis the maximizing interest, or other morally legitimate interests, will presumably depend in part upon whether there is a risk of near total exclusion from the dominant cooperative scheme. In other words, if a minority of individuals will simply not be able to participate at all in the economic mainstream of society unless societal resources are allocated to provide them with the special interventions they require, they have an exceptionally strong claim on resources. (This would certainly be the case for a Rawlsian theory of distributive justice or any theory that gives priority to the worst off, since being excluded from the basic cooperative scheme is presumably one of the worst liabilities an individual can have.) If a disability does not bar certain individuals from participation in a wide range of cooperative frameworks, including the dominant one of their society, but merely limits the effectiveness of their participation above some fairly generous threshold, then presumably their claim for special resources is weaker. Different types of general moral theories will give greater or lesser weight to the claims of the worse off, and this will result in different responses to the problem of exclusion.

According to some moral theories, at least, the numbers may count as well: within limits, the larger the genotypic minority requiring special allocations for health care or for education, the stronger their claim on resources. And it is worth stressing here that a theory need not be utilitarian in any thoroughgoing sense to make room for some consideration of the numbers.

Nor is it a matter of either opting for an absolute priority on improving the condition of the worst off or simply doing what improves the condition of the largest numbers of persons. A developed theory of the morality of inclusion might well include a limited priority for the worst off (giving them an especially weighty claim on resources needed to bring them up to some threshold of participation in the dominant cooperative scheme, to make them "normal competitors" in the language employed in Chapters 3 and 4), balanced by a principle that accords increasing weight to the conflicting interests of others as their numbers increase, once the worst off have reached the threshold of participation. Or, since the resources needed to bring the worst off of the worst off up to the threshold of participation may be virtually unlimited, a more appropriate balance might limit the commitment to bringing (all of) the worst off up to "normal competitor" status by a consideration of the opportunity-costs to the better off, if their numbers are sufficiently greater. These rough reflections are intended only to indicate the rich potential for working out a theory of the morality of inclusion.

CONCLUSION

In previous chapters we have argued that both justice and our obligations to prevent harm make genetic interventions to prevent disabilities not only permissible but also obligatory. We have also argued that the use of genetic interventions for enhancements, not just for the prevention or cure of disease, is also permissible if it occurs within the constraints of justice we have tried to specify.

This chapter has explored some of the most radical and disturbing challenges to the entire enterprise of genetic intervention – those forcefully raised by some members of the disabilities rights movement. The unifying theme of these challenges is that the new genetics, like the old eugenics, is exclusionary, despite its proponents' efforts to present it as an inclusive endeavor for human betterment through the conquest of disease. In the process of articulating and evaluating various arguments that purport to show the exclusionary nature of genetic intervention, we have seen how anticipated advances in genetic science raise in vivid and sometimes novel forms some of the most basic but neglected issues of ethical theory – problems we have grouped under the rubric of the morality of inclusion.

The new genetics does provide weapons for exclusion. This is undeniable, even though, as we have seen, there is nothing inherently exclusionary about the enterprise of improving human lives through the selection of characteristics by the application of genetic knowledge. Members of the disabilities rights movement have performed an invaluable service by alerting the public to the potential for exclusion which the new technology represents. Indeed, they have been pioneers in exploring the morality of inclusion, treading ground that most moral theorists have lamentably neglected. While the theorists have concentrated on the problem of how to distribute the burdens and benefits of social cooperation among those who have ready access to the cooperative framework, disabilities rights advocates have rightly emphasized that there is a more basic moral issue: How can our cooperative frameworks – and above all our attitudes toward those who have disabilities – be modified so as to achieve greater inclusion?

In spite of its potential for exclusion, the new genetics also creates hitherto unimaginable opportunities for including more people as effective participants in fulfilling forms of social interaction, through genetic intervention and the use of genetic knowledge to tailor environments to individual needs. An awareness of both the negative and the positive potential of the new genetics prompts a more systematic development of ethical theory – one that recognizes obligations of inclusion but that also acknowledges and articulates the limits of these obligations.

EIGHT

POLICY IMPLICATIONS

Newly informed of the origin of species and the mechanisms of evolutionary adaptation, Galton and the original eugenicists sought to apply their knowledge for the salvation and improvement of society. But the road was bumpy, their vision fogged, and the route unclear; before long, there were victims, and eventually, in the cataclysm of the Nazi years, the entire enterprise crashed. Today, it is standard practice to repudiate not only their beliefs, their biases, and their methods, but also their values and aims.

For two generations, it has been taboo to discuss the application of genetic knowledge to the design, management, and improvement of society. In light of our greater sophistication about heredity, this kind of thinking seemed pointless; and given the experience of many people with eugenics, it also seemed very dangerous. Genetic scientists and clinicians alike instituted a new orthodoxy, a practice that focused narrowly on the medical and on the individual. Their role was to be confined to providing information (and later, therapy) according to the wishes of the individual patient or client and without any thought of the impact of a particular intervention on society at large, whether for good or ill.

The social perspective on genetics, however, will inevitably be revisited as the revolution in genetic science and medicine progresses. As genetics permeates our lives, as more and more people come into contact with genetic screening, testing, and, eventually, intervention, we cannot fail to appreciate the fact that these individual encounters have effects on others. Governments and other payers with social responsibilities will be tempted to take these wider effects into account in deciding which services to offer to individuals. Because choices by individuals may sometimes have adverse effects on others, including the unconceived, public agencies may be moved to discourage or limit some of these options.

Moreover, our current aversion to social thinking about eugenics is not universally shared. The long-term leaders of Singapore and Malaysia have spoken favorably of old-style eugenics (Chan and Chee 1984), and the People's Republic of China recently enacted a "Law on Maternal and Child Health Care," which has eugenic provisions, including potentially coercive regulations on marriage and reproduction (*Nature* 1994; Qiu 1998). At least one community that perceives itself to be at particular risk has instituted a vigorous program of selection that has a marked eugenic flavor. The Dor Yeshorim organization, initiated by a rabbi, advises orthodox Jewish communities plagued by high rates of inherited diseases such as Tay-Sachs and Canavan disease. Dor Yeshorim offers tests for the genes in question to young people; matches that might produce diseased offspring are then discouraged by matchmakers (Wertz 1997; Landau 1994). Dor Yeshorim takes credit for the prevention of hundreds of cases of these diseases.

Our consideration of a range of ethical and social issues raised by advances in genetics stems from our conviction that these developments – both scientific and social – make it increasingly unwise to consider the ethics of genetics only at the individual level. What matters is not merely the ethics of the individual scientist, physician, or counselor, but the broader questions of justice, of claims for freedom and for protection from harm, and our obligations toward future generations. This book aims to provide a perspective for the development of public and institutional policy on genetics which takes these issues into account.

We will be cautious in pointing out the implications of our discussion for framing policy in the near to mid-term. Our account is stated in broad terms and in most cases would not imply support for specific regulations, laws, or practices until joined with detailed accounts of the individual problems these are meant to address and the likely effects and interactions of these measures. At the same time, the analysis we have provided of the implications of genetics for such issues as distributive justice, reproductive autonomy, and disability rights points us in particular policy directions. This final chapter both summarizes and extends our discussion of the practical bearing of our philosophical analysis.

WHERE DOES THE SHADOW OF EUGENICS FALL?

The Inevitable Comparison

The eugenics movement, which began to pick up steam about a century ago, marked the first attempt to apply the insights of evolutionary biology to our own species. However much the present genetic revolution may differ in its methods and its aims, those familiar with the career and consequences of the eugenics movement cannot easily avoid the comparison. Indeed, one of the signal differences between the new genetics and the old eugenics – vastly better science and technology – is simultaneously a potential cause for alarm.

As we noted in Chapter 2, one impediment to the realization of the grandest ambitions of the eugenics movement was its reliance, at that stage of scientific development, on selective breeding, pursued by methods that were ineffective (public appeals to choose mates on a eugenic basis), repugnant (involuntary sterilization), or both. The subtle and impressive methods of genetic engineering and the precisely targeted reproductive strategies born of genetic testing and screening provide us with tools that eluded the eugenicists even in their dreams. But if the eugenicists were wrong in their very inspiration, if the core values and inspiration were wrong-headed and evil, should we not be alarmed that more effective tools will soon exist for their realization? The description of Hitler's Luftwaffe as "Neanderthals in airplanes" vividly captures this concern: Modern technology guided by a primitive moral sense can produce horrific results.

Public Concern about Genetic Research

It is not surprising, then, that to a degree unprecedented in the annals of science and public policy, the Human Genome Project and attendant advances in genetic knowledge, technology, and basic science have been greeted by a chorus of demands for oversight, regulation, and even prohibition. Though legislatures in the United States have been relatively cautious in enacting specific measures, European parliaments have been bold, and several international groups are in the process of proposing protocols and conventions.

Some of these measures are specific regulations of the conduct of science and of the practices of insurers and employers. But in their

preambles, and in proposed conventions and protocols, are strongly
worded defenses of the inviolability and dignity of each person in the
face of a potentially dire genetic challenge. Expressions of concern
have been voiced on behalf of leaders of all major faiths and by
activists across the political spectrum. In Germany, a coalition of left-
leaning Greens and conservative religious groups wages a vigilant
campaign against complacent acceptance of promises of genetic progress. In the United States, a coalition of religious groups taking in the
entire political spectrum was organized to petition the president for
caution in genetic technology, a demand that ultimately resulted in
one of the first comprehensive governmental analyses of these issues,
the *Splicing Life* (1983) and *Genetic Screening and Counseling* (1983)
by the President's Commission on Medical Ethics.

These ethical and social issues present obstacles to progress in genetic science and clinical practice even if no legislative impediments
are enacted. In response to these public concerns, a good deal of
current writing on ethical, legal, and social issues in genetics has
sought to establish what we have referred to as "moral firebreaks."
The strategy has been to emphasize the risk or danger posed by certain
kinds of intervention, identified by one or another commonly encountered distinctions, and then to urge voluntary adoption or even legislation to ensure that actions of the suspect category are not undertaken. These distinctions include those between negative and positive
eugenics (i.e., discouraging reproduction among the "unfit" and encouraging the "fit" to multiply), between genetic intervention for individuals and for society, between treatment and enhancement, between eugenic and medical uses of genetic intervention and
information, and between germ cell and somatic cell genetic engineering.

Beyond Rules of Thumb

In our view, this strategy has only limited utility. Although we do find
a place for some of these distinctions in our own proposals, it is at
most as rules of thumb – supportable not because they demarcate an
important boundary of our moral world but because they denote a
point of convergence of diverse views or because they are a convenient
"bright line" whose use can be recommended since the rough-and-
tumble policy arena does not permit the use of finer distinctions. These

rules of thumb, being neither self-evident nor in themselves of arresting importance, obtain whatever authority they possess from higher-level principles of morality and justice.

A further motivation for pursuing our discussion at a higher level of abstraction is to take into account the possibility that consideration of the implementation of these rules in a future society might force a reconsideration of the rules themselves, as we would expect in keeping with the method of reflective equilibrium (i.e., adjusting theories and specific moral judgments in light of each other, together with other data, until a position of stability, not in need of further revision, is reached).

As we have noted repeatedly in this book, the genetic revolution provides the occasion for rethinking some of the basic concepts of moral and social philosophy. In our view, then, an approach that instructs us to get our moral bearings first and to set the terms of genetic policy thereafter falls victim to the challenge that the genetic revolution might someday pose to our current thinking about ethics. We expect that the broad moral guideposts we have outlined will bear further revision as new and unanticipated developments in genetic science, technology, and medicine require further elaboration and application to policy issues.

We make no effort to derive model statutes or regulations from our analysis, partly because we appreciate how hard it is to predict the scope and pace of genetic advances, and partly because we recognize that the sound application of ethical theory must be grounded in a wealth of empirical data about which we, as moral philosophers, have no expertise. There is a more positive reason, however, why we offer no concrete policy proposals: We have attempted to take a longer view of the issues, and this inevitably brings with it a loss of fine focus for objects in the immediate foreground. In addition, we gladly acknowledge the virtues of the division of labor, deferring to the valuable work that others are doing in advocating or criticizing various concrete policy initiatives, from regulations concerning the patenting of genes to proposals for eliminating genetic discrimination in insurance.

This book is devoted to determining the principles that might govern a just and humane society in the wake of the genetic revolution. We do not offer a comprehensive theory, but we do argue for and from a series of broad principles, most of which are consistent with contemporary liberal theories of justice. Our primary emphasis has been on equal opportunity, the prevention of harm, and on individual freedoms, but our treatment covers other principles as well, including those of citizenship and political participation, arguing broadly for an emphasis on inclusion – a value particularly pertinent to a genetic policy that seeks to steer away from the sins of the earlier eugenics. We trace a potentially important role for the state in setting and enforcing genetic policy. And although we argue for wide latitude in individual decision making in genetic matters, particularly in the context of reproduction, we do not regard this as implying the desirability of relying on markets in lieu of social policies based on principles of justice. The remainder of this chapter suggests various policy implications of these principles.

DISTRIBUTIVE JUSTICE

Our survey of the policy implications of our philosophical analysis begins with considerations of distributive justice. Much of the extant literature on ethical and social issues in genetics is concerned with "freedoms from . . . ," such as protecting the individual from threats to his or her privacy or freedom. It is unfortunate that in current writing on the genetic revolution, the problems posed sometimes crowd out the hopes fulfilled. Despite the profound moral challenges posed by these scientific advances, we believe that their promise far overshadows their danger. Accordingly, we turn first to an entitlement, that is, what each person should be able to expect from society by way of provision of genetic services.

The Right to Health Care

What does distributive justice require in public policy regarding clinical genetics and genetic intervention generally? To the extent that these genetic interventions constitute health care, we argue for social policies that ensure these services will be provided to those who need them. The contribution of genetic intervention to human well-being, however, is potentially broader than health care, and here we do not endorse the same kind of broad entitlement.

Access to Health Care: Equal Opportunity as Entitlement and Limitation Although we have not provided an elaborate case for universal access to health care, a subject that requires separate and extensive treatment, we have generally followed the lead of Daniels's

Just Health Care (1985) and the writings of other theorists in linking the requirements of justice to a broad entitlement to services needed to protect or restore species-typical functioning.

To be sure, this entitlement is limited by resource constraints. As citizens of a country in which spending on health care, measured both as share of gross domestic product (one seventh) and in absolute terms (around $1 trillion) dwarfs that of any other past or present, we are mindful of the diminishing returns of overspending on health. The gargantuan scale of the U.S. health care sector, however, is also the major premise in an argument against its lack of universality. While billions of dollars are spent on therapies of little or no value to patients, millions of people lack insurance even for the most important health care needs. Priorities in the system as a whole are not in order. Access to a broad package of health services, we have maintained, is required for justice, since it is needed to maintain fair equality of opportunity, which disease otherwise threatens to undermine.

Including Genetic Services in the Right to Health Care   This societal obligation extends naturally to clinical genetics. Our conclusion here is consistent with standard medical and insurance practices in industrial countries, including the United States. Although such services as genetic counseling are currently in relatively scarce supply, shortfalls can be traced not to any principled rejection of genetics as continuous with other forms of medical care but to the experimental status of much genetic testing and intervention and to the shortage of physicians and counselors with the appropriate training.

At present, the principal focus of clinical genetics is reproductive medicine. The accumulation of information regarding risks posed by genetic defects is rapidly accelerating and will increase the volume of useful services manyfold. This is not information that is easily absorbed by most patients. Even assuming maximum receptiveness and attentiveness to the explanations of physicians and counselors – an unrealistically optimistic assumption given what is at stake in reproductive decisions – patients must acquire familiarity with genetic diseases they may have never heard of before and must appreciate the significance of the statistical data about estimating the risks.

Providing this information without sufficient opportunity for absorption, questioning, and repetition is worse than useless, for in creating fear and even panic it can harm the patient and inadvertently steer him or her toward poor decisions. Most physicians in the United

States lack the training needed to provide even rudimentary genetic counseling, and patients must rely on clinical geneticists and genetic counselors. Yet the supply of well-trained professionals in this field is so limited that, in one estimate, if the cystic fibrosis gene were the subject of population-wide screening, all the professionals' working hours would be taken up with the counseling necessary for a thorough work-up (Wilfond and Fost 1992).

But reproductive medicine is just one domain of clinical genetics for the future. As genes are linked to more and more diseases of adulthood, from specific cancers to neurodegenerative diseases, millions of apparently healthy individuals in the United States alone will seek careful estimates of risk and advice on how these diseases might be avoided.

To the extent that genetic counseling and other services in clinical genetics constitute an integral component of the standard package of needed health care services, there is a pressing need to expand the training of physicians in clinical genetics and to build the infrastructure of counselors, testing laboratories, and the like needed to meet the anticipated need.

Because the United States at present relies on a system of private, competing health care providers and insurers to deliver care, an argument that supports a societal obligation to provide health care has implications throughout the system. One with special application to genetics is the double bind faced by individuals who are at risk for treatable genetic disease. For these patients, genetic testing is urgent, for a positive test shows the necessity of treatment, while a negative test would show that treatment would deliver no benefit and would allay fears of future illness as well.

Yet those with positive tests may be unable to buy health insurance policies that require individual assessments of health risks. Unless they are able to pay out of pocket for health care or to obtain free care, the test that points to the need for care also precludes it. This is a vexing problem for those with late-onset diseases such as hereditary hemochromatosis or genetically based colo-rectal cancer. It is even worse for children, whose parents may be reluctant to ask for testing in the fear that the entire family will be denied insurance and therefore access to care. This is precisely the experience of sufferers from Hippel-Lindau (VHL) disease, which causes brain tumors, necessitating MRI scans followed by surgical removal of malignant growths. It also affects the 600,000 Americans with polycystic kidney disease, for which care may be enhanced if done in connection with tests for the PKD1 gene (Beardsley 1996). The potential number of those adversely affected by these threats to insurability is much greater if we take into account Francis Collins's warning that these fears imperil the clinical mission of the Genome Project and genetic research as a whole.

These recommendations for incorporating beneficial genetic tests and interventions into an entitlement to health care and for expanding the educational and counseling infrastructure are entirely familiar and are accepted generally among those who agree, as we do, with the proposition that a just society must provide the basics of health care for all its citizens. But the extent of the entitlement to the services of clinical genetics is not fully determined by subsuming them under the general heading of needed health services. Some special features of clinical genetics engage our account of the basis of the societal obligation to provide health care, providing further reasons for ensuring access to these services but also a basis for considering their limitation.

Our analysis reinforces the case for a social obligation to provide genetic health services because of our reliance on an account of health care that places great importance on fair equality of opportunity. Opportunities of the range and type we are speaking of – that is, the broad array of paths of life, vocational, and otherwise – can be restricted by the sheer pain and disability inflicted by disease. But they can also be closed off by lack of access to information needed for effective planning, and in particular they can be truncated by erroneous information that the individual might come by in the absence of qualified professional counseling or as a result of inadequate services provided in health care settings. A genetically healthy woman who remains childless for fear of passing on the genes common in her family of origin is denied some of the opportunities of fulfillment that most can take for granted. The same would be true of a young man whose life plan was shaped by an erroneous expectation that his life would be cut short by an inherited condition that took the life of his relatives.

Limits on the Entitlement to Genetic Services   Resource constraints, however, limit the extent to which remedies for these deprivations can be offered under health care entitlements. The pattern of provision required by the opportunity account might omit certain genetic services for any of several reasons. In these early days of the genetic revolution, the benefit, if any, of new tests is often unclear for years.

In tests of uncertain significance, the information provided to the patient may have little value in medical decision making or life planning, or may even tend to lead patients into imprudent decisions. In poorly executed genetic screening programs in the past, for example, parents unlikely to have afflicted children have forgone childbearing, and at the time of this writing, geneticists have expressed concern that women who test positive for one or another form of the BRCA1 and BRCA2 (breast cancer) genes may imprudently rush to have preventive mastectomies.

Where the uselessness or hazard of genetic data derives from the fact that not enough is known, nor could be known, about the likely course of events following a positive diagnosis, this service might be a candidate for exclusion from the standard list of benefits in order to make effective planning feasible. This will remain the case even if, as is likely, strong or even intense demand for this information is expressed by patients themselves (particularly when prodded by those who profit from providing the tests).

At the time of this writing, BRCA1 and BRCA2 are deemed by most specialists to be of much too uncertain significance to make testing prudent among any but a small number of very high-risk women. Counseling before the administration of a test may be as important, for the purpose of avoiding harm, as counseling after a positive result; indeed, one result of counseling is often a decision not to submit to the test. This pattern is likely to be repeated for many years as one gene or another is discovered to have some statistical association with a disease, and the pressure on health care authorities to permit patients to make these allocation decisions may be unrelenting.

A second category of genetic services that might be excluded from a package of basic health services under the opportunity account, depending on cost, would be tests whose predictions may be reasonably certain and fully comprehensible but whose results might provide little or no assistance in making either life plans or medical decisions. Learning of the likely cause of death at an advanced age, assuming no prior accident, infectious disease, or injury, might be such a case, as long as nothing were known that could be done to head off this fate. This would not extend to late-onset conditions, such as Alzheimer's dementia, that are likely to necessitate long-term care and for which savings (and insurance, if obtainable) would be prudent at the moment of diagnosis.

A third category of genetic services that might not be provided for under a health system whose rationale lay in the opportunity account consists of those targeted not toward disease – that is, to restoration and maintenance of species-typical functioning – but to enhancement of the organism or to other changes in a patient's constitution that answer to what Daniels, following David Braybrooke, terms "adventitious needs" (Daniels, 1985). These are requirements for "contingent, idiosyncratic" projects rather than the "course of life" needs that human beings experience regardless of their personal choice of life plans. For the most part, these will be "enhancements" rather than "treatments."

As explained in Chapter 4, these demands are conventionally placed in the category of "mere preferences" and out of the category of "need" altogether. While we have not argued for any fundamental distinction underlying these categories, we have noted that for practical purposes the convergence of views among those supporting a range of theories of distributive justice on this boundary between what justice requires and what may remain optional provides support for policies that embody it.

These will join such medical practices as cosmetic plastic surgery (for patients who are not disfigured). We noted earlier that an argument based on opportunity exists for required provision of certain medical services that cannot reasonably be classified as treatments. Abortion is an example, with its important bearing on career and family planning. A similar case might thus be made for some genetic enhancements, if they also played an important part in meeting "course of life" needs, or if denying these services had an important adverse effect on opportunity.

Additional Arguments for Access to Genetic Interventions

The case for access to genetic services is not limited to citing their effect on opportunity and their efficacy in preventing serious harm. A second argument proceeds from the fact that the genetic revolution has been stimulated by large-scale public investment. The Human Genome Project itself is a tax-supported program of the Department of Energy and NIH, and many of the key advances in clinical genetics have derived from research supported by NIH grants. These funds were drawn from the population as a whole and their fruits should be returned to them.

To be sure, the field of biotechnology – including human genetics – has been developed by a hybrid public-private web of laboratories and facilities. Private venture capital has made it possible for many of the benefits of the genetics revolution to reach patients. But even in these cases, the scientists who constitute the chief assets of these companies typically develop their research in state-supported environments and retain a base within academia.

An additional reason for access to extensive genetic services is the role they play in supporting reproductive self-determination. We argued in Chapter 5 that protection of reproductive freedoms requires more than the absence of restraint. A potential parent will be in a position to make optimal reproductive decisions only if given a full account of any significant genetic risks, together with counseling on strategies and alternatives. Prospective parents who are afforded expert, extensive, and patient genetic counseling, where indicated, are in a much better position to make decisions that are best for themselves, other family members, and the well-being of any children they bring into the world.

SECURING EQUALITY

If People Are Not Equal Should We Treat Them So? Should We Make Them So?

Antiegalitarians sometimes talk as if their opponents refuse to face reality. Egalitarians, in their view, have to make believe that people are equally endowed with the talents and character traits conducive to fulfillment and success. Antiegalitarians charge that egalitarians know, in their heart of hearts, that people are not evenly blessed with these traits, yet that for fear of lending support to social policies that would take these differences into account, egalitarians insist that the differences do not exist.

To be sure, the antiegalitarian's egalitarian is a straw man. What virtually all egalitarian theorists wish public policy to promote is equality of treatment and equality of opportunity, which is in most respects as feasible in a population of diverse talents as it is in a group of exact peers. Nevertheless, in the antiegalitarian caricature, bad faith lurks just beneath the surface, for equal opportunity in a land of unequals would produce merely a meritocracy (which Herrnstein and Murray (1994) insist that the United States has already become), where success, since it would depend on talent, would be much too unequal for the egalitarian.

These authors argue in *The Bell Curve* that the Founding Fathers intended equality to hold only for negative rights, quoting Jefferson in praise of the "aristocracy of virtue and talent, which Nature has wisely provided for the direction of the interest of society . . . the most precious gift of nature."

Neoeugenic writers further from the mainstream have written hopefully of the ideological fallout of the Human Genome Project. Roger Pearson, long associated with *Mankind Quarterly*, funded by a foundation that has supported eugenic and racist research, writes in a recent issue of that journal:

Biological egalitarians are fearful that the knowledge acquired as a result of the Human Genome Project will destroy the plausibility of their universalist ideology. They are particularly concerned about the revival of scientific interest in group differences which will unavoidably result from the construction of "demic maps" tracing the genetics of regional populations of different evolutionary ancestry; and by throwing a sharp and revealing light on what had hitherto been a debatable area of human knowledge will explode the anti-evolutionary myth of universal biological uniformity.

Mankind Quarterly is generally regarded as a fringe journal, despite its many links to writers cited by such mainstream figures as Herrnstein and Murray, and the presence therein of sentiments like these does not in itself demonstrate that such views lie, like a poisoned aquifer, just beneath the surface of polite society. What is more notable for public policy purposes is the link that Pearson forges between the views of *The Bell Curve* and the Human Genome Project. Can we expect the project to encourage and legitimate these political views among people who already share some of Herrnstein's and Murray's skepticism about egalitarianism? How might these sentiments affect politics and public policy? Are they mistaken, and if so where does the mistake lie?

Our discussion engages this debate with two quite different responses. One replies to the claim that a view of justice that places a high value on equality and equal opportunity makes little sense unless we pretend that people have equal talent. The other asks what should be done in the event, however far-off and unlikely, that some of the differences in talent could be narrowed by deliberate genetic intervention.

Will Human Genomic Research Push Society to the Right?

Political debates over how much the state should intervene on behalf of equality and equal opportunity range generally across the familiar left-right spectrum. So, too, have accounts of the role of genes in social and economic success. Strongly hereditarian accounts of human talents tend to be favored by the right and disputed by the left, even though the contribution of heredity is ostensibly a scientific question that might be answered regardless of politics, because it is assumed that to the extent that talents are inherited they cannot be fostered (and opportunity cannot be equalized) by social reform.

Along with many others, we have pointed out that this latter assumption involves numerous non sequiturs, such as the unwarranted jump from the heritability of a trait to the inalterability of a character, and even from the inalterability of a character to the impossibility of environmental changes to reduce or erase the potential limitation (one remedy for myopia is eyeglasses; another is larger road signs). For these reasons, an egalitarian vision for the social order can consistently be espoused by someone who believes that talents are unequally distributed and even that these patterns of distribution reflect genetic differences in some cases. In this sense, egalitarians have little to fear from the revelations of human genomic research.

But what of inherited differences in talent that cannot be ameliorated, nor made moot by environmental changes? As Rawls and others have made clear, fitting tasks to talents need not involve putting the gifted at the top of the economic heap, either in perks or in pay. Furthermore, the very differences in talent and motivation that undoubtedly do exist can be turned into assets even for the worst-off, given appropriate incentive structures and redistribution. For the just society, as Rawls envisions it (1971):

A meritocratic society is [not] a danger . . . For . . . the difference principle [permitting inequalities only so long as they benefit the worst-off] transforms the aims of society in fundamental respects. This consequence is even more obvious once we note that we must when necessary take into account the essential primary good of self-respect . . . the confident sense of their own worth should be sought for the least favored and this limits the forms of hierarchy and the degrees of inequality that justice permits.

This is all that the moderately egalitarian liberalism of Rawls demands. It would call on the state for a much more active interventionist role on behalf of the less well off than we have seen in the United States for several decades, but it is does not demand that the egalitarian liberal deny the possibility that humans differ in natural ability or talent, and no discoveries turned up by the Human Genome Project will undermine this philosophy.

Must Everyone Have Access to Enhancements?

These considerations show that near-term advances in human genomic research do not threaten conventional redistributive liberalism by proving that not all are born equal. Still, the genetic revolution might pose a different kind of challenge: What if, in the far future, we are able not only to identify human inequalities but to do something about them? It is not worthwhile to engage the reader in an elaborate discussion of the options for the long term, since our speculation will almost certainly be out of date by the time it could have any application. Nevertheless, the contemplation of politics in connection with the genetic revolution cannot help but be drawn to the radical question: If we could literally reengineer the genetic code, should we make people more equal? If talents become even more subject to purposive distribution than now – if we learn how to rig the natural lottery – how should they be distributed in a just society of the future?

Perhaps it is enough to state that the contribution of genes to talents – traits that in any case are defined differently by particular cultures and markets – is so indirect and random that it is nearly nonsense to talk about "distributing" talents. But even if this prospect belongs in the realm of science fantasy, consideration of it might illuminate our choices should we acquire the powers to distribute talents even in very modest ways, such as boosting memory capacity.

With the prospect of taking steps to equalize human talents through genetic engineering nowhere in sight, nothing in our argument poses this as an urgent social task. Indeed, should human beings ever reach this stage of technological accomplishment, our argument would only suggest an attempt to ameliorate those genetic disadvantages that are most damaging to opportunity or that cause serious harms, rather than to bring all talents into line. In particular, there would be no justification in leveling down. Rawls, in his note on eugenics in *A Theory of Justice* (1971) argues that

it is not in general to the advantage of the less fortunate to propose policies which reduce the talents of others. Instead, by accepting the difference principle, they view the greater abilities as a social asset to be used for the common advantage.

This passage recalls the socialist eugenics of such figures as Muller, Brewer, and Serebrovsky (see Chapter 1), who proceeded from the premise of talent as a social asset. But for Rawls, the just society would tend toward equality. For

it is also in the interest of each to have natural assets. This enables him to pursue a preferred plan of life. . . . We might conjecture that in the long run, if there is an upper bound on ability, we would eventually reach a society with the greatest equal liberty and members of which enjoy the greatest equal talent.

In this view, a just society would permit inequality of talent, even if something could be done to equalize it, but (given the conjecture) it would eventually "level up" to the extent that the inequalities would disappear.

Although we do not believe that justice requires policies that enforce equality of talent for equality's sake (assuming, once again, that this were feasible), there might be occasions, particularly in a less-utopian stage in which justice has not been fully realized, for discouraging certain talent-enhancing steps that would widen existing gaps. These include zero-sum game situations in which an intervention is sought by a person, or by people for their children, that offer benefits only because they confer positional advantages on others: to be quicker, smarter, or taller, say, rather than to be long-lived or healthy, the benefit of which is only marginally related to the superiority it confers to the beneficiary in any competition with those with no access to the intervention. In these cases, what is good for one is thereby bad for others, and is undertaken in part for that reason. The inequality brought about would be objectionable not due to envy, but because of the commitment to ensuring that inequalities work to the advantage of all rather than to the detriment of all but the fortunate few.

Concern would also be justified for those individual gains that have the effect of raising the requirements for effective participation in important forms of social cooperation. As discussed in Chapter 7, the category of "disability" is to a considerable extent a social one, in the sense that the ability of an individual to participate fully in a group's affairs is a function both of the individual's particular assets and the demands of the social environment. Wheelchair-accessible buses are only the most obvious example. Well-engineered roads, for instance, can be safely negotiated even by those with slow reflexes, permitting the latter greater mobility. The same is true for a host of physical and cognitive limitations.

Our society has learned through its efforts to accommodate people with disabilities that in many cases lowering the barriers to participation need not be unduly burdensome to others. Still, many accommodations involve losses as well as gains. Tax codes and forms that might be fully comprehended by the cognitively impaired, for example, might be insufficiently detailed for efficient and fair allocation of tax burdens, and the gains for the few would not justify these losses.

And what of enhancements that do not inflict disability on those who lack access to them or that benefit simply by conferring competitive or positional advantage? We are familiar with parents who seek to give their children every advantage, without thereby lowering the chances of others, but while knowing that the children of others will not be similarly advantaged. Although there are always some interactive effects (if my child is admitted to a selective college, some other child is rejected; conversely, in a redistributive society my child's achievements will redound to the benefit of those left behind), these are not the main concern in such cases. Is there an injustice because of the gap between those who get and those who do not – an injustice, that is, because of the pure fact of inequality?

From the foregoing, our general answer would have to be "no," as long as the society were redistributive, as it would be, for example, if governed by Rawls's difference principle. But that principle was conceived to govern the allocation of resources regarded as "social," not "natural." In part this is because it is commonly thought that by definition only social advantages are distributable. If society is ever in a position to "distribute," through genetic engineering or genetic pharmacology, characteristics stemming from genes that have been classified as "natural" assets, it is not clear that redistributive principles permit inequalities. Indeed, as we have seen in Chapters 3 and 4, some of the most prominent and well-thought-out theories of distributive justice might be taken to imply that intervention in the natural lottery may sometimes be required.

It is difficult to engage this subject even speculatively, since we have little idea what these personal assets would be like. But those that afford their bearers greater fulfillment and enjoyment without much corresponding gain in productivity or social contribution could not return benefits to those left behind. Unless the resulting inequality would inflict harms on the worst-off – say, by tending toward class divisions, segmentation of society, or a lowering of self-respect – we do not see the necessity of public policy to prevent individuals from seeking these advantages even when not all can do likewise.

Enhancements versus Treatments

Inequality apart, the use of genetic techniques to enhance the human constitution rather than by way of prevention or cure of disease may give rise to some particular problems that are less likely to be posed by therapeutic interventions. Enhancement interventions may produce unanticipated and undesirable side-effects, and the gains obtained may be less tangible and less clearly desirable than relief from disease would be. This is a general reason to be less sanguine about enhancements than about treatments.

We conclude from these considerations that, even were the genetic revolution to progress to the point that reengineering of the human genome would prove possible and effective, no general obligation would exist to attempt to engineer equality. Pursuit by individuals of enhancements that might create unequal genetic endowments would be permissible in a society governed by the principles of justice that we presently recognize as desirable in our own society. The fact that these interventions constitute enhancements rather than treatments has no fundamental significance and ought not be used to support a public policy ban on all enhancements. Differential access to these enhancements ought to be restricted only when they threaten harm or unjust limitations on opportunity to others, as they might in conferring positional advantages on the fortunate or in imposing the great burden of disability or exclusion on the least favored.

FAMILIES

Reproductive freedom and the liberty to construct and conduct family life are potentially both enhanced and threatened by the genetic revolution. Advances in mapping genes have already provided potential parents with more information than has ever been available about the likely traits of their offspring. These screening and testing measures, together with a broadening range of reproductive techniques permitting testing and selection of embryos, even now afford some parents a measure of control over the kind of child they will have. In the future,

much more could be determined by planning and design through engineering techniques.

The authors of this book join in the current legal consensus and the
majority public opinion that support it in favor of a broad sphere of
reproductive freedom and endorse its institutional protection through
appropriate legal rights. At the same time, the technology that permits
reproductive decisions that will enhance the lives and opportunities of
children to come could also be used in ways that would harm these
children and limit their opportunities. Germ-cell genetic engineering
could visit these harms on many generations to come. The responsibility for using these techniques to good effect rests primarily on prospective parents, but we argue for a role for the state in some instances.
We will turn to these limits after a consideration of reproduction
freedom in light of the eugenic past.

Reproductive Freedom and Coercive Eugenics

In Chapter 6 we argued for wide but not unbounded latitude for
parents in determining the circumstances of reproduction and, to a
large extent, the kinds of genetic enhancements they secure in the
child's interest. This freedom is of crucial importance in public policy
regarding reproduction in the wake of the genetic revolution, in part
because reproductive freedom was the freedom specifically targeted for
curtailment by those eugenicists who supported sterilization and other
abridgments of this freedom in pursuit of social advancement.

As Diane Paul (1995) has pointed out, social attitudes toward reproductive freedom are so different today from the early decades of
this century, at least in the United States, that history is virtually
certain not to repeat itself. The state is not likely to begin any new
campaign of sterilization or other intrusion into reproductive freedom
for the sake of society's genes, no matter how much is learned about
what these genes do. Since involuntary sterilization and eugenics are
synonymous for many of those who warn of the danger of a recurrent
eugenics, this great change in the climate of opinion is a consideration
that can, in large measure, set these fears to rest.

Nevertheless, individual reproductive freedom is not fully secure. It
could be threatened not by the state, but by a variety of other agents,
ranging from social pressure to the actions of insurers. None of these
needs to have the force of law to have effect.

Genetic tests will foretell not only many characteristics that a child will have and will develop, but also the costs they will impose on others. As the "eugenic catechism" quoted in Chapter 2 indicates, such moral arithmetic was a constant theme of the old eugenics movement. This kind of thinking probably did help pave the way for the steriliza- tions and worse (Russo and Cove 1995). In our own time, we have experienced public resentment (with eugenic overtones) of the child- bearing proclivities of women on welfare, a subject that lends itself readily to politicians seeking to foment resentment against the poor. In this instance, there has been relatively little emphasis on greater use of abortion or even birth control, perhaps because the source of politi- cal support for curbing welfare benefits largely overlaps the socially conservative population, which tends to favor sexual abstinence, but the implication that reproductive practice should be altered to reduce social cost is open and explicit.

As it becomes clearer which prospective parents might transmit genes that produce conditions resulting in social costs, these individu- als might experience a social environment hostile to their reproductive plans and aspirations. Health insurers and employers could exert pow- erful pressure in an effort to avoid the costs of care for children with severe health care needs. Their influence could take the benign form of offering all manner of diagnostic tests or, more coercively, of threat- ening to withhold or not renew health insurance should the parents have children in the face of a positive test result.

The potential conflict between individual reproductive freedom and societal interests is real, although there is not a sense of crisis at present. There is for now a measure of breathing room. Our society can afford and should tolerate some cost-generating reproductive be- havior. Fortunately for all concerned, such behavior is unlikely to be a major phenomenon in any case. The interests of parents and poten- tial offspring are generally in alignment. Cases of parents wishing evil toward children unconceived are rather rare. And because parents generally benefit from healthy children and want their children to be healthy, the interests of parents and society are also generally aligned. This alignment projects into the future as well. As John Passmore (1974) has argued:[1]

Men do not love their grand-children's grand-children. They cannot love what they do not know. [But] they hope that those grand-children, too, will have grand-children to love. They are concerned, to that degree about their

---

[1] We thank Dr. Darren Schickle for bringing this passage to our attention.

grand-children's grand-children . . . as it were, an anticipation of their love. . . . By this means there is established a chain of love and concern running throughout the remote future.

As Passmore noted, this alignment is imperfect. Not all parents or grandparents mean well; some are negligent or inept. Our arguments support some limits on reproductive freedom. Parents ought not to bring into being children whose very existence involves so much suffering that theirs is a wrongful birth. The state might legitimately insist that prospective parents at risk of bearing these children avail themselves of tests that would predict the risks.

Moreover, potential children, we believe, should be ensured an "open future" that will secure a choice among a wide range of life plans, and any genetic interventions that would greatly restrict this range of choices would be unjust to the child. The state should therefore enjoin physicians from providing these particular services. It will not thereby be guilty of dictating to families which values they should live their lives by, for the point of this restriction is to preserve a choice of values rather than to predetermine the choices a child might eventually wish to make.

Restrictions on Parental Choice

The primary rationale for limiting parents' freedom of choice in genetic decision making in reproduction is protection of the child. As noted in Chapter 6, the notion of harm to the as-yet-unconceived child presents a philosophical mine field. Great care must be taken to avoid paradox, since, in many cases, the particular child "harmed" by mistaken genetic choices would not have come into existence had the "mistakes" not been made.

We have supported the commonsense view that parents act wrongly when they make reproductive decisions that result in their children suffering from handicaps and maladies that might have been avoided by wiser genetic decisions, and that public policies directed to the health and well-being of children have application in this genetic case as well. Since certain decisions made in the course of reproduction might have adverse consequences for other children and adults – including direct harms, disadvantage in positional benefits, and marginalization and exclusion in the (hypothetical) case in which those not provided with enhancements are in effect disabled – we favor also some legal restrictions on what parents may ask of genetic intervention on behalf of their children.

These restrictions, even in sum, are bound to be relatively minor. Stronger intervention on behalf of the public purse, of the children of parents seeking genetic services, or of other children who might be adversely affected might provide tangible benefits for these parties. But because of the basic alignment of interests, these should be regarded as the fair costs of a regime of robust liberty. In the absence of crisis, they must be counted as tolerable costs.

However, such unfortunate choices can be minimized by vigorous adherence to our first policy recommendation – the provision, at public expense if necessary, of greatly expanded clinical genetic services. Prospective parents who are adequately informed are in general less likely to make judgments that fly in the face of reason and needlessly burden their own children. The same holds true for parents who are provided with alternative means of having children, when the more customary methods threaten genetic harms. By bolstering the material conditions for reproductive freedom, the state can thus remove some of the potential pressure to curtail these freedoms.

CITIZENSHIP AND INCLUSION

The poor reputation of the eugenics movement is due in large part to its association with assaults on reproductive freedom. But we argued in Chapter 2, a more pervasive moral failing of eugenics was the zeal with which many of its mainstream adherents expressed opinions and endorsed initiatives that devalued and marginalized large segments of the public.

Perhaps the most important policy objective in guiding and regulating the social uses of the fruits of the genetic revolution will be to ensure that maximum benefit is obtained while avoiding the exclusion and stigmatization of any of our fellow citizens. If our society succeeds in this objective, we will have repudiated and triumphed over the baleful promise of the earlier mainstream eugenics movement; if not, we will have succumbed to the same moral failing. As with reproductive freedom, also a victim of that movement, certain costs must be judged worth incurring to preserve this value of inclusion based on equal respect – even if they seem to buy little that is more tangible.

Advances in genetic knowledge and techniques threaten to divide, marginalize, and exclude for two main reasons. One is the phenomenon of the so-called genetic ghetto, which threatens some of those identified as having defective genes with exclusion from the principal institutions governing social life. The other is the perceived threat to people with disabilities, some of whose advocates find in the promises made on behalf of the new genetics a theme that casts doubt on their very right to exist.

A Ghetto Walled by Data

People facing potential difficulties tend to have interests that are much more uniform in prospect and divergent after the fact (Daniels 1974; Gibbard 1983). When each of us is ignorant of what may befall us but all consider ourselves vulnerable, we have a personal, self-interested stake in banding together for mutual support in the face of a common threat. Once it is made clear which of us is actually threatened and which will emerge unscathed, the latter will perceive themselves as carrying a burden if their fortunes remain pooled. The burgeoning tide of knowledge about a person's genes and the bearing of these genes on health and other states is a case in point. The genetic veil of ignorance is about to be lifted.

It is not just insurance companies who stand to lose if a person with debilitating genes is included in the insurance pool; so, too, do the other insureds, unless they can easily transfer their patronage to an insurer more adept at avoiding these bad risks. Similarly, all persons seeking mates hope that their intended will love and accept them regardless of any problem genes they may later be found to carry; but once it is known who is afflicted and who is not (or who is badly afflicted and who is only slightly afflicted), each party is able to see clearly who is carrying the burden and who is sharing it. Unless genetic information is secured under a regime of strict privacy, a difficult task with any kind of information, the fault lines that divide us may become exposed and unbridgeable.

The genetic ghetto threatens because these bifurcations and divisions build on one another. For the reason stated earlier, it is doubtful that rights of genetic privacy will extend to customers wishing large life insurance policies. This may threaten the well-being of an individual's family (although the insurer would reply that the threat came from the gene rather than from the insurer). But the effect may be much greater when this person is told that a business loan he or she requires cannot be granted unless the applicant has successfully purchased a large insurance policy.

Public policy safeguards to protect against the formation of a genetic ghetto may have to attack the problem indirectly. Strict laws of privacy governing medical records have a role to play, but they cannot solve the problem alone. One reason is that information about genes can be, and usually is, gleaned without the use of DNA probes (e.g., through the taking of detailed family medical histories). It is difficult to devise a rule that bars consideration of more prosaic medical data with an eye for hereditary conditions. Another reason is that, as in the case of large-policy life insurance, it is not clear that each person should be able to gain an advantage by learning about his or her genes and refusing to tell.

In the end, a comprehensive approach to prevent the relegation of segments of the population into a genetic ghetto may require universal health insurance, with vigorous enforcement (if coverage remains in the private insurance market) of regulations that punish covert underwriting. We favor these measures on their own merits. Those who oppose them bear a special responsibility to consider carefully whether alternatives exist that would successfully block the formation of the genetic ghetto, and, if not, whether they agree with our contention that the avoidance of exclusionary tendencies is of overriding concern in the wake of the genetic revolution.

Devaluing the Less Than Perfect

One of the fears engendered by the new genetics is the prospect that an apparently healthy, "normal" person will wake up one day, in the manner of Kafka's metamorphosis, to be exposed as some kind of "defective" – a carrier of genes that will cause or hasten the development of some terrible condition and that would similarly brand and doom all the person's descendants. On that day, for reasons we have discussed, the affected individual faces the unwelcome prospect of being perceived as different, one of "those people," a person whose problems and prospects are at odds with the community rather than part of any shared fate, and one from whom others seek to be distanced in both contractual and personal social relationships.

To a "normal" person with these fears, people with disabilities might say, welcome to our world. People with disabilities have experienced social isolation and discrimination for a long time, and the ghetto that threatens those shown to harbor "bad" genes is the district in which people with disabilities already find themselves.

In one sense, the threat of the genetic ghetto is that, from the social point of view, the person with "bad" genes will suddenly become disabled – not in the sense of being unable to function, for many people with disabilities function well, in part because they have tailored their goals and habits to their abilities. But this person will share the social space inhabited by people with disabilities in the sense that much of his or her life will be affected by the exaggerated importance that others put on this one aspect of life.

Although lame or blind persons may think of themselves first in terms of other identities – men or women, Catholics, parents, Americans, teachers – for many with whom people with disabilities must interact they will be identified first of all as lame or blind. And much of the rest of a social interaction, near or long term, may be premised on this identification. Similarly, individuals shown to have "problem" genes may find themselves socially, professionally, and commercially isolated, rather than treated "as individuals" – that is, in keeping with the very complex set of physical, psychological, and social attributes that make up their personalities, which are trivialized and disregarded when identified simply as a member of a particular group.

Even if the new genetics offers the prospect of company, however, people with disabilities have no cause for cheer. Indeed, those whose status can be traced to inherited characters stand to suffer even further isolation and discrimination. The victims of sterilization in many countries during the heyday of the old eugenics (and of mass murder in Nazi Germany) were for the most part picked out not for their disabilities, but for having genetically transmissible disabilities. The threatened creation of a genetic ghetto might portend further exclusion and discrimination for this population.

As we discussed in Chapter 7, people with disabilities as a group face three further, potentially powerful, less tangible threats from the new genetics. One is that the possibility of screening for the genes associated with some disabilities will create a climate of opinion in which the birth of children with these conditions will routinely be regarded as an error or mistake, either in medical management or in parental judgment, or both.

The second, related fear is that the act of screening for and avoiding these births (whether by choice of gametes, by abortion, or by *in vitro* or *in utero* therapy) constitutes an expression of devaluation or animus, both on a personal and a social level, that will further stigmatize people with disabilities.

The third concern is that unequal access to genetic means for enhancement and health will both worsen the relative position of people with disabilities and increase the numbers of people with disabilities, since the societal norms for "normality" will change, with higher levels of functioning required for participation in social interaction and institutions.

Reducing the Risk of Exclusion

How ought public policy guard people with disabilities against these risks? Skeptics might view these alleged threats as vague and hypothetical – the creation of self-appointed rights advocates and their allies among bioethicists. After all, the chief portent of the new genetics for people with disabilities and for their potential offspring is amelioration. An understanding of the biochemical mechanism that leads from the Huntington's chorea and cystic fibrosis genes to their phenotypic expression is, first and foremost, an opportunity to devise a cure or palliative, extending lives and heading off the first symptoms of serious disease.

Secondarily, these advances in science offer sufferers from these conditions some hope, however distant, of bearing children without worry about bequeathing to them a painful and life threatening condition. How many would-be parents have remained childless for fear of passing on a dreaded family condition? And how many of these people regard the lack of children as a tragedy almost equal to the diseases themselves?

In comparison to the prospect of having biological children who are healthy, and perhaps of beating back the genetic disease for yourself, the rather abstract worries we have described here might understandably draw an impatient response. Every advance in medicine and science creates waves; if the benefits are great and the undesired side-effects diffuse and difficult to measure, should society put up the green light?

We side, in the end, with the skeptics on this issue. Genetics should not be held back out of general fears for the plight of people with disabilities. The gains are too great. More important, in regard to social justice, steps can be taken to counter the potentially damaging effects on people with disabilities.

The concern that the genetic ghetto will further marginalize people with disabilities can best be countered by vigilance against the creation of this ghetto. The ghetto would be bad for hitherto "normal" people, and doubly bad for people with disabilities, which is reason enough to strive to prevent its construction.

We recognize that this necessarily implies that some societal benefits will be forgone. For example, privacy laws help the individual in some ways but interfere with commerce and even with public health. And genetic registries that might be used in construction of ghetto walls are first justified by their real potential for catching criminals, clearing the unjustly accused, and identifying fallen soldiers. In each instance, the case for securing the immediate gain may seem stronger than the case for vigilantly combating the ghettoization of those with "problem" genes. This kind of social contest is familiar, however, from such arenas as First Amendment guarantees of free (if harmful) speech and civil liberties generally.

What of the three less tangible concerns of people with disabilities? It is understandable that individuals who have lived with inherited disabilities and diseases should feel that screening programs carry the implicit message that they should never have been born. The chief form of implementation of the "therapeutic" advantage of genetic screening has been that of avoiding the creation of afflicted children, rather than curing or ameliorating the condition of afflicted children. In this respect, genetics has differed from the other medical sciences. A cancer patient who encounters a medical volume on cancer screening can only wish that the book had been written earlier, so that he or she could have benefited. But the effect of a book on genetic screening would be that fewer people with that trait would even exist.

What should be the response of public policy? To some extent, the choice between screening and therapy is not either/or: The same genetic advances that locate a gene and permit screening also point out the direction for research on mechanisms and treatment. And the two approaches should not have to compete for the same funds if initiatives in either vein are independently worthy of public support.

This aside, however, the choice between screening and therapy is in part a decision to serve prospective parents versus affected individuals and their families. This kind of divergence of interests is not uncommon among advocates for individuals with disabilities or diseases. Grass-roots advocates for mentally retarded people, for example, are sometimes viewed as siding with parents and against the wishes of the retarded themselves in a variety of program choices, such as the maintenance of institutional living facilities. Thus the fact that some people with disabilities will hear a hostile message contained in the very idea of screening programs is not in itself a weighty argument against these programs.

It is not necessary to demonstrate that the programs are in the interest of persons with disabilities or the category of people with disabilities as a whole. If they serve the legitimate interests of others – prospective parents, including disabled prospective parents and the community as a whole – then a better response to the perceived hurt is through the kind of disabilities rights advocacy that is already practiced, aimed at bolstering the self-respect of people with disabilities, raising the consciousness of the public about what it is to have a disability, and exposing the extent to which disabilities are socially constructed.

In sum, the status of people with disabilities as valued and equal members of the community can be enhanced through familiar advocacy and policies; there is no need to take the extreme step of refusing to offer prospective parents the chance to have children unaffected by diseases they consider very burdensome.

The last of the concerns for people with disabilities dealt with in this book is the possibility that the boundary between them and fully functioning members of the community will be redrawn as genetic interventions bestow higher levels of functioning on some people – particularly if the lucky ones are those who can afford these benefits, and who would presumably also be enjoying the other advantages and opportunities that money can buy in our society.

At present, this risk is quite speculative. There are no memory-boosting genetic therapies that could boost the cognitive abilities of some so high that today's average person would seem mentally disabled. But in the long view, this is entirely possible, and we believe that it would be an injustice worth guarding against. Describing this as a matter of unjust inequalities among those who are effective participants in the most important forms of social cooperation fails to appreciate the nature of the problem. As with other issues in the realm of disability rights, what is at stake here is nothing less than the opportunity to be an effective contributor in social cooperation.

Again, we do not believe it is a favor to people with disabilities as a group, let alone to other members of society, to hold back genetic therapies, and even genetic enhancements on this account. People with disabilities have more to gain from these techniques than others do, since their deficits, real and perceived, serve to marginalize and exclude them.

In keeping with our general policy-guiding principles, we urge maximum progress in developing the genetic techniques and safeguards against exclusion. In this case, public policy should try to ensure that the benefits of genetic therapy and (particularly) enhancement are not distributed along class lines or selectively to those who already enjoy greater opportunity. Although we do not rule out the usefulness of these techniques even to the highest-functioning, most-able members of the population, the (perhaps unintended) risk of "disabling" already-vulnerable fellow-citizens by raising the ante on abilities needed to participate fully in society can be avoided by steps adopted toward that end.

Future public policy should put particular emphasis on ameliorating the condition of those who now have disabilities, thereby reducing inequalities in functioning, and should continue and extend present efforts to extend full participation and community membership to people with disabilities, erasing as far as we can the social disadvantages placed, without real necessity, on individuals with physical and cognitive limitations.

In sum, we concur with much of the substance of the disabilities rights critique of contemporary social institutions. We agree, moreover, that in some respects the advances promised by the genetic revolution threaten to exacerbate these problems. It is understandable that an affected person would suspect that, once screening programs come on line, those unaffected would regard people with disabilities as one of society's mistakes, and that affected individuals would perceive the programs as expressing disvalue for those of their kind, and perhaps thereby increasing the stigma associated with their condition. However, we do not share the view that these are inescapable interpretations and results of genetic advances.

We believe that the optimal response is not to retard the development of the techniques but to work to change the social conditions in which these advances might have the unfair results that disabilities advocates understandably fear. The problem lies not in our genes, but in their interpretation on a social level. One way we can resist the genetic determinism that constitutes part of the threat of greater discrimination is to demonstrate that we can, as a society, accommodate genetic advances while integrating, rather than marginalizing, people with disabilities.

STATE, SOCIETY, INDIVIDUAL, AND MARKETS

The Threat of the Eugenic State

In Chapter 2, we argued that eugenics as a social program is not necessarily statist (although history instructs us that the worst excesses of the movement were fueled by the power of the state). Eugenicists can and have argued in favor of the proposition that betterment of the race is a civic duty that each person should take seriously but one that ought not be imposed on the unwilling by an activist regime.

Still, the notion of eugenics as involving an intrusive state intent on overriding very private reproductive decisions persists because mainstream eugenics often indeed did favor such policies. Without the power of the state, the eugenics movement would not cast so dark a shadow. As already noted, historian Diane Paul has argued that eugenics, at least in its old form, is unthinkable at present (at least in the United States) in large part because reproductive freedoms are deeply entrenched in our legal and political culture. If anything, the trend is to grant even wider scope for self-determination, extending to the new reproductive techniques (Robertson 1995).

Eugenics as a Moral Obligation?

With the relatively minor exceptions noted in the preceding chapters (and repeated here), we support a rather expansive understanding of reproductive freedoms. Protecting these freedoms calls for legal authority over decision making to be vested in individuals contemplating reproduction.

However, one can be free to do that which one ought not to do. In making reproductive choices, as in deliberations generally, the interests of our fellow citizens, including members of generations yet unborn, are properly given weight by each person even when at liberty to make self-interested decisions that might conflict with general obligation to augment the well-being of others. With the few exceptions we have noted, the individual should be permitted to disregard the interests of third parties, including those yet unborn, since this privilege comes with the reproductive freedoms. This does not, however, imply that individuals should do so, and it may be appropriate to direct moral criticism at those who do.

It might even be good public policy for the state to encourage this kind of moral thinking. By way of analogy, Ronald Bayer (1989) has argued strongly both for rights of privacy for people at risk for AIDS and also for a strong, binding moral obligation not to behave, under protection of these rights, in a way that would endanger others.

Here our account has a common point of reference with the old eugenic program. The well-being of future generations ought to figure in people's moral calculations, but this kind of consideration is absent from contemporary civic education. It is easy to understand why. The disgrace attached to the eugenic movement and its Nazi manifestation is explanation enough: We risk invoking these terrible precedents if we so much as whisper that we expect the interests of descendants to be considered in reproductive decisions.

Perhaps this fear is justified, but we are unaware of any determinative argument that it is. Should it really be assumed that once we revive the eugenicists' admonition to consider the effects of our reproductive decisions on our descendants, we will also have to deal with much of the rest of the eugenic program?

Just as significant is the fact that the reproductive choice facing prospective parents today is not necessarily whom to marry, or whether to have children (virtually the only decisions that eugenicists could hope to influence), but which of our gametes will produce our own children – a choice exercised, as discussed earlier, in the context of both *in vitro* fertilization and post-conception termination of pregnancy.

The result of both these changes is that less is asked of prospective parents when they are encouraged to consider the interests of society, future and present, in making reproductive decisions. It may still be possible to have biologically related children even while guarding against harmful transmission, and people need not fear reproducing their own kind because their ancestors (or they themselves) may have been "shiftless," "feeble-minded," or "criminal." These considerations weigh against the fear that suggesting that prospective parents take the interests of future generations into account in making reproductive decisions is tantamount to reintroducing the entire regime of sweeping, scientifically unfounded programs of state control of reproduction for the most vulnerable parts of the population.

Presumably the genetics revolution will, in the more hopeful scenario, replace the vague and sweeping prescriptions of the old eugenics movement with more specifically targeted directives to be concerned about specific genes. Nevertheless, an argument can be made that in this new era there will be even more reason to pause before urging recognition of an obligation to protect future generations in reproductive decisions.

The Human Genome Project and related research will yield a huge increase in the number of genetic conditions that can be tested for and hence that we can worry about transmitting to our heirs. Propensities to disease that in the past were vaguely believed to "run in the family" will be known with some certainty to do so, and the route of these genes will be traced to the specific shoots of each branch of the family tree. And numerous genes will be discovered that we may never have contemplated, let alone guessed of their presence in our own genomes. Each of us will stand revealed as a Typhoid Mary many times over, bound to pass along dangerous or undesirable genes in each and every reproductive act. The fact that every other person is in a similar position may be some consolation but does not remove the dilemma.

Even if an obligation not to burden future generations with undesirable genes is taken seriously, it is obvious that reproduction will not grind to a halt. Indeed, morally serious people may welcome the chance to make informed moral choices about gene transmission, choices made blindly before the advent of the new genetics. Nevertheless, the drawbacks of this opportunity are already apparent. The possibility that screening will one day be accomplished by examining fetal cells in maternal circulation, a development just on the horizon at the time of this writing, presents the prospect of easily accomplished mass screening for any number of traits, exposing large numbers of parents not only to choices but also to possible social pressure to make those choices in socially approved ways. Eugenics thus enters through the "back door" rather than by state decree (Duster 1990).

Although reproductive freedom is unlikely to be undermined if a (relatively) few people with particularly dangerous or undesirable genes are alerted to their carrier status and alter reproductive decisions as a result, a comprehensive turn toward calculation of and due consideration for the genetic future in each person's reproductive decision

making might have a destructive result. Moreover, the parents' generation would not be the only losers.

We bequeath to future generations not just our genes but also our
patterns of family life and our sense of what matters when deciding
whether and how to have a child, just as we bequeath our commitment
to reproductive freedom. To the extent that this heritage is valuable, it
may offset some drawbacks denominated in genes, deficits in transmitted genes relative to what a more determinedly eugenic society might
offer its descendants. We describe this dilemma not because we hope
that people will willfully ignore the long-term effects of reproductive
choices but to point out a general reason for caution in advocating
state action to heighten public commitment to this end.

Eugenic Public Policy?

We have affirmed our support of broad and comprehensive freedom
in reproductive choice – protections and liberties that, had they been
in effect during the early decades of this country, would have gone a
long way toward countering and forestalling the worst eugenic abuses.
But this by no means exhausts the subject of a eugenic role for the
state.

The state can respect the right of individuals to reproduce without
any concern for the genetic consequences of their acts for future generations, but it may also seek to encourage responsible choices. It can
provide information that would likely be factored into these decisions,
and it can provide the means (including genetic tests and assisted
reproduction) to make possible reproductive acts that are likely to
result in the transmission of the most desirable genes. The state can
also seek to foster a climate of opinion in which these issues will be
seriously considered and in which public attention is directed to the
distant consequences of present-day reproductive choices.

Although these initiatives carry the risk that "facilitation" would
soon become pressure, there is no inconsistency between advocating
that the genetic welfare of future generations be given due consideration and a genuine commitment to free individual choice, which can
also be enhanced by state measures. Indeed, as we note shortly, the
need to enhance reproductive freedom specifies a continuing need for
state action in genetics.

The state, in our view, does have a legitimate role as guardian of
the genetic well-being of future generations. Though it is not currently

popular or common to say so, we find the *prima facie* case for genetic stewardship as persuasive as that for a state role in conserving nonrenewable resources, in ensuring that savings rather than deficits are our descendants' financial inheritance, in engaging in basic research in science and medicine with very long-term payoffs, and in affirming that our waste products do not have the potential to become toxic in the centuries to come.

If concern for our genetic future were expressed in terms of a determination to rid the land of radioactive wastes that might cause harmful mutations, few would take exception. Such an initiative would be regarded as an environmental safeguard, which it is, but it also involves a eugenic role for the state – and properly so, in our view. Indeed, just as the state is the principal agent acting in the interests of future generations in such fields as land and resource management, so too does a eugenic role for the state, if needed, fit into the standard categories of legitimate areas of concern for government.

Nevertheless, under conditions presently foreseeable – absent, say, a nuclear event whose radiation threatened the entire human genome – we find no need for an activist state eugenic policy. We base this claim on three premises, two of which have already been elaborated: the very general alignment of individual and social interests regarding reproduction and the lesser burden of eugenic practice due to advances in genetic science and technology. The third premise is that, for the foreseeable future at least, humanity is facing neither a "crisis of degeneration" calling for strong state action to avert disaster nor a requirement to make large-scale and significant enhancements in human beings through the use of genetic technologies.

Utopian Eugenics?

Since there will be neither an urgent need for remedial eugenic action nor an opportunity for gainful eugenic intervention by the state in at least the near future, there is no need for a rededication of the state to any comprehensive eugenic program. There is a "soft eugenic" alternative, however. Philip Kitcher (1996), in his advocacy of "Utopian Eugenics," recalls the emphasis of George Bernard Shaw and his circle on public education and encouragement, a much more acceptable eugenics than the genetic search-and-destroy missions carried out in U.S. mental institutions and German racial hygiene clinics.

In our view, however, there is at present little need even for this mild campaign, let alone more stringent measures. Our remarks on the need for a hugely expanded program of genetic services, together with the privacy protection and insurance regulation needed to integrate these services into the mainstream of medical practice, point toward policies that would have much the same effect without a hint of coercion. Education about genetics (rather than eugenics) both in the schools and in the news media can alert the public to the possibility of heading off avoidable genetic harms.

There might be further avoidance of tragedy (and, of course, expense) were the state to undertake eugenic education on a broader scale, but the residual burden may be the price society should expect to pay to avoid any return to the sorry historical record of the eugenics movement. It will be difficult, in the best of circumstances, to avoid slipping from a utopian vision of genetically healthy children to a much less savory attitude that holds that some people are much more valuable than others.

Contrary to Galton, we see neither the need nor the benefit of enshrining eugenics, conceived here narrowly as concern for the genetic constitution of future generations, as a public religion or anything close to it. Again, Galton's outlandish proposal stemmed from the fact that individuals would, in his view, have to be furnished with eugenic motivation adequate to overcome one of the strongest of human desires – the wish to bear genetically related offspring. Since this is neither necessary nor desirable at present, it is unnecessary to create a "Eugenics Church," even if it is not the state's established religion. Our argument applies with even greater force against any thought of state action that would violate hard-won reproductive freedom, as would sterilization or forced abortion, on the altar of eugenics.

These conclusions are the result of a weighing of benefits against short-term burdens and long-term concerns. As such, they might not yield a judgment that would apply equally well to other societies and to special contexts. The Orthodox Jewish communities that use the genetic services of Dor Yeshorim, described at the outset of this chapter, are well aware of the historical ironies involved when a Jewish group seeks to prevent the conception of certain individuals because of the genes they might have. Concerns over reviving the ideology that once threatened these communities with extinction, however, have been outweighed, in the judgment of those concerned, by the high concentration of the genes in question. Moreover, the manner and extent of intervention involved is tolerable to a community that maintains such traditions as arranged marriages (Rosner 1997).

China's law on maternal and child health care, also discussed earlier, has been defended as necessary in light of China's stringent curbs on population growth, which permit most Chinese families only one child. This limitation, defenders of the law have claimed, turns the attention of parents and the nation to "quality" as well as to quantity. While the details of China's law and the circumstances of its actual implementation are unclear as of this writing (Qiu 1998; Dikotter 1998), our impression is that even the special circumstances of China do not necessitate or justify the coercive requirements of the most controversial provisions of this law. Again, we view the occasional parental choice that might result in a net burden on society to be a price worth paying both for reproductive freedom and for maintaining and affirming the principle that each life is valuable.

Markets and Individual Liberty

Although we have endorsed the idea that concern for the genetic well-being of future generations is a proper function of the state, we have endorsed a policy, at least for the near term, of relative inaction. Our conclusions thus might seem to tally, in policy terms, with those who would reject any state role in this domain on more fundamental grounds, as an illegitimate extension of state authority and use of common resources.

On the contrary, we believe that the needed counterweight to the market is the state, acting both to regulate and, through taxation, to provide services. Together, these considerations indicate a significant role for the state in genetic policy, and we believe that a just society will need this kind of government intervention.

We have noted Robert Wachbroit's argument that the state has switched sides in the eugenics debate: Once the spearhead of "racial improvement," governments in Europe and North America now sponsor studies of ethical problems created by progress in genetics, and enact laws seeking to prevent discrimination against those with disfavored genes. The current risk of the grosser forms of exclusion of large numbers of people may be low. Evidence of exclusion from health insurance and employment is anecdotal (Billings 1992). Nevertheless, the potential for exclusion is great. As the cost of genetic tests falls and their accuracy increases, the temptation to use them to identify high-risk individuals will become stronger.

It is no secret that many of the virtues of markets, from the point of view of some participants, are simultaneously vices from the point of view of social justice. We have spoken of the fact that predictive information on predispositions to disease segments a society that had previously been united in a shared vulnerability by *ex ante* uncertainties. Markets permit the lucky, less vulnerable participants to detach their fortunes from those of their unlucky fellow citizens – a boon for those who can buy insurance at lower rates or who obtain jobs denied to those marked as genetically compromised, but also possibly (and, we believe, unjustly) disastrous for those adversely affected.

This fracturing of the common good will be exacerbated by the fact that genetic predispositions to disease are sometimes predictive of events long in the future, creating in effect a permanent divide between the unlucky individual and the rest of society, to the extent that markets permit people to detach their fortunes from those identified as genetic risks. When the goods secured by markets in genes are positional, as would arguably be the case with increased height for children, advantages won by some are by dint of logic disadvantages imposed on others.

State action to regulate markets as they distribute the fruits of the genetic revolution is necessary also for reasons familiar from other medical and scientific fields. Consumer protection of the sort provided in the United States by the Food and Drug Administration is needed for such services as genetic testing and screening on behalf of individual patients. Improperly performed, these tests can be as destructive as a dangerous drug or medical device. False positives for breast cancer genes may prompt unnecessary mastectomies in young women; false negatives for predispositions to serious disease might provide unwarranted peace of mind to individuals who, properly alerted to their condition, could take steps to remain healthy.

The apolipoprotein-E gene test, which can alert some subgroups of the population to a range of much higher than average probability of developing Alzheimer's dementia, presents a different set of considerations. Its results, for some individuals, may be less difficult to interpret, but nothing whatever can be done to head off dementia. Suicide attempts have been occasioned by positive test results. The point is not to ban these tests, but to ensure that their use is not simply governed by supply and demand.

The medical profession in the past exercised paternalistic control and protection of patients, for better and for worse, without any explicit mandate from the state. It might not play the same role in genetics, in part because of the direct financial participation by researcher-clinicians in genetic technology firms and because of the relatively poor understanding of genetics of many primary care physicians today. At a minimum, the state can encourage the medical profession to reflect on its appropriate role in protecting patients from unwise and hasty use of genetic tests and other genetic technologies by fostering the development of professional task forces on these ethical and clinical issues and the production of practice guidelines.

Commercial Genetics

Genetics and markets are linked not only on the demand side, through consumers, but on the production and supply side as well. Walter Gilbert, the Nobel laureate molecular biologist, has stated that not one prominent scientist in his field lacks financial ties to biotechnology companies (Gilbert 1992). This intermingling of basic science and venture capital is particularly problematic in a field that produces products that affect not only current lives but, potentially, generations unborn.

The introduction of constitutional changes in the genome by a commercial, competitive process that divides the population by risk category and that is immune from collective decision making and even public review is morally troubling (Dutton 1988). The concentration of authority in genetics in the hands of investors and executives in biotechnology companies gives a small number of people the ability to decide the direction of innovation and the conditions under which genetic services will be offered. These companies of necessity have a short-term orientation, which may slight valuable basic research, and profitability may hinge on successfully inducing demand (Dutton 1988; Culver 1995). Given the public's lack of understanding of genetics and genetic causation, and the seriousness of diseases linked to defective genes, the road to profit can lie through stimulating public fears.

Finally, state intervention in the market for genetic services is justified in some cases out of concern for future generations. We have mentioned the few restrictions we believe should be placed on prospective parents in making reproductive decisions, primarily those needed to secure their children an "open future." To the extent that this entails regulating and restricting markets for professional services, we believe this to be a proper state function.

Although we have endorsed a policy of benign neglect in pursuit of eugenic goals, both on the grounds that individual choices will tend to promote these ends anyway and that the tradition of individual liberty is itself a valuable legacy for future generations, unforeseen changes in genetic technology could alter this judgment. Discoveries of methods for delivering great benefits to future generations, particularly in prevention of disease but also conceivably in enhancement of skills and capacities useful in pursuing a broad range of plans of life, might create a *prima facie* case for government intervention, particularly if the intrusion were small and a laissez-faire approach could not be made to work.

We have presented a somewhat dialectical argument on the role of the state in genetic policy. Although our support is hedged in several ways, we do not reject the thesis that stewardship of the gene pool in the interests of future generations is an appropriate role for the state. And we have argued that recognition of this role is not incompatible with a proper respect for reproductive freedom in particular and for liberty generally.

At the same time, the terrible actions of governments in this century in the name of eugenics are warning enough to attach the highest importance to individual liberties. With few exceptions, individuals should make their own choices regarding reproduction and treatment, and there should be no retreat at all from the strong body of law and policy that presently protects these liberties in the United States and comparable countries. We are fortunate in that the general alignment of interests between parent and child also aligns the reproductive decision maker toward ends that are eugenic in the narrow sense of favoring the propagation of genes conducive to human well-being in future generations.

It is crucial to emphasize, however, that our support of individual liberty over state compulsion of the sort encouraged by the public health model does not translate directly into a brief for unregulated markets or an endorsement of the unalloyed personal choice model for genetic intervention. "Back-door eugenics" threatens individual liberties and well-being in a manner reminiscent of state eugenics programs, even if this outcome is the unintended effect of private decisions made on grounds of self-interest. The state must intervene as needed to protect the vulnerable from stigmatization and exclusion, as social justice requires, even though these interventions necessarily abridge the benefits that markets can provide to many.

Moreover, individual choice in some cases requires state intervention, since effective choices cannot be made without state subsidies and regulations ensuring access to services. Prospective parents need information and counseling, and may need clinical services to act appropriately on this intervention, and a policy oriented toward the individual as decision maker cannot ignore the need for state aid as well as state neutrality. And in light of the far-reaching effects that a market for genetic services can have, the state ought to act in its role as steward of resources and protector of future generations to ensure that genetic interventions are not based only on the prospect of short-term profit accruing to particular firms.

Liberal Neutrality and Democratic Decision Making

Thus far we have seen how the fruits of our analysis provide moral guideposts on the journey toward ethically sound public policy for a society with significant powers of genetic intervention. We have noted how reproductive freedom, the requirements of equal opportunity, the most basic obligations of inclusion, the child's right to an open future, and the obligation to prevent harm impose both negative and affirmative duties on the state and thereby shape the character of ethical public policy.

Our focus has been on the just society, not the good society. Yet in a pluralistic society such as ours, where no one conception of the good can be taken for granted, the public policy debate is not confined to rival conceptions of justice, nor is it limited to the prevention of harm. It is also the arena with competing conceptions of the good society.

Even if the demands of justice are fully met and both individuals and society have met their obligations to prevent harm, there would still be room for further public policy choices that would affect the character of society. The extent of this residual domain of public policy choice concerning the good society will depend on how robust the requirements of justice and the obligation to prevent harm are assumed to be. It will also depend on whether or in what sense the state ought to maintain a posture of neutrality with respect to competing conceptions of the good.

A familiar slogan of liberalism asserts that the state must observe a principle of neutrality. There is considerable controversy among liberal theorists, however, about the appropriate notion of neutrality (Kymlicka 1989). Perhaps the most plausible interpretation is what is called "neutrality of justification": The power of the state must not be used to pursue policies whose justifications depend on the assumption that certain substantive conceptions of the good are superior to others.

This conception of state neutrality appears to allow considerable space for public policy directed toward furthering a particular conception of the good society through the use of genetic technology or otherwise. If, as a result of fair democratic processes, legislation designed to pursue a certain ideal of the good society emerges, there should be no assumption that this ideal has been authoritatively pronounced to be superior, and hence there is no reason to conclude that the requirement of neutrality in justification has been violated. All that follows is that this ideal commands – for the present – the allegiance of the majority of voters.

It is, therefore, simply a mistake to assume that in carrying out democratically derived policies, the government or society is taking a stand one way or another on the justifications that the proponents of those policies advance to gain majority support for them. In that sense, the only public justification for democratic policy decisions is that they have been made democratically; hence the question of neutrality of justification simply does not arise.

The same point can be put in this way: Once the requirements of justice have been met, the outcomes of democratic processes are to be understood simply as expressions of preferences. Thus the justification for a public policy designed to further a certain conception of human improvement – assuming it operates within the bounds of justice – is not that the conception of the good it uses has been pronounced to be superior by the state, but rather that it is what the majority has chosen.

In principle, there is nothing more (or less) problematic about a public policy directed toward implementing a certain conception of human improvement through genetic means than there is about a policy of enriching the cultural opportunities of citizens or of building beautiful parks. In both cases, proponents and opponents of the policy may mistakenly assume that what they happen to value is objectively valuable, but this neither disqualifies them from attempting to gain democratic support for their projects nor bars the state from implementing their projects if they succeed.

The Permissibility of Rights-Respecting Genetic Perfectionist Policies

Through its democratic processes, a liberal society could decide to devote resources to the continual enhancement of desirable human characteristics – to embark on a process of genetic perfectionism – so long as in doing so it did not compromise its commitment to justice and the prevention of serious harm. Such a policy need not infringe on individuals' reproductive freedom, for example, if it only encourages rather than coerces or unduly pressures prospective parents to use enhancement technologies.

In other words, a just society of substantial powers of genetic intervention might have a public policy of eugenics in the broadest sense of that term – an effort to apply genetic science to the improvement of human beings. Alternatively, individuals and groups may, without transgressing liberal principles, work through the democratic process to try to block the efforts of others to further their conception of the good, either because they endorse a rival conception of the good or because they think the enterprise of genetic perfectionism is unwise or wrong.

Earlier we argued that it is not plausible for public policy to draw a bright line that allows individuals to use genetic technology for treatments but prohibits them from choosing to undertake enhancements. We have now reached a parallel conclusion for collective choice: There is no basis for a blanket prohibition of any public policy initiative designed to promote the use of genetic technology for improvement rather than just for the prevention of disease or disability.

The term "eugenics" may, if some get their way, be expunged from public policy discourse, but it is unlikely that we can avoid further debate about the wisdom or folly of collective efforts to use a knowledge of genes to improve humankind in the decades to come. We thus end this exploration of the ethics of genetic intervention where we began it – convinced that society can best prepare itself for the future not by reflexively dismissing the idea of improvement through genetic means as an unfortunate mistake of the past, but by reflectively exploring it with the aid of our best ethical thinking.

THE MEANING OF GENETIC CAUSATION

Elliott Sober

Genes do two things. They provide a mechanism of inheritance, and they influence how organisms develop. When genes do the former, they effect a connection between generations – parents pass genes along to their children. When genes do the latter, they participate in processes that occur within a generation; they affect how a fertilized egg – a single cell – divides and differentiates, and eventually becomes an adult, who has numerous traits that were not present at conception.

In saying that genes provide a mechanism of inheritance, the point of the indefinite article is to highlight the fact that there are nongenetic pathways whereby parents influence the traits of their children. A child who hears English spoken while growing up will come to speak English, but this is not because English-speaking parents transmit a gene for speaking English to their offspring. Imitation and learning can lead children to resemble their parents. Cultural context can engender additional similarities that are not genetically mediated; when children inherit money from their parents, this is neither genetic transmission nor learning.

When we turn to the second role that genes play, the indefinite article is again appropriate. Genes are one cause of the traits that organisms develop, but there are others. These nongenetic causes are lumped together under the heading of "environment." Genes contribute to an individual's being tall, but so does the amount of nutrition consumed when young. In discussing how development proceeds, it is important not to equate "genetic" influences with "biological" influences. How many calories you eat is a biological influence on your height, but this is an environmental, not a genetic, factor. To say that biology is relevant to a trait is not the same as saying that genetics is relevant. There is more to biology than genetics!

This point is easy enough to grasp in connection with an example like height, but it seems to get cloudy for many people when they think about psychological phenotypes. For example, in one controversial study, Simon LeVay (1993) performed autopsies on the hypothalmuses of a number of homosexual and heterosexual men, and claimed to find that a certain region – the INAH-3 nucleus – was smaller in the former group than in the latter. LeVay's claims have been disputed for many reasons; for example, the gay men examined had all died of AIDS, so the question arises as to whether the size of their nuclei was affected by the disease or by the treatments the individuals received. However, the point I want to make about this research concerns the fact that many people described LeVay's work as showing that there is a genetic basis of homosexuality. No such conclusion follows, even if LeVay is right that the two groups exhibit this neurological differ-ence. A difference in phenotype may be due to a genetic difference, an environmental difference, or both; the point does not change when one focuses on the phenotype of brain structure, or on a psychological phenotype like sexual orientation.

The two roles played by genes – in inheritance and in development – are illustrated in Figure A.1. Parents transmit genes to offspring during reproduction (R); genotypes influence phenotypes during development (D); and parental phenotypes influence offspring phenotypes when children learn (L) from their parents. The figure also depicts the fact that genes are not the only players in the processes in which they participate. Parent/offspring resemblance may be due to shared genes, to the fact that parents teach their children, or to the fact that both develop in the same environment. And the traits that an organism develops are a joint product of the genes the organism possesses and the environment in which the organism lives.

Of the two roles that genes play, one is much better understood than the other. The rules of genetic transmission are pretty clear. Genes reside in chromosomes, which are found in the nuclei of cells. Human parents have 46 chromosomes in each cell of their bodies; these chromosomes come in pairs, so there are 23 pairs. When parents produce sperm and eggs, each sperm and each egg receives one chro-mosome from each pair; each possesses 23 singleton chromosomes. When sex cells come together to form a fertilized egg, the genetic complement of 23 pairs is created anew. There is a great deal more to the physical processes involved in the formation of sex cells and in the way that sex cells come together to form a new individual, and some

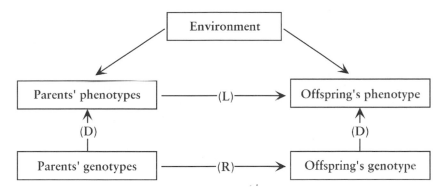

Figure A.1 The roles played by genes in inheritance and in development.

of these details are the focus of continuing research. Yet, in outline, the way genes behave in the process of reproduction is a known quantity.

Matters are very different when we ask how genes participate in the process of development. The initial stages of this process are well understood. Genes are pieces of DNA. Two pieces of DNA are physically different when they contain different sequences of nucleotides. Development begins with different pieces of DNA constructing different pieces of messenger RNA, which then are used to construct amino acids, the building blocks of proteins. These proteins then help construct still larger and more complex structures. A zygote has one cell. Genes cause the cell to divide and the daughter cells to specialize, so that the end product is an organism with many specialized cells – brain, liver, heart, etc. – that form specialized organ systems. In general, the more downstream developmental processes are, the less they are understood: a great deal is known about how genes produce proteins, but we still are vastly ignorant about how genes construct working livers and brains.

THREE MODES OF INTERVENTION

In spite of the fact that development remains a mystery in many respects, the current molecular revolution in biology is vastly expanding our understanding of how genes contribute to developmental outcomes. Scientists already are able to intervene in human lives in various ways, and the precision and pervasiveness of these interventions are bound to increase as we learn more. We can use Figure A.1 to identify three types of intervention that knowledge of genetics makes possible. To see how an individual's phenotype might be modified, consider the arrows that point, directly or indirectly, to that item in the figure. Two pathways of intervention were in use before the molecular revolution of the 1980s, although new knowledge will expand their domains of application. A third is still in its embryonic stage.

First, understanding which genes contribute to which traits allows people to control which genes are passed along from parents to offspring. This was the dream of the old eugenics movement. It lives on in the modern guise of genetic counseling. For example, potential parents can be tested for whether they carry a single copy of the Tay-Sachs gene; if each of them does, there is a one in four chance that their child will have two copies and so will have the disease. Parents, thus informed, may decide not to have children or to take the chance and abort the fetus if it turns out to have two copies. This intervention does not change the phenotype that a given individual comes to possess; it merely affects which individuals are conceived and allowed to be born. The use of this screening technique has significantly reduced the frequency of Tay Sachs disease – not by curing it, but by preventing individuals who would have had it from coming into existence.

Much of what is known about how to detect the presence of a gene and to predict its phenotypic effects predates the molecular revolution. Notice that it is not essential to understand the developmental details to put this intervention into practice. All that is needed is a test for whether parents have one copy of a gene that produces the target phenotypic condition when the gene is found in double dose. Powerful molecular techniques will greatly enhance this domain of knowledge. More traits in offspring, both good and bad, will be predictable (in that probabilities will be assigned to their occurrence) from genetic tests performed on parents.

The second pathway of intervention involves manipulating the environment. As we learn more about what genes do, we also learn more about how environments may be modified to compensate for defective genes. For example, PKU syndrome (phenylketonuria) is a genetic condition in which people are unable to digest phenylalanine. If they receive a normal diet that contains this amino acid, phenylalanine accumulates in their system, resulting in a severe mental retardation. But if they grow up in a different environment – one in which the amino acid is not present in their diet – they develop normally. Cystic fibrosis provides a second example. It is a genetic disease. People with cystic fibrosis often die of lung infections that occur because the mucus in their lungs is a breeding ground for bacteria. It has been found that the enzyme DNAase is able to break down the DNA in this mucus, thus reducing its viscosity. Here molecular biology has provided a new environmental manipulation, one that promises to improve the lives of many CF patients.

The third pathway of intervention is very much in its infancy, but it can be expected to become more and more available, across an ever-widening range of conditions. If individuals lack a gene that is needed to produce a given protein, then gene replacement therapy may allow working genes that do the job to be inserted into their cells. Likewise, if individuals have a gene that produces a destructive protein, new genes may be added that remove the protein or prevent it from being constructed in the first place.

One version of the condition called severe combined immune deficiency (SCID) results when two copies of a recessive mutation are present. The result is that a protein needed by the immune system is not produced. An experimental procedure has been tried on a small number of children in which they received DNA that causes the needed protein to be produced. The results have varied, but immune response has consistently improved, sometimes quite dramatically. Another example is a genetic condition that results in drastically elevated levels of LDL cholesterol. A young woman with hypercholesterolemia, who as a result had a history of severe coronary disease, had her LDL levels significantly reduced by a gene replacement therapy that involved modifying the genes in some of her liver cells. These two examples are still experimental procedures, so their general efficacy is at present unknown. It remains to be seen how many other phenotypes may be modified by similar techniques. Still, it seems clear that molecular biology will provide an ever increasing number of such interventions.

Early geneticists had no knowledge of the physical makeup of genes. The rediscovery of Mendel's work around 1900 led scientists to think of genes as hypothetical entities, known only by their effects on the phenotypes of organisms. The pea plants that Mendel studied produce smooth and wrinkled peas in predictable proportions; this allowed the inference that inside of those plants are entities – "factors" – that combine in certain ways and somehow cause phenotypes to appear. It was a major advance when Thomas Hunt Morgan and his school were able to establish in the early part of this century that genes are located in chromosomes. Even so, it remained true that the existence and nature of genes were things that could be gleaned only from the observable phenotypes of organisms.

The way in which genes actually produce phenotypes remained a mystery and science had no independent access to their physical makeup. The great leap forward effected by molecular biology is that the physical nature of genes and their contribution to developmental processes can be studied more directly. Genes are no longer thought of as hypothetical entities; rather, they are "factories." They start and stop work because of identifiable physical signals and they manufacture products, whose physical makeup can be analyzed.

In discussing these three possible types of intervention, which aim to influence the phenotypes that individuals develop, I have chosen diseases as my examples. Indeed, medical applications of this sort are pretty much the exclusive focus of present-day genetic counseling, genetically informed environmental manipulation, and gene replacement therapy. Still, what can be done for abnormal phenotypes may also be possible for normal ones. Just as science may provide techniques for changing a diseased phenotype into a healthy one, it also may be able to change a normal phenotype to one that is "better" than normal.

For example, if some interventions can prevent certain sorts of mental retardation, it is possible in principle that other interventions can change normal intelligence to above average intelligence. Not that it is easy to figure out how this type of intervention might proceed. Perhaps it is a simpler scientific task to identify genes that contribute to diseased phenotypes than it is to figure out how normal genes might be modified to produce "enhanced" phenotypes. And, of course, there may be ethical objections to interventions of this type. Still, the ability to intervene in this way is on the horizon as scientific knowledge expands. Figure A.1 applies just as much to "superior" phenotypes as it does to average or defective ones.

I place the term "superior" in quotation marks to signal the fact that it raises problems. Who is to say which traits are better? The Nazis thought in these terms, but their odious form of "racial biology" has long been exposed as the nonsense it always was. Although racists will be quick to use the term "superior," it is important to see that the issue I am pointing to does not disappear just by disavowing racism. When nonracists say that disease is less desirable than health, they are applying the terminology of better and worse.

If we try to say why it is better to be healthy than diseased, we inevitably are led to say that some unusual phenotypes would be better to have than the average phenotypes found in human populations. Mental retardation is less desirable than normal mental function, in part because retardation drastically contracts the range of worthwhile lives a person might be able to lead. However, this reasoning leads to a further conclusion – that enhanced mental function can be more desirable than average mental function if it expands the range of worthwhile options a person has. Of course, this does not mean that these two comparisons are equally weighty – that avoiding retardation and being average are exactly as important as avoiding being average and being a genius. The point is that if disease is worse than health, then it is hard to resist the conclusion that some rare traits would be better to have than traits that are "normal" in the sense of being average.

My claim is that from the point of view of biology, it makes sense to think of disease, health, and enhanced function as all falling on a single continuum. If intervening in the lives of individuals allows science to move them from disease to health, science may also be able to move individuals from being merely healthy to having enhanced function. The difference between a diseased and a healthy person may be due to their different genes, different environments, or both; by the same token, the difference between a normal healthy person and someone who has enhanced function in some respect (such as better lungs, better eyesight, better memory) may be genetic, environmental, or both.

FOUR KEY QUESTIONS

I now want to analyze more carefully the causal language that is used to describe the impact of genes and environment on an individual's phenotype. Figure A.1 was full of arrows that represent causal influence. What does it mean to say that genes are more important than environment (or vice versa) in the development of some phenotype? I said earlier that PKU and cystic fibrosis are "genetic" diseases, but then I described environmental interventions that prevent their development or ameliorate their symptoms. What does "genetic" mean in this context? I also said that speaking English is not a genetic trait, in that people acquire whatever language they hear while they grow up. But it also is true that individuals without genes do not end up speaking English, because they do not grow up at all; and a chicken exposed to spoken English will not end up speaking English, presumably because of the genes it has. So what does it mean to say that speaking English is environmental, not genetic?

To address these issues, it will be useful to consider four questions about the role that genes play in causing some trait that an individual has:

- Do genes causally contribute to the trait?
- How much do genes, as opposed to environment, contribute to the trait?
- Which genes contribute to the trait?
- How do these genes contribute to the trait?

These questions will have different answers, depending on the trait under discussion; what is true for speaking English is not true for Huntington's disease. The questions are listed in a certain order; typically, to answer a question further down the list, you have to answer earlier ones. In this sense, later questions are harder than earlier ones. My goal here is to clarify what these questions mean; I will not try to provide factual answers to these questions in connection with any particular trait.

All four questions assume a division between genes and phenotype on the one hand and between genes and environment on the other:

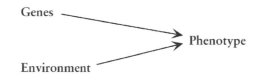

Phenotype and environment are defined in biology as "garbage can categories" – an organism's phenotype is all the traits it has other than its complement of genes. So all your morphological, physiological, behavioral, and psychological traits are part of your phenotype. The fact that someone is 5'8" tall, has brown eyes, high blood pressure, a certain blood type, lives in the Midwest, and likes jazz are all phenotypic traits. Similarly, an organism's environment includes any trait that it has other than the genes inside its body. How many calories you consume is part of your environment; your caloric intake, plus your genes, together influence how tall you grow.

Even things that are inside the organism's own body can count as part of the "environment" as far as the development of a given phenotype is concerned. For example, if an individual is born with some degree of immunity to a certain disease because it received antigens from its mother contained in the extrachromosomal part of the egg, these antigens are counted as part of the organism's environment. The antigens, plus the organism's genes, influence whether and how much immunity the individual will exhibit. Possessing a set of antigens might be considered a part of the environment as far as the development of immunity is concerned, but having those antigens is also a phenotypic trait that the organism possesses. Notice that the antigens are inherited *and* nongenetic. Now let's consider the four questions.

Question 1: Do Genes Causally Contribute to the Trait?

A set of genes can causally contribute to a trait without it's being true that those genes *suffice* for the trait. And it need not be true that those genes are necessary for the trait to be present. This is a general point about what the word "cause" means. Striking a match causally contributes to the match's lighting, but the striking is not by itself sufficient; oxygen has to be present and the match has to be dry. Similarly, you can get the match to light without striking it – for example, by using a magnifying glass to focus light on the head. Here are two illustrative examples:

- The defective gene in PKU syndrome causally contributes to the syndrome. However, a particular environment has to be in place – the presence of phenylalanine in the diet. So the gene is not sufficient for the syndrome.
- There is a defective gene that causes breast cancer. However, this gene is present in only a small percentage of women who contract breast cancer. The gene is not a necessary condition for the cancer.

These examples also show that when a phenotype has a genetic cause, this does not mean that the phenotype cannot be modified by changing the environment. As noted before, PKU syndrome can be avoided by modifying the diet. And it is possible that therapies will be discovered for women who have the gene for breast cancer that prevent the gene from doing its destructive work. Discovering genetic causes can provide insights into the types of environmental manipulation that would be efficacious.

Another point about question 1 is that it has to be understood in

Table A.1

Genes You Might Have	Language Heard as a Child	
	English	Chinese
G1	English	Chinese
G2	English	Chinese
G3	—	—

the right way. An organism will not develop at all if it has no genes. However, this obvious fact does not mean that genes automatically "contribute" to every phenotype we might consider. The reason is that "genetic contribution" means that genetic *differences* make a *difference* in whether you have a particular phenotype. For example, an organism cannot develop to the point where it is able to speak a language if it has no genes. However, this leaves open whether the genes you have make a difference in whether you will speak English rather than Chinese. Apparently, your genes make no difference in this regard, as seen in Table A.1.

The genes G1 and G2 each permit normal development, in which case the language you speak is determined purely by your environment. But suppose that G3 is a genetic configuration that causes a severe retardation that prevents a person from acquiring any language at all. If so, your genes affect whether you will learn a language or not, but they do not affect whether you will learn English or Chinese. Notice that this is entirely consistent with the fact that there are genetic differences between English speakers and speakers of Chinese. However, these differences do not *make* a difference; this is correlation without causation.

Question 2: How Much Do Genes, as Opposed to Environment, Contribute to the Trait?

When two causes both contribute to an effect, how are we to say how much each contributed, or which was more important? Consider an example due to Richard Lewontin (1974). Suppose two bricklayers build a wall. Each brings his own mortar, bricks, and tools to the site; they start at opposite ends, the one building from the right, the other from the left. We could determine which bricklayer contributed more to the resulting wall by counting the number of bricks in the wall that each had placed there. However, suppose that one bricklayer made the bricks and mortar and brought all the necessary equipment to the site, while the other used these items to put up the wall. Now it is impossible to say which bricklayer contributed more or to say how much each contributed in terms of some uniform measure.

The second version of the bricklayer example resembles the problem we face when we try to say whether genes or environment contributed more to a given phenotype. If Sally is 5'8" tall, it will not be true that her genes built 4' of her and her environment built the rest. Rather, her genes and her environment made different kinds of contributions, the net result of which was that she grew to a certain height.

Does this mean that question 2 is meaningless – that it makes no sense to ask whether genes or environment are more important causes of the resulting phenotype? No. It just means that we must pose the question in a different way. Rather than asking about the relative contributions of genes and environment to the phenotype of a single individual, we change the object of the preposition. We ask how genetic differences and environmental differences contribute to the differences in phenotype found in a population.

To see what this means, consider a simple experiment designed to show how genetic variation and environmental variation contribute to variation in height in a population of corn plants. In our experiment, the plants have either genotype G_1 or G_2; their environments provide either one unit of fertilizer (E_1) or two units of fertilizer (E_2). Thus, there are four "treatment cells" that a corn plant might occupy; it might be in E_1G_1, E_1G_2, E_2G_1, or E_2G_2. Suppose we plant four plots of corn, each containing a hundred corn plants, one for each of the four treatment combinations. How will the plants in one treatment cell differ in average height from the plants in others? Here are four possible observational outcomes that might be obtained:

	G_1	G_2			G_1	G_2			G_1	G_2			G_1	G_2
E_1	1	1		E_1	1	2		E_1	1	3		E_1	1	4
E_2	4	4		E_2	3	4		E_2	2	4		E_2	1	4
	(i)				(ii)				(iii)				(iv)	

In outcome (i), the genetic factor makes no difference; whether the plants have genotype G_1 or G_2 does not affect their height; it is the environmental factor – the amount of fertilizer the plants receive – that explains all the observed variation. Outcome (iv) is the mirror image of (i). In (iv), the fertilizer treatment makes no difference; the genetic variation explains all the variation in height. Outcome (iv) illustrates the idea of genetic determinism – the general thesis that an individual's phenotype cannot be modified by changing its environment. Outcome (i), on the other hand, illustrates the idea of radical environmentalism – the view that the only factor that influences an individual's phenotype is its environment. Outcomes (i) and (iv) thus support "monistic" explanations of variation in plant height; each suggests that only one of the factors considered made a difference in the observed outcome.

Outcomes (ii) and (iii), on the other hand, would support "pluralistic" conclusions. Each suggests that genetic and environmental factors both made a difference. However, they disagree about which factor mattered more. In outcome (ii), changing the fertilizer treatment yields two units of change in height, whereas changing from one genotype to the other produces only a single unit of change in height. In this case, the environmental factor makes more of a difference than the genetic factor. By the same reasoning, we can see that outcome (iii) suggests that genetic variation was more important than the environmental factor considered.

Although the four possible outcomes described so far differ in various respects, they have something in common. In each of these data sets, the change effected by moving from G_1 to G_2 does not depend on which environmental condition one considers. Similarly, changing from E_1 to E_2 has the same impact on plant height, regardless of which genotype the plant possesses. Results (i)–(iv) are thus said to be "additive" (or to show no "gene-environment interaction"). This is not the case for the following possible results:

	G_1	G_2		G_1	G_2
E_1	1	7	E_1	1	1
E_2	7	4	E_2	1	4
	(v)			(vi)	

In outcome (v), going from one unit of fertilizer to two increases height for plants with genotype G_1 but reduces height for plants that have genotype G_2. In (vi), changing genotype has an effect on plant height within one fertilizer treatment but not within the other.

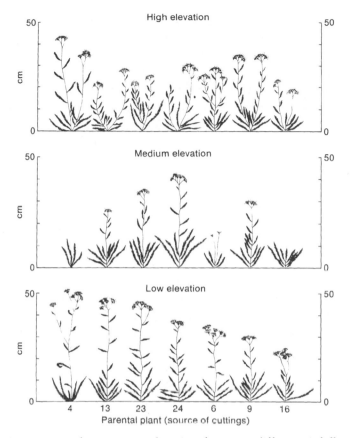

Figure A.2 Norms of reaction to elevation for seven different *Achillea* plants (seven different genotypes). A cutting from each plant was grown at low, medium, and high elevations. (Carnegie Institution of Washington)

Gene-environment interactions of the sort depicted in (v) and (vi) occur frequently in nature. Consider, for example, Figure A.2, taken from an introductory genetics textbook (Griffiths 1993, p. 14). It depicts the result of taking cuttings from each of seven plants in the species *Achillea millefolium* and growing them at high, medium, and low elevations. Notice that different environments have different effects on plant height; moving from medium to high elevation makes type 1 cuttings grow taller but reduces the height of cuttings from type 4; and even though moving from low to medium elevation reduces plant height in both types 2 and 3, it does so by different amounts.

The interaction effect depicted in (vi) shows that it can be overly simplistic to ask whether a phenotype is influenced by the environment. Notice that genotype $G2$ produces a different phenotype when the environment is changed, but genotype $G1$ does not. The same point holds when we ask whether a phenotype is influenced by genetic factors. Organisms reared in environment $E2$ produce different phenotypes depending on what genotype they have; organisms reared in environment $E1$ do not. We can look at the data in (vi) and make the summary statement, "the phenotype depends on both genotype and environment," but a more fine-grained analysis shows that genes make a difference in some contexts but not in others, and that the same is true of the environment considered.

This is not a merely academic fine point. An important discovery in AIDS research is that this disease is able to enter host cells by connecting with a protein found on the surface of CD-4 immune cells. Most human beings produce this protein, and so are vulnerable to the disease. However, it has recently been discovered that a small number of individuals possess two copies of a mutation in the normal gene CKR-5, which causes this protein not to be produced. These individuals are otherwise healthy; they also seem to be immune to the disease. Notice what this implies about whether AIDS is an environmental or a genetic condition. Before this mutation was discovered, it would have been natural to think that the disease is caused purely by an environmental insult – the presence of a virus; the difference between people with the disease and people without it is completely ascribable to the environment. But this recent discovery complicates the picture. For some people, not having AIDS is attributable to their genes, not to their environment. For many others, however, the disease remains an environmentally induced phenotype.

The simple 2-by-2 experiment we have described illustrates the basic idea behind the methodology that statisticians call the analysis of variance (ANOVA). It allows you to compare how much genes and environment contributed to a phenotypic outcome. A conclusion might be reached that "70% of the variation is explained by environmental differences and 30% by genetic differences." ANOVA quantifies the relative contributions that genes and environment make to phenotypic variation. It is important to bear in mind that this type of analysis is highly specific to the range of genotypes and environments considered. Even if changing from $E1$ to $E2$ has only a negligible effect on plant height, it is an open question whether changing to a new environment $E3$ would make a larger difference. Likewise, even if genotypes G_1 and G_2 perform similarly across a given range of environments, it is quite possible that genotype G_3 would behave quite differently in those same environments.

This point is relevant to understanding how the following two findings are quite compatible: a significant proportion of the variation in intelligence (as measured by IQ) found among individuals is attributable to genetic differences (Bouchard et al. 1990); and intelligence has been increasing steadily in 14 countries, including the United States, for several decades (Flynn 1987). When quantitative geneticists use ANOVA techniques, they typically study the range of genes and environments that are available at the time of their study; the results they obtain say nothing about whether the range of genes or environments has changed or will do so in the future, nor do the results predict what will happen should such changes occur. Even if the variation in height now found in a population is explained completely by genetic variation, it remains perfectly possible that the population will have a greater average height several generations later because nutrition has improved. The fact that genes significantly affect phenotypic variation does not mean that environmental interventions will be for naught.

I began my discussion of the 2–by-2 experiments on corn plants by saying that it makes no sense to apportion causal responsibility between genes and environment with respect to a single individual (Sally); this was why I shifted focus to the question of explaining patterns of variation in a population of individuals. However, it might appear that the ANOVA technique just described does allow one to explain the traits of individuals. Consider, for example, the data given in (ii); I will now present this set of data again, this time noting in the margins the average heights of individuals sharing the same environment, the average heights of individuals sharing the same genes, and, in the lower-right hand-corner, the grand mean – the average height of all the individuals in the experiment:

	G_1	G_2	
E_1	1	2	1.5
E_2	3	4	3.5
	2	3	2.5

Consider one of the individuals in the lower-right-hand cell of the 2-by-2 table of data who is 4 units tall. The average height in the whole population is 2.5. The difference between this individual's height and the grand mean $(4 - 2.5 = 1.5)$ can be decomposed into a difference between the average height of individuals with the same genotype as this individual and the grand mean $(3 - 2.5 = 0.5)$ and the difference between the average height of individuals living in the same environment and the grand mean $(3.5 - 2.5 = 1.0)$. Does this show that this individual's being 1.5 units above average in height is explained by her genotype making her 0.5 units above average and her environment making her an additional 1 unit above average? If so, her genes account for one third of her overshooting the average and her environment for two thirds.

I do not disagree. However, this is not the same thing as explaining why the individual is 4 units tall. Notice that if this individual had the same genes and the same environment but had lived in a population of different composition, her deviation from the mean might have been different, as would the breakdown between her genetic deviation and her environmental deviation. Yet the individual would still be 4 units tall; the genetic and environmental processes that determine her height would have been the same. ANOVA is an irreducibly population-level analysis; it can be used to describe how individuals are related to the populations they inhabit, but this is an entirely different matter from explaining why they possess the phenotypes they do.

One other conceptual point needs to be made about the logic of ANOVA studies. This concerns the relation of within-population differences to between-population differences. One of the most controversial subjects in the continuing debate about nature and nurture is the question of whether the observed difference between white and black Americans in IQ has a genetic basis. Murray and Hernnstein's *The Bell Curve* (1994) is the most recent attempt to muster evidence for the conclusion that it has; theirs was not the first effort, nor should we expect it to be the last. The point I want to make here is that their conclusion about group-level differences would not follow even if variation within the two groups had a significant genetic component.

Consider the following example, described by Lewontin (1970). Suppose a heterogeneous collection of corn seeds is planted in a single environment E_1. Since all the plants experience the same environment, all the variation in height must be due to genetic differences. Now suppose that a second experiment is performed in which the same collection of seeds is planted in a quite different environment E_2; once again, all the phenotypic variation in this experiment will be due to genetic differences. However, what should we say about the difference between the average height exhibited in the first experiment and the average height obtained in the second? This difference will be due entirely to the environmental difference between E_1 and E_2, since the two experiments tested the same range of genotypes. The fact that genetic differences explain phenotypic variation *within* two groups does not mean that genetic differences explain phenotypic variation *between* those two groups.

I hope this discussion makes clear what it means to compare the impact of genetic and environmental variation on variation in some phenotype. However, it leaves a related question unanswered. How are we supposed to find out what the contributions of genes and environment are if we cannot run a controlled experiment of the kind just described? Manipulations of the type just described are fine for corn plants, but ethics prevents us from cloning human beings and rearing them in identical environments. So how is it possible to say anything meaningful about the relative contributions of genes and environment to human height, much less to more subtle traits such as intelligence, aggressiveness, sexual orientation, or risk-taking?

A variety of techniques are used in the field of quantitative genetics to answer this question. These techniques involve assembling observations about individuals as they are. One approach is to study genetically identical twins who are reared apart. If two identical twins differ in height, this must be due to the fact that their environments were different, since they have the same genes. Suppose pairs of identical twins were more similar in height than pairs of unrelated individuals are. This would suggest that genes make a difference in how tall an individual grows.

Such methods are subject to various pitfalls. For example, in twin studies, it is important to investigate how much the environment of one twin differs from the environment of the other. Suppose that identical twins who are reared in separate households nonetheless receive the same number of Cheerios, and that this environmental factor is a powerful influence on how tall an individual grows. It will then turn out that twins closely resemble each other in height, but this is not simply because they have the same genes.

Bouchard et al. (1990) make this point in their report on the Minnesota twin studies, which involved comparing a set of identical twins who were reared together with about 100 pairs of identical twins who were reared apart. These individuals were subjected to about a week of psychological and physiological tests. Remarkably, the two groups each showed significant degrees of similarity; even more remarkably, they did not differ much in terms of how similar they were. For example, twins reared together are rather similar in how they scored on tests of "religiosity" (they exhibited a correlation of 0.49); twins reared apart also were quite similar (they exhibited a correlation of 0.51). Bouchard et al. (p. 227) point out that the twins reared apart in their study almost never grew up in extreme poverty and were almost never raised by illiterate parents. This means that these individuals had environments that were at least somewhat similar, and this fact has to be taken into account in interpreting the results. Some of the similarity found in identical twins (whether reared together or reared apart) will be nongenetic.

Other caveats apply to empirical efforts to estimate the genetic and environmental contributions to patterns of variation in some phenotype of interest. It is true that a number of studies in the past were sloppy. In addition, it would be naive to think that quantitative geneticists now do their studies without ever making mistakes. However, the fact remains that scientists learn from the errors of their predecessors; scrupulous studies are now being executed and they will become more numerous with the passage of time. The mistakes of the past should not lead us to dismiss twin studies and related inquiries *a priori*.

Question 3: Which Genes Contribute to the Trait?

Twin studies and similar methodologies in quantitative genetics can tell you that genes make a difference in the chances of having some trait; however, they fail to tell you which genes matter or how they have this effect. You may find that identical twins resemble each other in height far more than unrelated individuals do, but which genes on which chromosomes influence height and how do they do so? An answer to question 2 can leave you entirely in the dark concerning questions 3 and 4. This is both the strength and the limitation of quantitative genetics studies. They can go forward in total ignorance of developmental details; this is why the field of quantitative genetics developed before the molecular revolution of the 1980s and, indeed, before Watson and Crick discovered the chemical structure of DNA in the 1950s. Quantitative genetics is genetics without much attention to genes.

Mother   Father

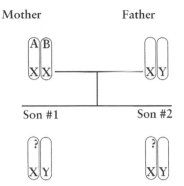

Son #1   Son #2

Figure A.3 Each brother inherited his one X chromosome from his mother. Since their mother has two X chromosomes, the probability is 1/4 that the brothers both inherited the one maternal X chromosome in which gene A is found. The probability that both brothers inherited their mother's single copy of gene B is also 1/4.

I now want to describe a study that aimed at providing insights into question 3. It was quite controversial because the scientists were not studying something innocuous like height in corn plants. They studied sexual orientation in human beings. This is the study by Dean Hamer and his associates (1993), in which they claim to have found a region of the X chromosome in males that causally contributes to homosexuality. Although a recent follow-up study failed to replicate Hamer's results, the point of interest here is to understand the logic of Hamer's investigation.

Recall an elementary fact about human genetics depicted in Figure A.3. Males are XY and females are XX. This means that males inherit their X chromosomes from their mothers. Suppose the mother is heterozygous at some location on her pair of XX chromosomes. This means that she has one copy of gene A next to a copy of gene B at that location. Now consider a group of such heterozygote mothers. Imagine that each has two sons who are not identical twins. What is the probability that they will both have A or both have B on their one and only X chromosome? The probability that son #1 has A is 1/2 and the probability that son #2 has A is also 1/2, so the probability that both have A is 1/4; similarly, the probability that son #1 has B is 1/2, which is also the probability that son #2 has B, so the probability that both have B is 1/4. This means that the probability of them matching (i.e., that both have A or that both have B) is $1/4 + 1/4 = 1/2$.

Suppose you wanted to know whether the genes at this locus on the

X chromosome, when present in males, affect their probability of having blue eyes. To find out, you might assemble 40 pairs of brothers, each of whom has blue eyes, and each of whom has a mother who is an AB heterozygote at some locus on her XX chromosomes. If these genes have no bearing on eye color, you'd expect that 1/4 of the brother pairs will match for A, 1/4 will match for B, and 1/2 will not match at all. In other words, if these genes do not affect eye color, you'd expect blue-eyed brothers to match at this locus about half the time. On the other hand, if you found that a very high proportion of the brother pairs match, this would be evidence that the locus in question influences eye color.

Hamer assembled 40 pairs of brothers whose score on a variety of self-report sexual orientation scales placed them at the homosexuality end of the spectrum, and whose mothers were heterozygotes for a marker placed at a certain region of their two X chromosomes. Hamer found that 33/40 of the brother pairs matched for the markers in question. This is evidence for the claim that genes in this region influence sexual orientation.

Suppose that these 33 brother pairs all have gene A. It would not follow that this gene suffices for homosexuality; there may be individuals, who are not in the study, who have the gene but are not homosexual. Nor would it follow that the gene is necessary for that phenotype to exist; it may be that this gene is present in only a small percentage of male homosexuals. An additional possibility is worth noting; it also is possible, given Hamer's finding, that the effect of gene A on sexual orientation is environmentally mediated. Let us consider a fanciful example to see why. Suppose that this gene makes boys have a freckle on their forehead and that this causes their parents to treat them in a certain way. Because of the way their parents treat them, boys with gene A tend to become gay. This may lead you to think that homosexuality in this scenario is environmental, not genetic. However, geneticists understand the contrast between genes and environment in such a way that they draw the opposite conclusion. When genes cause individuals to be reared in special environments, the resulting phenotype is said to be due to genes, not to environment.

Christopher Jencks et al. (1972) made this point in their book *Inequality* when they discussed the effects of racism on IQ. They used the following hypothetical example. Suppose that red hair is caused by genes and that the society we live in leads people to abuse red-headed children. If abuse lowers IQ, then redheads who live with their biolog-

Figure A.4 Two hypothetical causal scenarios by which genes for red hair might affect IQ.

ical parents and redheads who live with adoptive parents will suffer the same degree of abuse. The change in environment will not produce a change in the phenotype, because everyone in the society abuses redheads. The conclusion will then be drawn that IQ is genetic; the gene for having red hair is also a gene for lower IQ.

The analysis would be different if red-headed children were abused by their biological parents, but not by others. Then an adoption study would show that a difference in environment makes a difference in the IQ of red-headed children. Consider the two causal pathways shown in Figure A.4. In (a), the lower IQ of red-headed children is said to have a genetic cause. In (b), the lower IQ of red-headed children is said to be caused by their environment, not by their genes. The standard methodology in quantitative genetics says that the environment makes no difference in (a), but does make a difference in (b).

The possibility illustrated by this example is not merely hypothetical. As noted before, the Minnesota twin study found that identical twins reared apart are remarkably similar on a variety of measures. Bouchard et al. (1990, p. 227) speculate that this may be because "their identical genomes make it probable that their effective environments are similar. . . . Infants with different temperaments elicit differing parenting responses . . . children and adolescents seek out environments that they find congenial." The suggestion is that genes make an important difference in the phenotypes measured because different genes lead individuals to experience different environments. If so, the formula should not be "nature versus nurture," but "nature via nurture" (Bouchard et al. 1990, p. 228).

Question 4: How Do These Genes Contribute to the Trait?

Hamer's study, even if it were correct in every detail, throws no light on the developmental pathway from a gene to a trait. Question 3 has been answered, but question 4 has not. In a sense, question 4 is the hardest of the four. You have to do all the work involved in answering questions 1–3, and then you have to tackle a difficult developmental question besides. The reason that question 4 is difficult is that gene/ environment pairs do not directly produce phenotypes like height or sexual orientation or intelligence. Rather, genes produce gene products, which are chemicals. How these gene products interact with other gene products and with the environment is typically quite complicated. Somewhere downstream, the observable phenotype results.

There are examples of phenotypes in which the pathway from gene to phenotype is fairly well understood. Sickle-cell disease is caused by two copies of a recessive gene. People with two copies produce abnormal hemoglobin, which is the molecule inside red blood cells that carries oxygen from the lungs to the rest of the body. When these individuals are oxygen-deprived, for example, as a result of working hard, their red blood cells become sickle-shaped, thus blocking blood flow in capillaries. It is worth noting here that this fairly detailed grasp of developmental details has not yet resulted in the discovery of a viable gene replacement therapy. Knowledge and power do not always move exactly in tandem; some diseases are less well understood than sickle-cell anemia, but more effective therapies have been obtained nonetheless.

Examples like sickle-cell disease, in which science has discovered how genes contribute to the production of phenotypes, should not obscure the fact that when we shift to phenotypes such as sexual orientation, intelligence, risk-taking, and so on, question 4 represents a region of vast ignorance. As we descend from 1 and 2 to 3 and then to 4, the amount of knowledge we have at each stage vastly shrinks. There are many, many studies that purport to answer questions 1 and 2. As we have already seen, the methods of quantitative genetics permit these questions to be addressed even when science knows nothing about which genes might influence the phenotype under study and how they do so. However, when we look at questions 3 and 4, the range of phenotypes studied by science radically contracts. Typically, progress has been made for phenotypes, like sickle-cell anemia, that are diseases and are influenced by a small number of genes. It is a task for future science to try to achieve a more complete grasp of the developmental pathways that lead to nondiseased phenotypes.

Should we expect genes to be important in the explanation of normal function, just as they are relevant to the explanation of some, but not all, diseases? Let us be clear about what this question means. Genes help explain the difference between sickle-cell anemia and normal hemoglobin function. Is the same true of the difference between two varieties of normal hemoglobin function? Is it true for differences in intelligence, shyness, taste in music, etc., that all are normal? "Normal" is a vague term; it encompasses an array of phenotypes that are said to "fall in the normal range." Will genes be relevant to explaining differences within the normal range, just as they are often relevant to explaining differences between normal and abnormal?

It is a striking fact about work in quantitative genetics that genes are said to make at least some difference in virtually all phenotypes that have been studied (Bailey 1996). Even when traits like religiosity and political affiliation are studied by quantitative geneticists, they end up concluding that genetic differences among individuals matter, at least somewhat (Bouchard et al. 1990). Their question concerns how much genes matter, as compared to the environment. Not all these studies have been well executed, but quantitative geneticists keep getting better and better at avoiding mistakes. Even after all fallacies are removed and dubious interpretations are seen for what they are, we may have to live with the fact that the genetic contribution to any phenotype of interest is never precisely zero. This does not mean, of course, that genes make *all* the difference, or that they are *more important* than environment. Again, it is crucial to remember that genetic causality does not rule out environmental causality. Both influences exist. However, if genes contribute to variation in some phenotype of interest, more detailed questions remain to be addressed concerning which genes affect the phenotype in question, and how they do so; these are matters that future science will endeavor to answer.

CONCLUSION

It is often convenient to save breath or ink by neglecting to make explicit the relational character of certain claims. If I say that someone is a good musician, you will know roughly what I mean. But if you press for precision, I will have to say what benchmark of comparison I am using. The person in question may be good compared with the average player, mediocre compared with gifted amateurs, and decidedly poor when compared with the *crème de la crème*. This point is not news to anyone, but is part of our ordinary understanding of what such statements mean.

When we say that X is a genetic condition, full stop, it is easy to think that a complete statement has been made. The same conclusion seems natural when we say that Y is an environmentally acquired phenotype. However, such statements are no less elliptical than the statement that someone is a good musician. A condition has a significant genetic or environmental component only relative to a range of genes and a range of environments. Change the range of genes or the range of environments, and the conclusion about the condition may change as well.

In addition to emphasizing this fact about the relativity of claims concerning genetic causation, I also have tried to emphasize the difference between quantitative genetics and developmental genetics. Quantitative genetics studies have existed for about a hundred years; they long predate the molecular revolution. These studies can tell us whether genetic variation helps explain the phenotypic variation found in a population, but they are utterly silent on the question of which genes affect the phenotype and how they do so. Developmental genetics is the science that will make tremendous strides in coming years because of new techniques that allow scientists to investigate what genes do.

In fact, these two conclusions are not unrelated. A large measure of the power of molecular techniques stems from the fact that they allow scientists to modify the environments in which genes do their work. In addition, gene replacement therapy holds out the possibility that individuals can be furnished with new genes. Thus, interventions stemming from developmental genetics will have the effect of revising the range of environments and the range of genes that are available in human populations. As a result, it is not a mere flight of fancy to suspect that quantitative geneticists who now study a trait will reach conclusions quite different from the ones their successors will draw in the populations of the future. Heretofore, geneticists have studied the world of human variation; we now face a new age in which, for better or worse, they will possess the power to change it.

ACKNOWLEDGMENTS

My thanks to Michael Bailey, James Crow, and Hill Goldsmith for comments on an earlier draft.

METHODOLOGY

This appendix aims to address issues about the methodology of moral reasoning used in this volume. Because many, perhaps most readers will not be especially concerned about such issues, we have chosen to address them here, rather than impeding the flow of analysis in the text.

As much as at any time in the recent past, there is considerable controversy about the proper methodology for ethical analysis, especially in bioethics (Jonson and Toulmin 1988; Gillen and Lloyd 1994; Clouser 1994; Clouser in Gert 1996). Our purpose here is not to resolve these complex issues, only to make it clear that our choice of methodology is reflective (rather than reflexive), and to deflect what we take to be certain spurious but unfortunately predictable objections to our methodology. We are under no illusion that what we say here will render our work immune from methodological criticisms. We hope, rather, at least to clear the field of spurious criticisms to make room for serious ones.

THE METHOD OF REFLECTIVE EQUILIBRIUM

The Charge of Parochialism

In Chapter 1, we noted that we use a familiar method for moral inquiry, that of wide reflective equilibrium. That method is easily criticized – if represented in caricature form. In the end, the best defense of this method is to put it into action, as we have done, and let it be judged by its results.

There is another way to defend the method, namely, by emphasizing its apparent unavoidability, given the rejection of foundationalism. In simplest terms, foundationalism is the view that ethical theorizing must begin with indubitable or self-evident, unrevisable moral axioms and deduce subsidiary principles and concrete judgments from them. It is hard to see how any reasoned approach to ethics that rejects foundationalism can avoid relying on the process of mutual adjustment between principles and particular judgments, each conceived as revisable in the light of the other.

A foundationalist approach in ethical analysis is not promising for several reasons; we will not rehearse them all here, but we will mention two that are of special significance. First, the rejection of foundationalism in practical reasoning, including normative ethics, gains plausibility from its rejection in theoretical reasoning in the sciences. Absent a convincing account of why practical reasoning generally or ethical inquiry in particular is fundamentally different in this regard from theoretical reasoning, the cogency of antifoundationalist approaches in the philosophy of science lends weight to antifoundationalism in ethics. And once foundationalism is abandoned, it is hard to see how reasoned ethical inquiry can proceed without relying to some extent on the method of reflective equilibrium broadly construed (Rawls 1971).

Second, the idea of *wide* reflective equilibrium theory addresses perhaps the most common objection to the method – the charge that reasoning that begins with parochial moral beliefs can only end in parochialism, that the method simply systematizes and renders coherent the particular beliefs of the cultural or ideological group among whose members the practitioner of the method happens to be. This objection overlooks the resources of wide reflective equilibrium, which is wide in two senses: it ranges over a diverse set of moral-theoretical beliefs, including not only general normative principles and particular judgments but background moral concepts such as an ideal of the person and certain conceptions of the nature of social cooperation; and it also includes principles and concepts drawn from different ethical theories, traditions, and cultures, all of which are available to reflective and educated persons in our multicultural world. In a world in which the materials for reflection were severely limited by cultural insularity, the parochialism objection would be more telling than it is in our world.

The actual practice of ethical argumentation and consensus-building as it often occurs in medical institutions and in public policy debates concerning biotechnology illustrates, even if imperfectly, the resources of the method for transcending parochialism. To a large measure, the progress made in gaining reasoned and rather broad consensus on issues such as informed consent, the right to refuse life-sustaining treatment, and other areas of relative agreement in bioethics has been achieved by developing styles of argumentation that allow for considerable convergence of judgment among individuals and groups starting from quite different initial moral orientations, religious or secular.

The Communitarian Challenge

A predictable criticism of the styles of argument used in this volume is that they assume a "liberal-individualist" view of morality and that such a view is deeply flawed. More specifically, the charge would be that the account of the ethics of genetic intervention offered in this volume is biased in favor of individual autonomy and toward individual rights generally. Usually this criticism is voiced by those who are called communitarians, although aside from an animus against what they take to be liberalism, there may be little that all who go by this label have in common (Buchanan 1989). Later in this appendix we articulate the sense in which our view is liberal-individualist (and the senses in which it is not). For now, however, we only wish to emphasize that there is a sense in which the antifoundationalist character of the method of reflective equilibrium should be congenial to communitarians, and that from a communitarian perspective the source of the method's alleged parochialism – the fact that moral reasoning begins with a set of inherited cultural assumptions about the good, and so on – is a strength, not a weakness.

As we understand it, the method of reflective equilibrium is anti-Cartesian in two senses, not one. First, as already noted, it is antifoundationalist, rejecting any attempt to deduce ethical principles and judgments from indubitable or self-evident axioms, and accepting the inevitability that even the most basic starting points in the chain of argumentation are subject to revision. Second, it makes no pretense that the practitioner of the method can operate as a kind of moral "first man," freeing himself from the moral assumptions transmitted through the process of enculturation in the practices of his primary social group, in the way in which Descartes claimed to have freed himself from all traditional beliefs. Instead, the method of reflective equilibrium assumes that we begin *in medias res* as social-cultural beings, and that the various beliefs that provide the materials for the process of critical reflection are cultural products – they are not just my beliefs, but our beliefs.

If it were a tenet of liberalism that ethical reasoning does not begin within a cultural context of belief – or as MacIntyre puts it, a tradition (MacIntyre 1981) – then liberalism and the use of the method of reflective equilibrium would be incompatible. However, as we understand it, this is not a tenet of liberalism. All that liberalism – and the usefulness of the method of wide reflective equilibrium – requires is that even the most basic culturally inherited beliefs be in principle subject to revision as a result of critical reflection. If communitarianism goes further than this – if it holds not only that ethical reasoning must begin within a particular cultural tradition, but also that it cannot go beyond the assumptions of that tradition, that it cannot incorporate principles or ideals imported from outside the culture of origin, then communitarianism flies in the face of much human experience in our multicultural age. People do come to revise the assumptions of their culture of origin and in some cases to repudiate them and adopt those from other cultures. Indeed, in our world the boundaries between cultures or traditions are very hard to draw.

In our view, communitarianism, on its most plausible rendering, rightly emphasizes that ethical reasoning is always rooted in a cultural context, but it is not committed to the very implausible view that cultural contexts are, as it were, hermetically sealed, isolated social atoms. Understood in this way, communitarianism should find the method of reflective equilibrium congenial, at least if we assume that those of us who are practicing the method are part of a developing tradition of ethical reasoning about matters of public concern, a tradition of eminently social reasoning that seeks to develop a consensus in which people from a wide range of cultural and religious perspectives can participate.

There is another respect in which our approach should be congenial to thinkers who may broadly be described as communitarian. Our analysis, more so than most in bioethics perhaps, is deeply contextualized. We have situated our exploration of the ethical issues of genetic intervention historically, beginning with an account of the eugenics movement. In doing so, we have operated on the assumption that the historical context matters, that the experience of eugenics is profoundly relevant, not only from the standpoint of ethical theorizing, but also because both the actual public debate about and perception of the new genetics is inevitably colored by that experience.

Similarly, especially in the chapter on policy implications, we have proceeded on the assumption that the economic, legal, and popular cultural contexts within which genetic interventions will be deployed make a difference as to how the policy issues will take shape. And although we have concentrated primarily on the U.S. context and that of other economically developed liberal democratic societies, we have offered an analysis – drawing in part on our ethical autopsy of eugenics – of what might be called "ethical risk factors" regarding genetic intervention that is sensitive to contextual differences as well. In particular, we have argued that the greater risk in a country like the United States, which has relatively robust and entrenched legal rights regarding reproduction, comes from market-driven, rather than state-directed eugenics. It is our hope, therefore, that at least to some extent we have avoided one of the errors rightly or wrongly associated with liberal-individualist approaches: a failure to contextualize the prob lems under analysis.

THE LIMITS OF "PRINCIPLISM"

In recent years, voices of criticism have been raised against "principlism" in bioethics (Clouser in Gert 1996). To a large extent, the critics are, in our opinion, attacking a view that is at worst a strawman and at best a vulgarization of the framework for analysis advanced most prominently by James Childress and Tom L. Beauchamp in various editions of their influential book *Principles of Bioethics* (Beauchamp and Childress 1979). In simplest (and crudest) form, the antiprinciplists' complaint is that bioethics has been impoverished by an approach that mechanically applies to all issues a triumvirate of principles (autonomy, beneficence, justice – the so-called Georgetown mantra, named after the home institution of one of the authors of *Principles of Bioethics*).

If that is principlism, then it is obviously a flawed method, if one can call it a method. Our approach is not principlist in that sense, however. We do attempt to articulate principles, but we hope to have made it clear that the real work of ethical reasoning is quite complex and arduous and that principles must be argued for, refined, mutually adjusted to one another, and embedded in a coherent ethical theory that is sensitive to cultural, economic, and political contexts.

To make it even clearer that our analysis does not commit the sin of principlism, it will be useful to elaborate our earlier simplified account of the method of wide reflective equilibrium upon which we rely (Daniels 1996). The central methodological assumption of this volume is that the broadly coherentist view or "method" of justification that Rawls (1974) calls "wide reflective equilibrium" not only offers a promising account of the justification of ethical theories, but also gives valuable guidance for practical ethics. The process of working back and forth between our moral judgments about particular situations and general reasons and principles that cover particular situations is familiar to anyone who reasons about matters of right and wrong. Sometimes we use this process to justify our judgments, sometimes our principles.

We can still ask why we should accept the principles that explain our considered moral judgments. To answer this question, we must widen the web of justificatory beliefs. We must show why it is reasonable to hold these principles and beliefs, not just that we happen to do so. Seeking wide reflective equilibrium is thus the process of bringing to bear the broadest evidence and critical scrutiny we can, drawing on all the different moral and nonmoral beliefs and theories that arguably are relevant to our selection of principles or adherence to our considered judgments. Wide reflective equilibrium is therefore at the same time a theoretical account of justification in ethics and a process that is relevant to helping us solve moral problems at various levels of theory and practice.

The key idea underlying the method of wide reflective equilibrium is that we test various parts of our system of moral beliefs against other parts of our general system of beliefs, seeking coherence among the widest set of moral and nonmoral beliefs by revising and refining them at all levels. For example, we might test the appropriateness of a purported principle of justice by seeing whether we can accept its implications in a broad range of cases and whether it accounts for those cases better than alternatives. Rawls appeals to such a test in *A Theory of Justice* when he imposes a condition of adequacy on the principles chosen in his contract situation, requiring that they match our considered moral judgments in reflective equilibrium.

Our moral beliefs about particular cases count in this process. They have justificatory weight; yet they are not decisive, and what weight they have is provisional. Even firmly held beliefs about particular cases may be revised. For example, if a principle incompatible with such a firmly held belief about a particular case accounts better than alternatives for an appropriate range of cases we seem especially confident about, and if the principle also has theoretical support from other parts of our general belief system, we may revise our particular belief and save the principle. Unless we are willing to indulge in dogmatism and abandon all claim to reasonableness, we cannot insist on the particular belief without supplying reasons for doing so, and we must show that those reasons are superior to those in support of the principle that clashes with the particular belief.

Wide reflective equilibrium requires that we bring to bear all theoretical considerations that have relevance to the acceptability of principles, not just of particular judgments. These theoretical considerations may be empirical or they may be moral. Thus one task of ethical theory is to show how work in the social sciences, for example, has bearing on moral considerations.

It is very important to understand how diverse the types of beliefs are that are included in wide reflective equilibrium, as well as the kinds of arguments that may be based on them. They include our beliefs about particular cases; about rules and principles and virtues and how to apply or act on them; about the right-making properties of actions, policies, and institutions; about the conflict between consequentialist and deontological theories; about partiality and impartiality and the moral point of view; about motivation, moral development, strains of commitment, and the limits of ethics; about the nature of persons; about the role or function of ethics in our lives; about the implications of game theory, decision theory, and accounts of rationality for ethics; about human psychology, sociology, political and economic behavior; about the ways we should reply to moral skepticism and moral disagreement; and about moral justification itself.

As is evident from this partial list, the elements of moral theory are diverse. Moral theory, according to this method, is not simply a list of principles, as the principlist caricature would have it.

There is another, more sophisticated version of the antiprinciplist objection, which deserves more serious consideration. This is the view that there is something incomplete and inadequate about a conception of ethics that is concerned only with principles of action, understood as rules specifying what is right, wrong, and permissible – even if the list of principles is much richer than the Georgetown mantra, and even if the principles are embedded in a coherent web of nonmoral and moral beliefs.

Perhaps the most plausible interpretation of this complaint is that it overlooks the essential role of highly particularized judgment in the moral life and that hence it gives short shrift to **virtues**, so far as these are dispositions to judge and be motivated to act in the right way, in the right circumstances. In other words, antiprinciplism in some cases at least is a new name for an old ethical stance, one that has recently experienced a revival under the title of "virtue ethics": the rejection of a conception of morality that identifies it with a body of rules of action, that ignores or neglects the importance of virtues, and that places too much confidence in the usefulness of general principles as guides to a diversity of richly nuanced particular situations.

We reject the extreme version of this position, according to which an account of virtues can replace the articulation of a coherent and powerful set of moral principles. We cheerfully acknowledge, however, that a complete moral theory would give a prominent place not only to principles and to their limitations as guides for conduct, but also to virtues. We do not offer a complete moral theory, however, and the part of moral theory we have focused primarily on – that which provides guidance for how institutions ought to be structured – requires the articulation of principles. Principles are needed to evaluate existing institutions and to guide institutional design; reliance on the judgment of virtuous individuals (even if we could identify them without recourse to principles) is no substitute for principled public debate about the ethical character of our common institutions.

Nevertheless, much of what we have said regarding the morality of inclusion (especially in Chapters 3 and 7) pertains as much to virtues as to principles. This is also especially true regarding our ethical autopsy of eugenics, as well as our conclusions about the importance of combining a commitment to preventing disabilities with an attitude of respect for the equal worth of those who have disabilities. In that sense, our analysis is at least not guilty of the grosser sins of principlism.

A LIBERAL FRAMEWORK

The principles we began with (and have taken as revisable in the process of moving toward wide reflective equilibrium), as well as those with which we conclude our analysis in this volume, are in a broad sense liberal principles. Liberalism, however, is not one thing, and it is certainly not the thing that most who take themselves to be critics of liberalism are criticizing.

There are vigorous conflicts among liberal theorists, some of which we have explored in earlier chapters. (Consider, for example, the rival understandings of equal opportunity explored in Chapter 3.) However, there are some fundamental ideas that we believe are common to the most plausible variants of liberal moral-political theory, and which have played a formative role in our reflections. (The characterization of liberalism that follows owes much to lectures presented at the University of Wisconsin in the Spring of 1997 by Harry Brighouse.)

1. *Moral individualism.* From a moral point of view, it is only individuals who ultimately count. (Collectivities can have moral value, but only insofar as they affect the condition of individuals.)

2. *Equality of persons.* With regard to the most basic questions of morality and so far as the design of basic institutions is concerned, individuals count equally.

3. *The subjects of justice are persons who are capable of being critical choosers of ends.* At least so far as the justice of basic institutions is concerned, individuals are to be conceived as beings whose preferences and conceptions of the good are not fixed, but are rather subject to criticism and revision over time.

4. *The distinction between the private and public spheres.* Institutions that reflect a recognition of moral individualism, the moral equality of persons, and the capacity of persons to be critical choosers of ends will create and protect a significant private sphere in which individuals, either as individuals or as members of communities, can freely pursue and critically revise their own conceptions of the good. (And hence there are significant limitations on the use of public authority and the power of the state, including, on some accounts, the requirement of state "neutrality.")

These are not offered as a complete specification of liberalism, but will suffice for our purposes. Moreover, we will not attempt to defend these principles here – to do so would require a major treatise in political philosophy. It will be useful, however, to head off several common misinterpretations of these elements of liberalism.

First, it is crucial to understand that these are normative theses. They are not psychological generalizations intended to apply to all individuals in all societies. Nor are they ontological theses.

Thesis 1, moral individualism, is a claim about what ultimately matters from a moral point of view, not about what sorts of things

there really are. Hence, liberalism is quite compatible with the ontological view that there are irreducible social wholes or collectivities –
that groups exist and that they are not reducible to the existence of
individuals.

Thesis 2, the moral equality of persons, is not the claim that people
always recognize themselves or others as moral equals. Hence pointing
out that in some societies some people do not regard themselves as the
equals of others or that they cannot conceive of themselves as equals
is no criticism of liberalism.

Nor is Thesis 3 a psycho-social generalization about human beings.
It is about the relevance of a certain capacity of human beings, from
the standpoint of justice. As such, it is perfectly compatible with the
statement that many human beings never realize this capacity for
critical revisability, nor wish to realize it. So, for example, it is no
criticism of liberalism to point out that the "obsession with autonomy" is a Western attitude. Nor does the third liberal thesis imply that
people's preferences or conceptions of the good are formed independently of cultural influences, or that individuals ever completely free
themselves of the normative assumptions of their cultures of origin.

Similarly, the fourth liberal thesis is not to be confused with a
related empirical generalization – that all societies recognize a private
and a public sphere. It is compatible with it being the case that there
are societies that do not feature a clear distinction between a public
and private sphere, much less a recognition that the distinction is
important.

In large measure, the liberal tradition can be seen as an ongoing,
vigorous debate about what these four tenets mean, about what the
best justifications for them are, and about how best to realize them in
the social world. Because both their meanings and their justifications
are perpetually debated, it is incorrect to say they are dogmas of
liberalism.

Negative and Positive Rights: Freedom and Well-Being

Among the disputes that go on within the liberal tradition, two are
especially significant: the controversy over whether, or to what extent,
liberal justice includes positive rights, and the disagreement about
whether liberty or self-determination is a separate, irreducible value,
or a component of well-being broadly understood. Despite other differences, the authors of this volume endorse a view of the proper scope

of public authority and state action that includes positive rights. In other words, like most modern liberals, but unlike libertarians, we believe that justice toward persons conceived as critical choosers of ends requires the provision of certain goods that are valuable as flexible means that facilitate the critical formulation, revision, and effective pursuit of a wide range of conceptions of the good. Among these goods are health care services, especially so far as these facilitate the critical and effective pursuit of a conception of the good by preventing or removing harms and obstacles to opportunity.

We also believe that the liberal case for positive rights is greatly strengthened if the whole set of basic rights – negative as well as positive – is seen to be justified by appeal to a plurality of morally significant interests that persons have. In this sense, our view is not "rights-based"; we regard rights-principles as something that must be argued to, using the method of wide reflective equilibrium and in such a way as to emphasize the importance of rights as protectors for certain crucial interests.

The most important of these interests, somewhat crudely, are the interest in welfare and the interest in self-determination, where the latter is understood as the capacity to function as a critical chooser of ends. A person's interest *qua* critical chooser of ends, what might be called a self-determination (or autonomy) interest, consists in the achievement of optimal conditions for developing and exercising the capacity to formulate and rationally revise over time a conception of the good. This is not the only important interest, however; persons also have a morally considerable interest in effectively pursuing the ends that they set for themselves in their conceptions of the good and the attainment of which constitutes their welfare.

Different ethical theories, including different versions of liberalism, assert different connections between welfare and self-determination. On some theories, self-determination is merely a component, albeit a very important and weighty one, of a person's welfare comprehensively understood. According to other theories, self-determination is an irreducible, primary value, weightier than or at least as important as welfare. Each approach has its attractions and difficulties.

The most obvious difficulty for the second type of theory is that it immediately faces the task of either arguing convincingly that the interest in self-determination and that in welfare are always or generally compatible or, if they are not, how it could ever be good or rational for someone to sacrifice welfare for the sake of self-determination (Buchanan and Brock 1989). Fortunately for substantive ethical inquiries such as ours, in most cases the two views about the relationship between welfare and self-determination yield the same practical results. For this reason, although we have in several instances taken a stand on rather deep theoretical issues that divide liberals (such as the meaning of equal opportunity or the subject matter of theories of distributive justice), we have not found it necessary to do so here. Our analysis is compatible, we believe, with either resolution of this fundamental dispute in ethical theory.

Justifying the Liberal Framework

What justifies our reliance on a liberal framework for our ethical inquiry? The short answer is that, as our brief remarks about the method of wide reflective equilibrium indicate, we (like everyone else) must start somewhere. The longer and somewhat more satisfying answer is that we believe that a liberal approach to moral and political philosophy is to date the most carefully worked out and best defended approach available. In our opinion, there simply are no antiliberal or nonliberal (e.g., communitarian) moral-political theories that come close to the degree of systematic argumentation and power that we find in the writings of liberal thinkers such as John Rawls, Joel Feinberg, Ronald Dworkin, Thomas Scanlon, and Joseph Raz. Communitarian writings have tended to be criticisms of liberalism rather than constructive theories in their own right.

Finally, there is another reason – what might with some irony be called a communitarian reason – to explore the resources of a broadly liberal approach. We are attempting to provide guidance for a certain kind of society – a society like our own but with far greater powers of genetic intervention. Our society, at least in the basic contours of the political culture and legal structure in which issues concerning genetic intervention are likely to arise, is a liberal society – or at least strives to be. Hence we are doing what communitarians say we must: beginning the task of moral inquiry within a tradition, our tradition, and attempting to grapple with the problems of a particular society, our society.

REFERENCES

Note: We have had the good fortune to draw on two comprehensive histories of the eugenics movement, written in recent years by scholars who are not only good historians but who are also sophisticated in their insights into the philosophical and political issues the eugenics raised. These are the works by Daniel Kevles (1985) and Diane Paul (1995), listed below. Anyone familiar with these works will appreciate the depth and breadth of our reliance on them. Diane Paul has given guidance through much of the rest of the literature, extending even to the key to her filing cabinets, where copies of several of the more obscure items on the following list currently reside.

Adams, Mark, ed. 1990. *The Well-Born Science.* Oxford: Oxford University Press.

Allen, David B. and Norm Fost. 1990. "Growth Hormone Therapy for Short Stature: Panacea or Pandora's Box?" *Journal of Pediatrics* 117: 16–21.

Allen, Garland E. 1986. "The Eugenics Record Office at Cold Spring Harbor, 1910–1940: An Essay in Institutional History." *Osiris* 2nd Series. 2: 225–34.

   1980. "The Work of Raymond Pearl: From Eugenics to Population Control." *Science for the People,* July/August, 12(4): 22–8.

Aly, Gotz, Peter Chroust, and Christian Pross. 1994. *Cleansing the Fatherland: Nazi Medicine and Racial Hygiene.* Baltimore: Johns Hopkins University Press.

Anderson, W. French. January/February 1990. "Genetics and Human Malleability," *Hastings Center Report* 20(1): 21–4.

   1989. "Human Gene Therapy: Why Draw a Line?" *Journal of Medicine and Philosophy.* 14(1): 681–93.

   1988. *Human Gene Therapy: Preclinical Data Document.* Bethesda, MD: National Institutes of Health.

   1985. "Human Gene Therapy: Scientific and Ethical Considerations." *Journal of Medicine and Philosophy.* 10:3:275–91.

   1980. "Gene Therapy in Human Beings: When Is It Ethical to Begin?" *New England Journal of Medicine* 303:22:1293–7.

Arneson, Richard. 1989. "Equality and Equality of Opportunity for Welfare." *Philosophical Studies* 56(1): 77–93.

Asch, Adrienne. 1995. "Can Aborting "Imperfect" Children Be Immoral?" in John Arras and Bonnie Steinbock, eds. 4th edition, *Ethical Issues in Modern Medicine*. Mountain View, CA: Mayfield Publishing Co.

Bailey, J. 1996. "Can Behavior Genetics Contribute to Evolutionary Studies of Behavior?" in Crawford and Krebs, eds., *Evolution and Human Behavior – Ideas. Issues. and Applications*. New York: Erlbaum.

Bayer, Ronald. 1989. *Private Acts, Social Consequences: AIDS and the Politics of Public Health*. New York: Free Press.

  1981. *Homosexuality and American Psychiatry*. New York: Basic Books.

Bayer, Ronald and Cheryl Healton. (1989) "Controlling AIDS in Cuba: The Logic of Quarantine." *New England Journal of Medicine* 320 (15): 1022–4.

Bayles, M. 1976. "Harm to the Unconceived." *Philosophy and Public Affairs* 5(3): 292–304.

Beardsley, Tim. 1996. "Vital Data."*Scientific American* 274(3): 100–05.

Beauchamp, Tom and James Childress. 1979. *Principles of Biomedical Ethics*. New York: Oxford University Press.

Beauchamp, Tom and Ruth Faden. 1986. *A History and Theory of Informed Consent*. New York: Oxford University Press.

Berreby, David. 1996. "Up With People: Dwarves Meet Identity Politics." *The New Republic* 214(18): 14–19.

Billings, Paul, M.A. Kohn, M. De Cuervas, J. Bechwith, J.S. Alper, and M.R. Natowicz. 1992. "Discrimination as a Consequence of Genetic Testing." *American Journal of Human Genetics* 50(3): 476–82.

Boorse, Christopher. 1977. "Health as a Theoretical Concept." *Philosophy of Science* 44: 542–73.

  1976. "Wright on Functions." *Philosophical Review* 85(1): 70–85.

  1975. "On the Distinction between Disease and Illness." *Philosophy and Public Affairs* 5(1): 49–68.

Bouchard, T., D. Lykken, M. McGue, N. Segal, and A. Tellegren. 1990: "Sources of Human Psychological Differences – The Minnesota Study of Twins Reared Apart." *Science* 250 (4978): 223–8.

Brewer, Herbert. 1935. "Eutelegenesis." *Eugenics Review* 27(2): 121–6.

Brandt, Richard. 1979. *A Theory of the Good and the Right*. New York: Oxford University Press.

Brink, David. 1989. *Moral Realism and the Foundations of Ethics*. Cambridge: Cambridge University Press.

Broberg, Gunnar and Mattias Tyden. 1996. "Eugenics in Sweden: Efficient Care," in Gunnar Broberg and Nils Roll-Hansen, eds., *Eugenics and the Welfare State: Sterilization Policy in Denmark, Sweden, Norway and Finland*. East Lansing, MI: Michigan State University Press.

Brock, Dan W. and Allen Buchanan. 1989. *Deciding for Others: the Ethics of Surrogate Decision Making*. New York: Cambridge University Press.

Brock, Dan W. 1995. "The Non-Identity Problem and Genetic Harm: The Case of Wrongful Handicaps." *Bioethics* 9(2): 269–76.

  1992. "Quality of Life Measures in Health Care and Medical Ethics," in

Martha Nussbaum and Amartya Sen, eds., *The Quality of Life*. Oxford: Clarendon Press.

Buchanan, Allen. 1996. "Genetic Manipulation and the Morality of Inclusion." *Social Philosophy and Policy* 13(2): 18–46.

1995. "Equal Opportunity and Genetic Intervention." *Social Philosophy & Policy*, 12(2): 105–35.

1993. "The Morality of Inclusion." *Social Philosophy and Policy* 10(2): 233–57.

1990. "Justice as Reciprocity versus Subject-Centered Justice." *Philosophy and Public Affairs* 19(3): 227–52.

1989. "Assessing the Communitarian Critique of Liberalism." *Ethics* 99(4): 852–82.

1987. "Justice and Charity." *Ethics* 97(4): 558–75.

1975. "Revisability and Rational Choice." *Canadian Journal of Philosophy* 5(3): 398–400.

Burleigh, Michael, 1994. *Death and Deliverance: Euthanasia in Germany 1900–1945*. Cambridge: Cambridge University Press.

Burleigh, Michael and Wolfgang Wippermann. 1991. *The Racial State: Germany 1933–1945*. Cambridge: Cambridge University Press.

Carlson, Elof Axel. 1981. *Genes, Radiation and Society: The Life and Work of H.J. Muller*. Ithaca: Cornell University Press.

Carlson, Tucker. 1996. "Eugenics, American Style: The Abortion of Down Syndrome Babies." *The Weekly Standard*, Dec. 2, pp. 20–5.

Castle, William. E., John M. Coulter, Charles Davenport, Edward M. East, and William L. Tower. 1912. *Heredity and Eugenics*. Chicago: University of Chicago Press.

Chan, Chee Khoon, and Heng-Leng Chee. 1984. "Singapore 1984: Breeding for Big Brother," in Heng Leng Chee and Chee Khoon Chan, eds., *Designer Genes: I.Q., Ideology, and Biology*. Kuala Lumpur: Institute for Social Analysis.

Chesterton, Gilbert K. 1922. *Eugenics and Other Evils*. London: Cassell & Co

Clouser, K Danner. 1996. "Concerning the Inadequacies of Principlism," in Bernard Gert, ed., *Morality and the New Genetics: A Guide for Students and Health Care Providers*. Boston: Jones and Bartlett.

1995. "Common Morality as an Alternative to Principlism." *Kennedy Institute of Ethics Journal* 5(3): 219–36.

Cohen, G.A. 1993. "Equality of What?: On Welfare Goods and Capabilities," in Martha Nussbaum, ed., *The Quality of Life*. Oxford: Clarendon Press.

1989. "On the Currency of Egalitarian Justice." *Ethics* 99(4): 906–44.

Cohen, Joshua. 1995. "Amartya Sen: Inequality Reexamined." *Journal of Philosophy* 92(5): 275–88.

1994. "A More Democratic Liberalism." *Michigan Law Review* 92(6): 1506–43.

Collins, Frances. 1997. "The Human Genome Project." Lecture given at the Metropolitan Life Insurance Company offices in New York at the "Genetic Testing: Implications for Insurance" conference, June 23.

Committee on Assessing Genetic Risks, Division of Health Sciences Policy, Institute of Medicine. 1994. *Assessing Genetic Risks: Implications for Health and Social Policy*, in Lori Andrews, Jane Fullarton, Neil Holtzman, and Arno Motulsky, eds. Washington: National Academy Press.

Cook-Deegan, Robert, 1994. *The Gene Wars: Science, Politics, and the Human Genome*. New York: W.W. Norton and Co.

1990. "Genetics, Ethics, and Human Values," in Z. Bankowski and A.M. Capron, eds., *Genetics, Ethics and Human Values: Human Genome Mapping, Genetic Screening and Gene Therapy. Proceedings of the XXIVth CIOMS Round Table Conference*. Council for International Organizations of Medical Sciences.

Council for Responsible Genetics. 1993. *Genetic Engineering: Unresolved Issues – A Biotechnology Reader*. Cambridge, MA: Council for Responsible Genetics.

Culver, Kenneth W. 1995. "How Will You Measure Success?" *Gene Therapy* 14.

Daniels, Norman. 1997. "Mental Disabilities, Equal Opportunity, and the ADA," in Richard J. Bonnie and John Monahan, eds., *Mental Disorder, Work Disability, and the Law*. Chicago: University of Chicago Press.

1996. *Justice and Justification: Reflective Equilibrium in Theory and Practice*. New York: Cambridge University Press.

1994. "The Genome Project, Individual Differences, and Just Health Care," in Timothy Murphy and Marc Lappe, eds., *Justice and the Human Genome Project*. Berkeley: University of California Press.

1993. "Rationing Fairly: Programmatic Considerations." *Bioethics* 7(2/3): 223–33.

1991. "Is the Oregon Rationing Plan Fair?" *JAMA* 265(17): 2232–5.

1990. "Equality of What: Welfare, Resources, or Capabilities?" *Philosophy and Phenomenological Research* 50 (Suppl.): 273–96; reprinted in Daniels 1996.

1986. "Why Saying No to Patients in the United States is So Hard: Cost-Containment, Justice, and Provider Autonomy." *New England Journal of Medicine* 314: 1380–3.

1985. *Just Health Care*. Cambridge: Cambridge University Press.

Daniels, Norman and James E. Sabin. 1994. "Determining 'Medical Necessity' in Mental Health Practice: A Study of Clinical Reasoning and a Proposal for Insurance Policy." *Hastings Center Report* 24(6): 5–13.

1991. "Clarifying the Concept of Medical Necessity." *Proceedings of the Group Health Institute*. Washington, D.C.: Group Health Association of America, pp. 693–707.

Davenport, Charles. 1914. "The Eugenics Programme and Progress in its Achievement," in Moron A. Aldrich et al., eds., *Eugenics: Twelve University Lectures*. New York: Dodd, Mead and Co.

de Beaufort, Inez, Medard Hilhorst, and Soren Holm, eds. 1996. *In the Eye of the Beholder: Ethics and Medical Change of Appearance*. Oslo: Scandinavian University Press.

Diagnostic and Statistical Manual of Disorders (DSM-IIIR). 1987. 3rd edition – revised. Washington, D.C.: American Psychiatric Association.

Dickson, D. 1994. "Concern Grows Over China's Plans to Reduce Number of 'Inferior' Births." *Nature* 367: 3.

Dikitter, Frank. 1998. *Imperfect Conceptions: Medical Knowledge, Birth Defects and Eugenics in China*. New York: Columbia University Press.

Duster, Troy. 1990. *Backdoor to Eugenics*. New York: Routledge.

Dutton. Diana B. 1988. *Worse than the Disease: Pitfalls of Medical Progress*. Cambridge: Cambridge University Press.

Dworkin, Ronald. 1981. "What is Equality?" *Philosophy & Public Affairs*. 10(3):185–246 (Part I) and 10(4): 283–345 (Part II).

Eisenberg, L. 1976. "The Outcome as Cause: Predestination and Human Cloning." *The Journal of Medicine and Philosophy*: 318–31.

Elkins, Thomas E. and Douglas Brown. 1993. "The Cost of Choice: A Price Too High in the Triple Screen for Down Syndrome." *Clinical Obstetrics & Gynecology* 36(3): 532–40.

Englehardt, H. Tristram. 1974. "Disease of Masturbation: Values and the Concept of Disease." *Bulletin of the History of Medicine* 48(2): 234–48.

Feinberg, Joel. 1984. *The Moral Limits of Criminal Law: Offense to Others*, Vol. 2. New York: Oxford University Press.

1980. "The Child's Right to an Open Future," in W. Aiken and H. LaFollette, eds., *Whose Child? Children's Rights, Parental Authority, and State Power*. Totowa, NJ: Rowman and Littlefield.

1970. "The Nature and Value of Rights." *Journal of Value Inquiry* 4: 263–7.

Fisher, Irving. "Report of the President of the American Eugenic Society," American Eugenic Society, May 26.

Flynn, J. 1987. "Massive I.Q. Gains in 14 Nations." *Psychological Bulletin* 101(2): 171–91.

Fried, Charles. 1969. *An Autonomy of Values*. Cambridge, MA.: Harvard University Press.

Gallagher, Hugh G. 1990. *By Trust Betrayed: Patients, Physicians, and the License to Kill in the Third Reich*. New York: Henry Holt.

Gibbard, Allan. 1984. "Health Care and the Prospective Pareto Principle." *Ethics* 94: 261–82.

Gillon, Ranaan and Ann Lloyd. 1994. *Principles of Health Care Ethics*. Chichester, UK: Wiley.

Glover, Jonathan. 1999. *Humanity: A Moral History of the Twentieth Century*. London: Jonathan Cape.

1996. "The Moral Psychology of Human Cruelty." *Address to the Symposium on Bioethics and Human Rights, Physicians for Human Rights and International Association of Bioethics*. San Francisco, CA., November 25.

1988. "Mapping the Human Genome: Some Implications," in Office of Technology Assessment (OTA), *Mapping Our Genes: Federal Genome Projects: How Far, How Fast*. Contract Reports. Vol. 1. Washington, DC: Government Printing Office.

1984. *What Sort of People Should There Be?* New York: Penguin Books.

Glover, Noreen M. and Samuel J. Glover. 1996. "Ethical and Legal Issues

Regarding Selective Abortion of Fetuses with Down Syndrome." *Mental Retardation* 34(4): 207–14.

Gold, Martha, Joanna Siegel, Louise Russell, and Milton Weinstein, eds. 1996. *Cost-Effectiveness in Health and Medicine*. Oxford: Oxford University Press.

Graves L.M., and Cole F.H. 1945. "Memphis and Shelby County Tuberculosis Control Program." *American Journal of Public Health* 35(9): 934–40.

Griffin, James. 1986. *Well-Being: Its Meaning, Measurement and Moral Importance*. Oxford: Oxford University Press.

Griffiths, Anthony J.F., Jeffrey Miller, David Suzuki, Richard Lewontin, and William Gelbart. 1993. *An Introduction to Genetic Analysis*. 5th edition. New York: W. H. Freeman.

Guttman, Amy. 1981. "For and Against Equal Access to Health Care." *Milbank Memorial Fund Quarterly/Health and Society* 59(4): 542–60.

Hamer, D., S. Hu, V. Magnuson, and A. Pattatucci. 1993. "A Linkage Between DNA Markers on the X Chromosome and Male Sexual Orientation." *Science* 261(5119): 321–7.

Hanser, Matthew. 1990. "Harming Future People." *Philosophy & Public Affairs*. 19(1): 47–70.

Harris, John. 1992. *Wonderwoman and Superman: The Ethics of Human Biotechnology*. Oxford: Oxford University Press.

Health Security Act. 1993. Washington, D.C.: U.S. General Purchasing Office.

Heyd, D. 1992. *Genetics: Moral Issues in the Creation of People*. Berkeley, CA: University of California Press.

Holmes, Oliver Wendell. 1927. Opinion in *Buck v. Bell*, 274 U.S. 205, 207 (1927).

Hubbard, Ruth and Elijah Wald. 1993. *Exploding the Gene Myth*. Boston: Beacon Press.

The International League of Societies for Persons with Mental Handicap. 1994. *Just Technology*. North York, ON: Institut Roeher/Roeher Institute.

Jaroff, Leon. 1989. "The Gene Hunt." *Time*. 133(12): 62–7.

Jencks, Christopher, Michael Smith, Henry Acland, Mary Jo Bane, David Cohen, Herbert Gintis, Barbara Heyns, and Stephan Michelson. 1972. *Inequality – A Reassessment of the Effect of Family and Schooling in America*. New York: Basic Books.

Jonas, H. 1974. *Philosophical Essays: From Ancient Creed to Technological Man*. Englewood Cliffs, NJ: Prentice-Hall.

Jonson, Albert and Stephen Toulmin. 1988. *The Abuse of Casuistry*. Berkeley, CA.: University of California Press.

Karjala, Dennis. 1992. "A Legal Research Agenda for the Human Genome Initiative." *Jurimetrics* 32(2): 121–311.

Kay, Lily E. 1993. *The Molecular Vision of Life: Cal Tech, The Rockefeller Foundation, and the Rise of the New Biology*. New York: Oxford University Press.

Kevles, Daniel. 1992. "Out of Eugenics," in Daniel Kevles and Leroy Hood, eds., *The Code of Codes: Scientific and Social Issues in the Human Genome Project*. Cambridge: Harvard University Press.

1985. *In the Name of Eugenics*. Berkeley and Los Angeles: University of California Press.

Kitcher, Philip. 1996. *The Lives to Come*. New York: Simon and Schuster.

1992. *Vaulting Ambitions: Sociobiology and the Quest for Human Nature*. Cambridge, MA.: MIT Press.

Kuhl, Stefan. 1994.*The Nazi Connection: Eugenics, American Racism, and National Socialism*. Oxford: Oxford University Press.

Kymlicka, Will. 1989. "Liberal Individualism and Liberal Neutrality." *Ethics* 99(4): 883–905.

Larson, Edward J. 1995. *Sex, Race and Science: Eugenics in the Deep South*. Baltimore: Johns Hopkins University Press.

Leavitt, Judith Walzer. 1996. *Typhoid Mary: Captive to the Public's Health*. Boston: Beacon Press.

1986. *Brought to Bed: Childbearing in America, 1750 to 1950*. New York: Oxford University Press.

Leder, A. et al. 1986. "Consequences of Widespread Deregulation of the c-myc Gene in Transgenic Mice: Multiple Neoplasms and Normal Development." *Cell* 45:485.

LeVay, Simon. 1993. *The Sexual Brain*. Cambridge: MIT Press.

Lewontin, Richard C. 1997. "Science & 'The Demon-Haunted World': An Exchange." *New York Review of Books* March 6, pp. 51–2.

1992. *Biology as Ideology: The Doctrine of DNA*. New York: Harper Collins.

1974. "The Analysis of Variance and the Analysis of Causes." *American Journal of Human Genetics* 26: 400–11.

1970. "Race and Intelligence." *Bulletin of the Atomic Scientists*, March, 2–8. Reprinted in N. Block and G. Dworkin, eds., *The IQ Controversy*. 1976. New York: Pantheon, pp. 78–92.

Lindee, Susan and Dorothy Nelkin. 1995. *The DNA Mystique: The Gene as a Cultural Icon*. New York: W.H. Freeman.

MacGreggor, Francis C. 1979. *After Plastic Surgery: Adaptation and Adjustment*. New York: Praeger.

MacIntyre, Alastair. 1981. *After Virtue: A Study in Moral Theory*. Notre Dame, IN.: University of Notre Dame Press.

MacKenzie, Donald. 1976. "Eugenics in Britain." *Social Studies of Science* 6: 499–532.

Marx, Karl. 1844. "Economic and Philosophical Manuscripts," in David McClellan, ed., 1984. *Karl Marx: Selected Readings*. Oxford: Oxford University Press.

Mazumdar, Pauline M. H. 1992. *Eugenics, Human Genetics and Human Failings: The Eugenics Society, its Sources and its Critics in Britain*. London: Routledge.

McCormick, R. 1993. "Should We Clone Humans?" *Christian Century* 1148–9.

McMahon, Jeff. (1998). "Wrongful Life: Paradoxes in the Morality of Causing People to Exist," in Jules Coleman, Christopher Morris, eds., *Rational Commitment and Social Justice: Essays for Gregory Kauka.* Cambridge: Cambridge University Press.

Mehler, Barry and Garland Allen. 1977. "Sources in the Study of Eugenics #1: Inventory of the American Eugenics Society Papers." *The Wendel Newsletter,* # 14, June, pp. 9–15.

Morreim, Haavi. 1991. "Gaming the System: Dodging the Rules, Ruling the Dodgers." *Archives of Internal Medicine.* 151: 443–7.

Muller, Charlotte. 1985. "A Window on the Past: The Position of the Client in Twentieth Century Public Health Thought and Practice." *American Journal of Public Health* 75(5): 470–6.

Muller, Hermann. 1962. *Studies in Genetics: The Selected Papers of H.J. Muller.* Bloomington, IN: Indiana University Press.

   1950. "Our Load of Mutations." *American Journal of Human Genetics* 2(2): 111–76.

Murphy, Timothy F. and Marc A. Lappe, eds. 1994. *Justice and the Human Genome Project.* Berkeley: University of California Press.

Murray, Charles and Richard Herrnstein. 1994. *The Bell Curve.* New York: Free Press.

Narveson, Jan. 1973. "Moral Problems of Population." *Monist* 57(1): 62–86.

   1967. "Utilitarianism and New Generations." *Mind* 76:62–72.

National Center for Human Genome Research. 1994. *ELSI 1990-1995: A Review of the Ethical. Legal and Social Implications.* Washington, DC: National Institute for Health.

Nature. 1994. Editorial opinion. "China's Misconception of Eugenics." 367: 1–2.

Nelkin, Dorothy and M. Susan Lindee. 1995. *The DNA Mystique: The Gene as a Cultural Icon.* New York: W.H. Freeman.

Novack, Dennis H., Barbara J. Detering, Robert Arnold, Lachlan Forrow, M. Ladinsky and John C. Pezullo. 1989. "Physicians' Attitudes Towards Using Deception to Resolve Difficult Ethical Problems." *Journal of the American Medical Association* 261(20): 2980–5.

Nozick, Robert. 1974. *Anarchy, State and Utopia.* New York: Basic Books.

Nussbaum, Martha. 1993. "Non-Relative Virtues: An Aristotelian Approach," in Martha Nussbaum and Amartya Sen, eds., *The Quality of Life.* Oxford: Clarendon Press. pp. 242–69.

Nussbaum, Martha and Amartya Sen, eds. 1993. *The Quality of Life.* Oxford: Clarendon Press.

Parfit, Derek. 1986. "Comments." *Ethics* 96: 832–72.

   1984. *Reasons and Persons.* Oxford: Clarendon Press.

   1982. "Future Generations: Further Problems." *Philosophy & Public Affairs* 11(2): 113–72.

Passmore, John. 1974. *Man's Responsibility for Nature.* New York: Charles Scribner's Sons.

Paul, Diane 1996. "Culpability and Compassion: Lessons from the History of Eugenics." *Politics and the Life Sciences* 15(1): 99.

1995. *Controlling Human Heredity, 1865 to the Present.* Atlantic Highlands, NJ: Humanities Press.

1994. "Is Genetics Disguised Eugenics?" in Robert F. Weir, Susan C. Lawrence, and Evan Fales, eds., *Genes and Human Self-Knowledge: Historical and Philosophical Reflections on Modern Genetics.* Iowa City, IA: University of Iowa Press.

1992. "Eugenic Anxieties, Social Realities, and Political Choices." *Social Research* 59(3F): 663–83.

1991. "The Rockefeller Foundation and the Origins of Behavior Genetics," in K. Benson et al., eds. *The Expansion of American Biology.* New Brunswick, NJ: Rutgers University Press.

1984. "Eugenics and the Left." *Journal of the History of Ideas* 45(4): 567–90.

Paul, Diane and H.G. Spencer. 1995. "The Hidden Science of Eugenics." *Nature* 374(6520): 302–04.

Pearson, Roger. 1996. "Political Correctness and Research in Human Intelligence." *Mankind Quarterly* 36(4): 393.

1995. "The Concept of Heredity in Western Thought: Part Three, The Revival of Interest in Genetics." *Mankind Quarterly* 36(1): 73–104.

Perry, John. 1996. Personal Communication.

Peters, P.G. 1989. "Protecting the Unconceived: Nonexistence, Avoidability, and Reproductive Technology." *Arizona Law Review* 31(3): 487–548.

Pogge, Thomas. 1989. *Realizing Rawls.* Ithaca, NY: Cornell University Press.

Popenoe, Paul and Roswell H. Johnson. 1918. *Applied Eugenics.* New York: Macmillan.

Proctor, Robert. 1988. *Racial Hygiene: Medicine Under the Nazis.* Cambridge, MA: Harvard University Press.

Rafter, Nicole H. 1988. *White Trash: The Eugenic Family Studies 1877–1919.* Boston: Northeastern University Press.

Rawls, John. 1993. *Political Liberalism.* New York: Columbia University Press.

1982. "Social Unity and Primary Goods," in Amartya Sen and Bernard Williams, eds., *Utilitarianism and Beyond.* London: Cambridge University Press, pp. 159–86.

1980. "Kantian Constructivism in Moral Theory," *Journal of Philosophy* 77(9): 515–72.

1977. "The Basic Structure as Subject." *American Philosophical Quarterly* 14(2): 159–65.

1975. "The Independence of Moral Theory." *Proceedings and Addresses of the American Philosophical Association* 48(11):5–22.

1971. *A Theory of Justice.* Cambridge, MA: Harvard University Press.

Ricker, Ruth E. 1995. "Do We Really Want This? Little People of America, Inc., Comes to Terms with Genetic Testing." Position Paper, Little People of America, Inc.

Robertson, John A. 1997. "A Ban on Cloning and Cloning Research is Unjustified." Testimony Presented to the National Bioethics Advisory Commission, March.

1994. *Children of Choice.* Princeton, NJ: Princeton University Press.

1994b. "The Question of Human Cloning." *Hastings Center Report* 24: 6–14.

1986. "Embryos, Families, and Procreative Liberty: The Legal Structure of the New Reproduction." *Southern California Law Review* 59: 955.

Roemer, John. 1996. *Theories of Distributive Justice*. Cambridge, MA: Harvard University Press.

1989. "Equality and Responsibility." *Boston Review* 20(2): 3–7.

1985. "Equality of Talent." *Economics and Philosophy* 1(2): 151–88.

Roll-Hansen, Nils. 1996. *Eugenics and the Welfare State: Sterilization Policy in Denmark, Sweden, Norway and Finland*. East Lansing, MI: Michigan State University Press.

1989. "Eugenic Movement in Scandinavia." *British Journal for the History of Science* 22:335–46.

1988. "The Progress of Eugenics: Growth of Knowledge and Change in Ideology." *History of Science*. xxvi, 295–331.

1980. "Eugenics Before World War II: The Case of Norway." *History And Philosophy of the Life Sciences* 2(2):269–98.

Rothenberg, Karen. 1997. "Breast Cancer, the Genetic "Quick Fix" and the Jewish Community: Ethical, Legal and Social Challenges." *Health Matrix* 7(1): 97–124.

Russo, Enzo and David Cove. 1995. *Genetic Engineering: Dreams and Nightmares*. Oxford, W.H. Freeman/Spektrum.

Rydell, Robert W. 1993. *World of Fairs: The Century-of-Progress Expositions*. Chicago: University of Chicago Press.

Scanlon, Thomas M. 1989. "A Good Start: Reply to Roemer." *Boston Review*. 20(2): 8–9.

Scheidmandel, P. 1993. *The Coverage Catalog (3rd Edition)*. Washington, D.C.: American Psychiatric Association (Office of Economic Affairs).

Schneider, William. 1990a. *Quality and Quantity: The Quest for Biological Regeneration in Twentieth Century France*. Cambridge: Cambridge University Press.

1990b. "The Eugenics Movement in France, 1890–1940," in Mark Adams, ed., *The Well-Born Science*. Oxford: Oxford University Press.

Searle, G. R. 1976. "Eugenics and Class." *Social Studies of Science* 6: 217–42.

Searle, G. R. and Richard Soloway. 1991. "Demography and Degeneration: Eugenics and the Declining Birthrate in Twentieth Century Britain." *Albion* 23(1):164

Sen, Amartya. 1992. *Inequality Reexamined*. Cambridge, MA.: Harvard University Press.

1990. "Justice: Means versus Freedoms." *Philosophy and Public Affairs* 19: 111–21.

1980. "Equality of What?" in Sterling McMurrin, ed., *Tanner Lectures on Human Values*. Cambridge: Cambridge University Press.

Siever, Larry. 1997. *The New View of the Self: How Genes and Neurotransmitters Shape Your Mind, Personality and Your Mental Health*. Old Tappan, NJ: Macmillan.

Smith, G.P. 1983. "Intimations of Immortality: Clones, Cyrons and the Law." *University of New South Wales Law Journal* 6:119–32.

Soloway, Richard A. 1990. *Demography and Degeneration: Eugenics and the Declining Birthrate in Twentieth-Century Britain.* Chapel Hill: University of North Carolina Press.

Stepan, Nancy L. 1991. *The Hour of Eugenics: Race, Gender and Nation in Latin America.* Ithaca: Cornell University Press.

Stopes, Marie C. 1921. *Verbatim Report of the Town Hall Meeting.* October 27, 1921. New York: Voluntary Parenthood League.

Terry, C.E. 1913. "The Negro: His Relation to Public Health in the South." *American Journal of Public Health* 3:300–10.

United Nations. 1959. "General Assembly Resolution 1386 (XIV)." *Official Records of the General Assembly, Fourteenth Session.* 16, Supplement (A4249): 19–20.

United States President's Commission for the Study of Ethical Problems in Medicine and Biomedical and Behavioral Research. 1983. *Securing Access to Health Care.* Washington, DC: The Commission.

⸻ 1982. *Splicing Life: A Report on the Social and Ethical Issues of Genetic Engineering with Human Beings.* Washington, DC: The Commission.

Vehey, A. D. 1994. "Cloning: Revisiting an Old Debate." *Kennedy Institute of Ethics Journal* 4:227–34.

Wachbroit, Robert. 1994. "What is Wrong with Eugenics?" in Edward Edwin, Sidney Gendin, and Lowell Kleinman, eds., *Ethical Issues in Scientific Research: An Anthology.* Garland, NY, pp. 329–36.

⸻ 1987. "What's Wrong with Eugenics?" Report from the Institute for Philosophy and Public Policy, vol. 7, no. 2/3 (Spring/Summer), 6–8.

Wallace, Bruce. 1970. *Genetic Load.* Englewood Cliffs, N.J.: Prentice Hall.

Walters, L. 1990. *Gene Therapy for Human Patients: Information for the General Public.* Bethesda, MD: National Institutes of Health.

Walters, W.A.W. 1982. "Cloning, Ectogenesis, and Hybrids: Things to Come?" in W.A.W. Walters and P. Singer, eds., *Test-Tube Babies.* Melbourne: Oxford University Press.

Walzer, Michael. 1983. *Spheres of Justice.* New York: Basic Books.

Weindling, Paul. 1989. *Health, Race and German Politics between National Unification and Nazism 1870–1945.* Cambridge: Cambridge University Press.

Weiss, Sheila F. 1990. "The Race Hygiene Movement in Germany, 1904–1945," in K. Benson et al., eds., *The Expansion of American Biology.* New Brunswick, NJ: Rutgers University Press.

Wernimont, Brenda. 1997. "My Perspective as a Deaf Person Working with Geneticists." Hereditary Hearing Impairment Resource Registry, National Institute on Deafness and Other Communication Disorders.

Wikler, Daniel I. 1983. "Paternalism and the Mildly Retarded," in Rolf Sartorius, ed., *Paternalism.* Minneapolis: University of Minnesota Press, pp. 83–94.

⸻ 1978. "Persuasion and Coercion for Health: Issues in Government Efforts to Change Life Style." *Milbank Memorial Fund Quarterly* 56(3): 303–38.

Wikler, Daniel and Jeremiah Barondess. 1993. "Bioethics and Anti-Bioethics in Germany: What Must We Remember?" *Kennedy Institute of Ethics Journal* 3(1): 39–55.

Wilfond, Benjamin and Norman C. Fost. 1992. "The Introduction of Cystic Fibrosis Carrier Screening into Clinical Practice: Policy Considerations." *The Milbank Quarterly* 70(4): 629.

Wilson, Edward Osbourne. 1975. *Sociobiology: The New Synthesis*. Cambridge MA: Belknap Press of Harvard University Press.

Wisconsin v. Yoder. 1972. 406 U.S. 205.

Woodward, James. 1986. "The Non-Identity Problem." *Ethics* 96:804–31.

INDEX

abortion 3, 7, 36, 46, 49, 55, 106,
    120, 135, 156, 182–4, 204–5,
    210–11, 213, 226, 230–1, 233,
    237–41, 243, 250, 255, 261–2,
    265, 275–7, 280, 314, 323,
    329, 338, 350
achondroplasia 47, 49
adventitious needs 314
aggregation problem 232
AIDS 334, 348, 359–60
altruism 80–1, 88–9, 92, 174
American Eugenics Society 31, 54
American Journal of Public Health 52
Americans with Disabilities Act
    (ADA) 292

Bell Curve, The 45, 49, 316, 362
Brave New World 59, 164–5, 173
BRCA (gene) 313, 355

Canavan disease 305
capabilities 15, 33, 104, 106, 109,
    114, 116, 123, 125–37, 141,
    146, 148–54, 158–60, 174, 179–
    81, 186–7, 192–4
capability set 131–3, 135–7, 142,
    151
cells 265, 335, 347–9, 359
    somatic 6, 106, 191–2
    germline 6, 106, 192
    stem 6
    totipotent 6–7

character (choosing) 41, 43, 45, 50,
    166, 179, 215, 217, 343
cloning 2, 5, 14, 196–202, 209, 211
communitarianism 2, 20, 22, 176–7,
    373–82
cost-effectiveness 2, 11, 54–5
cystic fibrosis 8, 243, 311, 329–30,
    350–1, 353

deafness 47, 49, 281–4
    deaf culture 167, 281–4
degeneration 25, 37, 40–1, 52, 337
Department of Energy 314
determinism 91
    genetic 22–6, 80, 159, 161, 177,
    197–8, 201, 333
    and incompatibilism 91
disability 51, 61–2, 105–6, 117–18,
    126, 167, 182, 187–8, 202,
    210, 215, 226–7, 234–5, 243–
    7, 251–7, 266–7, 273–8, 284–
    8, 301, 312, 319–21, 331, 345,
    378
    disability rights 58, 305, 331
dominant cooperative framework 20,
    79, 259–60, 288–99
Dor Yeshorim 305, 338
Downs syndrome 3, 55, 243, 276–7,
    281
dysgenic 104, 231

embryo selection 9, 267, 275, 321
English Eugenics Education Society 31

395